T0379026

Modern Jewish Ethics since 1970

THE TAUBER INSTITUTE SERIES FOR
THE STUDY OF EUROPEAN JEWRY
    ChaeRan Y. Freeze, Editor
    Sylvia Fuks Fried, Editor
    Jehuda Reinharz, Editor
    Eugene R. Sheppard, Editor

THE BRANDEIS LIBRARY OF MODERN JEWISH THOUGHT
    Eugene R. Sheppard, Samuel Moyn, and Sylvia Fuks Fried, Editors
    David P. Briand, Managing Editor

This library aims to redefine the canon of modern Jewish thought by publishing primary source readings from individual Jewish thinkers or groups of thinkers in reliable English translations. Designed for courses in modern Jewish philosophy, thought, and intellectual history, each volume features a general introduction and annotations to each source with the instructor and student in mind.

Modern Jewish Ethics since 1970: Writings on Methods, Sources, and Issues
    Jonathan K. Crane, Emily Filler, Mira Beth Wasserman, editors
Hermann Cohen: Writings on Neo-Kantianism and Jewish Philosophy
    Samuel Moyn and Robert S. Schine, editors
Hasidism: Writings on Devotion, Community and Life in the Modern World
    Ariel Evan Mayse and Sam Berrin Shonkoff, editors
American Jewish Thought Since 1934: Writings on Identity, Engagement and Belief
    Michael Marmur and David Ellenson, editors
Spinoza's Challenge to Jewish Thought: Writings on His Life, Philosophy, and Legacy
    Daniel B. Schwartz, editor
Modern French Jewish Thought: Writings on Religion and Politics
    Sarah Hammerschlag, editor
Jewish Legal Theories: Writings on State, Religion, and Morality
    Leora Batnitzky and Yonatan Brafman, editors

FOR THE COMPLETE LIST OF BOOKS IN THE SERIES, PLEASE SEE
HTTPS://BRANDEISUNIVERSITYPRESS.COM/SERIES-LIST/

Modern Jewish Ethics since 1970

Edited by
Jonathan K. Crane,
Emily Filler, and
Mira Beth Wasserman

WRITINGS ON METHODS, SOURCES, AND ISSUES

Brandeis University Press
Waltham, Massachusetts

BRANDEIS UNIVERSITY PRESS
2025 © Brandeis University Press
All rights reserved
Manufactured in the United States of America
Series design by Eric M. Brooks
Typeset in Albertina and Verlag by Passumpsic Publishing

For permission to reproduce any of the material
in this book, contact Brandeis University Press,
415 South Street, Waltham MA 02453,
or visit brandeisuniversitypress.com

Library of Congress Cataloging-in-Publication Data
available upon request
Cloth ISBN: 978-1-68458-261-7
Paperback ISBN: 978-1-68458-263-1
Ebook ISBN: 978-1-68458-262-4

5 4 3 2 1

THIS PUBLICATION HAS BEEN MADE POSSIBLE
THROUGH THE GENEROUS SUPPORT OF
Steven L. Rachmuth, Brandeis Class of 2014,
in memory of Carl, Lotty, David, and Otto Rachmuth,
and Gilda and Mayer Milstoc.

ADDITIONAL SUPPORT WAS PROVIDED BY
The Program in Jewish Studies at Yale University
The Center for Ethics at Emory University
**The Center for Jewish Ethics at the
Reconstructionist Rabbinical College**

Contents

Foreword xiii
Introduction xv

I | Theories and Methods 1

1 | DOING JEWISH ETHICS 3

Aharon Lichtenstein | Does Jewish Tradition Recognize
an Ethic Independent of Halakha? 5

Louis Newman | Woodchoppers and Respirators: The Problem
of Interpretation in Contemporary Jewish Ethics 9

Michal Raucher | Conceiving Agency 14

2 | FORGING ETHICAL NORMS FROM JEWISH TEXTUAL SOURCES 19

Judith Plaskow | Standing Again at Sinai:
Judaism from a Feminist Perspective 22

Elliot Dorff | Love Your Neighbor and Yourself:
A Jewish Approach to Modern Personal Ethics 27

Shaul Magid | Ethics Differentiated from the Law 31

3 | ETHICS AND LAW 35

Robert Cover | Nomos and Narrative 37

Rachel Adler | Engendering Judaism:
An Inclusive Theology and Ethics 41

Alan Mittleman | Theorizing Jewish Ethics 46

David Novak | Jewish Social Ethics 50

4 | COVENANT 54

Emmanuel Levinas | The Levinas Reader 56

Walter Wurzberger | Ethics of Responsibility:
Pluralistic Approaches to Covenantal Ethics 60

Eugene Borowitz | Renewing the Covenant:
A Theology for the Postmodern Jew 65

Mara Benjamin | The Obligated Self:
Maternal Subjectivity and Jewish Thought 68

5 | CHARACTER/VIRTUE 72

    Jonathan Wyn Schofer | Self, Subject, and Chosen Subjection: Rabbinic Ethics and Comparative Possibilities 74

    Sarra Lev | Talmud That Works Your Heart: New Approaches to Reading 78

    Geoffrey Claussen | Musar in a White Supremacist Society: Arrogance, Self-Examination, and Systemic Change 82

6 | ETHICAL VALUES 87

    David A. Teutsch | Reinvigorating the Practice of Contemporary Jewish Ethics: A Justification For Values-Based Decision Making 89

    Tanhum Yoreh | Waste Not: A Jewish Environmental Ethic 91

II | **Communities** 95

7 | FAMILIES 99

    Gail Labovitz | Marriage and Metaphor: Constructions of Gender in Rabbinic Literature 101

    Jennifer A. Thompson | Reaching Out to the Fringe: Insiders, Outsiders, and the Morality of Social Science 105

    Rebecca J. Epstein-Levi | Person-Shaped Holes: Childfree Jews, Jewish Ethics, and Communal Continuity 108

8 | SPEECH 112

    Mark Washofsky | Internet, Privacy, and Progressive Halakha 114

    Matthew Goldstone | The Dangerous Duty of Rebuke: Leviticus 19:17 in Early Jewish and Christian Interpretation 118

    Lena Sclove | Beyond the Binary of Silence and Speech: What Jewish Liturgy and Spirals Reveal about the Limits and Potentials of Spiritual Caregiving for Survivors of Sexual Violence 121

9 | SOLIDARITY 126

    Aryeh Cohen | Justice in the City: An Argument from the Sources of Rabbinic Judaism 129

    Amanda Mbuvi | *Avadim Hayinu*: An Intersectional Jewish Perspective on the *Global Ethic* of Solidarity 135

10 | ECONOMICS 139

    Jill Jacobs | There Shall Be No Needy: Pursuing Social Justice through Jewish Law and Tradition 141

Aaron Levine | Economic Morality and Jewish Law 145
Samuel Brody | Jewish Economic Ethics in the Neoliberal Era, 1980–2016 150

11 | ZIONISM 155

Chaim Gans | A Just Zionism: On the Morality of the Jewish State 157

Ruth Gavison | Reflections on the Meaning and Justification of "Jewish" in the Expression "A Jewish and Democratic State" 161

Julie Cooper | A Diasporic Critique of Diasporism: The Question of Jewish Political Agency 166

12 | STATE POWER AND VIOLENCE 172

Geoffrey Brahm Levey | Judaism and the Obligation to Die for the State 175

Michael Broyde | Just Wars, Just Battles, and Just Conduct in Jewish Law: Jewish Law Is Not a Suicide Pact! 179

Melissa Weintraub | Does Torah Permit Torture? 183

Beth Berkowitz | Execution and Invention: Death Penalty Discourse in Early Rabbinic and Christian Cultures 187

Nadav S. Berman | Jewish Law, Techno-Ethics, and Autonomous Weapon Systems: Ethical-Halakhic Perspectives 192

13 | ENVIRONMENT 196

Michael Wyschogrod | Judaism and the Sanctification of Nature 199

Ariel Evan Mayse | Where Heaven and Earth Kiss: Jewish Law, Moral Reflection, and Environmental Ethics 202

Adrienne Krone | Ecological Ethics in the Jewish Community Farming Movement 205

Hava Tirosh-Samuelson | Religion and Environment: The Case of Judaism 208

III | Constructions of the Human 213

14 | ANIMALS 215

Aaron S. Gross | The Question of the Animal and Religion: Theoretical Stakes, Practical Implications 217

Rafael Rachel Neis | "All That Is in the Settlement": Humans, Likeness, and Species in the Rabbinic Bestiary 222

15 | GENDER AND SEXUALITY 227

    Daniel Boyarin | Dialectics of Desire: "The Evil Instinct Is Very Good" 230

    Tamar Ross | Expanding the Palace of Torah: Orthodoxy and Feminism 233

    Laura Levitt | Love the One You're with 236

    Max Strassfeld | Trans Talmud: Androgynes and Eunuchs in Rabbinic Literature 239

16 | GENES 245

    Paul Root Wolpe | If I Am Only My Genes, What Am I? Genetic Essentialism and a Jewish Response 247

    Robert Gibbs | Mending the Code 252

    Sarah Imhoff | Racial Standing: How American Jews Imagine Community, and Why That Matters 257

17 | DISABILITY 262

    Judith Z. Abrams | Judaism and Disability: Portrayals in Ancient Texts from the Tanach through the Bavli 265

    Tzvi C. Marx | Disability in Jewish Law 268

    Adrienne Asch | Recognizing Death while Affirming Life: Can End of Life Reform Uphold a Disabled Person's Interest in Continued Life? 272

    Julia Watts Belser | Improv and the Angel: Disability Dance, Embodied Ethics, and Jewish Biblical Narrative 276

18 | RACE 281

    Lewis R. Gordon | Afro-Jewish Ethics? 283

    Judith Kay | Jews as Oppressed and Oppressor: Doing Ethics at the Intersections of Classism, Racism, and Antisemitism 287

    Annalise E. Glauz-Todrank | Jewish Critical Race Theory and Jewish "Religionization" in *Shaare Tefila Congregation v. Cobb* 293

IV | Bioethics 299

19 | MEDICAL ETHICS 303

    Benjamin Freedman | Duty and Healing: Foundations of a Jewish Bioethic 306

Noam J. Zohar | Is Enjoying Life a Good Thing? Quality-of-Life
Questions for Jewish Normative Discourse 310

Toby Schonfeld | Messages from the Margins: Lessons
from Feminist Bioethics 314

Jason Weiner | Are There Limits to How Far One Must Go for Others?
Toward a Theoretical Model for Health Care Providers 318

Laurie Zoloth | Second Texts and Second Opinions:
Essays toward a Jewish Bioethics 321

20 | REPRODUCTION 326

Fred Rosner | In Vitro Fertilization and Surrogate Motherhood:
The Jewish View 329

Elie Spitz | "Through Her I Too Shall Bear a Child":
Birth Surrogates in Jewish Law 333

Don Seeman | Ethnography, Exegesis, and Jewish Ethical Reflection:
The New Reproductive Technologies in Israel 337

Sarah Zagar | Water Wears Away Stone: Caring for Those
We Can Only Imagine 342

21 | ABORTION 345

Dena S. Davis | Abortion in Jewish Thought: A Study in Casuistry 347

Rebecca T. Alpert | Sometimes the Law Is Cruel:
The Construction of a Jewish Antiabortion Position
in the Writings of Immanuel Jakobovits 351

Alan Jotkowitz | Abortion and Maternal Need:
A Response to Ronit Irshai 355

Ronit Irshai | Response to Alan Jotkowitz 359

22 | AGING/ENDS OF LIFE 362

Byron Sherwin | Jewish Views on Euthanasia 364

Ruth Langer | Honor Your Father and Mother:
Caregiving as an Halakhic Responsibility 369

Jonathan K. Crane | Narratives and Jewish Bioethics 373

Jeffrey L. Rubenstein | Can a *Goses* Survive for More Than Three Days?
The History and Definition of the *Goses* 377

Acknowledgments 381

Index 389

Foreword

A discrete field of Jewish ethics has emerged in North America as thinkers have sought to address the remarkable challenges posed by—and possibilities opened by—revolutionary technological innovations, climate change, sexual and gender identifications, and biomedical interventions that have stretched the beginnings and ends of life in fundamentally new ways. Jewish questions can sometimes seem perennial and unchanging: What is good and just? What is the right or virtuous thing to do? But what if the answers to these questions change as every facet of Jewish life does?

The diverse voices in this volume seek to systematically understand and determine the contours and substance of judgment when pressed by new technologies and the radically changing conditions of Jewish modernity. From their distinctive points of view, the authors engage perennial questions of ethics regarding the good, virtuous, and just, but do so in a dramatically new context for Judaism and Jews over the last half century. In these conditions, how exactly can Jewish sources and authority speak to the challenges facing individuals and communities? How ought Jewish belonging, obligation, and exclusion be legitimated or revised?

The importance of these questions is a good reason to welcome *Modern Jewish Ethics since 1970: Writings on Methods, Sources, and Issues* to the Brandeis Library of Modern Jewish Thought. This volume reflects the emergence of an entire new field of Jewish thinking that has come into its own.

Sylvia Fuks Fried, Samuel Moyn, and Eugene Sheppard, Editors,
The Brandeis Library of Modern Jewish Thought

Introduction

The present volume is a testament to the development of Jewish ethics as an academic field over the past five decades, marked by a distinctive set of priorities, themes, and methodological debates. As a field of study, Jewish ethics is characterized by deep engagement with the Jewish tradition—texts, practices, histories—alongside sustained critical considerations of the ways the tradition may (or may not) be employed to illumine questions of what is good, just, or virtuous.

From the beginning, the field of Jewish ethics has been marked by its engagement with other ethical traditions, as well as other fields of academic study. The opening portion of this introduction, therefore, introduces some continuities with earlier contributions to Jewish ethics, as well as some important contemporary influences that have helped to define the tenor, scope, and focus of the field. The second portion discusses some of the values underlying our editorial decisions about which readings and thinkers are featured in this book. The third portion provides an overview of the parts of the volume's structure and the general topics considered within them. The concluding portion of this essay then opens up the animating question behind this volume's existence: What is Jewish ethics?

Continuities and Influences in Modern Jewish Ethics

This volume begins its consideration of modern Jewish ethics around the year 1970. This portion of the introduction explains why this date serves as the emergence of this field.

When discussions of ethical topics—of what is good, just, or virtuous—appear in classical Jewish texts like the Torah, Mishnah, Gemara, and midrashim, they do not stand alone, but are rather woven into stories, aphorisms, laws, and biblical interpretation. While a student interested in ethical content could read these classical sources with an eye toward extracting Jewish ethical wisdom, the sources themselves are not organized around ethical topics and only rarely address ethical questions in an explicit way. One special resource for the study of early Jewish ethical ideas is *Pirkei Avot* (c. 250 CE), a collection of pithy aphorisms and pieces of wisdom attributed to early rabbis that became part of the

Mishnah. *Pirkei Avot* enumerates many principles and values that have become touchstones for Jewish ethical ideas, like the importance of being part of a community (*Pirkei Avot* 2:4) and of being generous to the poor (*Pirkei Avot* 1:5), and many scholars look to *Pirkei Avot* as a foundational source for later Jewish ethics. Yet even *Pirkei Avot* stops short of making arguments or giving sustained attention to ethical ideas.[1]

It is not until the medieval period that Jewish writers address ethics as a distinct subject, beginning in the ninth century with Saadia Gaon's magnum opus, *The Book of Beliefs and Opinions* (*Kitab al-'Amanat wal-l'tikadat*).[2] Saadia highlights ethics' importance by situating it as the concluding treatise in that book; everything else—beliefs, opinions, and all the rest—is background for, leads up to, and culminates in ethics. Central to his argument is the observation that humans comprise multiple elements: they are not just bone or muscle or nerve or thought. It is thus erroneous to assume that human behaviors should be done in favor of one element at the expense of all others. Were a person to behave exclusively according to one's appetitive, impulse, or cognitive capacity, it would be dangerous, antisocial, and contrary to the Judaic foundations Saadia discusses. Vital, then, is it for humans to constantly consider various options for their actions, sound reasons for those choices, and clear values to guide deciding among them.[3]

Good judgment thus becomes part and parcel to Jewish ethics. This was highlighted in the thirteenth century by Moshe ben Nahman's (also known as Nahmanides) reading of "Do what is right and good in the eyes of Adonai, that it may go well with you and that you may possess the good land Adonai your God promised on oath to your ancestors" (Deut. 6:18). Nahmanides saw in this teaching an acknowledgment that law can never be exhaustive: some circumstances will be novel, and Jews must discern, carefully, what is "good and right in the eyes of Adonai." In short, Jews need to figure out what is *lifnim mishurat hadin*, colloquially understood as "beyond the letter of the law." To do this, compromise may be necessary. For this reason, ethics, or good judgment, entails the difficult process of understanding (at least) what is right or legal and what is good or moral, and deliberating a course of action that best honors them, which may ensure that things "may go well with you" and your progeny.

A century before Nahmanides, Moshe ben Maimon (also known as Maimonides) brought Aristotelian virtue philosophy into such discussions about good judgment in his magisterial *The Guide of the Perplexed* (*Dalālāt al-Hā'irīn*, or in Hebrew, *Moreh Nebukim*).[4] Though Maimonides praises impulse control, he stresses that intellectual knowledge of the divine is what will induce the kind of *hesed* or lovingkindness that delights God. Virtue, righteousness, and integrity—all expressions of good judgment—are products of vigilant training and rigorous education. In short, one can learn how to make good judgments and one can put those judgments into action in part through the cultivation of certain character traits.

From such medieval foundations, ethics would be treated with gravitas by subsequent generations of Jewish scholars, though primarily as embedded in texts devoted to law, philosophy, or theology. Things began to shift in the modern period, especially with Immanuel Kant's challenge to embrace universalistic rationality—about which more will be said below. While sages of *musar* (character or virtue) ethics in the nineteenth century predominantly avoided this challenge, Hermann Cohen took up Kant's gauntlet in the early twentieth century to promote the idea of ethical monotheism in his 1919 magnum opus, *Religion of Reason: Out of the Sources of Judaism*.[5] Pushing deeper into the twentieth century, Franz Rosenzweig, Martin Buber, and Emmanuel Levinas[6] would, in their unique ways and diverse publications, echo Cohen's call for a Jewish ethics dissociated from law.[7] For them, the other, or relationality, should be the focus of an ethics worthy of being called Jewish.

Such discussions about the relationship between law, philosophy, theology, and ethics inspired a spate of publications in the 1970s, hence the decision to start this volume here. One of the most foundational in that wave was Aharon Lichtenstein's 1975 essay, "Does Jewish Tradition Recognize an Ethic Independent of Halakha?," featured as the first entry in this volume. Though Lichtenstein does not answer that question with much definitiveness, that essay, along with the volumes edited by Marvin Fox, *Modern Jewish Ethics: Theory and Practice* in 1975, and by Menachem Kellner, *Contemporary Jewish Ethics* in 1978, signaled the emergence of Jewish ethics as a distinct field within the larger ambit of Jewish studies.[8]

Concurrent with this new literature among Jews were the efforts across the United States and beyond by second-wave feminists. This larger movement gave voice to diverse perspectives challenging conventional assumptions about normativity, agency, inclusion, and responsibility, among other issues. Jewish communities were not immune to these swirling conversations and trends, as evidenced by the establishment in 1976 of *Lilith Magazine* and Cynthia Ozick's 1979 "Notes Toward Finding the Right Question," which prompted Judith Plaskow's response a few years later, "The Right Question Is Theological."[9] Such contributions pressed the point that in addition to interrogating *what* Jews ought to do (or not), a Jewish ethics meriting its name should also concern itself with *how* those arguments are made, by *whom*, and *why*. That is, a modern Jewish ethics needs to be a self-conscious enterprise, aware and critical of its voices and methods.

Within a few short years, new volumes asserted the emergence of Jewish ethics as a stand-alone field. The 1984 *A Book of Jewish Ethical Concepts: Biblical and Post-Biblical* by Abraham Bloch, the annotated bibliographies of modern Jewish ethics and morality by S. Daniel Breslauer in 1985–86, and Nachum Amsel's 1994 *The Jewish Encyclopedia of Moral and Ethical Issues* indicated scholarly as well as popular interest in this field.[10] By the end of the twentieth century, theologians like Eugene Borowitz, David Novak, Rachel Adler, and Jonathan Sacks, legal scholars like J. David Bleich and Elliot Dorff, biomedical ethicists like Fred Rosner and Avraham Steinberg, among a host of others, produced substantial contributions to the field, though as will be shown in this volume they deployed diverse methodologies to do so.[11]

Some of these scholars met in person at the annual conferences of the Society of Christian Ethics (SCE), an organization established in 1959. With membership among their ranks slowly rising, in the early 2000s this small group of Jewish ethicists forged a new entity—the Society of Jewish Ethics (SJE)—that would convene meetings alongside the SCE. They envisioned that this new SJE would vet its own proposals, and, like the SCE, facilitate dispassionate, cross-denominational, multidisciplinary, and deep conversations on all things Jewish ethics. The SJE membership steadily grew in number and disciplinary diversity. By 2015, the organization and field had sufficiently matured to warrant the establishment of a new publishing venue, *The Journal of Jewish Ethics* (JJE). Since then, the age-old debates about the relationships between law, philosophy, and theology, between agency, norms, and responsibility, and between tradition and change have continued in animated style in the pages of the *JJE*. However ragged the boundaries of contemporary Jewish ethics may be, the field broadly embraces diverse ways to theorize, observe, and enact good judgment.

Organizing Principles for This Volume

All edited volumes are a reflection of their editors' scholarly interests, deeply held commitments, and epistemic limitations. The present volume bespeaks the profound influence of methodological debates such as the ones mentioned above, and our subsequent editorial conviction that to focus on methods of reasoning is a compelling and generative way to study, and teach, Jewish ethics.

The field of Jewish ethics, we contend, is never far from foundational questions about how to do Jewish ethics, and these questions are inseparable from other kinds of scholarly conclusions or prescriptions.

In part because Jewish ethics is experienced deliberatively—that is, through encounters and discussions with others—this volume is organized not by stand-alone essays but by small sets of curated conversations between scholars from different time periods, academic subfields, and religious commitments (or lack thereof). These deliberate juxtapositions encourage scholars and students to develop similar meta-ethical analyses on Jewish ethics, broadly construed. These curated conversations feature anywhere between two and five voices that model distinct approaches to Jewish ethical questions, an intentional choice for scholarly and pedagogical reasons. Only one selection on a given theme could lead students to erroneously think it represents "the Jewish position"; conversely, an overly broad array of voices might suggest we were striving to be comprehensive. Instead, these curated conversations may serve as introductions to an array of methods, texts, and disputes across time and space.

When describing the book's parts and sections as "curated," attention is drawn to the role of the editors. The book explicitly reflects our distinctive editorial choices: not only which authors to include, but also with whom to invite them into conversation, and to what conversation they might contribute. Such choices are admittedly influenced by certain biases, too. For instance, there is an obvious tilt in the volume toward American voices, though a few scholars from Europe and Israel do chime in. All these choices are not self-evident but express editorial priorities for the volume. First, we maintain an explicit focus on methods of reasoning in addition to, or instead of, definitive ethical "answers" to a given topical query, and we invite readers to zero in on these explicit and implicit methodological turns at work in each selection.

Second, we present a picture of a developing academic field, from 1970 to the present. The volume works with the assumption that in seeing how and where scholars engage with one another's work, we may see the contours of a broad scholarly trend: What questions come up again and again? Which works are cited by scholars across a variety of settings? We acknowledge that since the emergence of the SJE in the early 2000s and the JJE in 2015, there have been far more publications in the field in recent years. The burgeoning of the field is reflected in this volume, which includes many more pieces from recent years than from the last decades of the twentieth century. With these developments in mind, readers can consider what the field is poised to become.

This volume features a wide array of thinkers from a variety of scholastic affiliations and a range of professional experiences. But, of course, selecting only scholarly essays necessarily excludes many other genres of literature that could potentially appear in collections of modern literature on Judaism and ethical reasoning. It means, for instance, that the genre of rabbinical responsa (individual or collective rabbinic answers to questions of Jewish religious law) is not represented in this book, despite its importance in some Jewish—particularly Orthodox—communities as a way of setting communal norms. So too the genre of the synagogue sermon, or *d'var Torah*, does not appear in this volume (though some of the selections do themselves make reference to responsa or sermons).

The emphasis on scholarly writing also excludes essays and books written in a popular idiom or for a wide, nonacademic, audience: opinion pieces in print or online sources, substantive social media posts, and other reflections of popular ethical discourse do not appear in this book. The decision to focus on the development of Jewish ethics as a *scholarly* field necessarily excludes these and other writings, even while we readily acknowledge the influence of popular works on scholarly writing (and vice versa). It is also true that scholarly publications often lag behind other kinds of writing, owing, in no small part, to the slow and capricious nature of academic publishing. As a result, many of the most prominent social debates as of this writing—such as analyses of artificial intelligence, or recent racial discourses in the United States, or the current Israeli incursion in Gaza—are only beginning to emerge in academic Jewish ethics. Some of the volume's most recent selections in particular suggest new directions for the field in the coming decades.

Finally, we intend this volume to be useful and accessible for teaching, a productive resource for undergraduates, graduate students, rabbinical students, and others. Each section of the book, and each curated conversation in the sections, is preceded by an introduction that considers some of the major questions and methodological disputes in those conversations. These editorial "interventions" are designed not only to give students some brief background for their reading but also to make it possible for teachers to assign some sections or selections without having to assign the whole book. And in the emphasis on "conversations" around a question, we hope to create the conditions for students to do meaningful comparative analysis of the methods and arguments of each thinker.

Structure of this Volume

This volume opens with a substantial section on theories and methods of doing Jewish ethics. Most of the selections attend to definitional questions—what is "Jewish ethics"?—and to fundamental methodological queries: How does one do Jewish ethics? This volume introduces some important, and ongoing, theoretical queries too: How do we know whether the ethical reasoning in question is "Jewish"? Which sources, themes, and resources repeatedly appear in works marked as Jewish ethics? How might the appropriateness of these sources and their deployment and interpretation be evaluated? The very first selection in this volume (Lichtenstein, mentioned above) even asks about the possibility of separating Jewish ethics from the ancient category of Jewish law at all, and if so, what the relationship is between the two ideas. The categories in this opening section are clearly best understood as foundational methodological themes across a broad spectrum of scholarly work in Judaism and ethical reasoning in the last several decades.

Yet although part 1, "Theories and Methods," introduces these fundamental questions and concepts, this section should not be understood only as a foundation on which "real" Jewish ethics can then proceed in the parts that follow. Rather, we believe that to reflect methodologically on the Jewish tradition and its intersection with ethics is already to have begun doing Jewish ethics—that, in fact, all work plausibly described as Jewish ethics also contains arguments and assumptions (marked or unmarked) about the correct ways of doing this work, of articulating good judgment.

The opening section certainly includes a number of selections whose chief arguments are meta-ethical; that is, they primarily consider how thinkers should proceed in their scholarship, whatever the precise nature of that scholarship. These selections still ground their theoretical work in particular texts or experiences. Louis Newman's essay in the section "Doing Jewish Ethics," for instance, considers arguments around euthanasia to make a broader argument about the limitations of classical Jewish texts for modern and contemporary ethics, while Sarra Lev's essay in the section "Character/Virtue" describes a particular semester of teaching Talmud to consider the relationship between reading practices and individual and communal virtue.

But part 1 also includes sections that attend just as much to a particular modern issue as to the broad methodological questions surrounding it. Michal Raucher's selection in the section "Doing Jewish Ethics," for instance, is excerpted from her book-length ethnographic study of ultra-Orthodox women in Jerusalem, and their distinctive experiences of pregnancy, parenthood, and bodily authority in male-dominated communities. The selection by Rachel Adler in the section "Ethics and Law" is an essential contribution to any study of Jewish feminist ethics and includes specific prescriptions for how Jewish rituals might be adapted in light of feminist critique. In such selections, the methodological arguments or overarching themes are inseparable from the authors' consideration of some particular ethical realm.

The remaining three parts are titled broadly: "Communities," "Constructions of the Human," and "Bioethics." In moving from general methodological queries directly to communities in part 2, we signal our assumption that the very first settings in which humans find themselves are in fact communal, not individual: people emerge into various kinds of families and groups, for better and worse, and must ask difficult questions about communal responsibilities and failures. Part 3 then moves to more specific questions about how to determine who is included in which communities and how to create circumstances for thriving. And part 4, on Jewish bioethics, introduces profound questions of medicine and bodily phenomena at all stages of life.

Crucially, however, many of the selections in these more "issue-based" sections could also find a home in part 1. Nadav S. Berman's essay on autonomous weapons systems in modern warfare, included in part 2, "Communities," in the section "State Power and Violence," considers the role of biblical narratives in contemporary Jewish law and ethics. Featured in part 3, "Constructions of the Human," Max Strassfeld's work on trans discourses in the section "Gender and Sexuality" analyzes the methodological complexity of deriving contemporary ethical conclusions from classical rabbinic literature. The fact that so many selections in this volume could be included in other sections is intentional: a way of marking that the boundaries between meta-ethical arguments and work on a particular ethical "issue" are by no means clear.

For each of the selections in this volume, we retained the original footnotes and citations for direct quotes or when we deemed them necessary for clarity. Footnotes in brackets indicate the editors' addition in order to explain a term or thinker referenced in the text.

What Is Jewish Ethics?

Implicit in the organization of this volume—and in its very existence—is our assertion that there is such a thing as Jewish ethics, and that it is a topic worthy of study. Other scholars have raised questions about whether it makes sense to speak of Jewish ethics at all. From the outset, we want to acknowledge some of the challenges inherent in the study of Jewish ethics and briefly explain how we think about them.

One reason to question whether one can speak of Jewish ethics is that there is not a specific term or concept that is precisely equivalent to "ethics" in classical Jewish literature. The study of ethics traces back to ancient Greek philosophers like Plato and Aristotle, who defined the study of ethics as an investigation into what kind of virtues lead to human flourishing. Ancient Jewish cultures, rooted in devotion to the Torah, had a different orientation. Jewish sages focused their studies on interpreting the Torah in an effort to discern what God wanted and expected of people. But even as classical Jewish writings focus on the study and practice of divine commandments, Jewish literature is intently interested in practices, principles, and character traits that allow for people and communities to thrive. Though there is not a discrete concept that is equivalent to "ethics," there is lots of content in biblical, postbiblical, and rabbinic writings that engages ethical ideas and navigates moral conundrums. On this basis alone, we think it makes sense to talk about Jewish ethics. And while there is broad overlap between the kind of actions and qualities that Greek philosophers associate with human flourishing and that Jewish sages associate with piety, the differences in focus, orientation, and language between Jewish teachings and the Western philosophical tradition are themselves illuminating.

One salient difference between Jewish teachings and the Western philosophical tradition is the form and structure of the Jewish literature that organizes ethical content. Rabbinic literature is largely commentarial, such that Jewish discussions of any given topic are dispersed across a vast corpus. For a study of Jewish teachings about the virtue of honesty, for instance, one might consult rabbinic commentaries on the biblical prohibition of false testimony, or on the biblical commandment to use fair weights and measures; one might look to legal traditions about honesty in business transactions in the early rabbinic compilation known as the Mishnah, and then trace commentary and discussion of these legal traditions in the Talmud and in talmudic commentaries; other rabbinic works might transmit exemplary stories about rabbis who tell the truth.

Yet another site for Jewish teaching is the tradition of rabbinic responsa, discussed above. Rabbinic teachings are not systematized, and the tradition is multivocal, so there might be a diversity of Jewish teachings on any given topic. This is in marked contrast to philosophical writing, which tends to be organized topically and presents arguments in a highly structured and well-reasoned way. Beginning in the medieval period, Jewish thinkers who were well versed in both rabbinic teachings and in philosophic texts sought to systematize Jewish teachings and lay things out in coherent topical arrangements. It might be, however, that differences in the structure and idioms of traditional Jewish and philosophic texts are more than differences of style, that they reflect different patterns of thought and different ways of weighing particular cases vis-à-vis general principles; that is, they demonstrate a different kind of good judgment. We see the different forms of Jewish ethical expression—in commentary, narrative, aphorisms, responsa, and legal dialectic—as an important source for theorizing about Jewish ethics.[12]

One consequence of the unruliness of classical Jewish discourse is that Jewish outlooks, methods, and principles do not always accommodate the taxonomies that philosophers use to characterize the different schools or approaches to the study of ethics. Students of moral philosophy distinguish among three main theoretical approaches: virtue ethics, consequentialism, and deontological ethics. Virtue ethics focuses on the qualities or dispositions of an ethical subject; consequentialism emphasizes the practical effects of any given ethical decision; and deontological ethics entails a focus on the duties, rules, and principles that should govern behavior. Jewish ethics does not fall neatly into any one of these categories. While the Jewish emphasis on commandments means that Jewish tradition is broadly oriented toward explicating duties, there are many Jewish works that focus on character.[13] Jewish legal discussions in talmudic literature are often dedicated to examinations of how edge cases or exceptional circumstances complicate rules and principles, and in these determinations, rabbinic decision-making is strongly oriented toward the practical considerations that characterize a consequentialist approach. This is just one example of how Jewish ethical tradition resists translation into philosophic discourse.

Another common set of distinctions that scholars make is between metaethics, historical ethics, and applied ethics. But as the pieces that we've selected indicate, Jewish ethicists don't maintain these distinctions: often, approaches to specific problems—applied ethics—are grounded in considerations of ancient texts, and it is only through a consideration of theoretical questions about the authority of these texts that Jewish thinkers can make a case for how ancient texts might speak to contemporary problems. In such investigations, the historical and the theoretical cannot be disentangled from the practical.

That Jewish textual discussions are not always legible to philosophers of ethics is not on its own a reason to challenge the notion that there is such a thing as Jewish ethics. But there are those who argue for the incommensurability of Judaism and ethics. Challenges to the very notion of Jewish ethics can come from either direction—from a perspective grounded in Western moral philosophy or from a grounding in Jewish thought.

The challenge from Western moral philosophy is not specific to Jewish ethics but can as easily be leveled against any particular religious tradition. At issue is the principle enshrined by Immanuel Kant that ethics need to be universal in its applicability. According to Kant's categorical imperative, the same rules need to apply to all people. Ethics is governed by reason and cannot discriminate with regard to a person's background or commitments. This universalizing principle puts Kantian ethics at odds with many aspects of Jewish tradition, which are oriented to the Jewish people in particular. While some elements of Jewish teaching address humanity as a whole, Jewish texts are overwhelmingly focused on obligations and experiences that distinguish Jews from others. Some contemporary Jewish ethicists take pains to highlight the universal aspects of traditional Jewish teachings,[14] while others emphasize the ways that Jewish thought has changed and evolved in response to the modern emphasis on the universal.[15] In this postmodern moment, many ethical thinkers are newly attuned to the ways that the modern, rationalizing rhetoric of universalism has often masked its own exclusionary logic, treating the distinctive concerns of Western Christianity as a standard by which all other cultures should be measured. For some of the thinkers represented in this volume, the particular idioms, concerns, and orientations that characterize Jewish discourse about morality, justice, and the human predicament provide a valuable counterbalance to Western patterns of ethical reasoning.[16] For feminist thinkers in particular, Jewish tradition offers a valuable corrective to Western biases.[17]

At the same time, there are Jewish thinkers who argue against the notion of Jewish ethics from another direction, contending that Jewish principles simply do not accord with the very idea of ethics. For some Orthodox Jewish thinkers, in particular, Judaism cannot accommodate ethics because when Jews face the kinds of questions that ethics addresses, these questions are most appropriately addressed by the dictates of Jewish law, or halakha. According to this way of thinking, ethical deliberation does not enter into things, because halakha alone is determinative of Jewish norms. For these thinkers, halakha and ethics are rival orders of normativity, and the two systems are incommensurable.[18] Some Jewish thinkers moderate this view slightly when they argue that there can be a role for ethics that accommodates the centrality of halakha, as an adjunct or supererogatory addition to halakha.[19] The pieces that we have gathered in the following sections construct the relationship between halakha and ethics in a diversity of ways. The approach we have adopted in shaping this book is to identify the question of halakha's relationship with ethics as one of the important theoretical questions for the field. Indeed, for us, Jewish ethics is precisely the field in which questions about halakha's authority and grounding can be investigated, interrogated, explicated, and deliberated.

We recognize that Jewish ethics is not just a set of propositions or principles, and it cannot be reduced to a single trajectory of thought or abstracted as an elaborate system of ideas. Jewish ethics is the field of study that engages Jewish texts, ideas, history, and experience in critical conversations about values and virtues, justice and good judgment, human relations and responsibilities. This volume presents some of these ongoing conversations to inspire more reflection, expansion, and debate.

Notes

1. For background on the history of *Pirkei Avot*, see Amram Tropper, *Wisdom, Politics, and Historiography: Tractate Avot in the Context of the Graeco-Roman Near East* (Oxford: Oxford University Press, 2004). For an explication of how *Pirkei Avot* and the classical rabbinic commentary *Avot d'Rabbi Natan* articulate the virtue ethics of the ancient rabbis, see Jonathan Wyn Schofer, *The Making of a Sage: A Study in Rabbinic Ethics* (Madison: University of Wisconsin Press, 2005).

2. Saadia Gaon, *The Book of Beliefs and Opinions*, trans. Samuel Rosenblatt (New Haven, CT: Yale University Press, 1976).

3. For an overall history of Jewish ethics, see Alan Mittleman, *A Short History of Jewish Ethics* (Malden, MA: Wiley-Blackwell, 2012); Elliot N. Dorff and Jonathan K. Crane, eds., *The Oxford Handbook of Jewish Ethics and Morality* (New York: Oxford University Press, 2012).

4. Moses Maimonides, *The Guide of the Perplexed*, trans. Shlomo Pines (Chicago: University of Chicago Press, 1963).

5. Hermann Cohen, *Religion of Reason: Out of the Sources of Judaism*, trans. Simon Kaplan (Atlanta: Scholars Press, 1995).

6. For more on Levinas, see part 1, section 4.

7. For example, see Franz Rosenzweig, *The Star of Redemption*, trans. Barbara Galli (Madison: University of Wisconsin Press, 2005); Martin Buber, *Between Man and Man*, trans. Ronard G. Smith (Boston: Beacon Press, 1955); and *Eclipse of God: Studies in the Relation between Religion and Philosophy* (Atlantic Highlands, NJ: Humanities Press International, Inc., 1988); Emmanuel Levinas, *Difficult Freedom: Essays on Judaism*, trans. Seán Hand (Baltimore: The Johns Hopkins University Press, 1990); Emmanuel Levinas, *Totality and Infinity: An Essay on Exteriority*, trans. Alphonso Lingis (Pittsburgh: Duquesne University Press, 1961); and Emmanuel Levinas,

Otherwise Than Being: Or beyond Essence, trans. Alphonso Lingis (Pittsburgh: Duquesne University Press, 1998).

8. Marvin Fox, ed., *Modern Jewish Ethics: Theory and Practice* (Columbus: Ohio University Press, 1975); Menachem Kellner, ed., *Contemporary Jewish Ethics* (New York: Sanhedrin Press, 1978).

9. Cynthia Ozick, "Notes toward Finding the Right Question," *Lilith* 6 (1979): 19–29; Judith Plaskow, "The Right Question Is Theological," in *On Being a Jewish Feminist*, 223–33, ed. by Susannah Heschel (New York: Schocken Books, 1983).

10. Abraham Bloch, *A Book of Jewish Ethical Concepts: Biblical and Postbiblical* (New York: Ktav, 1984); Daniel Breslauer, comp., *Contemporary Jewish Ethics: A Bibliographical Survey* (Westport, CT: Greenwood, 1985); *Modern Jewish Morality: A Bibliographical Survey* (New York: Greenwood, 1986); Nachum Amsel, *The Jewish Encyclopedia of Moral and Ethical Issues* (Northvale, NJ: Jason Aronson, 1994).

11. Most of these scholars are featured in this volume; see their selections for further information.

12. For examples of recent scholarship that engage the forms and style of rabbinic discourse as sources for Jewish ethics, see Emily Filler, "Classical Rabbinic Literature and the Making of Jewish Ethics," *Journal of Jewish Ethics* 1, no. 1 (2015): 153–70; and Mira Beth Wasserman, "Talmudic Ethics with Beruriah: Reading with Care," *Journal of Textual Reasoning* 11, no. 1 (2020): 4–23.

13. For study of the long tradition of virtue ethics within Judaism, see Geoffrey D. Claussen, Alexander Green, and Alan L. Mittleman, *Jewish Virtue Ethics* (Albany: SUNY Press, 2023).

14. See, for example, David Novak, *Natural Law in Judaism* (Cambridge: Cambridge University Press, 1998).

15. See, for example, Emil L. Fackenheim, *Encounters between Judaism and Modern Philosophy: Preface to Future Jewish Thought* (New York: Schocken, 1980).

16. See the pieces by Robert Cover in part 1, section 3; by Emmanuel Levinas in part 1, section 4; and by Benjamin Freedman in part 4, section 19.

17. See the pieces by Mara Benjamin in part 1, section 4; and by Toby Schonfeld and Laurie Zoloth in part 4, section 19.

18. Menachem Kellner, "Reflections on the Impossibility of Jewish Ethics," in *Moshe Schwarcz Memorial Volume* (Bar Ilan Annual, 22–23) (1987): 45–52. For an even stronger articulation of this view, see the condemnation of universalizing Jewish content in Michael Wyschogrod, *The Body of Faith* (San Francisco: Harper & Row, 1989).

19. This is the outlook that characterizes much of traditional *musar* literature. See the piece by Aharon Lichtenstein in part 1, section 1, for a more recent expression.

1 | Theories and Methods

> *Do what is right and good in the eyes of Adonai, so that it may go well with you . . .* Deuteronomy 6:18

Introduction

This volume opens with a substantial section on theories and methods of doing Jewish ethics—and in this regard, it is quite standard. This is the section in such volumes that most explicitly attends to definitional questions—what is "Jewish ethics"?—and to fundamental methodological queries: How do you do Jewish ethics? This volume includes some important, and ongoing, theoretical queries too: How do we know if the ethical reasoning in question is "Jewish"? Which resources do we see repeatedly in works marked as Jewish ethics? How might we evaluate the appropriateness of these sources? What guiding concepts or themes—classical or contemporary—are common in Jewish ethical reasoning?

Part 1 thus introduces pieces that exemplify this distinctive feature of contemporary Jewish ethics. Section 1, "Doing Jewish Ethics," presents pointed questions about the possibility and difficulties of this scholarship; it also introduces the volume's model of "curated conversations" on a given question. Each of these selections offers a critique of some reigning assumptions about the Jewish ethical endeavor, their respective eras a useful illustration of the debates emerging in the field. In the 1970s, Aharon Lichtenstein's question—is "ethics" distinguishable from halakha?—reflects the earliest scholarship in scholarly Jewish ethics, while Louis Newman's critical analysis in the 1990s bespeaks the ubiquitous appeals to classical Jewish sources for ethics as the field developed. Michal Raucher's 2020 book, meanwhile, critiques the enduring text-centric nature of Jewish ethics, pointing to ethnography as an equally valid—and perhaps more ethical?—method of reasoning.

Sections 2 and 3 can be understood as expansions on the foundational questions of the opening section. Section 2 delves more deeply into the use of Jewish texts for Jewish ethics, with debates about textual interpretation and critiques of what some scholars see as the overly limited canon of "useful" sources for modern ethical reasoning. Section 3 then resumes consideration on questions of law, its virtues and its limitations, in the construction of Jewish norms—where law refers not only to halakha but also to the idea of "law" as a governing structure for decision-making at all.

Part 1 also introduces some major concepts and themes in contemporary Jewish ethics scholarship. Section 4 focuses on the idea of covenant, a theme frequently invoked in this volume, while section 5 considers the possibility of cultivating virtues and section 6 speculates about the utility of "Jewish values" as a governing concept. Such themes are not necessarily unique to Jewish ethics, but the selections that are included below ground them in priorities, vernaculars, or histories that may be more particular to the Jewish tradition broadly construed.

These themes function something like overarching principles for Jewish ethical claims, featuring prominently in ethical reasoning regardless of the conclusions reached. Perhaps Jewish ethics should prioritize the idea of a covenantal relationship—whether divine-human or human alone—in drawing ethical conclusions. Or should it? So too with debates about ethical virtues, or the possibility of identifying communal values as a rubric for ethical decision-making: these are concepts employed by scholars of Jewish ethics across a wide variety of questions and conclusions. Readers are thus encouraged to approach every selection in this volume as a contribution to the conversation about what it means to do Jewish ethics, and do it well, whether these questions are explicitly marked as methodological queries or not. What resources, themes, and definitions are constitutive of this scholarship as the field has developed over the last half century?

1 | Doing Jewish Ethics

This volume is constructed with the assumption that Jewish ethics is always concerned with methods of reasoning. This means, of course, that the literature of this volume is as focused on how the thinkers come to their conclusions as it is on any what, or "position," on a topic. But contained within this broad question are many more specific queries whose answers are by no means settled. In a tradition whose most historically dominant normative category is law, halakha, is "ethics" a recognizable category at all? How might it differ from the processes or conclusions of halakha? What are the possible "sources" for Jewish ethical consideration? How do, or should, these sources "work" in service of contemporary ethical reasoning? And who may decide the answers to these questions?

The field of Jewish ethics is never far from such questions and their answers remain as contested as any particular normative ethical claim. Even as these debates continue, a body of scholarship categorized as "Jewish ethics" also continues — which is to say that thinkers who understand their work as belonging to "Jewish ethics" do their scholarship amid ongoing questions about whether that work should be categorized this way at all. (Sometimes it is the same thinker asking the question!)

It is perhaps fitting, therefore, that a volume confidently titled *Modern Jewish Ethics since 1970* opens with a 1975 essay by Rabbi Aharon Lichtenstein wondering whether Jewish ethics is even a recognizable category. Lichtenstein asks what might be understood as one of the "founding questions" of the field: How does "Jewish ethics" differ from halakha? That is, if halakha is the process of deriving communal norms from Jewish legal source-texts, what might it mean for these conclusions to not be already covered by this process?

The question is not (only) rhetorical. The Israeli scientist and philosopher Yeshayahu Leibowitz famously argued that Judaism recognized no normative framework outside of halakha; even the seemingly "ethical" commandments, regarding our treatment of our fellow humans, should be understood solely in a framework of divine command. Lichtenstein's essay probes this question of whether, or how, "ethics" might extend beyond, or exist alongside, Jewish legal reasoning, employing the rabbinic categories of *din* (legal judgment) and *lifnim mishurat hadin* (beyond the letter of the law) in his exploration. The reader will note that his conclusions depend largely on definitions; how we understand halakha will determine the degree to which we understand other non- or extralegal considerations to be at work.

Louis Newman's essay, by contrast, assumes the existence of a distinctive category called Jewish ethics. His now-classic critique also assumes that the sources of ethical reasoning are, chiefly, the classical textual sources of the Jewish tradition. But he insists on the subjectivity of textual interpretation, and the inherent challenges of appealing to classical Jewish texts for contemporary ethics, thereby making explicit a governing tendency of the field.

Like Newman, Michal Raucher assumes that "Jewish ethics" is a recognizable category. But in her departure from textually based arguments, she unsettles the assumption of Lichtenstein and Newman (and the field more broadly) that classical Jewish texts or later commentaries on the texts necessarily provide the primary foundation for any further reasoning. Exploring the lives of a contemporary group of haredi (ultra-Orthodox) women in Jerusalem as they discuss their pregnancies, Raucher observes that this experience furnishes the women with greater authority over their bodies, marriages, and medical decisions than their context might suggest. Raucher argues that this reality ought to occasion a rethinking of the assumption that texts and ensuing normative judgments are the sole, or best, foundations for Jewish ethical reasoning at all.

Each of these thinkers makes distinct arguments about what it might mean to do Jewish ethics, and to do it well. But they are not intended to "represent" the field as a whole, nor do their arguments and critiques exhaust the ongoing methodological debates in the field. Rather, we bring them together as an invitation for conversation with, and about, their assumptions, arguments, and critiques, and as an introduction to some of the major methodological questions seen throughout the volume.

AHARON LICHTENSTEIN

Does Jewish Tradition Recognize an Ethic Independent of Halakha?

Aharon Lichtenstein (1933–2015) was an Orthodox rabbi and leader of Yeshivat Rosh Etzion and held a PhD in English literature from Harvard University. Considered a towering authority on halakha in the contemporary world, he was awarded the Israel Prize for Jewish religious literature in 2014. Much of his work dealt with the interaction between Jewish law and the modern world.

From "Does Jewish Tradition Recognize an Ethic Independent of Halakha?" in *Modern Jewish Ethics: Theory and Practice*, ed. Marvin Fox (Columbus: Ohio State University Press, 1975), 62–88.

"Does the tradition recognize an ethic independent of halakha?" My subject is a simple factual question presumably calling for a yes-or-no answer. But what kind of Jew responds to salient questions with unequivocal monosyllables? Certainly not the traditional kind. Moreover, as formulated, this particular query is a studded minefield, every key term an ill-defined boobytrap. Who or what represents the tradition? Is the recognition de facto or de jure? How radical is the independence? Above all, what are the referents of ethic and halakha? A qualified reply is obviously required. . . .

The question is not what vestiges of natural morality continue to bind the Jew or to what extent receiving the Torah abrogated any antecedent ethic. It is rather whether, quite apart from ground common to natural and halakhic morality, the demands or guidelines of halakha are both so definitive and so comprehensive as to preclude the necessity for—and therefore, in a sense, the legitimacy of—any other ethic. . . . I am of course taking two things for granted. I assume, first, that halakha constitutes—or at least contains—an ethical system. This point has sometimes been challenged—most notably, in our day, by Professor Yeshayahu Leibowitz; but I do not think the challenge, albeit grounded in healthy radical monotheism, can be regarded seriously.[1] The extent to which halakha as a whole is pervaded by an ethical moment or the degree to which a specific mitzvah is rooted, if at all, in moral considerations are no doubt debatable. . . . As for the outright rejection of the ethical moment, however, I cannot

---

1. [Yeshayahu Leibowitz (1903–1994) was a prolific and influential Russian-Israeli philosopher and scientist at the Hebrew University of Jerusalem.]

find such quasi-fideistic voluntarism consonant with the main thrust of the tradition. One might cite numerous primary texts by way of rebuttal but a single verse in Jeremiah should suffice: "But let him that glorieth glory in this, that he understandeth and knoweth Me, for I am the Lord who exercise mercy, justice, and righteousness, in the earth; for these I desire, saith the Lord" (Jer. 923). The ethical element is presented as the reason for seeking knowledge of God, or, at the very least—if we translate *ki ani* as "that I am" rather than "for I am"—as its content. In either case, the religious and the ethical are here inextricably interwoven; and what holds true of religious knowledge holds equally true of religious, that is, halakhic, action. This fusion is central to the whole rabbinic tradition. From its perspective, the divorce of halakha from morality not only eviscerates but falsifies it.

Second, I assume that, at most, we can only speak of a complement to halakha, not of an alternative. Any ethic so independent of halakha as to obviate or override it, clearly lies beyond our pale. There are of course situations in which ethical factors—the preservation of life, the enhancement of human dignity, the quest for communal or domestic peace, or the mitigation of either anxiety or pain—sanction the breach, by preemptive priority or outright violation, of specific norms. However, these factors are themselves halakhic considerations, in the most technical sense of the term, and their deployment entails no rejection of the system whatsoever. . . . However elastic the term "tradition" to some, it does have its limits, and antinomianism, which for our purposes includes the rejection of Torah law, lies beyond them.

Essentially, then, the question is whether halakha is self-sufficient. Its comprehensiveness and self-sufficiency are notions many of us cherish in our more pietistic or publicistic moments. For certain purposes, it would be comfortable if we could accept Professor Kahana's statement "that in Jewish civil law there is no separation of law and morals and that there is no distinction between what the law is and what the law ought to be."[2] If, however, we mean that everything can be looked up, every moral dilemma resolved by reference to code or canon, the notion is both palpably naive and patently false. . . . There are moments when one must seek independent counsels. . . . Which of us has not, at times, been made painfully aware of the ethical paucity of his legal resources? Who has not found that the fulfillment of explicit halakhic duty could fall well short of exhausting clearly felt moral responsibility? The point to be emphasized, however

---

2. K. Kahana, *The Case for Jewish Civil Law in the Jewish State* (London, 1960), 28n (his italics).

—although this too, may be obvious—is that the deficiency is not merely the result of silence or ambiguity on the part of the sources. That may of course be a factor, requiring, as it does, recourse to inference and analogy to deal with the multitude of situations that, almost a priori, have not been covered by basic texts. The critical point, however, is that even the full discharge of one's whole formal duty as defined by the din often appears palpably insufficient.

"Rav Yohanan said," the Gemara in *Baba Mezia* cites, "'Jerusalem was but destroyed because they [i.e., its inhabitants] judged [in accordance with] Torah law within it.' Well, should they rather have followed the law of the Magians?! Say, rather, because they based their judgments solely upon Torah law and did not act *lifnim mishurat hadin* [i.e., beyond the line of the law]."[3] Nahmanides was even more outspoken.[4] In a celebrated passage, he explains that the general command, "Ye shall be holy" was issued because, the scope of the Torah's injunctions regarding personal conduct notwithstanding, a lustful sybarite could observe them to the letter and yet remain "a scoundrel with Torah license."

These passages contain strong and explicit language, and they answer our question plainly enough. Or do they? Just how independent of halakha is the ethic that ennobles us above the "scoundrel with Torah license?" If we regard *din* and halakha as coextensive, very independent. If, however, we recognize that halakha is multiplanar and many dimensional; that, properly conceived, it includes much more than is explicitly required or permitted by specific rules, we shall realize that the ethical moment we are seeking is itself an aspect of halakha. The demand or, if you will, the impetus for transcending the *din* is itself part of the halakhic corpus....

Once it has been determined that, in a given case, realization of "the right and the good" mandates a particular course, its pursuit may conceivably be as imperative as the performance of a *din*. However, the initial determination of what moral duty requires proceeds along different lines in the respective sphere. *Din* consists of a body of statutes, ultimately rooted in fundamental values but which at the moment of decision confront the individual as a set of rules.... Judgments are essentially grounded in deductive, primarily syllogistic reasoning. Metaphors that speak of laws as controlling or governing a case are therefore perfectly accurate.

3. *Baba Mezia* 30b.

4. [Moses ben Nahman (1194–1270), often known as Nahmanides was a medieval rabbinic scholar from Catalonia.]

Lifnim mishurat hadin, by contrast, is the sphere of contextual morality. Its basis for decision is paradoxically both more general and more specific. The formalist is guided by a principle or a rule governing a category of cases defined by *n* number of characteristics. The more sensitive and sophisticated the system, the more individuated the categories. Whatever the degree of specificity, however, the modus operandi is the same: action grows out of the application of class rules to a particular case judged to be an instance of that class or of the interaction of several classes, there being, of course principles to govern seemingly hybrid cases as well....

It goes without saying that Judaism has rejected contextualism as a self-sufficient ethic. Nevertheless, we should recognize equally that it has embraced it as the modus operandi of large tracts of human experience. These lie in the realm of *lifnim mishurat hadin*. In this area, the halakhic norm is itself situational. It speaks in broad terms: "And thou shalt do the right and the good"; "And thou shalt walk in His ways." The metaphors employed to describe it—"the ways of the good" or "the paths of the righteous"—denote purpose and direction rather than definitively prescribed acts.... In observing *din*, the Jew rivets his immediate attention upon the specific command addressed to him. His primary response is to the source of his prescribed act. With respect to *lifnim mishurat hadin*, he is "looking before and after," concerned with results as much as with origins. His focus is axiological and teleological.

Quite apart from the severity of obligation, therefore, there is a fundamental difference between *din* and *lifnim mishurat hadin*. One, at a more minimal level, imposes fixed objective standards. The demands of the other evolve from a specific situation; and, depending upon the circumstances, may vary with the agent....

Finally, the halakhic connection is relevant at a third level, when we are concerned with an ethic neither as decisor of specific actions nor as determinant of a field of values but as the polestar of life in its totality. Halakhic commitment orients a Jew's whole being around his relation to God. It is not content with the realization of a number of specific goals but demands personal dedication—and not only dedication but consecration.... Integration of the whole self within a halakhic framework becomes substantive rather than semantic insofar as it is reflected within the full range of personal activity. Reciprocally, however, that conduct is itself stimulated by fundamental halakhic commitment....

In dealing with this subject, I have, in effect, addressed myself both to those who, misconstruing the breadth of its horizons, find the halakhic ethic inadequate, and to those who smugly regard even its narrower confines as sufficient. In doing so, I hope I have presented my thinking clearly. But for those who prefer definitive answers, let me conclude by saying: Does the tradition recognize an ethic independent of halakha? You define your terms and take your choice.

LOUIS NEWMAN

Woodchoppers and Respirators: The Problem of Interpretation in Contemporary Jewish Ethics

Louis Newman (b. 1956) is a professor emeritus of Jewish studies at Carleton College, where his research and teaching emphasized Jewish ethics, the relationship between contemporary ethics and classical texts, and questions in applied ethics. He has also served as associate vice provost at Stanford University.

From "Woodchoppers and Respirators: The Problem of Interpretation in Contemporary Jewish Ethics," *Modern Judaism* 10, no. 1 (1990): 17–42.

The purpose of this study is to explore the ways in which Jewish ethicists derive answers to contemporary moral problems from traditional texts.... To illustrate this process and the hermeneutical issues to which it gives rise, I will focus on the contemporary Jewish ethical debate surrounding euthanasia.... Euthanasia has received a good deal of attention in recent years by Jewish ethicists of both traditional and liberal orientations.... Moreover, the situations in which questions of euthanasia arise in our time are largely unprecedented, owing to recent dramatic advances in medical technology.... At the same time, I want to emphasize that the interpretive problems raised here are in no way limited to this specific moral issue, or indeed to biomedical ethics generally. To the extent that this process of textual interpretation is central to all contemporary Jewish ethical discourse, so too are the methodological problems that accompany it ...

Translating traditional Jewish values into specific norms for ethical conduct in the modern world involves three steps: (1) identifying precedents from classical Jewish literature, (2) adducing principles from these texts, and (3) applying these principles to new sets of facts....

Let us begin by considering the difficulty of identifying precedents within the tradition for cases involving euthanasia:

> On the day that Rabbi Judah was dying, the rabbis decreed a public fast and offered prayer for heavenly mercy [so that he would not die]. . . . Rabbi Judah's handmaid ascended to the roof and prayed [for Judah to die]. The rabbis meanwhile continued their prayers for heavenly mercy. She took a jar and threw it down from the roof to the ground. They stopped praying [for a moment] and the soul of Rabbi Judah departed.[5]

> Sometimes one must request mercy on behalf of the ill so that he might die, as in the case of a patient who is terminal and who is in great pain.[6] . . .

Citing these sources, Solomon Freehof concludes that Jewish law sanctions passive euthanasia, at least in those cases in which the dying individual is incurable and/or in great pain. . . .

To others, however, such conclusions about euthanasia may not legitimately be derived from these texts. Asher Bar-Zev, for example . . . ultimately rejects it on the grounds that there is a qualitative difference between praying to God for death to come (or refraining from those prayers that presumably serve to sustain life) and taking active medical steps to hasten death. . . .

Do texts about praying for death to come have precedential value for matters of euthanasia? The fundamental problem in answering such a question . . . is simply that traditional sources do not come to us prelabeled to indicate which are relevant to the particular contemporary dilemma we happen to be facing. . . . Moreover, it is a matter of dispute among contemporary Jewish ethicists whether aggadic (non-legal) texts can serve as valid precedents for contemporary decisions at all. . . . Needless to say, one's decision to accept or reject one or more texts as precedential will greatly affect one's ultimate conclusion about what constitutes a Jewish view on issues such as euthanasia. Yet, even if all modern interpreters could agree on the body of traditional texts that constitute valid precedents, a second interpretive hurdle would remain, namely, how to articulate the general legal or moral principles embodied in these rules. . . . Certain traditional texts, for example, recognize a category of individual who is on the verge of death (*goses*) and specify what may and may not be done on that person's behalf.[7] These rules about the treatment of the *goses*, however, do not readily lend themselves to generalization and so the way in which they should

---

5. B. T. *Ketubot* 104a.
6. Rabbenu Nissim, commentary to B. T. *Nedarim* 40a.
7. [See part 4, section 22, for other considerations about the *goses* in Jewish ethics.]

be applied to modern cases of euthanasia remains a matter of considerable debate.

> It is forbidden to cause the dying to die quickly, such as one who is moribund (*goses*) over a long time and who cannot die, it is forbidden to remove the pillow from under him on the assumption that certain bird-feathers prevent his death.... But if there is something that delays his death, such as a nearby woodchopper making a noise, or there is salt on his tongue, and these prevent his speedy death, one can remove them, for this does not involve any action at all, but rather the removal of the preventive agent.[8] ...

Yet, even if all authorities could agree that traditional laws regarding the *goses* were applicable to contemporary cases of euthanasia, the principle underlying these cases is subject to several alternative interpretations. It is clear that the woodchopper is an impediment to the patient's death. But how are we to construe the nature of this impediment—as something physically removed from the person, as something that has no therapeutic value, as something not placed there by the patient or those caring for that person, or simply as anything whatsoever that prevents a person from dying....

While these traditional texts concerning treatment of the *goses* both proscribe taking any action that would hasten death and permit removing certain obstacles that forestall death, it is not apparent how such rules can be translated into general principles applicable to contemporary situations.... As a result, these texts can be applied to contemporary situations in a number of ways and, in any event, only with considerable reservation....

The third and final step in the interpretive process involves the application of general principles to contemporary situations. To do this the interpreter, once again, must determine the extent to which a new fact pattern does or does not correspond to the facts underlying previous rulings....

As we have seen, some view an artificial life support device as analogous to a woodchopper.... Some regard disconnecting a patient from such equipment as analogous to prayers offered for the death of those suffering or terminally ill. Others, as we have seen, call these analogies into question....

But my point in exploring the interpretive process ... is not primarily to note the fact that contemporary authorities, like their traditional predecessors, disagree about the meaning of specific texts.... Whatever other differences divide

---

8. R. Moses Isserles (Rema) on *Shulchan Aruch, Yoreh Deah* 339:1.

them, all modern Jewish ethicists are united in their perspective on both the meaning of texts and the role of the ethicist as an exegete.

The two working assumptions ... can be stated simply as follows. First, the source of contemporary values lies within the texts and, second, the job of the modern ethicist/exegete is to extract this meaning from the texts and apply it to contemporary moral problems. The texts themselves contain meaning and the interpreter merely retrieves this meaning and draws our attention to the inherent connection between the text and the contemporary world....

But in the view of many contemporary legal and literary theorists, this represents a serious misunderstanding of the interpretive process, of the meaning of texts and of the role of the interpreter in creating that meaning....

These views of interpretation challenge Jewish ethicists to look at textual study and exegesis in a new light.... The Jewish legal tradition does not really constitute a body of views and precedents that "speak for themselves" to contemporary issues.... It provides a rich resource of values and principles that Jewish ethicists, if they are committed to remaining within the tradition, must utilize. But the texts do not, either individually or collectively, dictate how to use or apply these resources.... The meaning that the interpreter finds in the text will change over time and will not be consistent from one interpreter to another....

Given a properly selected set of interpretive assumptions, the texts can be invoked to support a whole range of positions on such questions.... The very process of interpretation necessitates acts of judgment on the part of the interpreter—decisions about which cases constitute precedents, what the principles of those cases are, and how they should be applied to the case at hand.... It follows that the interpretive assumptions that readers bring to the literature play a decisive role in creating the very meaning that they attribute to the text. And if this is true generally, it is especially true for interpreters of classical Jewish texts, which are notoriously terse and ambiguous....

But, it will be objected, if we view the interpretive process in this way, do we not undermine the entire enterprise of contemporary Jewish ethics? ... To the extent that the meaning of a text lies as much in the activity of the interpreter as in the text itself, contemporary Jewish ethics becomes at least partly a matter of reading our values into the texts rather than deriving authentically Jewish views from them. And if eisegesis replaces exegesis, what is the point of doing Jewish ethics, or rather, what makes Jewish ethics Jewish and not just the subjective judgment of an individual reader?

In attempting to answer these questions, let me turn to a model of jurisprudence suggested by Ronald Dworkin.... Dworkin suggests that judges who interpret a legal tradition are doing much the same thing as authors who interpret the literary creativity of their predecessors. Indeed, he asks us to imagine a series of authors who write a novel one chapter at a time. Each author (after the first) inherits the work of earlier writers in the series and so is given a kind of limited creative license, for the author's literary imagination must work within boundaries (however fluid) that have been established by previous writers.... Dworkin proceeds to argue that,

> Deciding hard cases at law is rather like this strange literary exercise. The similarity is most evident when judges consider and decide common law cases; that is, when no statute figures centrally in the legal issue, and the argument turns on which rules or principles of law "underlie" the related decisions of other judges in the past. Each judge is then like a novelist in the chain.[9]

In my judgment, contemporary Jewish ethics can absorb this understanding of the interpretive process without losing its *raison d'être*, though the mental questions raised above will need to be answered in a new way....

On the level of semantics, Jewish ethicists should avoid talking about what specific positions "Judaism" sanctions on contemporary issues.... Accordingly, the rhetoric of ethics should change from "what Judaism teaches" to "what we, given particular interpretive assumptions and our particular way of construing the coherence of the tradition as a whole, find within the traditional sources." ... If contemporary Jewish ethicists presented their views in the more precise, qualified way that I have suggested, they would be forced to confront more self-consciously than they have their own role in the interpretive process.

With rare exceptions, these authors have attempted to defend their particular way of selecting and reading sources against other possible or actual readings. ... As a result, it could be said much contemporary Jewish discourse resembles a conversation in which the participants are talking past, rather than to, one another. If the foregoing analysis is substantially correct, it follows that any contemporary Jewish position is only as compelling as the interpretive assumptions

---

9. Ronald Dworkin, *A Matter of Principle* (Cambridge, MA: Harvard University Press, 1985), 159. Dworkin's distinction between advancing the current enterprise and striking out in a new direction has been challenged by Fish, who regards meaning as wholly a function of the reader's activity ("Working on the Chain Gang: Interpretation in the Law and in Literary Criticism," *Critical Inquiry* 9 (1982): 207–8).

on which it rests. To defend cogently any particular ethical position, then, requires that one offer reasons for adopting the interpretive stance that one has....

Moreover, given the obvious parallels between Jewish ethics as practiced by most contemporary authorities and Anglo-American jurisprudence, it is most unfortunate that Jewish ethicists have largely ignored developments in American legal theory.... If more attention were given to the literature in general jurisprudence, Jewish authorities might gain both a fuller understanding of the nature of legal interpretation and useful models for thinking about the interplay between the authority of a textual tradition and the freedom inherent in the exercise of judicial discretion.

Finally, in no sense do I wish to suggest, given the subjective nature of interpretation as I have described it, that Jewish ethicists should quit reading traditional texts.... I would propose that contemporary Jewish ethics be conceived, not as an attempt to determine what past authorities would say about contemporary problems if they were alive today, but as a dialectical relationship in which finally no sharp distinction can be made between our voices and theirs. ... Any reading of the texts that we produce, and any conclusions we draw from them, are as much our work as theirs. Those engaged in contemporary Jewish ethics surely need not quit reading texts, but just as surely they need to make more modest claims on their behalf.

MICHAL RAUCHER

Conceiving Agency

Michal Raucher (b. 1983) is an associate professor of Jewish studies at Rutgers University. Her work in anthropology of Judaism focuses on Jewish women in the United States and Israel, reproduction and reproductive justice, bioethics, and religious women's agency and authority.

From *Conceiving Agency* (Bloomington: Indiana University Press, 2020), 1–5, 9–11, 16–20.

A few months after I settled in Jerusalem, I received an email from a woman named Dina. Dina had heard about my research from a friend of hers....

I was nervous about calling Dina, but she was happy to hear from me and invited me to her apartment the following week.... [Her] youngest, about eighteen months, was cranky when I showed up at Dina's apartment on a Tuesday morning. Dina nursed him for most of our interview, which she said helped with the nausea. Although she was only about six weeks into her fifth pregnancy and not sharing the news with most people, she told me and allowed me into her life for the next year....

As she became more of a pregnancy expert, Dina also came to challenge the doctors and rabbis surrounding her.... During an ultrasound scan in the twenty-fourth week, the technician made a mistake and wrote down the wrong date of conception, making it seem like she was two weeks further along than she really was.... Dina tried to tell her doctor at each appointment, but he ignored her corrections. By the time she reached the ultrasound in the thirty-sixth week, Dina's doctor was very nervous about what he thought was a fetus that had stopped growing.... At this point, Dina got upset. She yelled at the doctor, "This is ridiculous. You obviously never listen to me. You never care what I say!" Dina stormed out of his office and did not return to the hospital until she was in labor at forty weeks. The baby was small but healthy when he was born. By her fourth pregnancy, Dina had gained sufficient embodied knowledge and reproductive authority to challenge the medical establishment.

Additionally, Dina, a devout haredi woman who grew up haredi, married a haredi man, and is committed to the haredi life, does not think her haredi rabbi has anything to teach her about what is permissible or forbidden during pregnancy. This is striking because rabbinic oversight has expanded in the last few decades as rabbis have increased their involvement in matters that were previously considered beyond their purview.... During our conversations, however, Dina struggled to think of a question she might ask her rabbi....

Although they are faced with patriarchal religious and medical authorities, haredi women find space for—and insist on—their autonomy from these authorities when they make decisions regarding the use of contraceptives, prenatal testing, fetal ultrasounds, and other reproductive practices. This autonomy, however, should not be read as freedom from religious life or the actions of an individual without any constraints. Instead, when haredi women assert that they are in a better position to make reproductive decisions, they draw on their embodied experiences of pregnancy, cultural norms of reproduction, and theological beliefs in their relationship to divine activity during reproduction....

The matrix of control surrounding a haredi woman's prenatal care might give one the impression that haredi women are restricted in their decision-making capacity and are limited in their authority over pregnancy. This was not what I found during my research with haredi women, however. They recognize this context and yet simultaneously talk about pregnancy as *their* space. When they are pregnant, they make decisions *without* their rabbis, husbands, or doctors, a fact that contradicted all my expectations....

I found that the embodied experience of pregnancy shapes a woman's ability to make decisions without male authorities and to develop a sense of authority over pregnancy-related decisions.... This sense of authority gives haredi women the ability to override the influence of the rabbis.... I argue that, paradoxically, the sources of a haredi woman's oppression are also the sources of her agency.

I show that the way haredi women make decisions about reproduction reflects a religious ethic distinct from the way Jewish bioethics frames its discourse. This gap between normative religious ethics and the strategies of religious participants necessitates a rethinking of the discourse of religious ethics. Scholarly discussions of ethics should account for the embodied, cultural, religious, and contextual experiences of individuals. I maintain that a haredi woman's agency over reproductive decisions is her reproductive ethic. Agency—built on bodily experience, bolstered by cultural and theological norms, and informed by socioeconomic context—shapes haredi women's reproductive autonomy. This is in contrast to those who see religious ethics as coming solely from sacred texts or rabbinic interpretations and legal applications. My findings speak to the relevance of normative religious and ethical doctrine in the lives of moral agents and the capacity of individuals to respond as moral agents to their situations. Ethics—and religious ethics in particular—must be viewed from the perspectives of embodied moral agents so that ethical discourse can better reflect the lived realities of ethics....

Reproductive agency refers to the ability to make decisions about the process of reproduction—contraception, abortion, prenatal testing, ultrasounds, and birth. [This term] is how I describe the authority that haredi women have over reproductive decisions. It is important to note that when I refer to women's authority, I am not referring to women as religious leaders, either formally or informally.... While many other scholars depict the haredi world as revolving around book learning and attentiveness to rabbinic instruction, these analyses have overlooked haredi women's distinct participation in haredi life.... My analysis demonstrates that haredi women lead religious lives distinct from their husbands' and that their reproductive experiences shape their theologies and their participation in the hierarchical structures of haredi Judaism....

It is important to note that my interlocutors would not describe their actions as demonstrating "agency" or having "autonomy." Although the haredi women

I spoke to discussed their knowledge (*yedah*) about pregnancy, their ability (*yecholet*) to make reproductive decisions, and their authority (*samchut*) over such decisions, they did not use the term "agency" or refer to themselves as "autonomous." . . . As a feminist ethnographer, I intend to prioritize the voices of my interlocutors and to use their interpretive strategies to describe their actions. At the same time, I am engaged in a contemporary conversation among scholars who resist simplistic, critical understandings of women in conservative religious traditions. Therefore, despite the fact that my interlocutors would not use the terms "agency" or "autonomy," I have found these to be helpful concepts in describing the tensions, negotiations, actions, and understandings of the haredi women who shared their reproductive narratives with me. . . .

Overwhelmingly, scriptural sources, religious doctrine and law, and central forms of religious authority have determined what Jewish bioethicists consider to be normative religious ethics. Haredi women demonstrate, however, that cultural, economic, theological, and embodied factors contribute to their reproductive ethic. This gap between normative religious ethics and the strategies of religious participants requires a rethinking of the discourse of religious ethics.
. . . I turn to Jewish ethics and suggest that ethnography must be incorporated as a corrective to the gap in normative ethics and practice. Ethics—and religious ethics in particular—must be viewed from the perspectives of embodied moral agents so that our ethical discourse can better reflect the lived realities of ethics. . . .

As I discovered such a significant gap between the professed importance of norms in haredi life and the lived experiences of haredi women—and, furthermore, the importance of women's lived experiences in their reproductive ethic—I began to consider whether normative religious ethics could benefit from more engagement with the ethnographic reality of ethics and, if so, what this would look like. This requires a shift in religious ethics from thinking about what books, laws, and authorities say one should do to what obstacles and approaches individuals face in making ethical decisions. . . .

Jewish ethics has been slow to adopt any ethnographic methods; instead, the field has been largely determined by various interpretations of Jewish law or readings from Jewish biblical texts. David Ellenson refers to this reliance on the text to find precedents and principles for Jewish ethics as "halakhic formalism." Users of this method presume that Jewish ethics are located in the legal texts because these texts carry the most authority in Judaism. . . . . While this methodology might include a consideration of contemporary morality, socioeconomic considerations, and the particular context of the situation, Dorff insists that what is Jewish about Jewish bioethics is its use of legal texts. . . .

Ethnography is both a more ethical approach for Jewish ethics and a historically accurate way of determining an ethical response in Jewish thought. Ethnography is more ethical not only because it appreciates context but also because it is attentive to feminist critiques of religious ethics.[10] Jewish ethicists Dena Davis and Ronit Irshai critique Jewish ethics for relying on rabbinic literature, which excludes women. They maintain that this void has an effect on moral deliberation and moral conclusions.[11] . . . Although feminist Jewish ethicists have advocated for the inclusion of women's voices in Jewish ethical discourse, this generally means the inclusion of more female scholars interpreting Jewish law. As long as bodily experience is overlooked, our ethical discourse will continue to ignore the subjectivity of those involved in the conversation.

I suggest reframing the discourse of ethics to reflect the lived realities and subjectivities of ethical decision-making. This requires a robust incorporation of ethnography into our ethical discourse. . . . But ethnography is not the only area where we should pay attention to the subjectivity of ethical agents. Normative ethics is not divorced from the embodied agents constructing moral codes. Individuals, informed by their subjective and embodied experiences, have determined normative moral discourse. In Jewish ethics, choosing which voice is authoritative and decisive in multivocal dialogic rabbinic writing is ultimately a moral choice each reader makes. In other words, contemporary bioethics scholars who claim to be using the rabbinic texts to inform their moral positions are actually relying on their moral positions first and searching for justification in the text second. . . . I argue that the reproductive ethics of haredi women in Jerusalem is, in fact, a Jewish reproductive ethic, just as much as ethical positions derived from scholarly reading of Jewish texts represent Jewish ethics. . . . The everyday experiences of religion cannot be separated from what is understood to be "official religion." Similarly, the everyday experiences of making ethical decisions cannot be separated from what we call "ethics." To construct this lived ethics, we must avail ourselves of a methodological tool not often used in ethics and especially not in Jewish ethics: ethnography.

10. Not all would agree that ethnography is a feminist method. Ethnography can violate many principles of feminism—namely, in that it is intrusive and exploitative of those very individuals that we seek to give voice to. See Judith Stacey, "Can There Be a Feminist Ethnography?," *Women's Studies Int Forum* 11, no. 1 (1988): 21–27.

11. [The work of both authors is included in part 4, section 21.]

2 | Forging Ethical Norms from Jewish Textual Sources

The primary resource for Jewish ethical thought and practice is the classical Jewish textual tradition, although the reliance on these sources for modern ethics is sometimes contested. Together, the Tanach (Hebrew Bible), particularly the five books of the Torah, Mishnah, and Babylonian Talmud are the foundation for a wide-ranging and extensive library of later Jewish writings, including commentaries, homilies, legal codes, legal decisions, and philosophic writings. Modern Jewish ethicists draw on these writings in developing theories of Jewish ethical thought and when seeking Jewish answers to ethical questions. This section presents three instructive examples of how contemporary scholars engage classical Jewish texts in their accounts of Jewish ethics. These three scholars focus on different parts of the Jewish textual corpus, and they bring very different questions, concerns, and assumptions to the texts they examine.

For some modern Jewish ethicists, the task of establishing Jewish ethical norms is largely continuous with the traditional practice of deciding questions of halakha. While halakha is commonly translated as "Jewish law," it diverges from other systems of law in some significant ways. Although it is traditionally understood to be an expression of God's will, it has seldom—if ever—functioned with the force of governing authorities to back it up. Moreover, the text that is foundational for halakha, the Babylonian Talmud, diverges from many works of law in its qualities of multivocality and indeterminacy. Traditionally, halakhic rulings were the purview of specially trained rabbis, experts in the interpretation of the Talmud and Talmudic commentaries. In the centuries following the publication of the Talmud, rabbinic authorities codified major areas of normative practice, and subsequent halakhic decision-making was largely limited to addressing new historical contingencies.

In the modern era, political upheavals and technological change introduced a host of new halakhic questions. At the same time, some thinkers (both Jewish and non-Jewish) began to question whether the Jewish textual tradition is truly a reflection of divine will and whether the dictates of halakha are consistent with universal ethical ideas. Today, the field of Jewish ethics includes a wide array of views on the authority of Jewish texts to weigh in on questions of Jewish normative practice. Some Jewish ethicists defer to traditional halakhic authorities, centering their accounts of Jewish ethics on the continuing tradition of halakhic decision-making. Other Jewish ethicists are strong critics of halakha, invoking ethical arguments that challenge core assumptions of the Jewish textual tradition. Still others look beyond the Jewish legal tradition and center Jewish ethical ideas on Jewish texts that are narrative or discursive rather than legal.

While the three pieces in this section all engage classical Jewish texts, their divergent interests and goals lead them to focus on different kinds of Jewish texts, and to deploy different modes of reading and interpretation. Judith Plaskow is a founding figure of the Jewish feminist movement and a pioneering thinker in the field of Jewish theology. She is committed to a transformation of Judaism that would be fully inclusive of the experiences and perspectives of women, and the starting place of her work is a searing ethical critique of the entirety of the Jewish textual tradition for its marginalization and exclusion of women. Her work focuses chiefly on core biblical narratives, beginning with the Torah's account of God's covenant with Israel at Mount Sinai. Even as she is committed to exposing and challenging the damaging ways that Torah texts silence and diminish women, she nevertheless looks to those texts as a central resource for building connections between the Jewish past and a transformed, inclusive Jewish future. Plaskow also finds a useful model in the classical rabbinic tradition of midrash, an imaginative mode of interpretation that diverges from the plain meaning of the biblical text so as to anchor new ideas and values in biblical stories and expressions. While Plaskow assigns no consistent ethical authority to classical Jewish texts, these texts remain central to her ethical vision for a feminist Judaism.

Elliot Dorff, a prolific scholar of Jewish ethics and a leading Conservative rabbi, looks to works of halakha to decide ethical questions; these he understands as the authoritative sources for establishing Jewish norms. At the same time, he acknowledges moral imperatives that come from outside Jewish texts and may be deployed to critique and change Jewish normative practice. In the selection below, he characterizes his own Conservative Jewish outlook on ethics as a middle position between Reform and Orthodox Judaism. As a Conservative halakhist, he brings a historical orientation to his interpretation of traditional Jewish texts, seeking to understand how any given text reflects its historic setting. Unlike more liberal Jews, he insists that authority for setting Jewish norms should rest with rabbis. Unlike some Orthodox Jews, he thinks halakha can change to accommodate new ethical insights.

Shaul Magid is a prominent scholar of modern Judaism as well as a rabbi. In his excerpt below, he criticizes the field of Jewish ethics for being far too narrowly focused on questions of law, normativity, and halakhic rulings. Magid broadens the field of Jewish ethical inquiry by explicating a text from the Hasidic tradition, a mystical movement focused on daily piety that emerged in Eastern Europe in the late eighteenth century. Magid argues that while halakha is an important element of Hasidic life, it is not seen as the primary locus for ethical development.

Though these pieces do not directly engage each other or even the same set of questions, they speak to each other in instructive ways. Plaskow and Magid, for instance, can be compared in the way they both depict Jewish ethics as being intimately tied to Jewish theology. Both Plaskow and Dorff discuss moral imperatives to change tradition, though they have very different ideas about the meaning and value of tradition. Dorff's piece is critical of Plaskow's pioneering feminist approach, while Magid pursues a corrective to what he sees as the field's overemphasis on legal issues, a tendency that Dorff typifies. The task of drawing ethical insights and arguments from an expansive, multiform textual tradition is no simple matter.

JUDITH PLASKOW

Standing Again at Sinai: Judaism from a Feminist Perspective

Judith Plaskow (b. 1947) is a scholar of religion, a theologian, and a pioneering leader of the Jewish feminist movement. Beginning in the 1970s, Jewish women who were inspired by Second Wave feminism began to bring a feminist critique to the structures and practices of Jewish communal life. While most Jewish feminist activists focused on increased access and participation for women, Plaskow argued that an emphasis on practice was not enough; change had to occur deep within the Jewish theological imagination, in how Jews thought about God, the Torah, and the nature of Jewish life. Standing Again at Sinai *is a foundational work of Jewish feminist thought. Plaskow is also a leading scholar of sexuality and religion and her writings on Jewish sexual ethics affirm and celebrate LGBTQ+ identities and experience. Plaskow is a professor emerita of religious studies at Manhattan College.*

From Standing Again at Sinai: Judaism from a Feminist Perspective (New York: Harper Collins, 1990), 25–31.

Chapter 2. Torah: Reshaping Jewish Memory

Entry into the covenant at Sinai is the root experience of Judaism, the central event that established the Jewish people. Given the importance of this event, there can be no verse in the Torah more disturbing to the feminist than Moses's warning to his people in Exodus 19:15, "Be ready for the third day; do not go near a woman." For here, at the very moment that the Jewish people stands at Sinai ready to receive the covenant—not now the covenant with individual patriarchs but with the people as a whole—at the very moment when Israel stands trembling waiting for God's presence to descend upon the mountain, Moses addresses the community only as men. The specific issue at stake is ritual impurity: An emission of semen renders both a man and his female partner temporarily unfit to approach the sacred (Lev. 15:16–18). But Moses does not say, "Men and women do not go near each other." At the central moment of Jewish history, women are invisible. Whether they too stood there trembling in fear and expectation, what they heard when the men heard these words of Moses, we do not know. It was not their experience that interested the chronicler or that informed and shaped the Torah.

Moses's admonition can be seen as a paradigm of what I have called "the profound injustice of Torah itself."[12] In this passage, the otherness of women finds

12. Judith Plaskow, "The Right Question Is Theological," *On Being a Jewish Feminist: A Reader*, ed. Susannah Heschel (New York: Schocken Books, 1983), 231.

its way into the very center of Jewish experience. And although the verse hardly can be blamed for women's situation, it sets forth a pattern recapitulated again and again in Jewish sources. Women's invisibility at the moment of entry into the covenant is reflected in the content of the covenant thaat, in both grammar and substance, addresses the community as male heads of household. It is perpetuated by the later tradition, which in its comments and codifications takes women as objects of concern or legislation but rarely sees them as shapers of tradition and actors in their own lives.

It is not just a historical injustice that is at stake in this verse, however. There is another dimension to the problem of the Sinai passage without which it is impossible to understand the task of Jewish feminism today. Were this passage simply the record of a historical event long in the past, the exclusion of women at this critical juncture would be troubling, but also comprehensible for its time. The Torah is not just history, however, but also living memory. The Torah reading, as a central part of the Sabbath and holiday liturgy, calls to mind and recreates the past for succeeding generations. When the story of Sinai is recited as part of the annual cycle of Torah readings and again as a special reading for Shavuot, women each time hear ourselves thrust aside anew, eavesdropping on a conversation among men and between men and God. As Rachel Adler[13] puts it, "Because the text has excluded her, she is excluded again in this yearly reenactment and will be excluded over and over, year by year, every time she rises to hear the covenant read."[14] If the covenant is a covenant with all generations (Deut. 29:13ff), then its reappropriation also involves the continual reappropriation of women's marginality.

This passage in Exodus is one of the places in the Tanach where women's silence is so deeply charged, so overwhelming, that it can provoke a crisis for the Jewish feminist. As Rachel Adler says, "We are being invited by Jewish men to re-covenant, to forge a covenant which will address the inequalities of women's position in Judaism, but we ask ourselves, 'Have we ever had a covenant in the first place? Are women Jews?'"[15] This is a question asked at the edge of a deep abyss. How can we ever hope to fill the silence that shrouds Jewish women's past? If women are invisible from the first moment of Jewish history, can we

---

13. [See part 1, section 3, for a selection by Jewish feminist ethicist Rachel Adler.]
14. Rachel Adler, "I've Had Nothing Yet, So I Can't Take More," *Moment* 8 (September 1983), 23.
15. Adler, "I've Had Nothing Yet," 22.

hope to become visible now? How many of us will fight for years to change the institutions in which we find ourselves only to achieve token victories? Perhaps we should put our energy elsewhere, into the creation of new communities where we can be fully present and where our struggles will not come up against walls as old as our beginnings.

Yet urgent and troubling as these questions are, there is a tension between them and the reality of the Jewish woman who poses them. The questions emerge out of a contradiction between the holes in the text and the felt experience of many Jewish women. For if Moses's words come as a shock and affront, it is because women have always known or assumed our presence at Sinai; the passage is painful because it seems to deny what we have always taken for granted. Of course we were at Sinai; how is it then that the text could imply we were not there?

It is not only we who ask these questions. The rabbis too seem to have been disturbed at the implication of women's absence from Sinai and found a way to read women's presence into the text. As Rashi[16] understood Exodus 19:3 — "Thus shall you say to the house of Jacob and declare to the children of Israel" —"the house of Jacob" refers to the women and "the children of Israel" refers to the men. The Talmud interprets Exodus 19:15 ("Do not go near a woman") to mean that *women* can purify themselves on the third day after there is no longer any chance of their having a discharge of live sperm (B. T. *Shabbat* 86a).

Apparently, women's absence was unthinkable to the rabbis, and this despite the fact that in their own work they continually reenact that absence. How much more then should it be unthinkable to us who know we are present today even in the midst of communities that continue to deny us? The contradiction between the Torah text and our experience is crucial; for, construed a certain way, it is a potential bridge to a new relationship with the tradition. To accept our absence from Sinai would be to allow the male text to define us and our connection to Judaism. To stand on the ground of our experience, on the other hand, to start with the certainty of our membership in our own people is to be forced to remember and recreate its history, to reshape Torah. It is to move from anger at the tradition, through anger to empowerment. It is to begin the journey toward the creation of a feminist Judaism.

* * *

16. [*Rashi* is an acronym for Rabbi Shlomo Yitzchaki (1040–1105), a rabbinic scholar of northern France who is the foremost commentator of the Torah and Talmud.]

Jewish feminists, in other words, must reclaim Torah as our own. We must render visible the presence, experience, and deeds of women erased in traditional sources. We must tell the stories of women's encounters with God and capture the texture of their religious experience. We must expand the notion of Torah to encompass not just the Five Books of Moses and traditional Jewish learning, but women's words, teachings, and actions hitherto unseen. To expand Torah, we must reconstruct Jewish history to include the history of women, and in doing so alter the shape of Jewish memory....

Perhaps the best example of the significance of memory in Jewish life is the Passover seder. On this most widely celebrated of Jewish holidays, families gather together not to memorialize the Exodus from Egypt but to relive it. As the climactic words of the seder say (slightly transformed!), "In every generation, each Jew should regard her or himself as though she or he personally went forth from Egypt.... It was not only our ancestors which the Holy One redeemed from slavery, but us also did God redeem together with them." But even this reliving would be pointless, or simply a matter of momentary experience, were it not meant to shape our wider sense of identity and obligation. Indeed, the experience and memory of slavery and redemption are the very foundations of Jewish religious obligation. "You shall not wrong or oppress a stranger, for you were strangers in the land of Egypt" (Exod. 22:20, altered). "I the Lord am your God who brought you out of the land of Egypt, the house of bondage" (Exod. 20:2). All the commandments follow. In the modern era, the memory of slavery in Egypt has also taken on more specifically political meaning. It has fostered among some Jews an identification with the oppressed that has led to involvement in a host of movements for social change—and has fueled the feminist demand for justice for women within Judaism.

The past as depicted in Jewish sources can be used not simply as a warrant for change, however, but also as a bulwark against it. If we need any further proof of the power of memory in Jewish life, we need only consider the ways in which the past is used against the possibility of innovation. Arguments against the ordination of women as rabbis, for example, are rooted not so much in any real legal impediment to women's ordination as in the fact that historically rabbis have been men. The notion of a woman as rabbi feels "un-Jewish" to many Jews because it is perceived as discontinuous with a Jewish past that makes certain claims upon its present bearers. On question after question, the weight of tradition is thrown at women as an argument for keeping things the way they are.

It is because of the past's continuing power in the present that, when the rabbis profoundly transformed Jewish religious life after the destruction of the Second Temple, they also reconstructed Jewish memory to see themselves in continuity with it. So deeply is the Jewish present rooted in Jewish history that changes wrought in Jewish reality continually have been read back into the past so that they could be read out of the past as a foundation for the present. Again and again in rabbinic interpretations, we find contemporary practice projected back into earlier periods so that the chain of tradition can remain unbroken. In Genesis, for example, Abraham greets his three angelic visitors by killing a calf and serving it to them with milk (Gen. 18:7–8), clearly a violation of the laws of kashrut, which forbid eating milk and meat together. As later rabbinic sources read the passage, however, Abraham first served his visitors milk and only then meat, a practice permitted by rabbinic law. Not only did Abraham and the other patriarchs observe the law given at Sinai, according to the rabbis, they actually founded rabbinic academies. Genesis Rabbah[17] 95:3 interprets Genesis 46:28, "And he sent Judah before him unto Joseph, *to teach* the way," to mean that he prepared an academy for the teaching of Torah. The point is not that such rereadings were a conscious plot to strengthen rabbinic authority—though certainly they would have served that function—but that it was probably unimaginable to the sages that the values they lived by could not be taught through the Torah. The links between past and present were felt so passionately that any important change in the present had to entail a new understanding of history.

All this has an important moral for Jewish feminists. We too cannot redefine Judaism in the present without redefining our past, because our present grows out of our history. The Jewish need to reconstruct the past in the light of the present converges with the feminist need to recover women's history within Judaism. Knowing that women are active members of the Jewish community in the present, even though large sectors of the community continue to define themselves in male terms and to render women invisible, we know that we were always part of the community—not simply as objects of male purposes but as subjects and shapers of tradition. To accept androcentric texts and contemporary androcentric histories as the whole of Jewish history is to enter into a secret collusion with those who would exclude us from full membership in the Jewish community. It is to accept the idea that men were the only significant agents in

---

17. [Genesis Rabbah is a classic work of midrash, or rabbinic interpretation of the Bible.]

Jewish history when we would never accept this (still current) account of contemporary Jewish life. The Jewish community today is a community of women and men, and it has never been otherwise. It is time, therefore, to recover our history as the history of women and men, a task that will both restore our own history to women and provide a fuller Jewish history for the Jewish community as a whole. Again to quote from Broner's[18] seder, "Mother, asks the clever daughter, / who are our mothers? Who are our ancestors? What is our history? / Give us our name. Name our genealogy."[19]

ELLIOT DORFF

Love Your Neighbor and Yourself:
A Jewish Approach to Modern Personal Ethics

Elliot N. Dorff (b. 1943) is a scholar of Jewish ethics and a Conservative rabbi. A professor at the University of Judaism, a seminary affiliated with the Conservative movement of Judaism, he has been a leading contributor to the Committee on Jewish Laws and Standards, the body charged with deciding questions of halakhic practice for the Conservative movement. As the author of numerous responsa on bioethics, gender inclusion, and other questions of halakha, his ethical arguments have had a formative role in shaping Jewish practice for Conservative Jews today. Dorff is the writer and editor of multiple book-length studies of Jewish ethics.

From Love Your Neighbor and Yourself: A Jewish Approach to Modern Personal Ethics *(Philadelphia: Jewish Publication Society, 2003), 15–19.*

Even if we are convinced that we should adhere to Jewish moral norms, how do we know what they are? Classical Judaism defines the moral in terms of God's will as articulated in God's commandments. Some modern theorists, however, have challenged the nexus between God's will and Jewish law, and some humanistic Jews have even denied that we should look to God's will in any form to

18. [Esther M. Broner (1927–2011) was an American Jewish feminist essayist, fiction writer, and liturgist who published one of the earliest feminist Haggadahs, or Passover rituals.]

19. E. M. Broner, "Honor and Ceremony in Women's Rituals," in *The Politics of Women's Spirituality: Essays on the Rise of Spiritual Power within the Feminist Movement*, ed. Charlene Spretnak (Garden City, NY: Anchor Press/Doubleday, 1982), 238.

define the right and the good. Even those who believe that Jewish moral norms are to be defined in terms of God's will and that Jewish law is the proper vehicle for knowing what God wants of us cannot rest with Jewish law alone, for the Talmud itself declares that the law is not fully sufficient to define morality, that there are morals "beyond the letter of the law" (*lifnim mishurat hadin*). Beginning, then, with Abraham's challenge to God, "Shall the Judge of all the earth not do justice?" (Gen. 18:25), one ethical question addressed throughout Jewish history has been the relationship between moral norms and God's word.

Another, more modern question, is this: If we assume that God's will defines that which is morally right and good, how shall we discern what God wants us to do now? Reform theories, such as that of Eugene Borowitz,[20] maintain that individual Jews should make that decision. They should inform themselves as much as possible about the relevant factors in the case and about the Jewish sources that apply, but ultimately individual Jews, rather than rabbis, should determine what God wants of us on the basis of their knowledge and conscience.

This Reform methodology raises major questions about how to identify any Jew's decision as being recognizably Jewish. Indeed, it makes it possible and even likely that there will be multiple, conflicting moral decisions, all claiming to be Jewish, because each and every Jew has the right to articulate a "Jewish" position on a given issue. This challenges the coherence and intelligibility of the Jewish moral message. Moreover, Borowitz's methodology depends crucially on the assumption that individual Jews know enough about the Jewish tradition and about how to apply it to carry out this task, an assumption that regrettably does not comply with reality.

Positively, though, Reform methodology empowers individual Jews to wrestle with the Jewish tradition themselves, and it encourages—even demands—that Jews learn more about their tradition in order to carry out this task. By making the decision depend on a specifically *Jewish* self, rather than an isolated, undifferentiated self, Borowitz also goes some way in the direction of explaining how such choices can be identified as specifically Jewish: Jewish choices come from self-identified and self-consciously Jewish people.

At the other end of the spectrum, most Orthodox theorists claim that Jewish law as it has come down to us should serve as our authoritative source for knowing God's will, and the more straightforwardly and literally we can read

---

20. [For a selection from Reform Jewish theologian Eugene Borowitz (1924–2016), see part 1, section 4.]

those sources, the more assured we can be that we have discovered God's will. No change is necessary or possible, for God has proclaimed these moral norms through the Written Torah (the Five Books of Moses) and the Oral Torah[21] that, Orthodox Jews believe, was given to Moses at Mount Sinai simultaneously with the Written Torah.

For those who affirm these beliefs, this methodology imparts a sense of assuredness that one knows how to identify God's will and why one should obey it: God demands that of you. On the other hand, this methodology rests, first, on the assumption that God's will is literally expressed in the Torah and later rabbinic literature; that is a conviction of faith that one either affirms or denies. Beyond that, to adopt the Orthodox approach one must believe that we have the exact expression of the divine will in hand in the texts that have come down to us. That assertion is largely undermined by the overwhelming evidence that biblical and rabbinic literature—including the Torah itself—were written at a variety of times and places. Moreover, even if one believes in the literal, divine authority of the Torah and rabbinic literature, one still needs to interpret and apply those sources, and that leaves plenty of room for human controversy and error. Thus this methodology does not deliver the certainty it promises to inform us what God demands. Finally, as some left-wing Orthodox rabbis have themselves noted, we still have to ask whether the law defines the entirety of our moral duty—and, I would add, whether the law might actually conflict with what morality demands.

Conservative theorists and rabbis (and a few Orthodox ones) use Jewish law as much as possible to know God's will (and hence the right and the good), and they pay attention also to Jewish theological convictions and Jewish stories. They combine this broader use of Jewish sources with a historical understanding of them. Thus, when it comes time to apply them to contemporary circumstances, Conservative theorists look carefully at the ways in which a given contemporary setting is similar to or different from the historical one in which a given source was written, in order to be able to judge the degree to which it should guide us today. They also look to the sources not so much for specific directions as for the principles that underlie past applications of Jewish law so

---

21. ["Oral Torah" is a term that refers to the classical rabbinic library, including the Mishnah, the Talmud, and works of midrash. These works were all transmitted as an oral tradition by the rabbis of ancient times and were subsequently committed to writing during the medieval period.]

that we can intelligently apply them to the modern context. For that matter, a historical understanding of the Jewish tradition requires that even past ethical principles themselves be subject to recurrent evaluation. Both past principles and past applications of them, however, are assessed with a bias toward conserving the tradition (and hence the name "Conservative"), such that the burden of proof rests on the one who wants to change a particular moral or ethical stance rather than on the one who wants to maintain what has come down to us.

This Conservative approach does not present a neat, clearly identifiable lesson on all moral matters in our day; on the contrary, it invites discussion and controversy. Moreover, it requires *judgment*; no source may be taken at face value, none is immune from evaluation. This is clearly not a methodology for the anal compulsive! Unlike the Reform approach, though, the Conservative methodology requires that such evaluation be done not just by individuals but by the community, thus preserving a greater degree of coherence and Jewish identity. It makes such decisions primarily through its rabbinic leaders, because they are the ones most likely to know what the tradition says and how to apply it to modern circumstances. Thus this way of discerning what God wants does not depend on knowledge and skills that most Jews lack. In contrast to the Orthodox approach, the Conservative one has the distinct advantage of historical awareness and authenticity, for it interprets sources in their historical context and, like generations past, combines received Jewish law with an openness to the moral sensitivities and needs of the time. It thus has a greater balance of the traditional with the modern, greater openness to learning from others, and greater flexibility.

Yet a fourth way of discerning God's will is that pioneered by Martin Buber,[22] developed further by Emmanuel Levinas,[23] and articulated in a contemporary feminist version by Laurie Zoloth-Dorfman.[24] In this approach we discover Jewish moral norms through our encounters with other human beings in one-to-one, direct interactions.

This approach, sometimes called "personalist" or even "feminist," suffers from the same problems that Reform individualism has: It is weak on Jewish identity, continuity, coherence, and authority. At the same time, it locates moral

22. [Martin Buber (1878–1965) was a prolific Jewish theologian active in Germany before World War II who is best known for his theory of dialogue.]

23. [See part 1, section 4 for a selection by French Jewish philosopher Emmanuel Levinas.]

24. [For a selection from Jewish bioethicist Laurie Zoloth, see part 4, section 19.]

decisions where they in fact lie, in the interaction among human beings. Moreover, it invokes the inherent authority another human being has over us simply by virtue of being another human being who faces us directly.

SHAUL MAGID

Ethics Differentiated from the Law

Shaul Magid (b. 1958) is a professor of Jewish studies who teaches at Dartmouth College. A scholar of modern Judaism and of Jewish thought, he studies diverse religious movements in modern Jewish life, including Hasidism, a pietistic movement that emerged in Eastern Europe in the late eighteenth century. Magid was ordained as an Orthodox rabbi but subsequently turned away from Orthodoxy and now serves as rabbi of a liberal, nondenominational congregation. In addition to his scholarship, Magid is a public intellectual at the forefront of Jewish communal debates about Zionism and the place of Israel in Jewish thought and identity.

From "Ethics Differentiated from the Law," in *The Blackwell Companion to Religious Ethics*, ed. William Scheiker (Malden, MA: Blackwell Publishing, 2005), 180–83.

One of early Hasidism's[25] great contributions to Jewish life and letters is its construction of a piety not dominated by the Neoplatonic division of body-soul and matter-spirit, but on the search for God in the mundane and everyday. This resulted in, among other things, a kind of non-ascetic Jewish piety. While remaining committed to an ultra-traditionalist lifestyle, Hasidism widened the scope of how one can serve God and, in some very significant ways, problematized the rabbinic dictum cited earlier that "God only dwells in the four ells of the law." But like other movements in traditional Judaism, Hasidism does not have a word for ethics. In this sense it faithfully inherits the rabbinic and later pietistic traditions of the past. However, Hasidism understands "ethics" (interhuman relations) as an expression of an internal disposition that halakha alone cannot fully cultivate. Halakha is defined as the formal set of requirements each Jew is obligated to perform in order to live in a full covenantal relationship with God.

25. [Shaul Magid describes Hasidism as "a Jewish revivalist movement" that joins spiritual renewal, pious devotion, and traditional practice. It emerged in eighteenth-century Poland (today's Ukraine) and spread rapidly across Eastern Europe.]

While halakha may encourage such a disposition of piety—that is, it may have ethics as part of its goal—it does not formally (i.e., legally) require it. Moreover, the fulfillment of halakha, even in a supererogatory manner, may not always result in ethical behavior. The disposition that the following Hasidic texts speak of is one of absorbing divinity, allowing it to become so much a part of one's being that one acts in the world as divine and subsequently treats the world (both the individual and the collective) as divine.

* * *

R. Menahem Mendel of Vitebsk was a contemporary of the Baal Shem Tov[26] and later became an influential part of the circle of the Maggid of Mezeritch (one of the spiritual heirs of the Baal Shem Tov). He immigrated to Palestine in 1777, living in Safed and Tiberias, where his collected writings and letters were completed. He is considered one of the most prominent figures in the first two generations of Hasidism.

His collected writings, entitled *Pri Ha-'Aretz* (lit. "fruits of the land"), presents a nuanced version of the Jewish idea of humanity's divine image and the part it plays in the expression of ethics (Mendel, 1987). The first part of the text addresses the question of preliminaries: that is, what is the existential posture necessary to create the possibility of being overcome by the divine? What is suggested is a stance of absolute impotence, emptying oneself of will to make room for the influx, and subsequent incarnation, of God.

This preliminary state of absolute impotence is required because R. Menahem Mendel holds that the core of one's humanness is the autonomous will that invariably interprets human action as sovereign and severed from God. Human beings, acting as independent volitional agents, will always see their actions as sovereign and independent of God. As a result, humans *qua* human cannot love, because love is divine. God is love and only God can love. And the only object of love is God. Therefore, in order to love, and thus to act ethically, one must become filled with God—one must create the context allowing love (God) to descend and overcome the volitional self. This emerges from a creative rendering of a midrashic passage. In describing the simultaneity of God's transcendence and immanence, the midrash states: "God is the place of the world but the world is not his place" (*Genesis Rabbah* 78:9; *Pesikta Rabbati*, 21). One half of this phrase is

---

26. [The Baal Shem Tov, or "Master of the Good Name," is Rabbi Israel ben Eliezer (1700–1760), the charismatic teacher who founded Hasidism.]

employed here, in one variant subtly substituting "world" for "humankind." That is, God's true residence in this world is the human being.

To be fully human is to become God-like. For R. Menahem Mendel, this requires the dissolution of volition. This experience of radical indwelling, which I maintain crosses over into incarnation, has two immediate consequences: first, it experientially affirms the human impotence that was merely posited earlier; second, and more importantly, it enables the individual to love.

> This [expression of] love results in connecting him to all creatures (*b'eyi 'olam*) and all human beings after realizing that this love is a love of grace that he did not merit in his own soul (M. *Rosh Hashanah* 1:2; Maimonides, Mishneh Torah, "Laws of Sabbatical and Jubilee Years," 13:13; and "Laws of Kings," 8:10). This is because it is impossible to create or merit this divinity. It is the will of God that it is given as a gift. If he gives this gift of love to another, his friend would be similarly inspired. And, his friend would realize that this gift is not from him [but from God].[27]

This experience of incarnation enables one to love all things because one sees how all things, even those that are evil (i.e., transgressors), share a divine source. The difference between one who loves and transgressors is that the latter have not yet opened themselves up to the experience of "incarnation" (divine indwelling) and still see themselves acting independent of God. One's ability to elevate those souls is equal to one's ability to love, for love, being divine, is that which elevates (elevation here being the act that reunites a thing with its source).

This ability is not procured simply by following the law. In fact, the law presents certain challenges to this ideal because the practitioner can easily err in seeing herself as an autonomous agent. . . .

Autonomous righteousness can only be false (and thus demonic) because, as autonomous (i.e., without God), it cannot be based on love. . . . A Torah without love does not result in elevation (of the self or another) but descent. . . . R. Menahem Mendel seems to be saying that hatred is exclusively a human trait, perhaps subtly invoking Genesis 6:5,[28] whereas only the divine can love. Therefore, in order for humankind to love, it must become divine, or at least be overcome with its own divinity.

---

27. R. M. Mendel, *Pri Ha-'Aretz* (Jerusalem: Masorah Press, 1987), 121, 122.

28. [Genesis 6:5: "The Lord saw how great was the human's wickedness on earth, and how every plan devised by his mind was nothing but evil all the time."]

Having established an incarnational ethics whereby love is dependent on the realization of one's inner divinity, R. Menahem Mendel turns back to the question of how that posture is cultivated.

> One must [always] contemplate: who do I fear? It is God, who fills all possible worlds, without whom nothing exists. What is the source of my existence? It is God. Where I am destined to go? Toward God. If that is so, what am I? There is no fear except the fear of God's glory. When one achieves this fear he will comprehend that it is also created by God and contains divine effluence, without which it would not exist. If one draws down this fear of God from its lofty place it will become compacted [in human experience] as love because any divine life force that is drawn down and implanted in this world is love. This will evoke love of God, resulting in "the descent of a thread of grace from the source of blessing" (B. T. *Hagigah* 12b). From there, *you will be like a watered garden, like a spring whose waters do not fail* (Isa. 58:11). (Mendel, 1987, 122)

"Who am I?" I am God's residence on earth, which enables me to love others whose divine potential I can also see. This love is the basis of ethics for R. Menahem Mendel because only love creates love, resulting in an interhuman (ethical) world that is really a Divine-divine world. To love is to be (fully) God-like, for only then can the divine in others be recognized. To be God-like is to be full of God and empty of self—it is to be incarnate.

3 | Ethics and Law

The very first selection in this volume asks whether there exists a category of "Jewish ethics" beyond the realm of halakha, Jewish law. Most (though not all) of the thinkers in this volume do indeed assume that there are many questions best considered in terms other than, or in addition to, legal ones. But the centrality of concepts of law and command in the Jewish tradition are undeniable. The biblical narrative of the Exodus, of course, tells a dramatic story of the Israelites at Mt. Sinai, of the commandments that God issues forth, and of the development of those commands throughout the Torah. But it is the development of Mishnah and Gemara, the foundational rabbinic commentaries of the postbiblical era, that have most contributed to the characterization of Judaism as a tradition of law. And, of course, each of these commentaries continues to invite further legal debate.

This section, therefore, is not the first occasion for readers to consider questions of Judaism and law. But this section is distinguished by its explicit attention to the concept of law as an essential tool for ethical repair. Importantly, the law in question does not necessarily refer to halakha, Jewish legal conclusions or reasoning, but to law as an umbrella term for rules of governance in a given context. The opening section by Robert Cover, for instance, comes from the realm of American constitutional law and might not seem to have an obvious connection to Jewish ethics or law. But Cover's essay, which presents a theory of how law is made, what inspires people to heed it, and how it changes, has been enormously influential for contemporary Jewish thinkers. It also introduces a theme that runs through each of the essays in this section: it is a profound error to imagine that law is separable from other categories of life and thought.

Cover's essay argues that "no set of legal institutions or prescriptions exists apart from the narratives that locate it and give it meaning.... Once understood in [this] context, law becomes not merely a system of rules to be observed, but a world in which we live." This argument, about the structures that give law meaning and also render it contingent, is essential for Rachel Adler's work in contemporary Jewish feminist ethics and theology. If law is inextricably connected to the narratives we tell about our world, then perhaps different narratives can give rise to more equitable systems of law. In her selection, Adler demonstrates the patently unequal and transactional features of traditional Jewish marital law, but rejects the notion that egalitarian communities should simply ignore the legal questions around Jewish marriage altogether. The excerpt below describes her creation of an alternative—though still thoroughly Jewish—legal framework for Jewish marriages, rooted in the rabbinic laws of business partnership instead of gendered acquisition.

The essays by Alan Mittleman and David Novak both consider the relationship between law and ethics, and the assumption that these represent entirely distinct categories. Mittleman's essay rejects the supposed binary between law and ethics in Judaism, which, he argues, is a serious misunderstanding of both law and ethics. He concludes, "It is impossible to decide which Jewish norms should be allocated to ethics and which to law because these categories are ill-suited to those norms." Novak's selection is excerpted from his book *Jewish Social Ethics*, a collection of essays on contemporary Jewish debates from the perspective of what he calls "traditional Judaism." In the introduction, Novak contrasts social ethics with "applied Jewish ethics," the latter requiring a legal response to a specific case. Rather than conceive of Jewish ethics simply as a set of halakhic rulings, Novak calls for "the enunciation of underlying principles" instead of "immediately applicable rules." In the excerpt below, Novak considers two different understandings of law—natural law and positivism—and argues that the idea of covenant helps draw the two approaches together.

The distinctive contribution of these essays, then, is not chiefly their discussion of "Jewish law," as the literature of modern Jewish ethics contains many such references, critical and sympathetic alike. The selections in this section insist that to meaningfully talk about law and ethics, we must consider not only "what the law says" but also what law *is* and *how* it works. Without such reflections, neither law nor ethics can be done well.

ROBERT COVER

Nomos and Narrative

Robert Cover (1943-1986) was a professor of law at Columbia University and Yale University, where he was awarded a Guggenheim Fellowship. His essay "Nomos and Narrative" (1983), a consideration of the role of shared communal assumptions in the construction of law, has been extremely influential in studies of Jewish law, ethics, and textuality.

From "Nomos and Narrative," *Harvard Law Review* 97 (1983): 4–68.

We inhabit a *nomos*—a normative universe. We constantly create and maintain a world of right and wrong, of lawful and unlawful, of valid and void.... The rules and principles of justice, the formal institutions of the law, and the conventions of a social order are, indeed, important to that world; they are, however, but a small part of the normative universe that ought to claim our attention. No set of legal institutions or prescriptions exists apart from the narratives that locate it and give it meaning. For every constitution there is an epic, for each decalogue a scripture. Once understood in the context of the narratives that give it meaning, law becomes not merely a system of rules to be observed, but a world in which we live.

In this normative world, law and narrative are inseparably related. Every prescription is insistent in its demand to be located in discourse—to be supplied with history and destiny, beginning and end, explanation and purpose. And every narrative is insistent in its demand for its prescriptive point, its moral. History and literature cannot escape their location in a normative universe, nor can prescription, even when embodied in a legal text, escape its origin and its end in experience, in the narratives that are the trajectories plotted upon material reality by our imaginations.

The normative universe is held together by the force of interpretive commitments—some small and private, others immense and public. These commitments—of officials and of others—do determine what law means and what law shall be. If there existed two legal orders with identical legal precepts and identical, predictable patterns of public force, they would nonetheless differ essentially in meaning if, in one of the orders, the precepts were universally venerated while in the other they were regarded by many as fundamentally unjust....

Just as the meaning of law is determined by our interpretive commitments, so also can many of our actions be understood only in relation to a norm. Legal precepts and principles are not only demands made upon us by society, the people, the sovereign, or God. They are also signs by which each of us communicates with others. There is a difference between sleeping late on Sunday and refusing the sacraments, between having a snack and desecrating the fast of Yom Kippur, between banking a check and refusing to pay your income tax. In each case an act signifies something new and powerful when we understand that the act is in reference to a norm. It is this characteristic of certain lawbreaking that gives rise to special claims for civil disobedience. But the capacity of law to imbue action with significance is not limited to resistance or disobedience. Law is a resource in signification that enables us to submit, rejoice, struggle, pervert, mock, disgrace, humiliate, or dignify. . . .

A legal tradition is hence part and parcel of a complex normative world. The tradition includes not only a corpus juris, but also a language and a mythos—narratives in which the corpus juris is located by those whose wills act upon it. These myths establish the paradigms for behavior. They build relations between the normative and the material universe, between the constraints of reality and the demands of an ethic. These myths establish a repertoire of moves—a lexicon of normative action—that may be combined into meaningful patterns culled from the meaningful patterns of the past. The normative meaning that has inhered in the patterns of the past will be found in the history of ordinary legal doctrine at work in mundane affairs; in utopian and messianic yearnings, imaginary shapes given to a less resistant reality; in apologies for power, and privilege and in the critiques that may be leveled at the justificatory enterprises of law.

The intelligibility of normative behavior inheres in the communal character of the narratives that provide the context of that behavior. Any person who lived an entirely idiosyncratic normative life would be quite mad. The part that you or I choose to play may be singular, but the fact that we can locate it in a common "script" renders it "sane"—a warrant that we share a *nomos*. . . .

I shall elaborate in more concrete form the processes by which even a single self-enclosed world produces a system of normative meaning. To do so I shall take the highly simplified case of the Bible—simplified because the Bible is a literary artifact of a civilization and no more captures the full range of contested possibilities of ancient Israel than any similarly small composite of our texts would capture the full range of our normative potential. Still, I think the Bible has something to offer as an illustration of the ways in which precepts and narratives operate together to ground meaning.

Imagine two legal systems, each with identical precepts dictating private and official action: the oldest son is entitled to succeed his father as head of the family and to receive a double portion of the family inheritance.... Contrast such an imaginary legal order with the one we find pictured in the Bible.

If a man has two wives, one loved and the other hated, and both the loved and hated have borne him sons, but the firstborn is the son of the hated wife—when he leaves his inheritance to his sons he may not prefer the son of the beloved wife over the elder son of the hated wife. He must acknowledge the firstborn son of the hated wife and give him the double portion. For he is the first fruit of his loins and to him is the birthright due. (Deut. 21:15–17)

The very casuistic phrasing of this precept suggests an extremely problematic psychodynamic. But the narrative materials in which the precept is embedded present even more complex dimensions of apparent contradiction and complication.

The Deuteronomic material has been included in a biblical canon together with a rich set of accompanying narratives.... These texts included: (1) the story of Cain and Abel, in which God accepts the sacrifice of Abel, the younger son, rather than that of Cain, the elder, and in which Seth, the third born, ultimately becomes the progenitor of the human race; (2) the story of Ishmael and Isaac, in which Ishmael, the first fruit of Abraham's loins, is cast out so that the birthright might pass to Isaac, the later son born of the preferred wife; (3) the story of Esau, the firstborn son of Isaac, who is denied his birthright by the trickery of Jacob, his younger brother; and (4) the story of Joseph and his brothers, in which Joseph—a younger child of the preferred wife—is favored by his father, dreams of his own primacy, provokes retaliation, and comes to rule over his brothers in an improbable political ascendancy in another land....

Now in order to understand any legal civilization one must know not only what the precepts prescribe, but also how they are charged. In the Bible there is no earthly or heavenly precept so heavily loaded as that of Deuteronomy chapter 21, verses 15 through 17, because there is no precept rendered so problematic by the narratives in which the law is embedded. This does not mean that the formal precept was not obeyed. Indeed, the narratives in question would lose most if not all of their force were it not for the fact that the rule *was* followed routinely in ordinary life. What is distinctive about the biblical narratives is that they can never be wholly squared either with the formal rule—though some later rabbis tried to do so—or with the normal practice. It is tempting to reconcile the stories to the rule by creating exceptions or by positing circumstances that would remove the case from the rule. These strategies may be useful to the later legist whose concern is a consistent body of precepts. Life in the normative world of the Bible, however, required a well-honed sense of where the rule would end and why.

In a society in which the norm of succession is relatively unproblematic, compliance or noncompliance, resistance or acquiescence may vary according to the contingencies of each instance calling for application of the rule.... But in every instance in the Bible in which succession is contested, there is a layer of meaning added to the event by virtue of the fact that the mythos of this people has associated the divine hand of destiny with the typology of reversal of this particular rule.... To be an inhabitant of the biblical normative world is to understand, first, that the rule of succession can be overturned; second, that it takes a conviction of divine destiny to overturn it; and third, that divine destiny is likely to manifest itself precisely in overturning this specific rule....

Thus, to know the narratives is not only to know of the psycho-familial complexities of succession, not only to see the motif of overturning the rule of succession as a vehicle for the problem of dynastic succession, but also to understand that motif as an expressive vehicle for the unresolved moral problems of geopolitics and as a potential source of sectarian division....

In the normative universe, legal meaning is created by simultaneous engagement and disengagement, identification and objectification. Because the *nomos* is but the process of human action stretched between vision and reality, a legal interpretation cannot be valid if no one is prepared to live by it. Certain thinkers may be dismissed as "merely" utopian, not only because they posit standards for behavior radically different from those by which we are accustomed to living, but also because they fail to posit alternative lives to which we would commit ourselves by stretching from our reality toward their vision....

The range of meaning that may be given to every norm—the norm's interpretability—is defined, therefore, both by a legal text, which objectifies the demand, and by the multiplicity of implicit and explicit commitments that go with it. Some interpretations are writ in blood and run with a warranty of blood as part of their validating force. Other interpretations carry more conventional limits to what will be hazarded on their behalf. The narratives that any particular group associates with the law bespeak the range of the group's commitments. Those narratives also provide resources for justification, condemnation, and argument by actors within the group, who must struggle to live their law.

To know the law—and certainly to live the law—is to know not only the objectified dimension of validation, but also the commitments that warrant interpretations.

RACHEL ADLER

Engendering Judaism:
An Inclusive Theology and Ethics

Rachel Adler (b. 1943) is a professor emerita of modern Jewish thought and Judaism and gender at Hebrew Union College, where she was also ordained as a rabbi in 2012. A Jewish feminist theologian, her work combines studies of classical Jewish texts and themes with normative theological and ethical arguments. She created the ritual of b'rit ahuvim, an egalitarian alternative to the traditional Jewish wedding ceremony.

From *Engendering Judaism: An Inclusive Theology and Ethics* (Boston: Beacon Press, 1998), 169–72, 174–76, 180–81, 190–96, 198–99.

Chapter 5: B'rit Ahuvim: *A Marriage between Subjects*

The [biblical] book of Hosea presents a dilemma: a husband who has appropriated a wife and assumed legal ownership of her sexuality finds that he wants not merely her fidelity, but fidelity freely given out of love. . . . He does not see that his two desires, the urge to possess and control absolutely and the yearning for a loving, willing partner, are irreconcilable.

These unresolved tensions between woman as possession and woman as partner are embedded in the classical liturgy upon which all modern Jewish wedding ceremonies draw. Two elements comprise this ceremony: a legal transaction in which the bride is acquired by a declaration of exclusive possession and a ring, followed by a liturgical celebration (*Sheva Berakhot*) that associates the new marriage with the covenantal reconciliation of God and Israel and depicts it as a new Eden for loving companions to inhabit. If we unpack the definitions of marital relationships underlying these two components, however, we find that they are mutually exclusive. . . . The traditional wedding ceremony, first treating the bride as a piece of property and then paradoxically depicting her as a covenanter, mirrors in its very structure the irreconcilable expectations implicit in patriarchal marriage.

To treat both parties consistently as persons rather than as property, we would have to reframe the legal portion of the ceremony in terms of partnership law rather than property law as it is currently categorized. Only then would the ceremony's legal component accurately reflect the kind of marriage to which egalitarian couples mean to pledge themselves. . . .

In the Bible, the verb to marry is simply *lakaḥat*, to take. If the woman is young and still under her father's roof, the husband or his agents give her father a bride price, *mohar*, for her. Whether the bride must consent is unclear. . . .

Deuteronomy describes a two-stage process for marriage. In an act of espousal, *erusin*, a man designates a woman to be his own. After an interval, usually about a year, the process of acquisition is completed by a second act, *nissuin*, in which the man takes the woman under his own roof and consummates the marriage. . . .

These texts depict the marriage of a young virgin as a private commercial transaction in which rights over the woman are transferred from the father to the husband. This commercial origin is reflected in the relational terminology. The word for husband is *ba'al*, the general term for an owner, master, possessor of property, bearer of responsibility, or practitioner of a skill. No specialized relationship term exists for wife; she is simply *isha*, woman. . . .

The mode by which women are legally transferred from one domain to another is called *kinyan*, acquisition, an act by which a subject unilaterally acquires specified rights over an object. *Kinyan* is essential in commercial transactions. . . . The basis for establishing that women are taken rather than reciprocally linked to men is an analogy between the language of taking in Abraham's purchase of the field of Ephron (Gen. 23:13) and the phrasing, "if a man takes a wife" (Deut. 22:13).

The rabbis pursue the analogy still further: women and fields can both be acquired though a transfer of money. The Mishnah specifies two other effective methods of acquisition. Women can be acquired by a deed (*shtar*) attesting to their acquisition, or they can be acquired through sexual intercourse, if such intercourse is for the purpose of appropriation. . . .

Although all three methods are legally effective, monetary acquisition (*kinyan kesef*) is . . . the one approved method for appropriating wives. What, precisely, is acquired by this means? Is it the woman's body, her services, or her sexual exclusivity? The rabbis themselves see the acquisition of wives as different from other commercial transactions. . . . One may buy a loaf of bread and share it with a neighbor, lend one's cloak to a chilled friend, sell it or give it away, but a man is not permitted to dispose of his wife in any of these ways.

The generic language of acquisition (taking) thus fails to express precisely those characteristics of matrimony the rabbis view as definitive: the transformation of status and category and the delineation of a boundary. To remedy these deficiencies, they turn to the language of sacralization and the metaphor of *hekdesh*, property set apart and earmarked as a pledge to the temple. Just as *hekdesh* simultaneously becomes reserved for sacred use and forbidden for secular use, so marital acquisition reserves a woman for one man and forbids her to others. In this limited sense, then, *hekdesh* is analogous to marital acquisition. . . .

How, then, is the metaphor of *kinyan* meaningfully linked to its literal sources? . . . What all the legally acceptable transactions have in common is that they are *unilateral* acts. Marriage cannot be initiated by the woman (*Kiddushin* 4b), nor can it result from mutual exchange (*Kiddushin* 3a, 6b). . . . *Processes in which both parties are active participants are explicitly rejected.* The man must take, and the woman must be taken. . . .

In contrast to the prosaic legal machinery that effects *kiddushin*, the second half of the Jewish wedding ceremony is poetic and allusive. It consists of a series of celebratory blessings recited over a cup of wine. . . . A later term, *Sheva Berakhot*, seven blessings, includes the introductory blessing over the wine along with six bridal blessings to add up to the sum of seven, the number of perfection. . . .

If *kiddushin* represents a sanctification through separation, then the *Sheva Berakhot* celebrate a sanctification through the holy coming-together that is covenant. They celebrate the cosmic process of wedding that occurs at all levels of sacred time and sacred history: making one, making joy, making new. Wedding is the beginning and end of time shaped into a circle and wreathed around the bridegroom and the bride. Wedding is creation and redemption, the origin of all bonds and their perfect mending, the first encounter of lover-equals and Zion's reconciliation with the lover she will no longer call my *ba'al*. This expansive metaphor of wedding strains at the limits of the *kiddushin* relationship it is meant to complement, and the strain cries out for relief. Either *kiddushin* must coopt the *Sheva Berakhot*, or the *Sheva Berakhot* must rise up and cast out *kiddushin*. This latter is the course I have chosen.

* * *

What are we to do when the words and gestures that effect marriage do not reflect but distort the event being celebrated in the life of the participants and their community? . . . Nontraditional Judaisms and even Modern Orthodoxy have sought to alleviate discomfort with the *erusin* portion of the wedding ceremony by liturgical innovations. . . . [There are] creative *ketubot* that articulate the couple's own visions of how the marriage is to be conducted [to] supplement or replace the standard *ketubah* form that attests the husband's responsibility to provide food, shelter, clothing, and sexual intercourse (*onah*) and records a financial settlement (now superseded by civil community property and inheritance laws) in the event of divorce or the husband's demise.[29]

These innovations, however charming and individualized, are halakhically impotent. They leave the legal structure of *kiddushin* intact, and that structure with its implicit definitions of the marital relationship legally supersedes any personal statements the bride and groom make to one another....

This is not to belittle the serious efforts couples have made to renovate the wedding ceremony. Their alterations reveal an instinctive understanding that a Jewish marriage is a legal ritual, and therefore it is important that the words that specify the commitments being made be words that the participants intend to honor....

We need a wedding ceremony that embodies the partners' intentions to sustain and strive with each other all their lives, to endure like the protagonists of the stormy but ultimately redemptive covenant marriage of biblical prophecy. This intention is not reflected in an act of acquisition. It can only be expressed by an act of covenanting.... The marriage agreement must specify the obligations that will form the fabric of the marriage. The partners must be able to make some promises to one another, even though promises are sometimes broken. And if a marriage loses its qualities as a *shutafut*, a partnership, people must be free to dissolve it.

For these reasons and others... partnership law, *hilkhot shutafut*, forms the legal basis for the contractual aspects of the *b'rit ahuvim* [lovers' covenant]. The model of a partnership reflects the undeniable fact that marriage is not only a social but an economic institution. But unlike the *ketubah*, which presumes that most economic power and resources belong to the male, the *b'rit ahuvim* presumes communal resources and requires joint decisions about their distribution....

The halakhic process of forming a partnership generally embodies three elements:

1. A partnership deed ...
2. A statement of personal undertaking in which partners committed themselves to certain acts on behalf of the partnership.

29. [The traditional *ketubah*, or Jewish wedding contract, reflects the historically transactional character of Jewish marriage.]

3. A *kinyan* or symbolic acquisition of the partnership. Partnerships were first understood as joint ownerships achieved by pooling resources. . . .

Kinyan, or symbolic acquisition of the partnership, is the third traditional element of partnership law embodied in the *b'rit ahuvim*, and it is fraught with difficulties. . . . It is essential to demonstrate that the couple intends to form a *b'rit ahuvim* and not to contract *kiddushin*. . . .

[I suggest] a form of *kinyan* that was used in ancient times exclusively for partnership acquisition: symbolically pooling resources in a bag and lifting it together. This gesture could not possibly be mistaken for an acquisition of *kiddushin*. Moreover, like the *b'rit* document and its stipulations, this ritual for acquiring pooled resources is another adaptable, expressive element of the ceremony: After the *b'rit* document has been read aloud and signed by the partners and by two witnesses, each partner places an object of some value in a bag provided for this purpose, perhaps specially designed or decorated. . . .

B'rit ahuvim, then, both is and is not a marriage. On the one hand, it formalizes a relationship between two lovers pledged to fidelity. Like any marriage agreement, it may be licensed and registered and thus recognized by the state, although at this writing that option is not yet available to gay and lesbian couples. But *b'rit ahuvim* does not meet the requirements for marriage under classical halakha, because one party does not acquire the other in the ceremony, nor is the couple's subsequent sexual intercourse meant to effect the woman's acquisition. While the *b'rit* contractors intend an enduring, monogamous relationship, they reject the power imbalance that characterizes *kiddushin* in favor of shared power and consensual decision-making about all aspects of the relationship, including its inauguration and, if required, its termination.

ALAN MITTLEMAN

Theorizing Jewish Ethics

Alan Mittleman (b. 1953) is a professor of Jewish philosophy at the Jewish Theological Seminary. His research and teaching focus on philosophical rationalism and Jewish thought, violence in the Jewish tradition, and the significance of religion in the modern world.

From "Theorizing Jewish Ethics," *Studia Humana* 3, no. 2 (2014): 32–42.

At least since the time of Moses Mendelssohn, Jewish modernists have decentered Jewish law and emphasized ethics as the salient category of Jewish representation.... But this is not to say that premodern Jews understood themselves solely within the framework of what we call law. Our concepts of law are no less problematic, when applied to traditional Judaism, than our would-be concepts of Jewish ethics. Common modern concepts of law are often positivistic; they are often tied to political concepts, such as sovereignty. They are in many ways ill-suited to map halakha....

At stake here is more than traditionalist Jews continuing to assert the indispensability of halakha. Bundled into the "traditionalist" claim is the view that halakha is not only necessary but *sufficient*; that halakha comprises *all* norms relevant to human conduct, at least for Jews. To assert that some other body of norms pertains, indeed, that some non-halakhic ways of thinking about norms are required is to detract from the omni-sufficiency of halakha ... Mere ethics seems to have a lesser pedigree or at least a more circuitous one.... Who is the subject of norms? Why is such a subject so bound? What relation does the subject's own reason and will have vis-à-vis norms? How do we, how can we know what is legitimately normative? If there is an independently cognizable realm of moral normativity over and against the halakha, then what do we need halakha for?

The scope and embodiment of norms is also at issue. Perhaps halakha, while irrefragably central, is not sufficient. Perhaps it recognizes its own insufficiency by commanding ethical counterweights, balances, and corrections.... But then again, if the halakha stipulates a need for a normative framework in excess of its own standards, ethics remains a creature of the halakha. If Jews are commanded (as they are) to go beyond the letter of the law (*lifnim mishurat hadin*), and the latter is thought to constitute ethics, then in what sense is ethics really separate from law? Ethics would be a moment internal to halakha....

There are, it seems to me, three broad positions that modern thinkers have taken on the relation of ethics to halakha/law. The first is that ethics ought to be the dominant category. Ethics forms the content, point, and purpose of halakha. . . . Let's call this position the sovereignty of ethics. The second point of view, which arguably arises historically as a reaction to the excesses of the first, is what I have called the omni-sufficiency of the halakha. On this view, Judaism is all law —ethics, as an independent normative sphere, cannot gain a toehold. . . . There might well be an independently cognizable or theorizable sphere of ethics, but it is *irrelevant* for Jews. . . . There is, for example, a great deal of Jewish biomedical ethics today that consists entirely of halakha applied to medical topics. On the view that advocates the omni-sufficiency of halakha there is nothing wrong with calling such work "Jewish biomedical ethics" as long as we understand "ethics" as a proxy for "halakha." This view assumes that all ethical problems are resolvable into legal problems and that legal problems can be resolved to greater or lesser satisfaction with the tools of, in this case, the rabbinic trade. . . . The strongest case for the exclusive dominance of the halakha was made by Joseph Soloveitchik.[30] . . .

A third position sees a division of labor between the two categories. Ethics picks up where the law leaves off. This is the view of the great medieval exegete, Ramban, and may also be said to characterize the whole tradition of *sifrut hamusar* (the literature of moral exhortation). On this view, halakha is necessary but not sufficient. . . . This division of labor between the inner and the outer is tacitly or explicitly assumed by those like Joseph Dan, who write on the history of Jewish ethics. Dan, in trying to constitute his subject matter, relegates ethics to an attitudinal accompaniment of the performance of mitzvot. There is something to be said for this view, of course, but it is also deeply problematic. It assumes, for example, that "ethics" and "halakha" are rather static terms that describe two categorically distinct domains of content, one explicable in terms of intentionality, the other in terms of performance. It probably fails as an incipient theory of action with its rigid dichotomy between act and intent. . . .

Another way of sustaining a law/ethics distinction, which avoids the inner/outer dichotomy, is to say that law is sustained by coercion and sanction while ethics is sustained by voluntary consent (albeit consent to fully normative imperatives). This is essentially a Kantian approach, distinguishing between perfect and imperfect obligations. . . .

30. [Joseph Soloveitchik (1903–1993) was an Orthodox rabbi, philosopher, and scholar of the Talmud.]

Now all of these views, their differences notwithstanding, share a common interest—to distinguish theoretically between ethics and law and to fix their conceptual relations. All thus presume that the terms designate categories that have in principle independent, identifying features. The categories of law and ethics, whatever the eventual relations between their contents, are prima facie separate and distinctive. It is this assumption that I want to criticize....

One reason the dichotomy seems so formidable is because the normative rules and conclusions of halakha sometimes violate the modern sense of justice, equity, fairness, and so on. Halakhic approaches to the status of women are a leading example of this. Insofar as halakha is particular to the Jews and ethics is thought to be universal, it is easy to frame this tension as one between law and ethics, a particular norm versus a universal standard. Conceptually, however, it would be just as easy to frame the tension as one between competing impulses, values, principles and goals within the halakha. The Jewish moral tradition is rich with such tensions and with the resources to negotiate them. Casting conflicts of value into the dichotomous terms of law and ethics can aggravate tensions rather than render them productive.

I suspect that "law" and "ethics" are proxies for Jewish uniqueness and particularity as against the standards, however idealized, of the general culture. The terms are needed rhetorically to protect distinctive Jewish territory or to subject it to criticism, whether internal or external. The real conceptual work that is being done with these terms is pragmatic rather than semantic: there is a fight going on over who represents Judaism, who has authority, what is the normative view. If you are a halakhist, you can be dismissive of a view if you can characterize it as mere ethics. If you are a liberal Jew, you get to critique the harshness of law in the name of something presumably higher and nobler. "Law" and "ethics" thus seem to be contrastive terms. They derive some of their sense, in these modern Jewish treatments, from their contrast to one another. One member of the pair acts as a foil for the other. If the writer holds to the omni-sufficiency of halakha, he needs "ethics" as his whipping boy. If the writer holds to the sovereignty of ethics, she needs "law" to provide the raw material for her idealizations or criticisms. Rhetorical and polemical needs drive the hypostatization of the terms.

In my view, the better way forward is to say that both "law" and "ethics" are terms that do not map entirely well over traditional Jewish materials. The Jewish tradition did not develop such a categorical distinction in the way that Western thought did. There is a holism about the Jewish normative order.... Like other traditional normative orders, Judaism did not distinguish between obligation and virtue; it did not see an opposition between obeying public norms and cultivating human excellence. The falling out of justice and virtue that marks modern ethics would be wholly unintelligible to a traditional Jewish moralist. It is an obligation of halakha to cultivate character, as much as it is an obligation to observe the Sabbath.... While a Western legal system wants to inculcate the attitude of law-abidingness, even law-affirmation, it is typically unconcerned with dispositions such as love, self-criticism, or awe. *Ahavat ha-briyot, heshbon ha-nefesh*, and *yirat shamayim* as these dispositions are called in Hebrew are as much elements of halakha as kashrut and festivals. It is impossible to decide which Jewish norms should be allocated to ethics and which to law because these categories are ill-suited to those norms. The integration of those norms into a complex whole requires theorizing in its own terms not in terms of borrowed oppositions and dichotomies.

What, then, of theorizing Jewish ethics? Is Jewish ethics a legitimate concept or should we avoid it? To the extent that we want to continue to speak about the normative dimensions of Judaism, and to speak of them in English, the use of such terms is unavoidable. Our aim should be to avoid using them thoughtlessly, using them in such a way as to generate confusion. A capacious and minimalist approach to the notion Jewish ethics would be best. I would suggest that we employ the term "Jewish ethics" to indicate "reflection on character and conduct."

"Jewish ethics" should not rival, dominate, or compete with other ways of thinking about the normative in Judaism. It should integrate not isolate those perspectives. It is not, properly conceived, the Judaism of the assimilated. It is that form of inquiry that seeks to evoke the wisdom of Judaism as it pertains to conduct and character, to what is entailed by the quest to live rightly and well.

DAVID NOVAK

Jewish Social Ethics

David Novak (b. 1941) is a professor emeritus of religion and philosophy, having taught at the University of Virginia and then the University of Toronto. Though he received rabbinic ordination from the Conservative movement, Novak went on to found and lead the Union for Traditional Judaism. He has done extensive work on Jewish-Christian relations in addition to publishing broadly in Jewish theology, law, philosophy, political theory, ethics, and biomedical ethics.

From Jewish Social Ethics (New York: Oxford University Press, 1992), 22–24, 33–38.

Chapter 1: Natural Law, Halakha, and the Covenant

Philosophers of law, certainly in modern times, can be divided into two main groups: legal positivists and natural law theorists. In essence, the difference between the two groups can be seen in their understanding of the relation of authority and right within a legal system.

Into which school of thought a modern philosopher of law fits can be ascertained by looking at his or her answer to the challenge made by an outstanding contemporary legal philosopher, Ronald Dworkin, that one constitute rights as "the one feature that distinguishes law from ordered brutality." A legal positivist would say that this distinction lies in *how* a legal system is ordered. . . .

Natural law theorists would say that this distinction lies in the purpose, the *why*, of a legal system. If a legal system's prescriptions are rational norms, that is, ordered toward objective human goods qua ends, which themselves transcend the system, then there is a sufficient distinction between these prescriptions and the commands associated with "ordered brutality," commands that serve no end other than the exercise of political power as an end in itself. . . .

One can see an antinomy between legal positivism and natural law theory, and the Jewish theologian must bear it in mind in his or her attempt to define the essential character of halakha. The antinomy is as follows:

Natural law is a body of norms, rationally apprehended, universally applicable, independent of the promulgation of any authority.	*Positive law is a body of norms, given for application in a particular society (and whomever it controls), dependent on promulgation by a particular authority.*

It seems that this position of legal positivism is the one that Jewish theologians would adopt in their essential characterization of halakha, for one can easily translate the positivist position into the following proposition:

Halakha is a body of norms, given for application among the Jewish people (and whomever they control), promulgated by God and subsequently by the rabbis authorized by God in the revealed sources: the Written Torah and the Oral Torah.

It seems that the adoption of a natural law position would require the authority of God's will as the prime authority of the halakhic system to be subordinated to a higher order of right. This seems to go directly against the transcendent theocentricity of Judaism, and hence it is not difficult to see why many Jewish theologians have willingly included themselves in the positivist school and have rejected the claim that halakha can be essentially characterized using natural law theory.

I propose that natural law theory is necessary for an adequate essential characterization of halakha....

The contemporary Sephardic theologian José Faur rejects the idea of natural law as "totally foreign to Jewish thought."[31] However ... he does see a necessary precondition to the acceptance of the commandments of the Torah. This precondition is the covenant, which Faur contrasts with the classical philosophical idea of nature, as the foundation of law.

The effect of this conception of religion is the establishment of a bilateral pact, a *b'rit*, between God and man which both parties freely agree to maintain a relationship between themselves. Thus conceived, religion for Judaism is a relationship between God and man, the sole ground of which is the free and mutual election of God and man....

In dealing with Faur's theory I propose three questions: (1) Are covenant and natural law in truth mutually exclusive ideas? (2) Is the *b'rit* in truth a "bilateral pact"? and (3) Is the human choice of God the same as God's choice of humans?

In the context of the covenant the first question breaks into two subquestions: (1a) Why does God choose to covenant with humans? and (1b) Why do humans choose to covenant with God? ... It seems to me that the best reason for the choice of the Jewish people to enter into the covenant with God, as we saw before, was their judgment that God's knowledge of their needs and his concern for them was sufficient reason for them to choose to accept his authority, to

---

31. José Faur, "Understanding the Covenant," *Tradition* 9 (1968): 41.

accept his laws as continually binding obligations, for the keeping of these laws itself is man's active participation in this same divine concern first manifest in Egypt.... In order for the people to know that God's commandments are right for them, they obviously have to possess some knowledge of what is right in general. This precondition is simply unavoidable.

The second question, namely, what enables the contract to endure, also involves natural law theory, for a contract presupposes the norm that promises are to be kept.... Without this presupposition, a contract would have no duration and would be, therefore, meaningless. This natural law precondition seems to be an integral part of the covenantal theory in Scripture. Israel is frequently (and rightly) accused by the prophets of being unfaithful to the covenant, that is, of not keeping to its word.... If the covenant is the foundation of the law... then covenantal faithfulness cannot be commanded by the Law inasmuch as it is already presupposed by the law itself....

I must seriously question Faur's definition of the covenant between God and Israel as a "bilateral pact." It is bilateral, of course, in the sense that both God and Israel are bound by it. However, it is not bilateral in terms of its initiation or its enduring authority. In a bilateral pact, a social contract, both parties enter the agreement as legal equals and the requirements of the contract are based on *their* mutual authority to obligate themselves and each other. In the *b'rit*, on the other hand, God initiates the covenant as sovereign, the goals of the covenant are set down by God, and the authority of the covenantal requirements is the will of God alone when there is human resistance to it. This does not mean that humans cannot freely accept or reject the covenant. If they could not do that, they would not be morally responsible for it.... In constituting what is involved in this freedom to accept or reject the covenant and its norms, we have seen that natural law theory cannot be avoided....

It seems, viewed from the scriptural and rabbinic sources of Jewish theology, that God's choice is fundamentally different from human choice.... Just as nothing required God to create the world, nothing required God to make a covenant with Israel....

The choice of humans, however, seems to be much more limited in that it is only the freedom to respond or not. The prime obligation already exists; humans in no way create it or even cocreate it.... It is this point that makes the *b'rit* for humans unlike a contract.... In a contract, written or tacit, there is always the assumption that the agreement is initiated in mutual freedom and maintained in mutual freedom. Thus, it is always assumed that the contractual partners have other good options both before initiation of the contract and after its expiration. But in the *b'rit*, these other options are only God's; for humans, the covenant is coeval with life. "To love the Lord your God and to listen to his voice and to cleave unto him: that is your life and the length of your days . . ." (Deut. 30:20).

In this sense, then, the covenant is like natural law in that it is unavoidable. Accordingly, just as the fact of human sociality makes such norms as the prohibition of murder necessary, so does the covenant make the prohibition of adopting the religious practices of the gentiles (Lev. 18:3) necessary. Without the former, society disintegrates; without the latter, the covenantal community disintegrates. . . .

We have seen heretofore that the covenant presupposes natural law and human freedom of choice, that is, human freedom to respond or not to God's covenant, based on rational judgment. It does not, however, presuppose human freedom of will, that is, the freedom either to initiate the covenant or to terminate it. Both decisions are God's alone. . . .

Nevertheless, the halakha and its development seem to manifest a role for human freedom over and above the choice to respond or not to what God has commanded. In this sense, the covenant seems to call forth not only a human response but, moreover, human initiative, even autonomy of sorts. . . . This freedom of innovation is broader than the freedom of choice presupposed by the covenant and its revealed law.

This power of human innovation entails the limitation of revelation to make room for this essentially human contribution to the covenant. . . . In rabbinic law the humanly appointed authorities can make either positive enactments (*taqqanot*) or restrictions (*gezerot*), and they have the power to repeal this legislation (*bittul*)—at least in principle. In fact, the greater bulk of the halakhic system is not from direct scriptural revelation but from human reason, ultimately operating *for* the sake of the covenant. . . .

Positive rabbinic law, precisely because it is humanly ordained, involves natural law factors in its very initiation, in the setting forth of its grounds. In divinely revealed positive law, natural factors are immediately present only in the conditions for human response to the commandments of God. However, even here, we assume that the reasons for the divine decrees are far better than those we see more readily in humanly instituted law because of the greater wisdom of God. Indeed, part of the messianic hope is that we will fully understand God's law so that it will immediately persuade us and require no external coercion. At this time we will fully and immediately understand the law of God in all its manifestations.

4 | Covenant

The English word "covenant" is the most common translation of the biblical Hebrew word *b'rit*, as when God, speaking to the soon-to-be-renamed Abraham, says, "I will establish My covenant between Me and you, and I will make you exceedingly numerous" (Gen. 17:2). Or when God speaks to Moses in Exodus 19, saying, "Now then, if you will obey Me faithfully and keep My covenant, you shall be My treasured possession among all the peoples" (Exod. 19:5).

Other common English synonyms include "promise," "contract," or "pact," and each of these words, like covenant, is contested, and evokes a set of assumptions, associations, and questions that are not so easily answered. This volume is replete with references to "the covenant" and its centrality in much Jewish thought and ethics. The writers in this section, however, insist on stopping well before questions about this or that ethical dilemma and ask what it means to be in any *relationship of obligation* at all. From this foundation, we can begin to ask questions about this relationship. For instance: Who are the parties in this relationship? How do they mark its establishment? What obligations are incumbent upon each party? How do they know? And what happens if they fail?

This section is devoted to these kinds of questions in the context of Judaism and ethical responsibility. In his essay, "The Pact," for instance, the philosopher Emmanuel Levinas presents an interpretation of a Talmudic discussion about biblical covenants and finds at its heart the absolute obligation of each person for another. His conclusions, in keeping with his general philosophical orientation, express the uncompromising nature of our obligations to respond to the needs of the other, even at immense personal cost. This, Levinas says, is what it means to truly form a community of ethics: "In the covenant, when it is fully understood, in the society which fully deploys all the dimensions of the law, society becomes a community."

Levinas's insistence on the absolute communal and ethical nature of covenant is highly influential in modern Jewish ethics, not least in the work of the other writers in this section. That is, whatever the theological or denominational differences between these thinkers, they share the assumption that any covenant between Jews and others, human or divine, must contain profound ethical demands to be worthy of the name.

Walter Wurzberger argues that Judaism, correctly understood, is founded on the singular relationship between a God who has made specific and exclusive demands, and the people Israel, who must obey. Wurzberger repeatedly contrasts himself with other, more liberal thinkers, writing that "unlike many prominent Jewish ethicists, I am approaching this subject from a traditional Jewish perspective, accepting halakha as the supreme normative authority. For me, halakha represents the revealed will of God." But Wurzberger insists that this commitment does not detract from but rather creates what he calls "covenantal ethics." Such an ethics may overlap with our moral intuitions but will always be subject to the absolute demands of God.

Eugene Borowitz and Mara Benjamin concur that the meaning and ethical significance of covenant is misunderstood until relationships of obligation are at the center. But they also suggest that we rethink the way these relationships work. Borowitz, for his part, argues that "the Jewish self has its roots in the Jewish people's historic relationship with God," but that we should not assume that this relationship is static or its content predetermined. He calls this "our personal-yet-folk intimacy with God"—where "folk" indicates the theological and communal nature of Jewish life, without which, he argues, Judaism will not survive. At the same time, the fact of this communal obligation does not necessary tell modern Jews how they ought to display this "continuing faithfulness"; to determine this is the task of all Jews who continue to affirm the meaningfulness of this covenant.

Benjamin, meanwhile, appeals to her own experience as a parent raising children to reconsider the terms of obligated relationship. The biblical description of a covenantal relationship between God and God's "children," the people Israel, is a common metaphor from antiquity to the present. But Benjamin, reflecting on the unrelenting and often gendered demands of parenting, flips the metaphor on its head: it is the child, who needs constant help to be fed, dressed, cleaned, and soothed, whose acute needs determine the parent's response. Who, then, Benjamin asks, has more "power" in this relationship? Who has determined the rules of this "covenant," and who is obligated to "obey"? The gendered implications of this turn are not inconsequential. Jewish law, after all, includes some commandments that are traditionally obligated only upon adult males. But in parenting, it is often a woman who finds herself cast as the obligated "responder" to children's needs. Thus Benjamin issues a challenge to past and present theorists of covenant: How might it change our understanding of its ethical significance if we dramatically reenvisioned the kind of relationship we understand a covenant to be?

EMMANUEL LEVINAS

The Levinas Reader

Emmanuel Levinas (1906–1995) was a leading French philosopher of the twentieth century. Born in Lithuania, he initially went to France to study philosophy at the University of Strasbourg. Levinas made enduring contributions to two scholarly worlds, publishing works of secular philosophy that build on the work of his teacher philosopher Edmund Husserl, and also serving as a Jewish educator, teaching and writing on Jewish thought and classical Jewish texts. He is best known for putting ethics at the heart of philosophy, giving primacy to the other over the self, and ascribing transcendence to the face-to-face encounter with another person.

From *The Levinas Reader*, ed. Seán Hand (Cambridge: Basil Blackwell, 1989), 211–26.

Chapter 13: The Pact
B. T. *Sotah* 37a–b:

They turned their faces toward Mount Gerizim and opened with the blessing etc. Our rabbis taught: There was a benediction in general and a benediction in particular, likewise a curse in general and a curse in particular. (Scripture states): to *learn*, to *teach*, to *observe* [keep], and to *do*; consequently there are four (duties associated with each commandment). Twice four are eight and twice eight are sixteen. It was similar at Sinai and the plains of Moab; as it is said, *These are the words of the covenant which the Lord commanded Moses* etc., and it is written, *Keep therefore the words of this covenant* etc. Hence there were forty-eight covenants in connection with each commandment.... R. Simeon b. Judah of Kefar Acco said in the name of R. Simeon: There is not a single precept written in the Torah in connection with which forty-eight times 603,550 covenants were not made. Rabbi said: According to the reasoning of R. Simeon b. Judah ... it follows that for each Israelite there are 603,550 commandments. (And forty-eight covenants were made in connection with each of them.) What is the issue between them? — R. Mesharsheya said: The point between them is that of personal responsibility and responsibility for others [*the responsibility of responsibility*]....

[B. T. *Sotah* 37a–b] presents itself as a commentary to chapter 27 of Deuteronomy, but it also refers to chapter 7 of Joshua....

Chapter 27 of Deuteronomy expounds the recommendations made by Moses to the people of Israel for a ceremony that will take place at a later date, when, after Moses's death, at the end of their peregrinations in the desert, the people shall enter the Holy Land.... The place where the ceremony is to be performed is indicated; two mountains stand there, Mount Ebal and, beside it, Mount Gerizim. After the stones have been set up there, and the Torah inscribed, there is a second recommendation, in verse 5: "And there you shall build an altar to the Lord your God, an altar of stones; you shall lift up no iron tool upon them." ... Iron, probably the basis of all industry, is in any case fundamental to all war.... From verse 11, Moses's recommendations concern the positioning of the people on Mounts Ebal and Gerizim "for the ceremony of the Covenant" being planned. Six tribes are to stand on Mount Gerizim "to bless the people" and six others "shall stand upon Mount Ebal for the curse." In this way, will not everybody, blessed or cursed, be visible to everybody else? Throughout the ceremony anticipated here, all the members of society will be able to see each other....

Allow me now to give you the last version of this scene, taken from the Mishnah itself (32a) to which the Gemara that contains our text is attached....

> Six tribes ascended the summit of Mount Gerizim, six tribes ascended the summit of Mount Ebal and the priests [the *Cohanim*] and Levites with the Ark were stationed below in the center [as in Joshua], the priests surrounding the Ark, the Levites (surrounding) the priests, and all Israel on this side and that side....

A question that was about handwriting has been transformed into one about the language used! This third version of the pact refers to the account in Joshua but uses the formulae of Deuteronomy. The pact that, according to Deuteronomy, was concluded in the presence of all the tribes in front of an altar whose stones, from the very earliest texts—texts that belong to a civilization that aspires to have no wars—are untouched by any tool of iron; the pact that, in Joshua, includes women, children and foreigners, has, in this Mishnah become truly universal: its law is written in seventy languages. A message addressed to humanity as a whole! The real meaning of this apparently particular ceremony, performed by a people whose members can all look upon one another, a community that one gaze can encompass, is that *all* human beings are included in the legislation in whose name the pact is concluded....

This universality is rooted, in some way, in a society that makes itself entirely visible to its members congregated on the two mountain tops, visible as if on stage. From the outset the society that values the intimacy of its twelve tribes looking at each other, and that aims to be one community, is already available or reaching out to humanity as a whole.

I have offered you here a precise example of the way an idea can develop as it passes from the written law to the oral law. The oral law claims to discuss the contents of the written law. But the actual knowledge of the oral law is greater still. It goes beyond the obvious meaning of the passage studied, but remains within the spirit of the global meaning of the Scriptures.

* * *

Let us return to our text. It is about to reveal to us the various dimensions of this pact concerning the Torah, those aspects that are there to ensure that a community whose members are practically face to face retains these interpersonal relations when its members turn their gaze toward humanity as a whole. The distinction between community and society belongs to an immature stage of social thought. The adoption of the law that is the foundation of this society brings with it, for those men who adopt it in the proper manner, the possibility of remaining in contact, face to face with each other.

Our rabbis taught: There was a benediction in general and a benediction in particular, likewise a curse in general and a curse in particular. (Scripture states): to *learn*, to *teach*, to *observe*, and to *do*; consequently, there are four (duties associated with each commandment). Twice four are eight and twice eight are sixteen....

In Deuteronomy, the same laws are proclaimed with curses for the man who transgresses them and blessings for the man who obeys them. Curse and blessing, that makes two: two independent ways of adhering to the same law, for the man who undertakes to keep it....

But we also know—if we refer to Deuteronomy 5:1 and Deuteronomy 11:19—that the Torah brings with it four general obligations: to learn it (*lilmod*), to teach it (*lelammed*), to observe it (*lishmor*), to carry it out (*la'asot*). Four covenants are included within the Covenant, sixteen pacts within the pact. Such arithmetic can be astonishing. I will return to this point later. Let us say, speaking generally, that in what we simply call the adherence to the law the rabbinical doctors distinguish sixteen dimensions.

Sixteen dimensions! But there are still more! If the rabbinical calculations are correct, the Torah was handed down on three different occasions. According to Exodus, the first time was at Sinai; the second time, according to Deuteronomy, was in the plains of Moab; and the third time—we have just seen—was between Ebal and Gerizim. And each time, we have said, there were sixteen acts of adherence, which makes forty-eight altogether. You will see that there are still more....

Forty-eight covenants? We can do better. "Rabbi Simeon ben Judah of Kefar Acco said in the name of Rabbi Simeon:"—this is the same Rabbi Simeon that disputed the importance of the ceremony at Gerizim—"There is not a single precept written in the Torah in connection with which forty-eight times 603,550 covenants were not made." The number of covenants made in the course of these three ceremonies is said, then, to be 603,550 times 48. Where does this figure of 603,550 come from? It represents the number of Israelites standing at the foot of Sinai. But why do we multiply by that number? Because the Covenant concerning the revealed law does not have the character of an abstract and impersonal juridical act; rather, its acceptance establishes living bonds with all those adopting the law. Within this Covenant each person finds himself responsible for everyone else; each act of the Covenant expresses more than six hundred thousand personal acts of responsibility. The forty-eight dimensions of the pact become 48 x 603,550. This might, of course, raise a smile. It is a large number. But it is not an infinite one. The Israelites, more correctly described as men participating in a common humanity, answer for each other before a genuinely human law. In the making of this Covenant the relationship between one person and the other is not a matter of indifference....

It is not necessary to gather on the mountains of Ebal or Gerizim, to gaze at length into each other's eyes, for there to be a situation in which everyone looks at everyone else. Everyone looks at me. Let us not forget the seventy languages in which the Torah is read. The Torah belongs to everyone: everyone is responsible for everyone else. The phrase "Love your neighbor as yourself" still assumes the prototype of love to be love of oneself. Here, the ethic is one that says: "Be responsible for the other as you are responsible for yourself." In this way we avoid the assumption about self-love that is often accepted as the very definition of a person. But we have not finished yet: "Rabbi said ... there is not a single precept written in the Torah in connection with which forty-eight times 603,550 covenants were not made, it follows that for each Israelite there are 603,550 commandments. (And forty-eight covenants were made in connection with each of them.)" Doesn't this repeat what we heard a moment ago? The Gemara asks this question: "What is the issue between them?" And R. Mesharsheya finds it: "R. Mesharsheya said: The point between them is that of personal responsibility and responsibility for others [the responsibility of responsibility]." One is not only responsible for everyone else, but responsible also for the responsibility of everyone else. So forty-eight must be multiplied by 603,550, and the product multiplied by 603,550 again. This point is extremely important. A moment ago, we saw a part played by something resembling the recognition of the Other, the love of the Other. To such an extent that I offer myself as guarantee of the Other, of his adherence and fidelity to the law. His concern is my concern. But is not my concern also his? Isn't he responsible for me? And if he is, can I also answer for his responsibility for me? *Kol Yisrael 'arevim zeh lazeh*, "All Israel is responsible one for the other," which means: all those who cleave to the divine law, all men worthy of the name, are all responsible for each other.

This must also mean that my responsibility includes the responsibility taken up by other men. I always have, myself, one responsibility more than anyone else, since I am responsible, in addition, for his responsibility. And if he is responsible for my responsibility, I remain responsible for the responsibility he has for my responsibility. *Ein ladavar sof*, "it will never end." In the society of the Torah, this process is repeated to infinity; beyond any responsibility attributed to everyone and for everyone, there is always the additional fact that I am still responsible for that responsibility. It is an ideal, but one which is inseparable from the humanity of human beings. In the Covenant, when it is fully understood, in the society that fully deploys all the dimensions of the law, society becomes a community.

WALTER WURZBERGER

Ethics of Responsibility: Pluralistic Approaches to Covenantal Ethics

Walter Wurzberger (1920–2002) was a philosopher, rabbi, and leader of Modern Orthodoxy. Born in Munich, he emigrated to the United States after Kristallnacht. A student of Rabbi Joseph Soloveitchik, he served as a congregational rabbi and as editor of the journal Tradition.

From *Ethics of Responsibility: Pluralistic Approaches to Covenantal Ethics* (Skokie, IL: Varda Books, 2001), 9–30.

Chapter 1: Foundations of Covenantal Ethics

The Jewish conception of piety places special emphasis upon ethical conduct. The Torah defines "the way of God" as the "doing of righteousness and justice."

One is made acutely aware of the primacy of the ethical dimension in the Torah's account of the legislation promulgated at Marah. Even before Israel entered into the Sinaitic Covenant, there was need for laws governing interpersonal relations....

Although all *ritual* commandments (with the exception of the prohibition of idolatry), including even the observance of the Sabbath—the very cornerstone of Judaism—are set aside when necessary for the preservation of life, ethical laws are in a different category. Murder or acts of sexual immorality or idolatry may not be committed even if the perpetration of these crimes is deemed indispensable to the saving of one's life....

As opposed to paganism and pantheism, the God of monotheism completely transcends nature.... In the realm of the *is*, God's will generates the laws of nature, which all creatures necessarily "obey." But in the realm of the ought, God is the Author of prescriptive rather than descriptive laws. Unlike the laws of nature, the moral law does not create facts but establishes norms or standards governing the spiritual realm....

The Talmud goes so far as to declare that the Torah served as the blueprint for the creation of the world. Natural law theories base ethical norms on the facts of nature. The Talmudic doctrine reverses the order and asserts that nature is so constituted as to make possible the realization of the divine purposes (the *ought*)....

Many provisions of the halakha clearly fall within the purview of ethics. Yet it is, nonetheless, questionable whether we are really justified in speaking of a "Jewish ethics." After all, in Leviticus such a fundamental ethical norm as "Love thy neighbor as thyself" is subsumed, together with numerous ritual laws, under the overall precept of "Ye shall be holy." As far as the Torah is concerned, no distinction is made between ritual and ethical laws. They form a seamless whole, indispensable for the becoming of a "holy people."... Any transgression of a divine command, whether it is ritual or ethical in nature, amounts to an infringement of the proprietary rights of God, the Creator and the Owner of the universe....

A number of eminent thinkers contend that, since halakha functions as the sole normative authority of Judaism, there can be no such entity as Jewish ethics, in the literal sense of the term.

In radical opposition to this view, I ... show that Judaism in fact transcends such narrow legalism and, for all its theocentric orientation and emphasis upon obedience to the law, it endows moral judgments with genuine religious import.

I employ the term "Covenantal Ethics" to describe my approach, which seeks to reconcile unconditional acceptance of halakha as the supreme normative authority with the recognition that our intuitive moral judgments, even when they cannot be grounded in explicit provisions of the halakha, possess religious significance....

I look upon halakha as an indispensable component but not as coextensive with the full range and scope of the Jewish normative system. I deliberately avoid the term "Halakhic Ethics," preferring to speak of "Covenantal Ethics." In my view, Jewish ethics encompasses not only outright halakhic rules governing the area of morality, but also *intuitive* moral responses arising from the covenantal relationship with God, which provides the matrix for forming ethical ideals not necessarily patterned after legal models. To use Erich Fromm's terminology, Judaism provides for an "ethics of responsibility" as well as for an "ethics of duty" or an "ethics of obedience."[32] ...

To be sure, the belief that an ethical norm should be obeyed in response to a divine imperative rather than for purely ethical reasons by no means detracts from the intrinsic moral character of the norm itself. Judaism demands total commitment to the service of God. Every action, be it self-regarding or other-regarding, be it inspired by self-interest or ethical concerns, ideally "should be performed for the sake of God."

It may be argued that this type of theocentric orientation results in a state of affairs where the intrinsic ethical properties of our norms become totally irrelevant, since ethical duties are performed solely as religious obligations. But to affirm the primacy of the religious dimension does not entail the repudiation of moral authority. Since for Judaism God represents the highest possible moral authority, obedience to His command is not merely a religious but also a moral requirement.

This explains why Judaism has no need for the Kierkegaardian doctrine of "the suspension of the ethical," which demands that whenever moral imperatives clash with religious commandments, we must subordinate our ethical concerns to the higher authority of the religious. Once God is defined as the supreme moral authority, obedience to divine imperatives emerges as the highest *ethical* duty. Thus, Abraham's readiness to sacrifice Isaac cannot be invoked as a paradigm of the "suspension of the ethical." On the contrary, it was a perfectly

---

32. [Erich Fromm (1900–1980) was an influential German-American psychologist and psychoanalyst.]

moral act. Abraham does not cringe before the absolute power of a demon, but rather obeys the command of the supreme moral authority....

We are still left with the question: If an act is moral because it possesses certain intrinsic qualities rather than because it was commanded by God, is it possible to speak of a Jewish ethics? As long as we maintain that there are objective grounds for ethical beliefs, there can be no difference between Jewish and any other ethics....

At this point it must be emphasized that as long as one subscribes to the notion that ethical statements are objectively true or false, religion really has nothing to contribute to the content of ethics. Its sole function in the realm of morality would be to provide additional sanctions, motives, and incentives to inspire obedience to ethical norms. It, then, would be as nonsensical to speak of a Jewish ethics as it would be to refer to a Jewish mathematics or a Jewish chemistry. Were the Jewish moral code merely to prescribe what objectively is morally right or good, then the covenantal basis of ethical norms would have no bearing upon their meaning, validity, or significance....

The belief that ethics must ultimately operate with culturally conditioned intuitions need not necessarily lead to historicism, relativism, or skepticism. It is one thing to state that knowledge of moral principles is influenced by historical or cultural contingencies, and another to maintain that there are no objectively true principles, because all morality is merely the product of human invention. The fact that our moral beliefs may be incorrect, because they are perceived through the prism of our cultural and historic situation, must not be confused with the thesis that moral judgments are purely relative to a given historical situation....

From the vantage point of Jewish Covenantal Ethics, the entire problem as to why ethical imperatives override all other considerations completely disappears. The moral *ought* is absolute, because a divine command constitutes, by definition, the ultimate normative standard. From a traditional Jewish point of view, it is precisely because moral norms are grounded in divine imperatives that they present themselves authoritatively and demand unconditional obedience.

* * *

Most modern systems of ethics ... rely on a single property from which specific norms are deduced. Jewish Covenantal Ethics is pluralistic and reverses the process. Its points of departure are a variety of specific norms such as prohibitions against murder, perjury, robbery, or fraud. General ethical principles are secondary. They are derived by extrapolation from these norms....

In Jewish ethics an explicit legal norm always takes precedence over a general moral principle, even if the latter seems to reflect the general thrust of the legislation of the Torah....

This emphasis upon obedience to the law does not—contrary to widely held belief—reduce Jewish ethics to legalism. A trenchant observation by R. Naftali Tzvi Yehudah Berlin, in a comment on the verse "Ye shall be unto Me a kingdom of priests and a holy people" (Exod. 19:6), strengthens our claim that Jewish morality transcends mere obedience to explicit rules of a legal code. R. Berlin notes that, although the Torah contains numerous specific commandments, the Sinaitic Covenant cannot dispense with the general norm "to become a holy people," because ever-changing historic realities make it impossible for any finite set of specific legal ordinances to meet the requirements of all possible contingencies....

Because mere obedience to a set of formal rules as specified by the Torah is only a necessary but not a sufficient condition of ethical propriety, another source of moral authority must be found....

Obviously, within a theocentric framework there is no room for autonomy in the literal sense of the term—that is, a human self that is self-legislating and its own source of obligation. Human beings are responsible to God rather than to themselves. To quote Micah,[33] "to do justice and to love mercy" is a response to "what God demands of thee," not a self-imposed duty.... Saadia defines "rational commandments" not as self-imposed duties but as divine commandments that may be apprehended by our cognitive faculties and that do not require for their validation any reference to a supernatural act of Revelation.[34] ...

It must be emphasized that ... there is no suggestion that the promptings of the conscience may be pitted against explicitly stated norms of the Torah. The Will of God represents the supreme authority to which all other considerations must be subordinated. Conscience is merely complementary to the explicitly revealed provisions of the law; it supplements but does not supersede them. The role of conscience is limited (1) to discern the Will of God for situations that do not come within the purview of explicit legal norms and (2) to function as a hermeneutical principle to be employed to help ascertain the meaning and range of applicability of laws when their formulation contains an element of ambiguity....

Far from constituting an independent normative authority, conscience merely

---

33. [Micah 6:8.]
34. [Saadia Gaon (892–942) was a medieval Jewish rabbi, exegete, and philosopher.]

provides, in consonance with supernatural Revelation, an instrumentality through which the divine will may be discerned. It would be the height of arrogance to challenge the validity of an explicit divine imperative on the ground that it runs counter to our own ethical intuitions. . . .

In the event of conflict with explicit halakhic requirements, all ethical, aesthetic, intellectual, or prudential considerations must be set aside. . . . The revealed word of God is the highest normative authority, which must be obeyed unconditionally and must not be subjected to the scrutiny of our autonomous moral perceptions. . . . What matters from a theoretical point of view is that in cases where ethical considerations are perceived to clash outright with explicit and unambiguous halakhic provisions, we are duty-bound to follow in Abraham's footsteps and subordinate the promptings of our human conscience to the superior authority of divinely revealed imperatives. In the final analysis, they constitute the supreme ethico-religious standards of evaluation.

EUGENE BOROWITZ

Renewing the Covenant:
A Theology for the Postmodern Jew

Eugene Borowitz (1924–2016) was a leading theologian of Reform Judaism who influenced generations of Reform rabbis as a professor at the Hebrew Union College-Jewish Institute of Religion in New York. A Reform rabbi trained in philosophy, he developed an approach to Judaism called "covenant theology," and founded Sh'ma: A Journal of Jewish Responsibility.

From *Renewing the Covenant: A Theology for the Postmodern Jew* (New York: The Jewish Publication Society, 1991), 214–17.

Chapter 15: Covenant, Not Chosenness

We shall not arrive at a theory of robust Jewish duty as long as we do not transform the Enlightenment's self into a Jewish self, the kind of person I contend our religious experience has shown many of us we are. . . . The notion of Covenant as relationship . . . provided me with a metaphor keyed to the involvement of the whole self yet pointing to the priority of the Jewish people in our relationship with God—the Covenant being made with the folk as a whole, not with Jews as isolates.

This understanding of the sociality of the self explains how one of our major societal ills, privatism and its associated loneliness and depression, intellectually derives from taking persons atomistically rather than as intrinsically social. The same is true in the Jewish community. The theological root of Jewish nonobservance is the doctrine that we are persons-in-general who happen-also-to-be-Jews. But if Jewish particularity does not require external legitimation and has a self-validating quality, theologies built on the primacy of universal selfhood can never give adequate dignity to being one-of-Israel. Moreover, with the modern notion of universalism itself now revealed as particular to a given sociocultural situation, our intuition of the universal dignity of human selfhood itself requires a particular base, one that Covenant/covenant provides.

Where the self-in-general finds its ground in the Noahide covenant with God, the Jewish self has its roots in the Jewish people's historic relationship with God. This Covenant-Jew is no schizoid person-in-general who incidentally though gratefully participates in Jewish ethnicity but is a Jew/person at once, in utter existential depth. Throughout biblical times, the Israelites maintained a sufficient number of these people oriented to God and folk that they became a critical ethnic mass and the choosing/chosenness of the Covenant came into being. Today that critical core group has dwindled perilously and simple ethnicity must carry a burden of continuity that it cannot long sustain. . . . Jews living as part of a community bound today, as for millennia, in a true relationship with God will find their individual responsibilities arising from being commanded as part of our personal-yet-folk intimacy with God. God's quality exalts the relationship, making its entailments compelling. At the same time we, the humans who must live out the Covenant as given selves in a specific time and place, determine how our tradition must be continued, modified, or newly expressed to reflect our continuing faithfulness. . . .

From the covenantal perspective, one can see two primary spiritual challenges facing contemporary Judaism, the one taken up most notably by the Jews of the state of Israel, the other by diaspora Jewry, though both communities share each other's concern. In the former case, an extraordinary historic opportunity, seized by Jewish initiative and courage, enabled our people to reassert its ethnicity with a fullness of land and sovereignty we had not known for two millennia. The Covenant classically involved our people living as a nation and attempting to deal with realpolitik within the tensions of survival/sanctification. Zionism at its best has pursued this Covenant-ideal, and in the many ways the state of Israel has fulfilled this unique theo-political vision it has exalted the spiritual life of Jewry worldwide.

At its best, diaspora Jewry has pursued the other great spiritual opportunity of this era: to discover what it might mean to be an enfranchised self as a believing Jew. Our emancipation prompted us to radically amplify our tradition's high regard for individual dignity and the place of human interpretation in delineating covenantal obligation. Two centuries of experience have led us to attach such religious worth to democratic pluralism that we have sought to reshape personal and communal Jewish life in its terms. As a result, modern Jews have been uncommonly effective workers for our society's improvement and have brought a historically unparalleled tolerance into Jewish communal affairs.

By covenantal standards, neither of these agendas should be permitted to become the exclusive concern of our people.... We can say that the bipolarity of Covenant has now made itself manifest geographically. Jews of the state of Israel, who seek ever better ways of expressing covenanted nationhood today ... know they need to give significant attention to the modern reinterpretation of God's grant of individual dignity.... The converse holds for world Jewry. The individualism that motivates its admirable voluntarism and pluralism also causes its thoughtful leaders to worry about its limited sense of ethnicity and community....

Despite this theoretical chasm and the consequent tensions that have roiled our community, a considerable measure of communal goodwill has persisted among us. Much of this can be ascribed to Jewish realism, to our revulsion at doing the antisemites' work for them after all we have suffered. No small part of it also arises, I suggest, from our intuition of our common meta-halakhic foundation. Covenantally, caring non-halakhic Jews can be understood as fervently seeking to serve God as participants in the Jewish people's historic relationship with God and guided by its tradition, though convinced that Covenant-faithfulness today mandates their deviance from the past. They persist in seeking communal unity because they believe that what binds them to all Jews far exceeds what separates them.... One can best gain insight into people's Jewishness by judging with what personal seriousness they take it. A Judaism that functions essentially as a leisure-time activity or occasional adjunct to one's core concerns seems an unworthy expression of covenantal identity regardless of the ideological label its bearer claims. By contrast, Covenantal selfhood begins with the effort to base one's life on one's Jewish faith and then seek to give it expression in all one's ways. Wherever such devout non-Orthodox Jewishness makes itself evident it will, I am convinced, evoke a certain measure of respect from many of those who, in principle, consider it deviant.

MARA BENJAMIN

The Obligated Self:
Maternal Subjectivity and Jewish Thought

Mara Benjamin (b. 1972) is a scholar of Jewish thought and religious studies who teaches at Mount Holyoke. In 2024, Benjamin was awarded a Guggenheim Fellowship to pursue constructive theological work on Judaism and climate change.

From *The Obligated Self: Maternal Subjectivity and Jewish Thought* (Bloomington: Indiana University Press, 2018), 23–32.

Chapter 2: Love

In the initial weeks and months of caring for my first child, I noticed that moments of seemingly primal protectiveness came and went; the intensity of my attachment to my daughter waxed with proximity and physical contact and waned without it. Over time, some of her gestures, noises, or expressions consistently melted me; others were reliably frustrating.... The curiosity, astonishment, wonder, and terror of being responsible for another human being's life did not disappear; indeed, my own sense of vulnerability grew with the baby to whom I was ever more recognizable and whom I increasingly sought out. All of this seemed quite far from the pacific constancy of motherlove I had naively anticipated.

By contrast, the love and responsibility I came to know seemed remarkably reminiscent of religious forms of praxis with which I was familiar. In Jewish theology and practice, love is active and behavioral: God loves a particular people, Israel, with special intensity, and the covenant God makes with Israel mediates this love and obligates both parties. Love, furthermore, can be commanded, and this commanded love is performative. A daily praxis of service constitutes the proper response to divine love.

Juxtaposing embodied, maternal experiences of love and biblical expressions of divine love ... illuminates both the human and the divine. God's "firstborn," Israel, occasions intense disappointment, rage, pride, vulnerability, and anguish, just as children provoke in their human mothers. But the maternal position also parallels that of the people of Israel in the covenantal relationship, for the visceral imperative to care for one's children is accompanied by a visceral imperative to love them. "Thou shalt love YHVH your God . . . me!"—is also the cry of the infant. Both sides of the covenanted relationship between God and Israel, as envisioned in Scripture and rabbinic tradition, reveal aspects of maternal love, and maternal experiences, in turn, give material reality to the nature of divine love.

* * *

The connection, so common in daily life for parents, between profound love and profound disappointment, frustration, and rage, has long confounded religious philosophers in contemplating God. Divine wrath, like maternal ambivalence, seems a contradiction in terms. But the emotional intensity of maternal caregiving reveals the seamless continuity between God's affection and fury as portrayed in the Hebrew Bible....

Emotional whiplash, a function of intimate, daily contact, can surprise new parents with its intensity. Yet experiences in which repetitive, time-consuming, emotionally, and sensorially taxing work of caring for children beget love soon become familiar to any adult responsible for his or her child's material needs and daily well-being. Love emerges within the contradictions of caring for a child. It lies in the gap between the struggle to get an exhausted, cranky child down for a nap and longing to tiptoe in to gaze on or smell him as he sleeps....

The bond of obligation, as explored in the previous chapter, brings with it a degree of "bondage," and mothers experience these volatile oscillations precisely because of that bondage. Inescapability gives the tether its tautness, its potency for every imaginable emotional register. A mother who yearns for her child's warm skin at other times recoils from being clung to or touched; a mother who shouts or spanks may immediately be consumed with regret or self-castigation; a mother seeking to shelter her helpless fledging finds instead a fully realized other whose volition and capacities are abruptly unfamiliar.

An honest reckoning with the prismatic variety of experience engendered by obligation and love helps us understand the Pentateuchal God's passion for the vulnerable, dependent other to whom he is indissolubly bound.[35] The God of the Pentateuch is a character for whom love is wound up with vexation and fury: no sooner does he show tenderness for Israel than he explodes in rage; his patient care can quickly devolve into a punishing outburst when he finds his people insufficiently mindful of him. God's love is expressed in declarations and acts of protection and favor, but it is also manifested in the disappointment and indignation that result from Israel failing to make good on God's beneficence.

---

35. Here and throughout, I use the male pronoun when speaking of male-gendered portraits of God in biblical and rabbinic texts.

These oscillations are evident to Israel in inexplicable graciousness and nearly indiscriminate plague, an alternation that expresses the moral ambiguity of the universe and the ambiguity of the people of Israel's experience of God....

A usable understanding of love cannot separate divine love from the specific nature of God's concern. God's grand gestures of caretaking are equally—perhaps even proportionately—indexed to his vicious outbursts of frustration. Both stem from the nature of the covenant and God's role in initiating it. God "conceives" and "births" a people to love, a people who will, by definition, also drive him crazy. The oscillations between these extremes are terrifying, disorienting, destabilizing for all involved—child and mother, Israel and God. Yet they are produced by the intense care that defines the relationship....

Separating love from wrath, as Marcionites ancient and modern have attempted, obscures this existential responsibility's effect on the core of the self, activating it on all affective levels. God, as portrayed by the biblical authors, cannot disengage from Israel, as much as he might want to; such is the nature of covenant. God has "bonded" with Israel and thus experiences moments of bondage as a result. This bond, unbreakable once forged, comes from a wellspring at the heart of God's being. When Israel abandons or dismisses God's gift, God's sorrow, rage, and resignation are inevitable. All of these emotions testify to the nature of covenant, which finds its earthly expression everywhere in maternal experience....

Maternal experience of caregiving as love illuminates God's love for Israel and Israel's response in the performance of mitzvot. Maternity offers, in this way, a corrective in a culture that defines love strictly as an involuntary emotion, as irrational and therefore radically uncontrollable. While Jewish sources recognize that love includes this mysterious, uncontrollable, and unwilled dimension, they also suggest that rigorous, active practice can cultivate love.

The Torah repeatedly enjoins Israel "to love" various objects: God, the neighbor, the stranger. This commanded love is manifested in observable behavior. To "love God"—especially in Deuteronomy, a text that emphasizes this idea—has a primarily practical, behavioral meaning; the command instructs the listener "to be loyal to him, to walk in his ways, to heed his mitzvot, to do them," and so on: all activities that (unlike emotion) can be commanded....

Parental caregiving manifests this performative aspect of love. Most of the time, affective state is not the key factor that drives parents to attend to their children or prevents them from doing so. Primal, visceral love of one's child, as powerful as it can be, does not always (or perhaps even usually) tell a parent what to *do* vis-à-vis one's child any more than does one's equally primal frustration or rage.... This reorientation counters romanticized, sentimentalized notions of maternal love, according to which "intuition" rather than reflection guides maternal practice. Proper human action in daily life cannot rest or fall on enthusiasm, zeal, or intensity of feeling; certainly one cannot rely on these feelings to keep a dependent creature alive. Parents execute their daily acts of diaper-changing, cleaning, and feeding their young children as an expression of their love, but childrearing demands that acts of service continue even when parents don't want to attend to their children and when they don't feel affectionate toward them.

Likewise, the people of Israel are to perform mitzvot out of, and as the expression of, their love of God. The validity of the performance does not depend on whether an individual is gripped, moment to moment, by a sense of gratitude or love of God. Instead, performance becomes a means by which action can be regulated.

Maternal activity testifies to the role of performance in generating disposition. To spend many hours caring for one's child involves activity and participation, not standing and observing from afar. Intimate, repeated caregiving actions enable us to notice the creases and folds in chubby limbs; an inventive method of scooting across the floor; the sudden, arresting appearance of a new gesture—hand on hip, arched eyebrow; the squeal of delight and fear when a dog walks by; the need to move constantly; the slowing of breath as a child releases into sleep. Time and care transform a generic person into a unique person; to "discern, learn, teach, appreciate, do, and fulfill" the commandments of Torah transform Torah into a treasured gift....

A mother gives, often unstintingly, to her child not because she "chose" him, and not because of any particular qualities he has, but because he is hers. And once a child becomes "one's own," love of and responsibility to a child lead parents to levels of devotion they could never have imagined....

The love that is nurtured in caring for one's child is alert and attuned to that specific self, to a unique body and temperament. To note that maternal love is "interested" is not to imply that it is conditional but rather to appreciate its dynamism. Parents cannot know in advance which of a child's qualities are transitory and which are enduring, but they nonetheless watch and participate in the whole of a child's changing, embodied existence. God's love for his people is maternal love amplified: dynamic, volatile, and keenly attentive.

5 | Character/Virtue

Many of the sections in this volume are devoted to Jewish communal debates and challenges, and as such the foundational "actor" in these considerations is a communal one. This approach often assumes, before any question is asked, that the answer will apply to a collective—that it will determine how "we," a given Jewish community, should respond. This section is distinguished by its emphasis on individuals—and the ways individuals might accurately evaluate, reflect upon, and build up our own character. In modern theories of ethics, this orientation is usually termed "virtue ethics." Theories of virtue ethics emphasize the necessity of cultivating a deep goodness of individual character, and living in the world in ways that reflect that goodness. We can distinguish the virtual ethical approach from deontological ethics (emphasizing duties, or rules, of behavior) or consequentialism (emphasizing the potential consequences of behavior). Of course, these theories are by no means entirely separate from one another; rather, the difference is perhaps in where the emphasis is placed. Virtue ethics emphasizes sustained discernment of our own instincts, limitations, and ability to change.

These emphases are central to the selections in this section, each of which reflects on processes of ethical self-cultivation in some Jewish context. Jonathan Wyn Schofer and Sarra Lev's essays are both grounded in classical rabbinic literature, while Geoffrey Claussen considers a biblical narrative.

Schofer points out that although rabbinic literature displays profound commitments to what we might call "ethics" and "self-cultivation," these commentaries themselves have no "overarching concepts either for the self/person or for ethics." Schofer thus offers overarching categories for describing the world of ancient rabbinic character formation, arguing that close study of this distinctive group's approach to self-cultivation may contribute to comparative studies of ethical systems and formulating constructive ethical norms, both in and outside Judaism.

Lev's approach is explicitly pedagogical; they reflect on a Talmud class they created with the explicit intention of encouraging students to learn Talmud with the goal not only of making strides toward textual mastery but also of continually interacting with the material as a "summons" to personal reflection. In this class, as Lev tells it, the goal would be "to treat the texts of the Talmud as if they exist to help us achieve holiness. . . . It is a text that pushes our buttons and by which we can be pushed to become ever more reflective, understanding, empathetic, discerning, and expansive."

Geoffrey Claussen introduces us to *musar*, which he characterizes as a tradition "focused on cultivating virtues and resisting vices." The practice of *musar*, in Claussen's description, requires *heshbon ha-nefesh*, an "accounting" of one's own soul requiring constant self-examination. Claussen introduces *musar* in the context of a broader contemporary issue: white supremacy in the United States, which he diagnoses as—among other things—an expression of arrogance, the "disposition to believe that, and behave as if, one is superior to others." Arrogance is, of course, a serious vice, and Claussen argues that it can manifest itself in ways expected and unexpected.

Heshbon ha-nefesh, ethical "summons," subject formation: such are the terms these selections employ to describe the process of creating a virtuous self. But importantly, each of these authors is quick to argue that individual practices and internal accounting are not separate from broader social and cultural movements. Schofer points out that the rabbinic discourse of individual self-cultivation is only intelligible in "the broader culture that the rabbis inhabit." Lev asks in their introduction, "Can we read Talmud to create a kinder, more compassionate, empathetic, and self-reflective society?" And Claussen emphasizes that inasmuch as white supremacy is a structural phenomenon, *musar* must mean "humble self-examination that leads to systemic change." Such claims suggest that studies of character and subjectivity are as inseparable from the communities and cultures in which they develop as any other ethical approach.

JONATHAN WYN SCHOFER

Self, Subject, and Chosen Subjection: Rabbinic Ethics and Comparative Possibilities

Jonathan Wyn Schofer (b. 1967) is an associate professor of religious studies at the University of Texas at Austin, where he teaches and researches classical rabbinic literature alongside ethics, embodiment, and subjectivity.

From "Self, Subject, and Chosen Subjection: Rabbinic Ethics and Comparative Possibilities," *Journal of Religious Ethics* 33, no. 2 (2005): 255–91.

Early rabbis had a large vocabulary through which they set out norms for action and character: ideals that the sages prescribed for students, the ways that the tradition (*torah*) interacted with basic impulses (*yetzer, lev*), and the motivations and emotions that a person was to maintain in relation to God, particularly love (*'ahavah*) and fear or reverence (*yir'ah*). Through such categories, and others, they discussed the nature of human emotions and desires, ideal states, and ways to transform oneself to attain such ideals. That is, they were concerned with ethics and self-cultivation, yet they had no overarching concepts either for the self/person or for ethics. A study of rabbinic ethics, then, cannot rely only upon native rabbinic terminology, but also requires a careful use of contemporary categories. In this paper, I first set out basic features rabbinic ethics in the sources I examine, and then I present accounts of "ethics," the "self," and the "subject" that I argue are appropriate for expositing this particular case. My theoretical work aims not only to open up an account of this cultural group, but also to contribute to descriptive, comparative, and constructive ethics more broadly....

The center point of my analysis is a large compilation entitled *The Fathers According to Rabbi Nathan*. Despite the attribution to "Rabbi Nathan," it is not a single-authored text, but one compiled by anonymous editors over several centuries, roughly from the second to the eighth centuries CE and probably for the most part in Roman Palestine.

Rabbi Nathan is often characterized as a commentary upon a highly influential collection of ethical maxims known as *Avot* or *The Fathers*. *The Fathers* has become the most commented-upon text in all of the rabbinic literature, in part because of its incorporation into Jewish liturgy.... *Rabbi Nathan* itself is arguably the largest and most significant collection of rabbinic ethical instruction. Examples of its maxims include:

The Men of the Great Assembly ... said three things: Be patient in judgment, raise up many disciples, and make a fence for the Torah (Schechter and Kister, 1997, 2; *Avot* 1:1).

[Yose ben Yoezer says]: Let your house be a meeting place for the sages, sit in the very dust of their feet, and drink with thirst their words (Schechter and Kister ,1997, 27; *Avot* 1:4).

Rabbi Yehoshua says: The malicious eye, the bad impulse, and hatred of creatures cast a man out from the world (Schechter and Kister, 1997, 62; *Avot* 2:11).

Rabbi Nathan has for its base maxims such as these, and then it comments on them through a variety of genres, including midrash, narrative, and further epigrams. ... The stories have certain common themes that center upon the importance of Torah, or rabbinic tradition, and reasons why the reader can and should engage with it.

The account of Rabbi Akiva opens by emphasizing the transformative impact of Torah upon emotions and desires that are said to emerge from the "heart." When the story begins, the hero is an uneducated man who understands neither the workings of nature nor the text of the Bible. He sees a rock that has been worn away by water.... Rabbi Akiva draws from the words a teaching that finds hope for shaping his heart through Torah:

What was the start of Rabbi Akiva? They said: He was forty years old and had not studied anything. One time [Akiva] would stand at the mouth of a well. He asked, "Who chiseled out that rock?" They said, "The water, which continuously falls upon it, every day." They said, "Akiva, do not you read in Scripture, 'Water carves away rocks ...'"(Job 14:19). Rabbi Akiva reasoned on his own from the minor to the major case: just as the soft chips away the hard, how much the more so that the words of Torah, which are hard as iron, will hollow out my heart, which is flesh and blood [Schechter and Kister, 1997, 28–29].

Rabbi Akiva places the figures of water and stone on a continuum of soft-hard, stating that "the soft [water] wears away the hard [stone]." ... He asserts that the heart is not hard stone, but soft and receptive flesh and blood. Torah is not soft water, but hard iron. If soft water can wear away the stone, then iron-hard Torah has more than enough power to "hollow out my heart." According to these new metaphors, Torah is a highly powerful agent that can bring a rapid transformation of the receptive heart.

Along with the analysis of these metaphors, it is important to note that the hermeneutical move that generates the teaching—the interpretation of Job 14:19—actually reverses the simple or contextual meaning of the verse. The full verse says, "Water carves away rocks, its torrents wash away earth, so You destroy human hope." Yet Rabbi Akiva interprets the verse in a way that brings him hope for hollowing out his heart. This point is important for seeing the complexity of "Torah" for late ancient rabbis. Many of them saw their Scripture as divine, and they used very strong metaphors to convey its authority and power over themselves, but at the same time their modes of interpretation reveal tremendous amounts of freedom and creativity in their actual encounter with its discourse.

* * *

Rabbi Nathan includes multiple genres of instruction, all of which are permeated by tropes (metaphor, metonymy, hyperbole, and other figures of speech). These modes of expression, and the ethics conveyed through them, include four features that are particularly salient....

1. The sources I examine are discursive, and they also uphold discourse, or language-in-use, as crucial for ethics. The teachings of the sages, the words of Torah, and concepts and tropes describing God are all central to the process of a rabbinic student transforming himself into a sage. The discourse preserved in *Rabbi Nathan* is pedagogic, in that it both presents ethical motifs and ideals and aims to impact the listener or reader in a direct manner. An appropriate theoretical frame will center upon such pedagogical discourse and needs to address not only the ideas and images presented by the discourse, but the function of the discourse itself in ethics—including an account of the relations between discourse, the self, ethics, and the broader culture that rabbis inhabit....

2. Rabbi Nathan is an example of metapractical discourse, for through categories such as Torah and divine justice, rabbis reflect upon practices that are developed and articulated in other sources.... The text addresses the reader—specifically a male who takes on the authority of the rabbinic sages, their Torah, and their account of God—and instructs in correct comportment and action. Rabbis teach, offer powerful metaphors, attempt to persuade, and do many other sophisticated things regarding ethics, but I am not convinced that they "theorize" in anything like the ways that contemporary ethicists do.

3. The ethics of *Rabbi Nathan* presumes and orients the reader toward rabbinic law (halakha). Occasionally, the text discusses specific legal matters, but more generally the law is implied through the concept of Torah, which contains not only law . . . but rather includes both legal and nonlegal . . . materials. Rabbinic law is also implied through motifs such as "serving" God, which centers upon observance of the commandments. An appropriate account of character ethics, then, needs to include deontology as a crucial component.

4. A common theme that runs through *Rabbi Nathan* is that one attains the character of a sage through subordination to particular authorities with the goal of, in various senses, internalizing aspects of them. In the passages quoted above, this dynamic is expressed through the tropes of sitting at the feet of the sages and drinking with thirst their words, and in the commentary through letting one's heart be shaped by Torah as metal upon flesh. The text presents three key points of religious authority—the sage, Torah, and God—and the central argument of my descriptive study centers upon the place of these external authorities in the process of ethical transformation. Theoretically, a challenge is to address the roles of subordination, internalization, and authoritative others in the self-cultivation of religious elites. In many cultural and religious contexts, people attain virtues and forms of freedom through entering into subordinate relations with particular authorities. This important dynamic is, I believe, still undertheorized, despite much work that comes close to the mark.

SARRA LEV

Talmud That Works Your Heart: New Approaches to Reading

Sarra Lev (b. 1964) is a rabbi and associate professor of classical rabbinic literature at the Reconstructionist Rabbinic College. They co-founded Bat Kol, a feminist house of Jewish text study, where they served as rosh yeshiva.

From "Talmud That Works Your Heart: New Approaches to Reading," in *Learning to Read Talmud: What It Looks Like and How It Happens*, eds. Jane L. Kanarek and Marjorie Lehman (Boston: Academic Studies Press, 2019), 175–202.

Some years ago, a rabbinical student who was several weeks into his first semester of Talmud study approached a colleague of mine and said, "When you teach me Talmud, you are assuming this is the *first* time that I am studying it." ... The student then continued, "This is not the *first* time I am studying Gemara ... this is the *last* time. I will never open this book again. So, you'd better teach me what you want me to know." ... There is something important to be learned here. At best, this student feels that the Talmud cannot be harmonized with his values and, at worst, that it is downright immoral. This student is not alone. Every semester, there is at least one student who enters my class already hating the Talmud.

These students echo feelings that I myself have had on reading certain passages, and yet, I am compelled by the Talmud—by its depth and by the *way* in which it is traditionally studied. So, I ask myself, "Can we read Talmud to create a kinder, more compassionate, empathetic, and self-reflective society?"

"Reading to work the heart" is far less clear-cut than other reading methods. ... I am asking [my students] to read Talmud by addressing its moral (and immoral) issues. I want to teach them how to read *all* of the stories, including those in which the rabbis reject saving a non-Jew's life if it would mean transgressing Shabbat; those in which they debate the mechanics of sex with a three-year-old girl; and those in which they (on more than one occasion) even commit murder. I want to provide students the opportunity to use their encounters with rabbinic texts to deepen themselves in multiple ways: as individuals, in their relationships with others, and in their relationship with the material itself. And so, I premiered the course "Talmud Through a Moral Lens." ... I wanted to know: Is there a way to read Talmud that will help us grow, even when the Talmud *itself* does not reflect our values? What qualities can we cultivate in ourselves through encounters not only with the Talmud's "friendly" sides but even (or perhaps, particularly) with its "unfriendly" ones? In short, I wanted to know if there is a way to read Talmud that not only "works the brain," but also "works the heart."

The way I determined to set about this was to treat the Talmud as a new genre—which I will call "summons." By that, I mean to treat the texts of the Talmud as if they exist to help us achieve holiness, not by telling us what is or what should be, but by impelling us to interact with the text. It is a text that pushes our buttons and by which we can be pushed to become ever more reflective, understanding, empathetic, discerning, and expansive....

When I have taught Talmud in the past, I have noticed two opposite ways that students experience the text—for some, it feels remote and alien, while for others, it feels intimate, sacred, and infallible. The first student will reject the texts. The second will run circles around the texts to make them conform to what he/she believes the text should say or wants it to say, ultimately opening the text to presentism, ethnocentrism, and egocentrism. Neither group's response allows for complex analysis.

Both my choice of texts and my teaching require a careful balance between making the strange familiar and making sure that the familiar is not *too* familiar....

"Working the heart" is meant to cause a disruption in what Paulo Freire calls "circles of certainty," by identifying (and dispelling) responses to a text that are entirely based on what we *think* we know.[36] But, while trying to dispel the predisposition to "know and judge," I also want to keep my students close enough so that reading Talmud *matters*. How can they truly meet the Other, if they do not feel at all attached to the text? Reading the Talmud as "summons" demands the ability to hold both enough distance to quell our assumptions and enough familiarity to feel something, to create meaning. I want the students to grow through *getting to know* a text that is laden with religious meaning, is entirely foreign, and yet, they can claim as their own....

For this class, I chose texts in which the message (and many times the plot itself) was unclear, and they could legitimately be read in a number of ways and on multiple levels.... Additionally, if a text had elements with which the students

36. [Paulo Freire (1921–1997) was a Brazilian philosopher of education and the author of *Pedagogy of the Oppressed*.]

might disagree, that friction itself could stimulate conversation. I did not want to alienate them entirely with "terrible texts" merely to provoke discussion and regress into sensationalism, and yet, I wanted to deal head-on with highly problematic material....

In what follows, I will use B. T. *Yoma* 23a, a story about a priestly murder that we studied during the semester. The story had intricacies that could lead to in-depth conversations, and was both familiar (murder) and strange (Temple practice) at the same time:

> Our rabbis taught: It once happened that two priests were neck and neck as they [raced] and ascended the ramp [to the altar]. One of them ran ahead.... He took a knife and thrust it into [his competitor's] heart. R. Tsadok stood on the steps of the Hall and said: "Our Brothers of the House of Israel, listen! Behold it says [in Torah], 'If a corpse is found in the land then your elders and judges shall go out...' (Deut. 21:1) For whom shall we bring the heifer whose neck is to be broken? On [behalf of] the city or on [behalf of] the Temple Courts?" All the people burst out weeping. The father of the [stabbed] boy came and found him while he was still in convulsions. He said, "May he be your atonement. My son is still in convulsions and the knife has not become impure." [His remark] comes to teach that the purity of their vessels was graver for them than the shedding of blood....

I then had the students read... the father's statement in a variety of tones of voice, asking them to experiment with different emotions behind the tones expressed. Some students read the father's words... somberly, as a wish or a hope for the priestly clan that either his son, the (still pure) knife, or some other "this" should atone for the murder. Others read them... as didactic. Some students suggested that however one reads the statement, the father is likening his dying son, stabbed with a knife normally used for sacrifice, to a sacrificial animal used for atonement....

Did the father care more about the purity of the knife than his son's death? Were his words ironic or sincere? Was his voice breaking or was he indifferent and unmoved by his son's death? Was he included in those who cared more for their vessels or was he reprimanding them? Without veering from the text in any way, multiple interpretations emerged from this exercise. The more that new options for reading were introduced, the less certain students became of their original readings, responses, and judgments; and the less likely they were to extract simplistic moral lessons from the text....

Achieving a balance of differentiating between ourselves and the Other, while still understanding and empathizing with the Other, would not emerge from solely intellectually analyzing the text. We needed a process to shape the nature and extent of that encounter. The more we pulled at the material, in order to know the texture of every thread, the more we exercised that skill, and the more we were able to translate it into our understanding of *many different* "Others." But pulling at the threads is only one essential aspect of this process. *How* we pulled was equally essential. While the reader must come to know and understand the text on its own terms, she must also cultivate an ability to see herself in those who appear within the pages of the Talmud and in their circumstances. Once we had accomplished the complex analysis of the text, we needed to take the reading to the next stage—understanding how the text summons us to become our best selves....

I did not want the text to become a jumping-off point from which to just talk about ourselves or to flatten the text's depth by glibly applying our own experiences to it. Avoiding reductionism and cultivating the above skills and characteristics, first and foremost, required keeping the discussion close to the text, even while self-reflecting. In order to maintain depth and complexity, we did this while reading the text and through class discussions. Maintaining the variety of perspectives we had accumulated in stage 1 allowed the students more entry points into the material *and* offered them much richer material for analyzing their own behaviors.... I wanted my students to understand that while perhaps they *could* judge the text the way they originally had (whether positive or negative), they must not *necessarily* do so. Indeed, in each text, we took time to question particular judgments based on elements in the text and to introduce alternative and equally plausible readings....

My purpose throughout was to cultivate an encounter that views the text as summons, a call to look within, not only by leading with bridging questions (such as that above), but by *explaining* the types of questions that this approach requires as we apply the text to our own lives: "What is it that I am not understanding about these opinions or behaviors?" "What information do I need to collect to understand more?" "How can I read this differently if I approach it with compassion?" "What will I learn about myself if I meet this text without beginning at a place where I am right?" All of these questions serve to bridge between the text and the reader, not by *leaving* the text and *moving* to the reader, but by applying parallel methods to understanding ourselves as readers and to understanding the text itself.

GEOFFREY CLAUSSEN

Musar in a White Supremacist Society: Arrogance, Self-Examination, and Systemic Change

Geoffrey Claussen (b. 1979) is a professor of religious studies at Elon University, where he teaches Jewish texts, thought, and ethics. He received rabbinic ordination from the Jewish Theological Seminary.

From "Musar in a White Supremacist Society: Arrogance, Self-Examination, and Systemic Change," in *No Time for Neutrality: American Rabbinic Voices from an Era of Upheaval*, eds. Michael Rose Knopf with Miriam Aniel (2021), 352–68.

In this essay, I consider the arrogance of white supremacy through the lens of the tradition of *musar*, the Jewish ethical tradition focused on cultivating virtues and resisting vices. White supremacy is much more than an expression of arrogance—it is also an expression of injustice and many other vices, and it is embedded within many ideas, policies, laws, institutions, and systems. For white-identified people in the United States, resisting expressions of arrogance is only one aspect of the work that is required to resist white supremacy. But I suggest that it may be an important part of that work. And for those of us who are white-identified and seek guidance from Jewish tradition, it may be valuable to reflect on *musar* traditions regarding arrogance, humility, and the ways that these dispositions shape and are shaped by ideas, policies, laws, institutions, and systems.[37]

According to some *musar* traditions, arrogance is prohibited by the Torah in Deuteronomy 17:18–20. That passage appears on the surface (*peshat* level) to be only a warning for male, Israelite kings, but some sources see a comprehensive *prohibition* on arrogance for kings—and, certainly, those who are not kings as well. The text . . . teaches that if the people of Israel decide to establish a monarchy . . . their king must be bound by rules including the following:

> When he is seated on his royal throne, he shall have a copy of this Teaching [*Torah*] written for him on a scroll by the Levitical priests. Let it remain with him and let him read in it every day of his life, so that he may learn to revere

---

[37]. This essay is addressed to those who are white-identified and interested in guidance from Jewish tradition, whether or not they personally identify as Jewish or see themselves as belonging to Jewish communities. For a recent essay directly addressing white Jews and racism within Jewish communities, see Sandra Lawson, "I'm a Black Rabbi. I've Never Been in a Jewish Space Where I Wasn't Questioned," June 12, 2020, https://forward.com/opinion/448654/im-a-black-jew-i-have-never-been-in-a-jewish-space-where-my-jewish.

the Lord his God, to observe faithfully every word of this Teaching as well as these laws. Thus he will not act arrogantly toward his fellows or deviate from the Instruction [*Mitzvah*] to the right or to the left.

The king, it seems, should keep a Torah scroll with him and continually read it, so that he will be filled with reverence and humility....

But, unfortunately, if the king is reading the words of the Written Torah, a fair portion of what the king will read will *not* help him to see all people as created equal. If the king continues reading *Parashat Shoftim*, for example, he will read God's instructions for conquering the land of Canaan and annihilating its inhabitants: "You shall not let a soul remain alive. No, you must exterminate them" (Deut. 20:16–17)....

We might imagine how, amidst a military campaign, the king reads from his portable Torah scroll: "you shall not let a soul remain alive, but you must exterminate them." The king could read this and resolve to be more humble, not to inject his own personal desires into the Torah but only to do what it says, and he goes out and humbly orders the execution of the inferior peoples around him —humbly, not deviating from the Torah's instruction to the left or to the right. ... It is easy to think that one is being humble even when one is upholding the worst forms of supremacism....

Consider another tradition that invokes the commandment to the king, one that appears in the writings of the eleventh-century Jewish philosopher Bahya ibn Pakuda. Bahya was the author of *The Book of Direction to the Duties of the Heart*, a book focused on how the Torah should guide one's inner life and inspire one to continually take stock of one's soul. Bahya's book is often described as the foundational work of *musar* ("moral discipline"), the tradition of Jewish reflection and practice focused on cultivating virtues and resisting vices....

Bahya was also the first Jewish thinker to introduce the phrase often translated as "moral accounting," "soul accounting," "taking stock of the soul," or "self-examination"—in Hebrew, *ḥeshbon ha-nefesh*, a Hebrew term invented to translate the equivalent phrase that Bahya used in Arabic. Bahya taught that it is an obligation at all times to inspect and take an accounting of the condition of one's soul, looking out for traces of arrogance and considering how one could be more humble, and mistrusting one's impulse to think that all is fine with one's moral and intellectual life.[38] ... Bahya explains this obligation in part with

---

38. See Bahya ben Joseph ibn Pakuda, *The Book of Direction to the Duties of the Heart*, trans. Menahem Mansoor (Oxford: Littman Library of Jewish Civilization, 2004), 380, 389, 399.

reference to the verses about the king quoted above: if the king is commanded to work toward humility every day of his life, so too all of us must have an obligation to do so, continually: "Self-examination is binding upon each person . . . at all times, with every blink of one's eyes and with every breath one takes, if this is possible." . . .

In the United States, we live in a society pervaded by racial biases, especially anti-Black and anti-indigenous biases. . . . White-identified people in the United States are socialized to believe that being white is ideal and to view Black people, indigenous people, and other people of color as inferior. . . . Seeking to preserve our sense of our own goodness, we insist that we are not complicit in upholding white supremacy. But we often are. . . .

Those of us who are white have ḥeshbon ha-nefesh work to do as we examine our complicity with white supremacy and pursue greater justice. Those of us who are white Jews may see such work as an essential part of our Jewish practice, one that fits within the *musar* tradition. . . . And this tradition of *musar* can, I think, offer resources to those seeking Jewish traditions that may inform antiracist commitments.

Reading the Torah, even "every day of one's life," will never be enough. . . . Reading the Written Torah does not easily lead to treating all human beings as created in God's image; having correct beliefs does not easily lead to correct behavior. The work of *musar*, of cultivating moral discipline, must involve daily attention to the patterns and prejudices to which we have been habituated, often since childhood. . . . At the heart of the work of *musar* . . . is the commitment to mistrusting our impulse to think that all is fine with our souls and our world. . . .

Awareness that we are not as good as we think we are is also essential for keeping our efforts in perspective. This is especially important given the tendency of those devoted to the work of moral introspection to view themselves as morally superior to those who do not engage in such work. . . .

Introspective practices focused on antiracism, though they may aim to counter arrogance, may have this same effect, leaving practitioners with a sense of superiority. . . . Certainly, when we are (however unconsciously) seeking to feel better about ourselves, or when we seek to display how we humbly accept our guilt, we are not humbling ourselves at all. . . .

Even more significantly, focusing on the virtues of personal antiracist work may distract us from working for political changes that will better alleviate human suffering. Scholar Charisse Burden-Stelly's critique of how contemporary antiracist literature fails to challenge exploitative systems of racial capitalism is instructive here.... A focus on reducing white racial arrogance can lead white people to take up far too much space, centering our inner work and distracting from systemic changes.[39] ...

As such, those engaged in inner work can be like the Israelite king who is dedicated to cultivating humility and ... engaging in self-examination every day of his life—but whose self-examination does not sufficiently account for the suffering of the oppressed and who becomes known more for his piety than for ensuring just systems.... His reverential dedication to the Written Torah leaves him in a position of arrogance—unable to hear the voices of those who are most marginalized under the existing system, such that unjust suffering continues unabated....

There are some models of *musar* that detach character formation from politics. From these perspectives, the work of *musar* involves focusing on one's private, inner life and not on matters of public affairs.

But we see from the model of the king that character is inseparable from politics. The king's cultivation of humility matters in part because it will shape the ideas, laws, policies, institutions, and systems that he upholds; and these will ultimately shape his character as much as his character will shape them. Equitable laws that ensure, for example, that "you shall not judge unfairly" will cultivate greater humility. Laws that require the killing of Canaanites will distort the king's soul, cultivating a greater sense of superiority and greater arrogance.

So too, the cultivation of humility by white Americans matters *in part* because of how it will shape ideas, laws, policies, and systems. Will we have the humility to see our own complicity with white supremacy? Will we overcome our comfort with unjust systems? In challenging those systems, will we have the humility to follow the lead of those who are racialized and most oppressed by our current systems? Will we work for systems that ensure greater equity?

But laws, policies, and systems ultimately shape our character as much as character can shape laws, policies, and systems. Just laws that counter inequity are conducive to greater humility. Unjust laws that further inequity are conducive to greater arrogance and to damaging our souls.... So too with unjust laws promulgated by Israelite kings: unjust laws will distort the souls and damage the personalities of kings and the others who will not deviate from their unjust instructions. Statutes that dehumanize the Canaanites will provide a false sense of

---

39. Charisse Burden-Stelly, "Caste Does Not Explain Race," *Boston Review*, December 15, 2020, https://bostonreview.net/race/charisse-burden-stelly-caste-does-not-explain-race.

superiority, relegating persons to the status of things. The same is true of racist systems today. Halting the arrogance that leads to dehumanization, exploitation, and oppressive systems is important *musar* work; and so is combatting unjust systems that distort souls, damage personalities, create false senses of superiority, and relegate persons to the status of things. We require *musar* that will help to turn our attention away from ourselves and toward ensuring greater equity.

6 | Ethical Values

A conventional understanding of Judaism holds that, in contradistinction to fickle contemporary society, it espoused a set of unchanging values at its inception. For example, Nachum Amsel[40] starts *The Jewish Encyclopedia of Moral and Ethical Issues* with this claim:

> In an age when society's values are rapidly changing and are constantly called into question, many people are searching for a more fixed, permanent value system that can provide an anchor for identifying right and wrong and that will allow a person to find meaning in his or her daily endeavors. Judaism's unchanging value system has remained consistent and constant throughout the ages and has thus given meaning to millions of Jews for the past three thousand years.[41]

Such an approach assumes that "Judaism" is a singular and clearly defined phenomenon. It also simultaneously contends that "Jewish values" exist and are clear, identifiable, immutable, perfectly transmitted, and wholesomely applied. Were this the case, variations across communities and eras would be negligible and disputes about values and norms absent. Modern ethics would be rather like a form of archaeology, uncovering and interpreting past norms for present issues.

As the selections in this book exemplify, modern Jewish ethicists are skeptical (or highly critical) of this conceptualization of Judaism. While some contemporary scholars do embrace this static view and insist that Judaism articulates an unchanging set of values, many others offer different methodologies vis-à-vis values. Some philosophically investigate the very term (values) and query the relationships between values, principles, and good(s), all within Jewish texts and contexts.[42] Others put contemporary issues into conversation with (what they identify as) Jewish

---

40. Rabbi Nachum Amsel is director of education at the Destiny Foundation in Israel.

41. Nachum Amsel, *The Jewish Encyclopedia of Moral and Ethical Issues* (Northvale, NJ: Jason Aronson, 1994), 1.

42. Some examples include Kenneth Seeskin, *Autonomy in Jewish Philosophy* (Cambridge: Cambridge University Press, 2001); David Novak, *Covenantal Rights: A Study in Jewish Political Theory* (Princeton, NJ: Princeton University Press, 2000).

values.⁴³ The selections below provide additional ways to engage values: one procedural and discursive, the other historical.

David A. Teutsch argues that while moral reasoning is necessary, it alone is insufficient to generate moral action. Communal deliberation is critical. Moreover, that deliberation is particular, by which he means that Jews exist in certain times and places and what they should do needs to be tailored to their unique circumstances. Through this iterative process, a community's values thus have a significant role in shaping norms for contemporary Jews who understand themselves unbound to halakha.

Tanhum Yoreh's study, by contrast, "uses the methodology of tradition [sic] histories to produce an intellectual history of the prohibition against wastefulness."⁴⁴ This intellectual history of the imperative *bal tashchit* (do not waste) involves deep consideration of value and values. In this selection, Yoreh distinguishes intrinsic from instrumental values. Conventionally, humans are understood to *be* intrinsically valued, whereas anything nonhuman *has* instrumental value. Another conventional idea is that of hierarchy, that some are more valuable than others. These distinctions help prioritize which interests shall be championed when human and nonhuman interests conflict. Such reasoning engenders a kind of consequential calculus whereby "if . . . then" thinking leads to communally sanctioned action, and in the case of the environment, these actions most often favor humankind's interests.⁴⁵

Such scholarly pieces raise some questions. For instance, if there are values to take seriously in contemporary Jewish ethics, which values are most salient? How should those values then lead, guide, and constrain personal and communal decision-making? And what should be done when values come into conflict: Which ones should take precedence, who shall decide, and how?

---

43. To illustrate: regarding the topic of strangers, strangeness, and justice, see Shmuly Yanklowitz, "Strangers, Immigrants, and the *Eglah Arufah*," *Milin Havivin* 6 (2012–2013): 66–77; Aryeh Cohen, *Justice in the City: An Argument from the Sources of Rabbinic Judaism* (Boston: Academic Studies Press, 2012); Joy Ladin, *The Soul of the Stranger: Reading God and Torah from a Transgender Perspective* (Waltham, MA: Brandeis University Press, 2019).

44. Tanhum Yoreh, *Waste Not: A Jewish Environmental Ethic* (Albany: State University of New York Press, 2019), 1.

45. For a completely different application of the *bal tashchit* imperative, see David Novak, "Nuclear War and the Prohibition of Wanton Destruction," in *Jewish Social Ethics* (New York: Oxford University Press, 1992), 118–32.

DAVID A. TEUTSCH
Reinvigorating the Practice of Contemporary Jewish Ethics: A Justification for Values-Based Decision-Making

David Teutsch (b. 1950), a professor emeritus of contemporary Jewish civilization, was president of the Reconstructionist Rabbinical College, where he established and directed the Center for Jewish Ethics. His scholarship focuses on Jewish theology, ethics, liturgy, and organizational leadership. He held leadership positions in the Academic Coalition for Jewish Bioethics, the Society of Jewish Ethics, the National Havurah Committee, and the Conference of Presidents of Major American Jewish Organizations, among other organizations.

From "Reinvigorating the Practice of Contemporary Jewish Ethics: A Justification for Values-Based Decision-Making," *The Reconstructionist* (Spring 2005): 4–15.

Reinvigorating Jewish ethics is critical to the future of Jewish culture, to the relevance of Judaism to contemporary Jews, and to the positive influence of Judaism in the world. But how can that be accomplished? What is the ground of moral life, and given the current nature of American Jewish life, what is a plausible moral decision-making process? . . .

Congregation-based communities can only have substantial influence on the moral lives of their members if they develop a shared ethos and intensive relationships. Values-based decision-making (VBDM)[46] is designed to create a moral dialogue that reinforces values, creates consensus, and builds community.[47]

46. [The steps of VBDM are as follows, according to the article cited next:
1. Determine facts, alternative actions, and their outcomes.
2. Examine relevant scientific and social scientific approaches to understanding these.
3. Consider the historical and contemporary context, including the history and rationales of Jewish practice.
4. Look for norms that might exclude some actions.
5. Assemble and weigh relevant attitudes, beliefs, and values.
6. Formulate decision alternatives.
7. Seek consensus (if a group is deciding).
8. Make the decision.]

47. For a fuller methodological discussion of values-based decision-making, see my article, "Values-Based Decision-Making," *The Reconstructionist* 65, no. 2 (Spring 2001): 22–28.

VBDM is a multistep process that requires fact-finding, exploration of Jewish tradition, determination of actions excluded by norms, and discovery of relevant values and ideals. Consideration of alternative courses of action can then take place in light of consequences, values, and ideals. This process is one of self-education and not just decision-making. It can work both for individuals and for groups when they are facing decisions with sufficiently important impact and a substantial moral component.

Over the last fifteen years, VBDM has become common in Reconstructionist congregations. The need for moral discussion and a community consensus around ethical practice provides a powerful rationale for VBDM. It is designed to help raise consciousness about vocabulary, and to help establish communal norms and practices that add depth and meaning to Jewish culture. By empowering people to engage in this process as a community, we also help them to discover the means to carry their set Jewish values and norms into application in their own lives.

* * *

Of course, if the study stage of VBDM is not done with care, people will simply bring with them their American individualist perspectives, patiently wait until the study step of VBDM is over, and assert their American values. That can derail the educational phase and empty the process of its Jewish content. When that occurs, the purpose of VBDM is circumvented. VBDM only works as effective Jewish guidance if there is genuine and substantial engagement with Jewish culture—texts, traditions, and values. Otherwise, VBDM may still result in effective decision-making—it's just not Jewish. A Jewish community committed to Jewish culture ought to be true to its identity.

This is not to say that Jewish values are unchanging—Reconstructionists in recent decades have expanded Jewish tradition to include values like democracy and inclusion. Cultures evolve. But values held by individual Jews are not necessarily Jewish values; that is an issue with which each Jewish community must wrestle. When a claimed value is in tension with inherited beliefs, practices, or norms, careful Jewish study and exploration of the issues are warranted.

The decision to make a significant change should be accompanied by soul-searching and trepidation, with careful thought about implications for social justice and the future of the Jewish people. The response to "giving Jewish tradition a vote" ought not to be "it doesn't speak to me." Tradition votes only when we listen carefully. Only listening and agonizing can validate a veto. Some communities may not start by examining Jewish tradition. This invalidates their decision-making process. However, if a community avoids engaging Jewish tradition, that flaw would carry over to other decision-making processes, unless it turns over decisions to a rabbi who takes Judaism seriously, or to another leader with similar knowledge and commitment. This would involve the betrayal of other values....

VBDM is not a panacea. It can fully invigorate the moral life of a Jewish community only when it includes a substantial educational process, when the leaders of the community create currency for Jewish moral terminology, and when the study of Jewish texts and maintenance of Jewish traditions are ongoing parts of the life of the community.

The central importance of community in a Jewish ethical system suggests that we ought to make major personal investments in the creation and maintenance of community. Without community there will be no vehicle to preserve and convey Jewish culture. Because of the cultural setting in which we live, democratic, inclusive community is the model that makes the most sense. While developing the technologies to create and reinforce such community is a challenging and ongoing task, the rewards of community involvement have intrinsic benefits that more than justify that challenge.

TANHUM YOREH

Waste Not: A Jewish Environmental Ethic

Tanhum Yoreh (b. 1980) serves as a professor of environmental humanities and worldviews and beliefs at the University of Toronto. His award-winning research delves into many aspects of religion and environment, with a special focus on wastefulness, consumption, and simplicity. His recent monograph, Waste Not, *received critical praise.*

From Waste Not: A Jewish Environmental Ethic (Albany: State University of New York Press, 2019), 45–48.

Multiple layers of meaning can be found in . . . midrashic sources.[48] First and foremost, it is important to point out that *midrash halakha*[49] treats the legal

48. [*Sifre*, Deuteronomy, *Shofetim*, piska 203–4; *Midrash Tannaim*, Deuteronomy 20:19–20; *Sifre*, Leviticus, *Kedoshim*, 10:6–7.]

49. [*Midrash halakha* is a classic genre of rabbinic exegesis of biblical laws.]

boundaries of the prohibition to cut down fruit trees more broadly than the wartime context of Deuteronomy 20:19. While not yet relating to the edict as a blanket prohibition against wastefulness, it does extend the prohibition to non-war situations. This appears to be a first step in expanding the prohibition to include all forms of wastefulness and destruction.

Two central themes arise in these three midrashim [see note 50]. The first is the notion that there is a hierarchy between humans and nonhumans, and also within the nonhuman world through the preferential status given to fruit trees over their non-fruit-bearing counterparts. This preferential status within the nonhuman world appears to be a spillover from the superiority of humans over the nonhuman world because of the sustenance fruit trees provide. The second theme, which is intricately connected to the first, is that the two interpretations offered for *ki ha'adam etz hasadeh*[50] seemingly represent different worldviews with regard to the value of the natural world. One is that the fruit trees are a future source of food, and long-term sustainability should not be compromised unnecessarily, even in the heat of battle. This worldview gives the fruit trees status because of their instrumental value. It protects them because of their utility. The other worldview suggests that the natural world might have inherent value. Fruit trees are defenseless, unable to escape a marauding army; no benefit is gained through their needless destruction and as such it is prohibited to destroy them.[51]

The problems posed by hierarchical worldviews and the intrinsic vs. instrumental value of anything nonhuman have been some of the central debates within environmental discourse, and there is no consensus on a "winning" approach. Both can offer environmental protection under different premises. . . . Nevertheless, it is relevant to our subject matter to understand which worldviews in the field of environmental ethics are most similar to the worldviews represented in these particular midrashim. . . .

Scholars of religion and environment, especially from within the monotheistic traditions, have found it challenging to abandon the notion that humans are morally superior to nonhumans. For instance, even though environmental philosopher Holmes Rolston III argues that there is no fundamental conflict

50. ["Are trees of the field human . . . ?" according to the New Jewish Publication Society translation of Deuteronomy 20:19. This is a notoriously ambiguous verse.]

51. The reason we cannot determine with certainty that the midrash espouses this view is because here, too, it is possible that protecting the defenseless trees may ultimately be just a way to inculcate humans with moral values, ultimately making both approaches resonate as anthropocentric.

between human and nonhuman interests; where conflict does exist, human interests take precedence.[52] This view appears to be consonant with the midrash, insofar as it protects both the fruit trees and human interests. Within environmental thought, the main conflict with this position would be with deep ecologists such as Arne Naess and George Sessions,[53] who base some of their philosophy on Baruch Spinoza's notion that there is no hierarchy in nature.[54] While the midrash itself appears to establish legal parameters through which fruit trees are protected, deep ecologists and ecofeminists would argue that the very notion of hierarchies allows for humans (or, for ecofeminists, men) to dominate the natural world (and women), ultimately resulting in ecological crisis.

It could, of course, be argued that the fruit trees have no inherent value and that they are only protected by virtue of their instrumental value. The fact that human life can be sustained (at least in part) by fruit does not necessarily attribute any value to the tree; it only confirms that humans have inherent value and that sustaining human life is paramount. This view is consistent with that of environmental philosophers such as Bryan Norton, who argues that there is no inherent value in nature, yet this does not prevent humans from protecting the environment. Instead, Norton champions the idea of "weak" anthropocentrism, an ethic through which humans do not have the license to unreservedly exploit the environment. In fact, according to Norton, when viewed holistically, it becomes apparent that long-term human sustainability depends on environmental protection.[55] For Norton, the two interpretations presented in the midrash might ultimately just be versions of "weak" anthropocentrism.

A point that deserves further consideration from an environmental perspective is the idea in *Sifre*[56] (and in later commentaries) that the prohibition against

---

52. Holmes Rolston III, *Environmental Ethics: Duties and Values in the Natural World* (Philadelphia: Temple University Press, 1988), 62–71.

53. [Arne Naess was a twentieth-century Norwegian philosopher who coined "deep ecology," and the American environmentalist George Sessions helped develop that concept.]

54. Peter Hay, *Main Currents in Western Environmental Thought* (Bloomington: Indiana University Press, 2002), 42.

55. Bryan Norton, *Toward Unity among Environmentalists* (New York: Oxford University Press, 1994), 240.

56. [*Sifre* are works of *midrash halakha* commenting on either the biblical book of Numbers or of Deuteronomy.]

destroying fruit trees includes taking action to prevent water from reaching the tree. The environmental cost of human activities is often neglected due to its indirect nature. In addition to the direct, obvious, and immediate consequences of human actions, one could derive from this midrash the importance of understanding the indirect consequences of human actions.

11 | Communities

> Hillel says: Do not separate yourself from
> the community.   Pirkei Avot 2:4

Introduction

Jewish sources across the ages highlight the importance of community, promoting virtues and practices that cultivate connection and cohesion, and emphasizing collective flourishing over and above the interests of individuals. Rabbinic writings distinguish between two overarching sets of commandments: duties that human beings owe to God (*bein adam la-makom*) and responsibilities that bind human beings to one another (*bein adam la-havero*). The distinction between these two categories is sometimes characterized as a distinction between ritual and ethical commandments, but it is important to note that community is the context in which *both* sets of obligations—the ceremonial and the interpersonal—are lived out. The required quorum of a minyan of ten worshipers for the full liturgy is just one example of how Jewish ritual and ceremonial life presume a communal context. Ritual practices thus reinforce Jewish ethical teachings about the primacy of communal belonging and participation. Jewish life is fundamentally a communal endeavor.

Even as the value of community is a consistent theme in Jewish ethical discourse, what "community" means varies from age to age and from thinker to thinker. In rabbinic sources, ethical responsibilities are constructed on a model of concentric circles, where one owes the most to those who are in closest proximity: one attends first to one's family's needs, then to the needy Jews in one's town, and then to needy Jews in more distant places (e.g., B. T. *Bava Metzia* 71a). Sources like these probably never squared with the messy realities of communal life, but they are especially remote from social life in the twenty-first century, as social media and global economics bring us into relationship with people across the world, even as group identities fragment and proliferate across intersecting lines of gender, race, nationality, class, and ideology. The writings gathered here illustrate how scholars seek to bring Jewish ethics to bear on changing conceptions and experiences of social life.

The sections that make up this part are arranged along two trajectories that intertwine.

One trajectory traces a progression from the smallest units of social groupings to the largest, moving from family to other solidarities to the state to the environment. A second trajectory examines the modes of connection that organize and bind these social units: language, economics, and violence. The sections move in a spiral: from the most intimate organizations of community to the most vast, and from the most benign currents of connectivity to the most lethal.

Section 7 focuses on the foundational unit of human sociality, the family. While the importance of family is emphasized in Jewish ethical writings from ancient times through the present, the structures and meanings of family are perennially changing. The pieces in this section make ethical arguments that Jewish thinking with regard to marriage and childbearing must change to better accord with values of egalitarianism, human dignity, and gender liberation.

Beyond the intimate circle of kinship ties, social relationships are established through acts of speech and communication. Section 8 highlights the ways speech is deployed to navigate relationships between the self and community. Traditional Jewish sources come from a time when speech was largely confined to immediate face-to-face relationships and emphasize the power of the tongue to do harm; since then, revolutions in technology have remade the power and reach of human communication. This section brings together research on classical conceptions of speech ethics and efforts to address contemporary concerns. But the acceleration of technological change means that new ethical questions arise far more quickly than they can be substantively addressed through research, deliberation, and scholarly publication. The piece by Mark Washofsky is an example of how Jewish ethicists address the innovations of the digital age, but—having been published in 2014—it does not address the more recent intrusions of big data or the extent to which social media platforms have reshaped social relationships, much less the vast potential of artificial intelligence.

The connectivity and mobility that the contemporary world affords means that communal affiliations and social bonds are increasingly matters of volition. While ancient people's communal ties were constrained by the places of their births, contemporary people navigate where to draw lines of "us" and "them," forging bonds that extend across lines of difference. Section 9 examines the ethics of solidarity, mutual care, and belonging in social groups. In section 10, we turn to a different engine of human relationality: economics. Though few Jewish ethicists attend to economic topics, our selections here highlight the degree to which business practices, the distribution of wealth, and the treatment of workers are all expressions of communal flourishing, and as such, important topics for Jewish ethics.

Sections 11 and 12 address the most overarching structure that dominates social life, the modern state. Section 11 focuses in on the distinctive ethical questions raised by Jewish statehood and the history of the state of Israel. This section demonstrates how the particulars of history—of Jewish dispersion and oppression, and of the conflicts between Israelis and Palestinians—condition ethical discussions about Israel's claims to land, sovereignty, and power. Section 12 looks more broadly at the ways that all states wield power, violence, and control, bringing together discussions of war, torture, conscription, and capital punishment.

Section 13 zooms out to the most encompassing context for social life, the environment. Emerging from different disciplines and employing different methodologies, the scholars in this section all argue for ecological ethics out of the sources of Judaism.

The discussions in all these sections configure ethical action within a matrix of relationships, embedding Jewish ethics within social life. In the face of new technologies, rarefied economics, and corrosive politics, Jewish ethical discourse maintains its orientation to relationality, collective responsibility, and community.

7 | Families

More than an important topic of Jewish ethical thought, the family is also a central setting in which Jewish ethical teachings are enacted and inculcated. For much of Jewish history, it was the family or household—not the individual—that constituted the foundational unit of Jewish society. The family has been the setting in which much of ritual life is centered, including the observance of Sabbath and holidays, daily prayer, mourning rites, and traditions governing eating and sex. Family is also the site for living out Jewish values such as filial piety, marital fidelity, and caregiving. (One aspect of family life that is emphasized in both the Torah and rabbinic literature are practices of purification that regulate sexual relationships called the laws of "family purity"; we address this topic in part 3, section 15.)

In biblical sources, family inheritance is the vehicle for the perpetuation of the covenant between God and Israel and for the settlement of the land of Israel. In the rabbinic period, family becomes a central locus for religious life after the destruction of the Temple in Jerusalem, when family homes are reconceived as "small sanctuaries." In modern and contemporary Jewish life, values of egalitarianism and personal freedom are often invoked to justify changes in the configuration of family life.

The opening chapters of Genesis set forth two key principles that reverberate through later Jewish discussions of family ethics. First, in Genesis 1:28, God blesses the newly created humans with the charge, "Be fruitful and multiply and fill up the earth." This blessing resonates in the strong emphasis that Jewish cultures have placed upon childbearing and childrearing: procreation as both divine imperative and divine blessing. But while Genesis 1 characterizes the relationship between the first human male and the first human female primarily in terms of the imperative to procreate, Genesis 2 introduces the idea of companionship. In this account, God is prompted to create a partner for Adam because "it is not good for the human to be alone" (Gen. 2:18). This second biblical account has often provided a foundation for Jewish ethical understandings that value marriage and family as sites of human connection, love, and care. The outlooks encapsulated in these two biblical principles together have helped shape Jewish discourse on the family, with some Jewish works relating to family primarily as an institution for the propagation of children and the management of economic goods while others emphasize relationality, virtues, and values.

In recent decades, the overturning of gender hierarchies has been one important vector of change in Jewish families. Another has been an upsurge in marriages between Jews and non-Jews in diaspora communities. While there are many marriages between Israelites and non-Israelites depicted in the Bible, Jewish endogamy became a norm during the rabbinic era and was reinforced for hundreds of years by imperial regimes that prohibited Christians and Muslims from marrying Jews. Jewish emancipation brought an end to some external barriers to intermarriage, but most Jews persisted in seeking marriage partners from within the Jewish community. Today, intermarriage is a flash point in Jewish life, as nearly half of diaspora Jews marry non-Jews. While liberal Jewish institutions encourage the full participation of intermarried Jews, their non-Jewish partners and relatives, and the children of intermarried couples in Jewish life, many centrists and traditionalists continue to describe intermarriage as a national threat or tragedy.

The readings in this section offer examples of how contemporary ethical thinkers seek to expand or transform conceptions of the Jewish family in keeping with values of egalitarianism, human dignity and choice, and gender liberation. Talmudic scholar Gail Labovitz offers a critique of the rabbinic conception of marriage, arguing that rabbinic laws and rituals of Jewish marriage presume and perpetuate a conception of women as property to be acquired by men. Jennifer A. Thompson addresses what many in recent decades have called a "continuity crisis" in Jewish life, challenging the view that rising rates of intermarriage and declining affiliation with Jewish organizations should be characterized as signs of communal decline or cast in moral terms at all. Rebecca J. Epstein-Levi identifies other problems with the dominant discourse of Jewish continuity, arguing for a vision of continuity that emphasizes communal flourishing rather than biological reproduction.

GAIL LABOVITZ
Marriage and Metaphor: Constructions of Gender in Rabbinic Literature

Gail Labovitz (b. 1966), a Conservative rabbi, is a professor of rabbinic literature at the American Jewish University in Los Angeles, where she teaches rabbinical students at the Ziegler School of Rabbinic Studies. In her scholarship, she brings an interest in gender to the analysis of classical rabbinic literature, focusing primarily on the Babylonian Talmud.

From *Marriage and Metaphor: Constructions of Gender in Rabbinic Literature* (New York: Lexington Books, 2009), 250–54.

I disagree with the conclusions of many other scholars who have claimed that language and rites of acquisition in rabbinic marriage are not "really" an acquisition, or are an acquisition of something other than the woman (be it property she brings into the marriage, or exclusive sexual rights), or are merely "symbolic," or represent a model that rabbis inherited but from which they progressively moved away or disavowed. Judith Hauptman,[1] to take just one of many possible examples, argues that rabbinic developments such as the *ketubah*[2] and provisions for female consent to betrothal indicate that the rabbis were moving "From Purchase to 'Social Contract'": "Marriage became a relationship into which two people entered. Even though the man and woman were not on equal footing, they worked out the details between themselves."[3] Closer examination, however, demonstrates that the lack of "equal footing" between men and women brings us back to the ownership metaphor. Even if Hauptman's characterization of women as participants in marital negotiations is correct, we might ask just how many details of her marital relationship such a woman was really in a position to negotiate....

I have repeatedly demonstrated in this work the number of aspects of rabbinic marriage that remain structured by a model of ownership—from the legal formalities by which a woman enters a marriage (understood as a purchase), through her expected duties and role as a wife (often comparable to those of

1. [Rabbi Judith Hauptman is a feminist Talmudic scholar who taught at the Jewish Theological Seminary.]
2. [A *ketubah* is a Jewish marriage contract.]
3. Judith Hauptman, *Rereading the Rabbis: A Woman's Voice* (Boulder, CO: Westview Press, 1998), 67–68.

slaves, particularly female slaves), to the means by which she might leave the marriage (structurally parallel to the manumission of a slave). A similar question can be asked about provisions for female consent to a marriage. As Laura Levitt[4] has framed this problem (regarding liberal marriage in Western societies, but applicable to rabbinics as well), "To freely agree to be a slave is not an act of volition.... Once married, it is precisely a woman's consent that can be used to justify all subsequent infringements on her agency."[5] The reference in Levitt's work is to sexual agency and a question that long challenged male jurists: whether wives have the right to refuse consent to sexual contact, such that husbands may be held legally accountable for raping their wives. However, I find the issue, as posed by Levitt, applicable also to agency in other areas of married life, such as control over property and one's own labor. To consent or even negotiate to be acquired, with all the limitations on personal agency that such an acquisition imposes, is a paradoxical exercise of agency indeed.

In truth, though, it is not so much the specific details of previous works on rabbinic constructions of marriage and (thereby) gender that I have set out to challenge in this work, but rather the underlying, and often unacknowledged (even unconscious), question that typifies so many of these works—are women or are women not property in the rabbinic system? As I have stressed over and over, it is the precise tension between wives imagined as ownable—as something purchased, as houses and fields and slaves—and yet also as persons with rights to such things as conjugal satisfaction and ownership of property and financial remuneration in case of widowhood or divorce, that establishes this construction of marriage and gender relations based in metaphorical reasoning.... Repeatedly, creatively, and fully in keeping with the cognitive importance of metaphor, the rabbis construct a woman wife who is not, and yet is (like) property....

At my own wedding, in the summer of 1988, my husband placed a ring on my index finger and proclaimed (before two male, Jewishly observant friends chosen as witnesses), "You are *m'kuddeshet*[6] to me with this ring, according to the law of Moses and Israel." If Peskowitz and Joshel and Murnaghan[7] are cor-

---

4. [Laura Levitt serves as a professor of religion, Jewish studies, and gender studies at Temple University. See section 15 to read one of her selections.]

5. Laura Levitt, *Jews and Feminism: The Ambivalent Search for Home* (New York and London: Routledge, 1997), 66–67.

6. [Betrothed.]

7. [Miriam Peskowitz is a scholar of rabbinics, women, and gender; Sandra Joshel is a

rect in warning that when we study male-authored discourses we are always at risk of reproducing their "restricted perspectives," this is all the more true when we base our own religious practices on these discourses. Classical rabbinic discourse on marriage, and on many areas of Jewish life and practice, is by no means a thing of the past, confined to distant, historical works of literature. Practices observed to this day by significant segments of Jewish communities have traceable roots—back through such works as Jewish legal codes, responsa literature, and Talmudic commentaries—in the works authored by the rabbis of late antiquity. Rabbinic literature continues to occupy a position of authority and canonicity for many modern Jews and Jewish movements. Although I approach the rabbinic marital metaphor as a scholar, it is hardly a subject that is purely "academic" for me. In 1988 CE, in Philadelphia, Pennsylvania, I was—legally at least—"purchased" as surely as if I were living in a rabbinic community in Caesarea in 200 CE, or Maḥoza in 400 CE.

The purchase model of marriage still underlies the way Jewish divorce functions; that is, halakhic divorce remains a unilateral act in which the husband releases the wife. In the premodern and modern periods, this has contributed to the phenomenon of *agunot*, "chained" women whose husbands refuse to issue divorces or who use the threat of withholding a divorce to extract money, child custody, and/or favorable divorce terms from their wives. Such women, if they wish to abide by Jewish law, are unable to remarry. As recently as 1998, the Orthodox halakhic scholar J. David Bleich[8] (as just one example) demonstrated, in an argument *against* the validity of another proposed method for freeing women from such marriages, how easily a "former, harmful justification" of marriage laws—that is, the metaphor of woman as ownable—can be mobilized to women's material detriment:

> The legalistic essence of marriage is, in effect, an exclusive conjugal servitude conveyed by the bride to the groom. All other rights, responsibilities, duties, and perquisites are secondary, and flow therefrom.... Understanding that the essence of marriage lies in the conveyance of a "property" interest by the bride

---

professor of history at the University of Washington, focusing on women in antiquity; Sheila Murnaghan is a professor of Greek at the University of Pennsylvania, focusing on epics, historiography, and gender.]

8. [Rabbi J. David Bleich is a professor of Talmud at Yeshiva University.]

to the groom serves to explain why it is that only the husband can dissolve the marriage. As the beneficiary of the servitude, divestiture requires the husband's voluntary surrender of the right that he has acquired.[9]

The Lieberman clause[10] in my *ketubah* is meant to protect me from the fate of becoming an *agunah*. Yet this solution can readily be characterized as a cure for the symptoms rather than the disease; it does not seek to alter the legal underpinnings of marriage and divorce, that is, metaphors of property and ownership, which allow for the possibility of *agunot* in the first place....

I have to consider that any form of Jewish religious practice, ritual or literary or otherwise, that continues to utilize metaphors and constructions of women as ownable retains the power to do material harm to Jewish women's lives. That does not exclude practices that I have participated in in the past, or might be invited to participate in in the future. Of course, the work done here is an essential step; as Claudia V. Camp[11] observes, "Recognition of the function of folk theories provides a certain, if still uncertain, leverage for dislodging damaging ones.... Recognizing that this model *is* a model, and not some innate description of reality, provides the only possibility that exists for beginning to deconstruct it."[12] To make visible, however, is not itself to deconstruct (in the sense of undoing), and it is certainly not to begin the vital work of reconstructing and/ or building something new in place of the old: "The only real solution to such a powerful, world-constructing metaphor is another metaphor of equal power. ... The world will not change if only a void is offered in return."[13]

---

9. J. David Bleich, "*Kiddushei Ta'ut*: Annulment as a Solution to the *Agunah* Problem," *Tradition* 33, no. 1 (1998): 114.

10. [The Lieberman clause, named after Jewish Theological School professor Saul Lieberman, stipulates that a couple commits to securing a divorce from a *bet din* (rabbinic court), so as to ensure that the woman can remarry.]

11. [Claudia V. Camp is a professor of religion at Texas Christian University.]

12. Claudia V. Camp, "Metaphor in Feminist Biblical Interpretation: Theoretical Perspectives," *Semia* 61 (1993): 27–28.

13. Camp, "Metaphor in Feminist Biblical Interpretation," 28.

JENNIFER A. THOMPSON

Reaching Out to the Fringe:
Insiders, Outsiders, and the Morality of Social Science

Jennifer A. Thompson (b. 1976) is the Maurice Amado Professor of Applied Jewish Ethics and Civic Engagement at California State University at Northridge. Her research bridges the social sciences and Jewish ethics.

From "Reaching Out to the Fringe: Insiders, Outsiders, and the Morality of Social Science," *Journal of Jewish Identities* 8, no. 1 (2015): 179–200.

[The article excerpted here is based on her study of how the popular Jewish media—newspapers and websites created by Jewish organizations for Jewish audiences—reported on demographic studies of American Jewish life between the years 1973 and 2014. Thompson argues that while social science research can serve discussions of Jewish ethics by establishing certain facts, the task of interpreting these facts demands other kinds of investigation.]

Jewish media use of social science to support insider/outsider distinctions starts from the fear that the Jewish population is in decline, and assumes that this fear has an obvious moral meaning. The question of whether the Jewish population is in numerical decline can be resolved, to some extent, through social scientific study. The moral meaning of this question, however, is not properly an object of quantitative empirical inquiry. Social science can explore the attitudes of American Jews concerning the moral meaning of its perceived decline. However, this is a question embedded in a religious context concerning the Jewish people's relationship with God and its mission in the world. . . .

The problem with disguising religious questions as scientific ones is that it makes religious questions appear to be less complex and deep than they are. Suggesting that Jews should be convinced to join synagogues or marry other Jews on the basis of the utility of these actions for Jewish continuity, as demonstrated by correlations found in analysis of surveys, does violence to Judaism itself. It strips away the context in which these actions have taken place traditionally—a context that assumes a shared idea of the good life. Shared ideas about the good life and the common good are precisely the content of the moral questions underlying social scientific study of American Jewry and its ostensible decline. These ideas are precisely what must be better articulated and understood. An investigation into how, if at all, American Jews share an idea of what it means to be Jewish together might find that the moral meanings at stake for American Jews are different than the categories typically investigated in social scientific study of this population. In other words, what moral meanings might attach to intermarriage and affiliation with Jewish institutions besides the choice to be an outsider or the inability to engage with Judaism due to ignorance? Qualitative social scientists such as Keren McGinity, Samira Mehta, Bethamie Horowitz, and I have pursued some of these questions[14] but of this group of social scientists, only Horowitz was cited in my sample, and only once. Social-scientific approaches that might disrupt insider/outsider distinctions are not getting much attention in Jewish media discourse. But even if there were substantial media discussion of such social-scientific approaches, such discussion would not be a substitute for sustained moral analysis that openly recognizes its religious sources.

Such sustained moral analysis, in turn, could lead to new avenues for Jewish communal leaders to explore, beyond currently emphasized insider behaviors. Sociologist Debra Kaufman has pointed out that constructions of "authentic" and "inauthentic" Judaism privilege certain people's experiences over others —particularly the experiences of insiders such as Orthodox men over those of outsiders such as women and liberal Jews.[15] In the articles discussed above, the experiences of insiders are presumed to be the ones that are valid, authoritative, normative, and right. Outsiders, in contrast, are assumed to require education through outreach and then assimilation and adaptation to the norms of insiders through joining Jewish institutions and participating in their activities. The unaffiliated are depicted as being in need of reform or rehabilitation so that they may participate in "real," "authentic" Judaism in its institutional form.

The language of affiliation and outreach is shorthand for the questions: Who is an insider, and who is an outsider? Who belongs? Whose Judaism is authentic or legitimate? The language of outreach and affiliation constructs categories of Jews: those who need help, and those who offer help. Certainly there are many

---

14. Keren McGinity, *Still Jewish, and Marrying Out: Jewish Men, Intermarriage, and Fatherhood* (Bloomington: Indiana University Press, 2014); Samira K. Mehta, *Beyond Chrismukkah: The Christian-Jewish Interfaith Family in the United States* (Chapel Hill: University of North Carolina Press, 2018); Bethamie Horowitz, *Connections and Journeys: Assessing Critical Opportunities for Enhancing Jewish Identity* (New York: UJA-Federation of Jewish Philanthropies, 2000; Thompson, *Jewish on Their Own Terms* (New Brunswick: Rutgers University Press, 2013) and "'He Wouldn't Know Anything': Rethinking Women's Religious Leadership," *Journal of the American Academy of Religion* 81, no. 3 (2013), 644–668.

15. Debra Kaufman, "Measuring Jewishness in America: Some Feminist Concerns," *Nashim: A Journal of Jewish Women's Studies and Gender Issues* 10 (2006): 84–98.

Jews who are glad to accept such help, who are eager to learn more about Judaism in the contexts in which such help is offered. Implicit in such offers, however, is the idea that those to whom outreach is directed practice or possess a Jewishness that is inauthentic or faulty....

Content analysis of articles containing "National Jewish Population Study" or "NJPS" shows that Jewish media have been preoccupied with distinctions among Jews along insider/outsider lines, and that survey data are used as authority for these distinctions, even though there are lots of other things that the survey reports themselves treated as equally important. Through selective interpretation by community leaders and journalists, population surveys have been endowed with a moral authority that the social scientists who created them may not have anticipated or intended. This endowment of moral authority on population studies undercuts the moral authority of more traditional sources, such as Jewish textual sources and communities themselves.

Using social science as the measure of good Jewishness creates an impoverished moral discourse. However, attending to moral discourse will require addressing head-on disagreements about the nature of Jewish religious authority in the lives of contemporary American Jews. It might require debate across denominational lines about which traditional texts matter most, and how to interpret them. It might require recognition that agreement about these topics might never be reached. That recognition may be unsettling. In contrast, using social science to organize our moral discourse allows American Jews to pretend they are talking about something quantifiable and ostensibly provable. Using social science to perpetuate Jewish continuity may perpetuate a certain number of Jews, but it cannot create Jewishness itself.

REBECCA J. EPSTEIN-LEVI

Person-Shaped Holes:
Childfree Jews, Jewish Ethics,
and Communal Continuity

Rebecca J. Epstein-Levi (b. 1987) teaches Jewish studies and gender and sexuality studies at Vanderbilt University. As a scholar of Jewish ethics, she seeks to engage traditional rabbinic texts with questions and approaches drawn from feminist and queer theory. Her first book, When We Collide: Sex, Social Risk, and Jewish Ethics (2023), *argues that the Talmud's discussions of sex can be generative touchstones for thinking expansively about virtue ethics and a wide range of social relationships.*

From "Person-Shaped Holes: Childfree Jews, Jewish Ethics, and Communal Continuity," *Journal of Religious Ethics* 49, no. 2 (2021): 226–44.

Over the past several decades, significant areas of Jewish thought and practice have grown to accommodate a wider range of gender roles and expressions, sexualities, and family structures, and the language of professional Jewish ethics increasingly reflects this. However, Jewish culture, and professional Jewish ethics when it addresses the topic, remain overwhelmingly pronatalist. Jewish discourse overwhelmingly frames reproduction as a core Jewish value, and thereby frames the choice not to bear or raise children as contrary to Jewish values. To remain childfree, according to this framework, is to selfishly prioritize one's individual desires over and against the welfare of one's community....

On a basic level, that most Jewish discourse is basically and strongly pronatalist is unsurprising. Even at a halakhic level, procreation is commanded, at least for men, who are obligated in the mitzvah (commandment) of *pru urvu*, to be fruitful and multiply. Furthermore, a minoritized and frequently persecuted group that has spent most of its history in diaspora and underwent a massive, industrial extermination attempt in which six million of its number were slaughtered might reasonably be expected to have a strong interest in its own physical reproduction. And, indeed, recent voices on the matter are likely to appeal precisely to the Holocaust and, more generally, to what Salo Baron[16] famously referred to as the "lachrymose conception"—as it were—"of Jewish

---

16. [Salo Baron (1895–1989), who taught at Columbia University, was considered by many to be the greatest Jewish historian of the twentieth century.]

history" when they stress the urgent need for Jews to bear more Jewish children, using the term "Jewish continuity." . . .

Thus choosing to have Jewish children becomes the fulfillment of a communal duty, while choosing not to have children is figured as selfish and individualistic. Yet the overwhelming focus of this kind of pronatalism is directed toward encouraging young Jews to marry other Jews and procreate within Jewish nuclear family units—a fundamentally modern, individualist structure. Even if this comes accompanied by calls for respectable social support policies—egalitarian parental leave, strong social safety nets, community funds for Jewish education, and so on—the call for this reproduction to occur within a nuclear family model remains basically unchanged. Nor, of course, do these calls address the fact that some people, Jews included, simply do not wish to bear or raise children—and that such Jews are, in fact, also members of the Jewish community toward whom the community bears some reciprocal responsibilities.

These simplistic dichotomies of "selfishness/duty" and "individual/community" thus obscure the fact that modern Jewish pronatalism is much less robustly invested in community as it could be. Situating reproductive continuity as primary and prior to other forms of continuity places fertile heterosexual couples at the center of its overall account of continuity in a way that is atomizing, isolating individual couples from their communal networks and minimizing or erasing the contributions nonreproductive agents contribute to the flourishing *and* overall continuity of the community as a whole. In this way, I argue, shifting the moral focus somewhat from fertile heterosexual couples in a way that robustly and unregretfully includes childless and childfree-by-choice adults within its sphere actually allows the possibility for a more robust and nourishing account of Jewish community, continuity, and care than a simple nuclear-family-centered pronatalism ever could. . . .

[T]hree stories from B. T. *Ketubot* 62b demonstrate what I call "person-shaped holes" in the narrative—states of being, institutions, structures, and situations that demonstrate or facilitate children's development and flourishing and which, by their very presence, imply the unrecognized labor of people other than those children's parents. The stories occur one right after the other, as part of a longer series of anecdotes about sages who leave their spouses and children in order to spend several years immersed in Torah study. All appear, at the outset, to be stories of indifferent husbandhood and fatherhood that focus on the tension between duties to spouses and children, and the duty of and desire for intensive, all-consuming Torah study. On closer examination, however, the reader can unearth person-shaped holes in each text, which, in turn, allows them to imagine possibilities for a variety of roles for communal care and generational continuity—roles which may be neglected or obscured here, but which are vital nevertheless....

Primary among the points these texts illuminate is the recognition that nurturing the next generation and creating the conditions in which that next generation can flourish requires not merely the efforts of biological or even social parents but the work of numerous others. This is true whether these others work in direct relationship with children or whether they work to create a world in which dedicated work with children can take place more easily....

Continuity is not merely about producing children, or even about providing primary care for those children. Continuity is about creating a community that supports the flourishing of all generations in ways both direct and indirect. It is not limited to individual family units or types of contribution; rather, it is a collective obligation that different members of the collective carry out in different ways....

What does this mean for Jewish communities? First, it means that we must strenuously resist attempts to reduce the project of "Jewish continuity" to simple pronatalism. "Remember that we suffered" is *not*, in fact, an adequate ethical warrant for making people's wombs communal property, and genuine continuity ought not be synonymous with reproductive coercion. Second, it means that we must rethink rhetoric that erects a binary opposition between individualistic and community-oriented actions and choices, and instead recognize that communities are composed of particular individuals who depend upon the community and all of whose flourishing the community has an obligation to support. Continuity, then, means continuously participating in the creation and maintenance of a community that fosters the flourishing of all members and all generations, in both direct and indirect ways. Theologically, it means thinking about the range of ways God may sustain and support God's people. It means being able to imagine that the mitzvah of *pru urvu* [be fruitful and multiply] might include those who might model that face of God who, as my friend put it, "is, perhaps, happily childfree but always willing to meet her parent friends for coffee while someone else looks after the kids."[17]

In practical terms, this means that all Jews may indeed have an ethical obliga-

---

17. Wendy Love Anderson, personal correspondence, July 28, 2020.

tion to contribute in some way to some sense of "Jewish continuity," broadly defined. No given Jew, however, is obligated to carry out that duty in any specific fashion. No Jew is specifically obligated to undergo a pregnancy or to impregnate someone else, or to commit to the project of parenting. Every Jew, however, is obligated to work toward a Jewish community in which all members of all generations can thrive and in which no one's work is uncompensated or made invisible. Genuine continuity, and truly sustainable, humane community dragoon no person's gonads. They do, however, require us to recognize, acknowledge, and compensate the myriad forms of labor that all of us contribute to our collective futurity. They depend on ensuring that no person becomes a person-shaped hole.

8 | Speech

Jewish ethical teachings emphasize the power of speech. According to Proverbs 18:21, "Death and life are in the power of the tongue." Discussions of Jewish speech ethics oscillate between circumspection about the dangers of harmful speech and the promotion of truth-telling and other positive speech acts. While classical Jewish sources acknowledge the potential of words that are true and well-chosen to do good, they emphasize the danger of speaking out of turn much more. Scriptural prohibitions against false testimony, cursing, and gossip are the foundation for a vigilance about speech that is expressed in Jewish liturgy: the prayerbook includes a personal petition to "guard my tongue from evil," to be recited at the end of prayer three times a day, and the public confession for the season of repentance includes no fewer than eleven speech-related transgressions in its litany of sins. The interdiction against *lashon hara*, or evil speech, prohibits not only slander but also saying true things about another person because such gossip might cause shame and other harm. Traditional Jewish teachings about speech ethics were consolidated by Rabbi Yisrael Meir Kagan (1838–1933) in an influential work called the *Sefer Chofetz Chaim*, "Book of One Who Desires Life," a reference to Psalms 34:13–14: "Who is the man who desires life . . . Guard your tongue from evil and your lips from speaking guile." The work highlights the grave seriousness of shaming another in public.

In the contemporary context, the advent of the internet has all but eroded the distinction between private and public speech that classical Jewish writings presume. The penetration of social media into social, economic, and political life magnifies and proliferates the impact of speech. Today, gossip and lies can spread instantly across the globe so that *lashon hara* not only destroys lives but also changes the outcomes of elections. At the same time, the reach of social media enhances the transformative potential of speech to effect positive change. The #MeToo movement is one recent social movement that has centered on public speech as a vehicle for liberation. This movement in particular has prompted a reconsideration of traditional Jewish speech ethics by illuminating the gendered aspects of communication, highlighting how the traditional emphasis on refraining from speech serves to isolate and further marginalize those who are already vulnerable and disempowered and often victimized by vested interests.

In different ways, the three selections in this section all reflect the heightened power of speech for good and for ill in contemporary life. For Mark Washofsky, the rise of social media necessitates renewed attention to the importance of speech ethics. He grounds a right to privacy in the Jewish principle of *kvod habriyot*, or human dignity, and on this basis, argues for limiting and regulating the access governments, corporations, and others are granted to personal information. (For further discussion of how values and principles are deployed in Jewish ethical reasoning, see part 1, section 6.) He goes on to argue that such a defensive posture vis-à-vis the internet is not enough, however; the rise of information technologies requires individuals to embrace a new commitment to reticence, taking responsibility for safeguarding their own privacy.

While Washofsky affirms and extends a traditionalist vigilance with regard to speech, Matthew Goldstone's work uncovers an ancient counterbalance to such circumspection in his explication of the biblical commandment to offer rebuke in Leviticus 19:17. While Goldstone's historical study does not explicitly address contemporary challenges, his emphasis on rebuke enlivens a long neglected aspect of Jewish speech ethics, the power of the tongue to promote virtue. In a sense, Goldstone's explication of how the Torah and its early interpreters understood the potential benefits of speaking out about wrongdoing provides a usable history for contemporary ethicists who valorize speech as a foundation for social reform.

Lena Sclove complicates the celebration of speech and the vilification of silence that the #MeToo movement advanced. She takes issue with the presumption that speaking about sexual violence is always a path toward healing for survivors of abuse, identifying the ways that pressure to speak can be as damaging as pressure to keep silent. She describes a speech ethics where the prerogative to speak or to keep silent is a central aspect of human autonomy and flourishing.

MARK WASHOFSKY

Internet, Privacy, and Progressive Halakha

Mark Washofsky (b. 1952) is a leading ethicist in the Reform movement of Judaism. A Reform rabbi and professor emeritus at the Hebrew Union College-Jewish Institute of Religion who chaired the Responsa Committee of the Central Conference of American Rabbis for over twenty years, he is the foremost theorist of progressive halakha. His scholarly oeuvre of books and articles illustrate and explicate how the Jewish legal tradition remains vital and relevant for Reform Judaism. The selection excerpted below is like much of his work in that it joins an explication of legal theory and a practical engagement with ethical problems in contemporary life.

From "Internet, Privacy, and Progressive Halakha," in *The Internet Revolution and Jewish Law*, ed. Walter Jacob (Pittsburgh: Rodef Shalom Press, 2014), 81–142.

I would argue . . . that this accepted rhetoric of privacy, which emphasizes the defense of the individual against unwanted surveillance of his or her personal affairs, whether the intruders be governments, businesses, or hackers, is by itself an inadequate response to the contemporary challenge. The internet age has introduced a new range of threats to our privacy. Our concern is no longer exclusively with old-fashioned sorts of intrusion—the peeping Tom, the prying journalist, the wiretapper, and the electronic eavesdropper whose trespasses originate from without—but increasingly with the newer forms of intrusion that emerges from within, that we ourselves facilitate and allow into our personal space. The internet enables us to upload as well as to download, to produce as well as to consume digital content. Its technologies, particularly the new social media, permit and entice us to transmit a great deal of personal data to an electronic realm over which we exert very little control, a social network where our lives of necessity become an open e-book. This is the difference that the internet makes, the unique threat that the World Wide Web poses to our privacy: its invitation to live our lives increasingly online and in public, to the point that we might be said to have waived any "reasonable expectation" of privacy[18]

---

18. The phrase, which has become a well-known formula in American privacy law, seems to have originated with Justice John Marshall Harlan's concurring opinion in *Katz v. United States*, 389 U.S. 347.

and, indeed, to have rendered that concept essentially meaningless. If in fact we enjoy "zero privacy" in the age of the internet, the blame lies not solely or even primarily with unwanted, external intruders but with ourselves.

Any cogent and coherent halakhic discussion of privacy in the age of the internet will accordingly have to advance beyond the conceptual boundaries that have heretofore defined the subject. The current halakhic discourse on privacy, much like that in Western law, speaks mostly to the protection of the individual from damage caused by others invading his personal realm. The new discussion of which I speak will have to focus upon protecting the individual from the damage that he brings upon himself. It will have to acknowledge that we will not make much headway in protecting our internet privacy from the unwanted attention of others without first addressing our own conduct. And here is where it really does help to be Jewish, for the same fundamental principles that lie at the base of the traditional halakhic discourse on privacy also provide us with the intellectual resources needed to frame an adequate response for the challenge of our time. I refer, in particular, to the concept of modesty (*tzniyut*) and of human dignity (*kvod habriyot*). It is to these principles we must appeal in the name of safeguarding our personal privacy in the current technological environment.

Let's begin with *tzniyut*, which . . . is cited as the basis for several of those existing "privacy" provisions of Jewish law. The concept, to be sure, can be a problematic one for liberal Jews. Today, we tend to associate the word *tzniyut* with the set of rules, social mores, and customary practices that comprise the particularly Orthodox definition of "modesty" in the relationship between the sexes. That definition diverges sharply from progressive values, based as it is upon assumptions of specific gender roles that we do not share.[19] Yet *tzniyut* extends far beyond the realm of sexual conduct. The term speaks as much of "restraint" as of modesty, expressing the value of moderation and humility in all spheres of personal behavior. Its linguistic root appears in the famous injunction of the prophet Micah (6:8) to "walk humbly (*hatzne'a lekhet*) with your God." The humility of which that verse speaks, according to its Talmudic interpretation (B. T. *Sukkah* 49b), concerns neither gender norms nor sexual modesty but the conduct expected of us when we bury the dead, escort the bride to the *chuppah*, and (by extension) when we give *tzedakah* to the poor. The commentators understand this as an exhortation to personal restraint: one should perform these

---

19. For a classic description of the expectations that *tzniyut* places upon females as opposed to males see Yad, *Ishut* 24:12ff.

and, indeed, all other mitzvot humbly and with moderation, so that one does not draw unnecessary attention to oneself....

This theme of restraint—the word "stringency" might also fit—applies precisely to our subject. *Tzniyut* is the Jewish value that teaches us to practice restraint in self-expression, to behave mindfully and moderately when online, to think carefully before we share our lives with the denizens of the virtual universe, to consider the potential outcome of our actions before we post, upload, blog, text, or tweet. There is nothing essentially illiberal or nonprogressive in this message; in fact, there is much we can and ought to learn from it. Accordingly, it is essential that we liberal Jews recover this value and make it our own, that we develop a specifically liberal Jewish discourse and teaching concerning *hilkhot tzniyut*, the rules of self-restraint in social and personal behavior. Some encouraging efforts have already been made in this direction, with more, hopefully, to follow. The argument here is that we have little choice but to do so. To protect what is left of our personal privacy in the age of the internet, we must practice the traits of *tzniyut*. We must learn to restrain our tendency to live our lives increasingly in the virtual world, to share the facts and photos and data of our lives with the universe that lies on the other side of our computer and smartphone screens.

Yet *tzniyut* by itself is insufficient; the principle of *kvod habriyot* is, for two reasons, its necessary complement. First, as I have argued, "human dignity" is the fundamental principle that undergirds the entire discussion of privacy in the halakha. Without a substantive sense of what our "dignity" requires of us, it is unlikely that we will value our privacy enough to take concrete steps to protect it. Second, to speak of the need for "self-restraint" may raise concerns among some in our community....

Since the eighteenth century, liberal political thought has stressed the importance of such values as individual liberty and freedom of expression, and to the extent that we liberal Jews share in this outlook, we are rightly disturbed by the admonitions of those in political, social, or religious authority to "watch what we say," even in the name of securing some important end. An objection of this sort would parallel the objection... that some legal scholars have lodged against the "right to privacy" in the common law and in American constitutional discourse, namely that the enforcement of privacy rights is at some level inimical to the exercise of free expression in a democratic society....

There can be, in other words, a very real tension between liberty and security. And this is why *kvod habriyot* is so vital to this discussion. To affirm a substantive conception of human dignity is to overcome the liberty-vs.-security dichotomy, to deny that we must choose between them, to assert that the values of personal freedom and self-restraint do not contradict each other. To declare a commitment to *kvod habriyot* is to acknowledge the overriding importance of restraint in the way we conduct our personal and interpersonal affairs. It is to remind ourselves that freedom is not an end in itself. As Edward Bloustein[20] put it in his discussion of American privacy law, "What provoked Warren and Brandeis to write their article[21] was a fear that a rampant press feeding on the stuff of private life would destroy individual dignity and integrity and emasculate individual freedom and independence."[22] ....

The survival of freedom, that is to say, is conditional upon our willingness to honor the essential dignity of each member of our community. Self-restraint, the reasonable limits that we can and do accept upon our personal expression, is the price we pay to secure this end. These restraints are set by our basic sense of self-respect, that modicum of dignity that we demand for ourselves and therefore are prepared to guarantee to others, that we cannot yield or forego and still hope to fulfill our human potential. Dignity is as essential to us as freedom; indeed, we actualize our freedom precisely when we use it within the boundaries dictated by *kvod habriyot*. And the respect that we accord to those boundaries is what we mean by the "value of privacy."

---

20. [Edward Bloustein was a professor of law in the 1960s before becoming president of Rutgers University 1971–1989.]

21. [Samuel D. Warren II was a Boston lawyer in the latter part of the nineteenth century, whose Harvard University classmate, Louis D. Brandeis, finished first in their class (Warren was second) and went on to serve as an associate justice on the Supreme Court of the United States 1916–1939. They went on to co-author Samuel D. Warren and Louis D. Brandeis, "The Right to Privacy," *Harvard Law Review* 4 (1890): 193–220.]

22. Edward Bloustain, "Privacy as an Aspect of Human Dignity: An Answer to Dean Prosser," *New York University Law Review* 39 (1964): 971.

MATTHEW GOLDSTONE

The Dangerous Duty of Rebuke:
Leviticus 19:17 in Early Jewish and
Christian Interpretation

Matthew Goldstone (b. 1985) is a Conservative rabbi and scholar of ancient Jewish and Christian literature who serves on the faculty and administration of the Academy for Jewish Religion in New York, a pluralistic seminary. This excerpt is from the introduction to his first book, The Dangerous Duty of Rebuke: Leviticus 19:17 in Early Jewish and Christian Interpretation *(2018). The piece illustrates how biblical interpretation grounds discussions of Jewish ethics historically and in contemporary scholarship.*

From *The Dangerous Duty of Rebuke: Leviticus 19:17 in Early Jewish and Christian Interpretation* (Leiden: Brill, 2018): 1–25.

Introduction

What is the extent of our responsibility to respond to the shortcomings of others? If a friend, family member, or colleague commits an offense do I have an obligation to confront them? How do I offer constructive criticism without damaging my relationship with another person? These questions seem to reverberate strongly within the contemporary Western world, in which the notion of individual rights and autonomy is so pronounced. To challenge another's actions impinges upon their freedom. Yet, to say nothing encourages them to continue their transgressive behavior unimpeded and ultimately degrades the moral fiber of society at large. Although based in a significantly different social setting, texts from late antiquity also respond to the complexity and urgency of these questions. This book engages with these key questions by exploring fundamental discussions about the nature of interpersonal responsibility contained in early Jewish and Christian texts.

The Bible commands that: "You shall not hate your kinsfolk in your heart. Reprove your kinsman, but incur no guilt because of him" (Lev. 19:17). This verse describes a duty to challenge others who transgress rather than harboring animosity or simply overlooking their infraction. But this Levitical injunction provides little guidance on the practical performance of rebuke. Daily life presents us with many situations in which we might consider speaking out against someone for doing something wrong. But how does one actually go about chastising another person? It is no simple task to tell someone that they have erred. Is it even worthwhile to speak up or should such confrontation be avoided? Early Jewish and Christian sources that interpret the Levitical command to rebuke grapple with these acute questions and in this way conceptualize the nature of a person's responsibility for the failings of others....

Narrowing in on the rebuke clause itself ("Reprove your kinsman"; Lev. 19:17b), we find that this act permits multiple connotations. The commandment to reprove utilizes the Hebrew root י.כ.ח, which carries a number of different meanings: decide, prove, argue, reprove, convict, appoint, declare, etc. Several scholars have argued over the "primary" connotation of this verb as it appears in the conjugation used by our verse. Some see private "reprimand" as the verb's primary sense. Others believe a judicial meaning of "determining what is right" is primary....

The ambiguity over the primary connotation of the words for rebuke in Leviticus 19:17b is not simply a quality of this Hebrew root alone. As Kugel[23] argues, different exegetical possibilities are latent in the verse itself depending on whether one reads it in isolation or in the broader context of the preceding verses.[24] Looking at Leviticus 19:17 on its own (or together Lev. 19:18), one gets the impression of a private, moral activity. The charge not to hate one's "fellow" (אָחִיךָ) implies that one has a somewhat personal relationship with the other party.[25] In addition, the commandment to love one's fellow speaks to one's interpersonal relationship. Moreover, the aforementioned terms and linguistic elements that focus the reader's attention back to the self (כָּמוֹךָ [like you], בִּלְבָבֶךָ [in your heart] and the second person suffixes) also give the impression of an interpersonal interaction.

In contrast to this personal sense of rebuke, the broader context of Leviticus 19:11–18 might suggest a more legal framing. Leviticus 19:15 reads, "You shall not render an unfair decision: do not favor the poor or show deference to the rich; judge your kinsman fairly." According to J. R. Porter,[26] this verse "begins a series of instructions designed to safeguard the proper administration of the law."[27]

---

23. [James Kugel is a professor emeritus of classical and modern Hebrew literature at Harvard University.]

24. James Kugel, *In Potiphar's House* (Cambridge, MA: Harvard University Press, 1994), 229–31.

25. As Schwartz points out, this term indicates a close relationship between the subject and the other party; Baruch Schwartz, *The Holiness Legislation: Studies in the Priestly Code* (Jerusalem: Magnes/The Hebrew University Press, 1999), 322.

26. [J. R. Porter is a professor emeritus of theology at the University of Exeter.]

27. J. R. Porter, *Leviticus: Cambridge Bible Commentaries on the Old Testament* (New York: Cambridge University Press, 1976), 154.

Consequently, he interprets the prohibition against hatred in Leviticus 19:17 as forbidding "hatred against a man accused of a crime" as this would "make an impartial verdict difficult."[28] The connection between Leviticus 19:15 and 19:17 is underscored by the parallel language employed to refer to the other party. This section as a whole (Lev. 19:11–18) continually switches between a few different appellations: "your fellow" (רֵעֶךָ), "your kinsman" (עֲמִיתֶךָ), "your countrymen" (בְּנֵי עַמֶּךָ), and "your brother" (אָחִיךָ). However, the same term, "your kinsman" (עֲמִיתֶךָ) appears in both Leviticus 19:15's discussion of proper judging and Leviticus 19:17's command to rebuke. This parallel terminology strengthens the link between these two verses in particular, heightening the judicial sense of the root י.כ.ח. in our rebuke clause.[29]

The personal (or moral) and judicial dimensions of rebuke mark an important point of ambiguity in the understanding of our verse. However, when it comes to practical application, this ambiguity is transformed into a tension over the proper audience and setting for administering rebuke. If rebuke is intended as a personal action, then it should ideally be performed in private so as not to embarrass the other party or encourage them to defend themselves against the accusation before their peers. By contrast, if rebuke is meant to be understood judicially, then this implies a more public and exposed context in which a person's transgressions are aired openly. The driving coercive force behind rebuke similarly hinges upon one's understanding of this dimension. Personal rebuke implies a morally driven change of heart motivated by an offender's recognition of having harmed the rebuker. Judicial rebuke, on the other hand, conveys more institutional force that compels the transgressor to comply or else face possible communal sanctions.

The tension between a private and a public setting may also be amplified by the doubling of the root י.כ.ח. In Leviticus 19:17, the biblical root appears in the form of an infinitive absolute plus imperfect (הוֹכֵחַ תּוֹכִיחַ). (Jacob Milgrom[30] suggests that "the infinitive absolute *hôkeaḥ* before the verb *tôkîaḥ* is used to lay emphasis on an antithesis."[31] This antithesis is the tension between the internal hatred described in Leviticus 19:17a and open rebuking recommended by Leviticus 19:17b where in הוֹכֵחַ תּוֹכִיחַ implies "open reproof." In Milgrom's understanding, the infinitive absolute helps to overcome one's "psychological barrier"

---

28. Porter, *Leviticus*, 155.

29. Schwartz, *The Holiness Legislation*, 321–22.

30. [Rabbi Jacob Milgrom (1923–2010) was a professor of Hebrew Bible at the University of California, Berkeley.]

31. Jacob Milgrom, *Leviticus 17–22* (New Haven, CT: Yale University Press, 2000), 1648.

against expressing their grievances to their fellow.[32] The biblical author is quite aware that people may be hesitant to confront others and thus stresses the need for such exposed dialogue. This "antithesis" between the internal and the external, the hidden and the exposed, magnifies the tension between private and public settings for rebuke.

LENA SCLOVE

Beyond the Binary of Silence and Speech: What Jewish Liturgy and Spirals Reveal about the Limits and Potentials of Spiritual Caregiving for Survivors of Sexual Violence

Lena Sclove (b. 1991) is an activist and spiritual leader with a background in chaplaincy. At the time of this publication, she is studying for the rabbinate with Aleph, the Jewish Renewal movement.

From "Beyond the Binary of Silence and Speech: What Jewish Liturgy and Spirals Reveal about the Limits and Potentials of Spiritual Caregiving for Survivors of Sexual Violence," in *Applying Jewish Ethics: Beyond the Rabbinic Tradition*, eds. Jennifer A. Thompson and Allison B. Wolf (Lanham, MD: Lexington Books, 2023), 67–84.

Sexual violence can be a cataclysmic rupture in a life—a moment of pivot, where there is "before" and "after" and a life is cut down the middle. Sexual violence is *any experience that is sexual in nature that one lives through outside their realm of choice or agency.* That includes rape, sexual assault, and power-based personal violence, but it also includes experiences that survivors may not have the words to describe. Each person processes and experiences trauma differently and does so within particular social contexts. Some may not respond to sexual violence as if a major life interruption has occurred. Nevertheless, many people in a survivor's life will seek to help them on a "journey of healing" after this rupture, with an eventual end point of cure and finalized healing. They may falsely assume that recovery from traumatic violence follows a linear path, starting from the worst event in a person's life, then proceeding to support from a terrific therapist, psychiatrist, chaplain, rabbi, or doctor, to arrive at a new life of being "back to who you were before." But many survivors do not experience this.

32. Milgrom, *Leviticus 17–22*, 1648.

Unfortunately, social and cultural notions of the process of healing often can deepen the harms survivors experience. These notions celebrate certain kinds of survivor narratives, paths and presentations of "healing," while devaluing or rejecting others. White, cis, able-bodied women, especially famous ones in film or at elite colleges, are often pushed to share, while people of color, queer, trans, and disabled folks are more likely silenced, minimized, and advised to stay quiet....

Silencing is not the only approach commonly taken. It is also common for friends, family, therapists, and medical providers to encourage the survivor, particularly cis-white-able-bodied-wealthy-woman survivors, to publicly tell their story—both as part of a process of healing on a personal level and to help other survivors or society as a whole heal from rape culture—on the grounds that to expose oneself *willingly* will be corrective and empowering and that in *not* saying something, one presumably allows more harm to be done by the perpetrator. Silencing is harmful, but so too is this push to "break the silence."

This impulse toward healing through telling goes far back in history. Michel Foucault[33] traces the history of "confession" as a central component of the history of sexuality. He writes of the growing conviction, from Christianity and into the scientific medical model, that to tell the deepest secrets, particularly of sexuality, is the way to freedom, healing, and ultimately the path to understanding the "truth" of the "self."[34] Writing in 1993, Linda Martin Alcoff and Laura Gray-Rosendale[35] saw that "the principal tactic adopted by the survivors' movement has been to encourage and make possible survivors' disclosures of our traumas. This strategic metaphor of 'breaking the silence' is virtually ubiquitous throughout the movement."[36] While all of these ideas may be undertaken out of concern for the survivor, the reality is that this understanding and approach is deeply troublesome.

For one, it wrongly assumes that the event itself is assumed to be the worst of it, and that a journey of healing will follow from that point of earth-shattering.

33. [Michel Foucault (1926–1984) was a French philosopher and historian of ideas; he taught at many universities throughout Europe and the United States.]

34. Michel Foucault, *The History of Sexuality*, vol. 1 (New York: Vintage Digital, 2012), 60.

35. [Linda Martin Alcoff is a professor of philosophy at Hunter College, City University of New York; Laura Gray-Rosendale is a professor of English at Northern Arizona University.]

36. Linda Alcoff and Laura Gray, "Survivor Discourse: Transgression or Recuperation?" *Signs: Journal of Women in Culture and Society* 18, no. 2 (1993): 261, doi.org/10.1086/494793.

But this is often not the case. Beyond that, the theory of healing through telling falsely assumes that the journey will be linear, contained, and will have an end point of cure and finalized healing, skipping over the realities of how trauma recovery is more like a spiral than a straight line....

The pressure to tell one's story is also concerning. Telling one's story often not only does not result in healing, complete or otherwise, but also can actually deepen the harms a survivor experiences or even cause new ones.... Alcoff and Gray report, "Many survivors are put in risk of physical retaliation by disclosure and may also face difficulties on their jobs, negative repercussions for their supportive relationships or the welfare of their children, and debilitating emotional trauma."[37] Any amount of harassment only reinforces the survivor's deep feelings of being in danger. And the result can be a new rupture in the survivor's life: that of being famous for one of the very worst of their moments.

Some survivors may feel empowered and emboldened by voluntarily sharing their stories publicly and holding perpetrators accountable. However, perpetrator accountability must not come at the expense of survivors. While well-meaning allies may suggest that a survivor's storytelling can be healing and empowering, this suggestion places responsibility on survivors themselves to change the very systems and power dynamics that harmed them. Perpetrators, and the systems that train, raise, and protect them, are once again off the hook. The founder of the #MeToo movement, Tarana Burke,[38] has worked to shift the burden to those who are responsible. She has said that survivors are always being told "tell your story" and that while doing so can be cathartic and important, "repeating that doesn't help you, though. Reliving that doesn't help you."[39] ...

Asking survivors to tell their stories both for their own healing and to prevent others from being harmed puts a lot on the survivors' shoulders. This is not to say that telling publicly is a "wrong choice," but rather that *to direct* a survivor in this direction, without a full conceptualization of the further silencing and abuse that exposure could bring, is not to honor them with the empowerment of making informed choices. When survivors experience harms as a result of trusted caregivers' encouragement to share their stories, they can feel betrayed....

37. Alcoff and Gray, "Survivor Discourse," 281.

38. [Tarana Burke, activist and community organizer, is considered the founder of the "Me Too" movement.]

39. Aisha Harris, "She Founded Me Too. Now She Wants to Move Past the Trauma," *New York Times*, October 15, 2018, https://www.nytimes.com/2018/10/15/arts/tarana-burke-metoo-anniversary.html.

What can Jewish prayer in conversation with the image of a spiral offer as insight into the work of spiritual care for survivors of sexual violence, given the problems I outlined earlier? Jewish prayer is not intended to be done once a year on a big holiday like Rosh Hashanah or Yom Kippur, nor is it intended to just be done once a week on Shabbat. The invitation to return to the themes of creation, revelation, and redemption daily, several times each day, conveys a message that there is wisdom in regularity and repetition. The invitation to say these words and visit these themes again and again in daily life is significant. While the words of the liturgy don't change, the inner experience of the person praying does. As human beings we are constantly in flux, and this is no less true of an individual navigating the aftermath of sexual violence. The *siddur* (prayer book) itself is "our Jewish diary of the centuries,"[40] and points to traumas in Jewish history and mythology, such as enslavement and escape, and the destruction of the Temple. The words and stories are revisited, as are the silences between the words, but the relationship to them changes as the person praying spirals through time. So too the survivor changes their way of relating to what happened, as time passes. At times the traumatic event(s) can feel quite close, at others there is more distance, but as near as they might feel in the moment, as much as it might feel like "it's all happening again," the spiral never fully overlaps or crosses. The lines remain parallel even as the distances between them shifts.

The spiral shows fluidity and change, even in coming near again. Posttraumatic experience can involve a great deal of returning and repetition, in the form of flashbacks and nightmares, and this can be magnified by what is asked of survivors by loved ones and caregivers. As the spiral is traversed again and again, just as the prayers of creation, revelation, and redemption are recited several times every day, the nature of the trauma, the impact it has on a life, and the way a survivor makes sense of it, can shift. This is important because it does not suggest that there will be some future "healed and cured" day when there is no longer any need to be in relationship with what happened. Rather, there is space to allow for transformation in *how* the experience is related to. There is hope and empowerment in this possibility. It is flush with reality, and doesn't suggest brushing anything away. Rather, it invites abiding with the truth of the moment, while making space for hope in change, because change is inevitable.

40. Lawrence A. Hoffman, ed., *My People's Prayer Book, Vol 1: The Sh'ma and Its Blessings* (Woodstock, VT: Jewish Lights, 1997), 1.

* * *

All of the benefits that I have just underscored can happen with much greater ease when those surrounding the survivor are not in a rush to see a finish line, to reach redemption before what needs revealing has been revealed, to build the creation of a new chapter before expansion out of narrowness has been tasted, to arrive at revelation, the sharing of stories, before the depth of chaotic un-creation has been acknowledged and honored. If prayer stands between life and death, and spiritual caregivers are often asked to provide prayer to those in crisis, then the willingness to *stand one's ground* in the in-between place, *with* the survivor, is to transcend the binary of silence and speech.

9 | Solidarity

Judaism emerged historically in a complex landscape of diverse religious traditions, political structures, and tribal affiliations. One of its central tasks was to delineate membership, deciding who was included in the Jewish people and who was not, whether that boundary was permeable, and how it could be navigated. This task was and continues to be a vexing one.[41]

Figuring out who counts in the "we" implicates privileges, rights, and responsibilities. Not only that, but these determinations also influence how others not (yet) "us" are to be regarded and treated. Conventional studies on these issues speak in terms of universalism and particularism and often construe membership as a mutually exclusive category: one is either *in* or *out* of the group. Contemporary deliberations, by contrast, increasingly resist such binary thinking by invoking the language of justice, fairness, solidarity, and intersectional permeability. These terms resist clear and uncontroversial definitions, and so it is not surprising that they prompt debate.

Recent discourse on these interlocking topics has, in some large measure, converged on the notion that Jews—however understood—can and should care extensively about and for those deemed as other. The issue has become of late not if but to whom such Jewish allegiance is owed and how it should be expressed. Tension sometimes arises, however, when the impulse and duty to extend welcome and hospitality (*hachnasat orchim*) is put into conversation with the duty of protectionism (*ḥezkat yishuv*). Discussion and debate about these and related topics are not confined to academic discourses; activists, clergy, and organizational and political leaders offer their visions through petitions, sermons, resolutions, platforms, and policies, as well as op-eds, blogs, podcasts, and other public-facing genres.

Two recent scholarly voices are included here. Amanda Mbuvi aims to be in conversation with the initial declaration of a "global ethic" by the 1993 Parliament of the World's Religions, while Aryeh Cohen lays out a vision of "what a just city

---

41. See Michael Walzer, Menachem Lorberbaum, Noam J. Zohar, and Ari Ackerman, eds. *The Jewish Political Tradition*, vol. 2, *Membership* (New Haven, CT: Yale University Press, 2006).

should be." To address these topics, Mbuvi and Cohen draw significantly from classic Jewish sources, from the biblical book of Exodus and from rabbinic sources, respectively. Another commonality between them is the reliance on narrative. Mbuvi looks to the stories of Moses and Pharaoh and the Pesach seder, while Cohen plumbs those of rabbis found in the Talmud. They also share a significant rhetorical feature: each discusses his or her own personal identity. One goal of such self-disclosure, often understood as an offspring of feminist scholarship, is to assist readers connecting with the lived experience of the author and thereby inculcate trust; another is to clarify how an author's social position and experience might impact their scholarship.

While more could be said about elements and strategies common to these pieces by Cohen and Mbuvi, it's where they differ that is perhaps the more interesting. Cohen offers a book-length meditation not just on citizenship but also on the just city. In his view, the city as such is no less a religious agent morally obliged to care for its diverse denizens as individuals are for other persons. To make this argument, he uses the modern French philosopher Emmanuel Levinas's notions of a "humane urbanism" to develop ways of living that are more attentive to the impacts of one's actions. With Levinas as his muse, the language of "I" and "other" pepper Cohen's project on justice. (See part 1, section 4, for a selection from Levinas.)

Mbuvi, by contrast, digs into the themes of authenticity, identity, and belonging. Though the idea of solidarity links them all, her approach emphasizes the lived experience of intersectionality insofar as it enables individuals to understand the multiple groupings in which they live and operate. Through careful analysis of the Pesach theme of *avadim hayinu* (we have been slaves), Mbuvi demonstrates a first-person-plural strategy for thinking about solidarity as the most fundamental underpinning for all norms. Her essay thus meditates on how "we" and "they" operate through the stories of Moses and Pharaoh and the transformation of the Israelites from Egyptian slaves (*avadim*) into worshipers (*avadim*) of Adonai.

These distinctions notwithstanding, both Cohen and Mbuvi—and many others who address these and related topics—agree that solidarity, however construed, cannot remain hypothetical: it is and must be performative. Though solidarity may also be a character trait or *middah*, it is no armchair virtue or ethic.[42] It requires

---

42. On solidarity as a trait, see chapter 9 in Geoffrey Claussen's edited volume *Modern Musar: Contested Virtues in Jewish Thought* (Philadelphia: Jewish Publication Society, 2022).

active engagement in complex societies, local and global alike. Yet questions remain about whether solidarity refers to "in-group" alliances (between, say, Jews over here and Jews over there) or "cross-group" relations and about how to negotiate multiple solidarities. Both Mbuvi and Cohen encourage solidarities that push against the parochial. Which rationales for self-protective principles might problematize Jewish arguments for a just city or global ethic?

ARYEH COHEN

Justice in the City:
An Argument from the Sources
of Rabbinic Judaism

Aryeh Cohen (b. 1958), professor of rabbinic literature at American Jewish University, is an ordained rabbi and scholar of Talmud, Jewish ethics, and social justice activism. Cohen's activist and academic work delves into issues of race, immigration justice, nonviolent direct action, veganism, and interrelated concerns.

From *Justice in the City: An Argument from the Sources of Rabbinic Judaism* (Boston: Academic Studies Press, 2012), 8–14, 69–83.

Introduction

I argue that the literature of the rabbis—and especially the Babylonian Talmud, the central canonical text of rabbinic Judaism—paints a compelling picture of what a just city should be. A just city should be a *community of obligation*. That is, in a community thus conceived, the privilege of citizenship is the assumption of the obligations of the city toward others who are not always in view. These "others" include workers, the poor, and the homeless. They form a constitutive part of the city.[43]

The goal of this project is to ground a conception of justice in a tradition of rabbinic discourse centering on the Babylonian Talmud. This theory of justice that I seek to propose is significantly drawn from that textual tradition, while it is also based on a contemporary ethical and philosophical framework. Most prominently, I am indebted to the twentieth-century French Jewish philosopher Emmanuel Levinas[44] for a framework of interpersonal ethics that allows me to see rabbinic ethics more clearly and to ask sharper questions about rabbinic ethics. At the same time, I am indebted to the Babylonian Talmud and the textual tradition it generated to enhance or critique what I consider to be Levinas's asymmetrical obsession with the Other....

The hermeneutic engagement itself brings to bear or is itself imminently

---

43. For this reason, in this work, I use the Greek term *polis* interchangeably with *city* and identify the latter as a community of obligation. A *polis* denotes not only a randomly assembled mass of humans who by chance live together. A *polis* in the Greek sense is the end result of a natural tendency of humans to congregate and create communities. A person, in the Aristotelian philosophical tradition, is a *zoon politikon*, a political being.

44. [See part 1, section 4, for a selection from Emmanuel Levinas.]

intertwined with a necessary sociality. Studying together in actuality or theory implicates both author and reader in a process of persuasion that is grounded on a textual moment. When we place a text between us either metaphorically (as in this [essay]) or in actuality (if we were sitting around a table), we engage in an activity one of whose steps is entering into the parameters of a textually bounded moment. There is a notion of a "shared project" in the attempt to understand together or dialogue through the text. This notion is not dissimilar to constitutional interpretation, in that there is a premium placed on the legal interpretation arrived at being grounded in the textual situation (i.e., the Constitution or the Bill of Rights), rather than merely in this or that principled belief. For this type of textual reasoning to take place, the text that is mediating or generating the dialogue (and which, in this specific way, will ultimately ground the interpretation) must be a text that generates a certain level of respect or have at least a patina of gravity. One need not have a declared fidelity to the text (though one might, as in the case of the Constitution), but one must have at least a level of respect for the text.

Through this joint study of a text—in the case of this [essay], rabbinic texts—I invite you into a discourse on an issue of import without having to develop an argument from first principles. The unfolding of the subsequent dialogue is informed by the fact that it is mediated through a text that is part of a tradition. This connection to tradition brings to bear a certain hermeneutic seriousness that might be called inspirational. By this I mean that in our dialogue, there is an intention to "follow in the footsteps" of the implications of a *sugya*[45] in the Babylonian Talmud, where implications would be arrived at through what might be a generous, though discursively rigorous, reading of that *sugya*. The sociality of the hermeneutic situation implies that the consequences of the engagement will be, or are intended to be, applied outside this specific engagement....

This [essay], to some extent, is an attempt to flesh out Emmanuel Levinas's notion of a "humane urbanism."[46] I read this generally to mean a practice of living such that I am attentive to the consequences—immediate and ultimate—of my actions upon those whom I do not know but who share this city with me.

Levinas states the goal of his philosophical exploration as "maintaining, within anonymous community, the society of the I with the Other-language and

---

45. [A *sugya* is a section of Talmud exploring a particular question or theme.]

46. The term is found in his essay "Cities of Refuge," which appears in the collection *Beyond the Verse: Talmudic Readings and Lectures* (London: Athlone Press, 1994).

goodness."[47] This dense statement is the translation of his philosophical insight into the working of the *polis*. The goal is to see the interactions between people—between the I and the Other, or between myself and another person—within an anonymous community, as sites or moments of justice. For Levinas, it is coming face-to-face with the other person, which is referred to here as "language," that removes the Other from anonymity and instills an obligation on the part of the I toward the Other—this is referred to here as "goodness."

One of the important things to note here is that the reason Levinas speaks of the "I" and the "Other" rather than "myself and another person" is to distinguish between the two people in a complete way. The basic characteristic of another person is that she is not me—that is, she is not the same as me; and therefore, also, I am not able to glibly understand her as a slight variant of me. This is what Levinas refers to as the philosophical mistake of assimilating the Other into the Same.

Navigating those anonymous interactions justly is dependent upon my recognition that the Other is beyond my grasp and my ability to completely understand, assimilate, and, especially, make use of or exploit. This leaves me only the ability to listen to, to hear, to learn from, or to be commanded by the Other. I am deprived of the ability to control, to own, to enslave. In an anonymous community, in a non-intimate relationship with the many people whom I don't "know," I am still obliged to maintain this society with the Other. My obligation to the Other is forced upon me by my recognition of my asymmetrical relationship with another person—the Other is transcendent. This latter idea is somewhat counterintuitive to the current ethos of American culture. The political culture of the United States is a culture of rights, while the popular culture is a culture of individual expression and entitlement. Levinas's understanding of the relationship between the self and the Other is a relationship of obligation—that is, I am obligated to the Other person from the moment of the first meeting or interaction....

Chapter 3: Geographical Boundaries and the Boundaries of Responsibility

... In this chapter, I will argue that out of rabbinic Judaism, a model of responsibility emerges that, while recognizing the poor and homeless in society

---

47. Emmanuel Levinas, *Totality and Infinity: An Essay on Exteriority*, trans. Alphonso Lingis (Pittsburgh: Duquesne University Press, 1969), 47.

—citizen and noncitizen—as groups in need of care and deserving of support and shelter, sees the answer also in political terms. The responsibility is placed on the city as a community defined by obligation toward those who reside in its boundaries. The boundaries of obligation are not the geographical boundaries of intimacy or municipality. The central argument in this chapter is that the boundaries of responsibility redraw and exceed the boundaries of intimacy, community, and municipality.

The texts that I will introduce in this chapter are grounded in a biblical ritual that attempts to adjudicate responsibility for the ownerless places in between cities, and responsibility toward people who may pass through cities anonymously. The rabbis used this biblical ritual as a grounding for the principle that the boundaries of responsibility extend beyond the geographic boundaries of intimacy—village, community, neighborhood....

The biblical ritual [about the ownerless corpse] is found in Deuteronomy, chapter 21.[48] ...

A whole chapter of Mishnah is devoted to this ritual—the last chapter of tractate *Sotah*. The chapter of Mishnah interrogates every point of possible ambiguity in the biblical ritual. What if the man is not found on the ground but in a tree? Where on the body do you measure from? The head? The navel? What happens if one witness claims to have seen the murderer, while the second witness claims to have not seen the murderer?[49] What happens to the animal if after it was brought to the stream, yet before it was killed, the killer was found? The questions continue on and on....

The feeling of responsibility is immediately translated into legislation as the Talmudic discussion continues, citing another *baraita*.[50]

Rabbi Meir would say: We coerce accompaniment, for the reward for accompaniment has no measure.

This is the final step in articulating the responsibility placed upon the city. In the Deuteronomic ritual, we first find the elders responsible because of geo-

---

48. [This is a rite of expiation for when a dead body is found lying out in the open and the killer is unknown: Leaders take measurements to determine which town is closest to the corpse, then elders from that town break the neck of a young heifer over a dry riverbed and priests wash their hands over the heifer, proclaiming their innocence. The biblical ritual is discussed in Mishnah *Sotah*, chapter 9.]

49. Rabbinic law demands two witnesses.

50. [A *baraita* refers to a teaching not incorporated into the Mishnah.]

graphic location to the blood impurity that must be purged. ("Your brother's blood cries out to me from the soil" Gen. 4:10.) The Mishnah assigns a more specific responsibility that the *baraita* thickens. A stranger passing through town is owed, it seems, food and protection. Finally, Rabbi Meir[51] codifies this responsibility....

Rashi explains what the coercion might look like: "A positive commandment which presents itself to a person, and he does not want to fulfill it; for example, they say to him 'make a sukkah' and he does not make it ... they beat him until his soul departs." This, according to Eidels,[52] is what "coercion" is. It is not peer pressure or religious guilt. It is not even "moderate physical force" to use a current euphemism. It is violent persuasion. Not that the full force of the violent persuasion needs be deployed in every given situation. However, the possibility of the full force of institutional judicial coercion hovers in the background of any discussion.

This move, that we just outlined above, from purging blood guilt to accepting municipal responsibility for strangers and which is traced from Torah to the statement of Rabbi Meir, is accompanied by another move. The story and ritual in Deuteronomy focuses on the *sadeh*, the ownerless space between towns. The statement of the elders as now understood focuses on what happens in cities. Only cities that have a court are considered under this legislation,[53] and it is the city (or, for Maimonides explicitly, the court) that bears the responsibility. The *baraita* and Rabbi Meir's statement move us directly into the urban arena. The Talmud is no longer concerned with what happened on the road. The concern is with what happened in the city, and what will happen in the city in the future....

The *levayah*[54] of the dead also reinforces the basic structure of accompaniment. It is a reaching out toward another, a gesture that has no hope of being repaid. It is not a gift in the anthropological sense—a gesture that creates an obligation. It is only an answer to a commanding of the other, the stranger in the Levinasian sense.

The obligation to accompany another is an obligation to cross boundaries. In

---

51. [Rabbi Meir was a second-century Palestinian *tanna*, or sage.]

52. [Rabbi Shlomo Eidels (also known as Maharsha) was a sixteenth-century Polish rabbi, famous for his commentary on the Talmud.]

53. Cf. Mishnah *Sotah* 9:2: "If he was found next to a city which had no court, they would not do the ritual. We only measure from a city which has a court." It is the *existence* of the court that defines a place as a *city* that is to be held responsible.

54. [*Levayah* refers to escorting the dead toward burial, as in a funeral.]

accompanying the dead, the boundaries that are crossed are those between life and death. The gesture is not one that is dependent on a sense of mutuality since there is no possibility that the dead will repay the kindness. Accompaniment is a stretching across fixed boundaries, whether of a city or of life....

The logic of *levayah*/accompaniment says that the justness of a city is a function of the web of relationships between "strangers," between people who are anonymous to each other. If people can fall into a place that is beyond anybody's responsibility, this is a reflection on the justness of the city itself. This is when the city needs to atone.

The performance of accompaniment as a practice exists for both the individual and the city. The actual accompaniment of guests out of one's house as the invoking of the Abrahamic ideal is a token of remembrance that the boundaries of responsibility extend beyond the boundaries of intimacy. In our daily lives, the practice of reaching out beyond ourselves is also a performance of accompaniment. Finally, in the life of a city, when budgets are being decided upon, when scarce resources are being allocated, the response to the stranger has to be the center of the discussion. Eradicating the existence of the "ownerless places" has to be the first and not the last priority. The very fact of widespread homelessness, of people suffering and dying because they cannot afford health care, of people going hungry, shatters the illusion that we live in a just society.

AMANDA MBUVI

Avadim Hayinu:
An Intersectional Jewish Perspective
on the *Global Ethic* of Solidarity

Amanda Mbuvi (b. 1976) served as vice president for academic affairs at Reconstructionist Rabbinical School, the first Jew of Color in a leadership role at any American rabbinic institution. A scholar of Hebrew Bible, she is drawn to vivid narratives and how they connect with current identities.

From "*Avadim Hayinu*: An Intersectional Jewish Perspective on the *Global Ethic* of Solidarity," in *Multi-Religious Perspectives on a Global Ethic: In Search of a Common Morality*, eds. Myriam Renaud and William Schweiker (New York: Routledge, 2021), 85–99.

This chapter responds to the *Global Ethic*[55] from a Jewish perspective, taking a central aspect of its "minimal *fundamental consensus* concerning binding *values*, irrevocable *standards*, and *fundamental moral attitudes*"[56] and exploring one of the primary ways that it lives in Judaism, an exploration that leads to some broader consideration of its relationship to Judaism. The analysis focuses on the idea of solidarity as developed by the biblical book of Exodus and appropriated through the holiday of Pesach (Passover). It considers both individual and communal dimensions and relates the dynamics of intergroup relationships to the dynamics of individual membership in the Jewish people, engaged here through Exodus as B'nai Yisrael. Like the Passover seder, the analysis moves from the present moment to the ancient past and back again, grounding personal experience in collective memory. It uses hybrid Jewish identities to illuminate the larger context of intersectionality[57] involved in living out Jewish tradition in a world based on a different set of values. I will show how recognizing such intersectionality can provide the impetus for developing diverse alliances and for the "transformation

---

55. [The *Global Ethic* refers to "Towards a Global Ethic (An Initial Declaration)," an initiative ratified by the Parliament of the World's Religions in 1993 and expanded in 2018.]

56. See "Towards a Global Ethic (An Initial Declaration)" (Chicago: Parliament of the World's Religions, 1993, 2018), henceforth the *Global Ethic*.

57. [Intersectionality, coined by Kimberlé Crenshaw in 1989, builds on feminism's critiques of interlocking structures of power, privilege, and discrimination, to better understand the complexities of group and individual identities.]

in individual and collective consciousness" that the *Global Ethic* envisions as necessary to address contemporary problems.[58]

I am a Bible scholar and a reader of texts. Living with the Hebrew Bible in this racial world has led me to focus on identity and the competing narratives that seek to give structure to life in community. My initial attempts at sketching out a position on Judaism and the *Global Ethic* were dogged by discomfort about representing the Jewish people. "Jewish" straddles the categories of religion and ethnicity, leading to tension between (1) the Jewish tradition's view of identity and belonging and (2) the dominant US view of identity and belonging. Jewishness according to Jewish tradition sometimes conflicts with Jewishness according to American society. You can be halakhically Jewish but not "look Jewish" since, in this society, Jews are imagined as (sort of) white people. As an interracial African American Jew, I am intimately acquainted with this tension. My relationship to the Jewish people has involved a struggle with racial impostor syndrome—a set of insecurities that arise among those whose bodies, families, or predilections don't correspond to their normative sense of what it means to be a member of a group to which they putatively belong.

As I engage the idea of solidarity in this essay, I will not approach it from the perspective of "representative" Judaism but from my own perspective. I will embrace the Pesach directive to envision myself as part of the Exodus and enter into the logic of the holiday. Pesach involves commemorating the movement from a life of slavery in Egypt to a life of freedom as the people of YHWH, using storytelling to dissolve the distinction between past and present and constitute the Jewish people across space, time, and other boundaries.

* * *

Central to Pesach is the idea that the Exodus is not something that happened a long time ago to other people. It is something that is current for each of us. And so we say *avadim hayinu*: we have been slaves. The grammar of *avadim hayinu* designates a particular kind of relationship between the speaker and the experience of slavery. Ancient Hebrew verbs have something called aspect rather than tense. They do not situate actions in accordance with time as a stream that only flows in one direction, from the past to the future. Rather, these verbs invoke actions as complete or as incomplete, in their entirety or in

---

58. Ibid.

medias res.[59] Translators of ancient Hebrew usually choose English verbs in the past tense for Hebrew verbs invoking completed actions and English verbs in the present or future tense for Hebrew verbs invoking incomplete actions. However, to fully appreciate the ethical richness of the formulation *avadim hayinu*, it is necessary to enter into the temporality of ancient Hebrew. . . .

When Jews say *avadim hayinu*, we are refusing to let the experience of slavery fade into the background as we develop a sense of self rooted in growing prosperity. We remain first generation refugees. In keeping with that identification with the outsider, we have a special sensitivity to the word "we." Our experience with universals teaches us that they generally don't include us, an exclusion that always threatens to spill over into violence. . . .

As conceptualized by my invocation of Jewish tradition, being authentically human refers to living into a kind of spiritual wholeness and health that fulfills the intention of the existence of the human species. In the book of Exodus, this notion of authentic humanity stands in contrast to the alternative presented by and centered on Pharaoh. Rather than distinguishing between better and worse ways of living into one's humanity, Pharaoh's version distinguishes between those humans who count and those who matter less, or not at all. It attributes authentic humanity only to a select group, applying different rules to those within that group and those without. . . .

As distinct as these two worldviews are, it is important to recognize that these two groups do not exist in simple binary opposition. The people who live with these ways of conceptualizing and constituting community are not neatly sorted into one camp or the other, a point illustrated by the ambiguity surrounding the identity of the midwives in Exodus. The text identifies Shiphrah and Puah as "midwives to the Hebrews" (Exod. 1:15), leaving open the question of whether they are Hebrew or whether they are Egyptians who work with Hebrews. Regardless of the answer, they, like everyone in the book, are impacted by the exercise of the power of Pharaoh and the power of YHWH. They receive Pharaoh's command to kill Hebrew babies and they must answer to him when they do not comply, having chosen a course of action rooted in fear of YHWH rather than fear of Pharaoh (Exod. 1:17).

By prominently featuring the decision made by midwives who might be

---

59. ["Medias res" refers to starting not at the chronological beginning but sometime or somewhere else.]

Egyptians, Exodus foregrounds the question of where the Egyptians will find blessedness—as people of this Pharaoh or as people of YHWH? Exodus does not depict a conflict between two groups, but rather between two sources of authority promoting different conceptions of solidarity. Everyone must choose which call they will heed: Pharaoh's or YHWH's. . . .

The Torah itself does not refer to the mixed multitude again, which could mean that they maintained a separate existence and went on to their separate destiny. Or it could mean that they became part of B'nai Yisrael. My goal here is not to settle the matter as a point of interpretation or to pass judgment on other interpreters. Rather, engaging Exodus in the spirit of Pesach, I am examining the kind of solidarity created when we say *avadim hayinu*. Seeing ourselves in the Exodus story means that we who partake in the seder have to choose between different ways of understanding what it means to be an "us" and how we fit into the world. Identifying with or alongside B'nai Yisrael means that we choose the Genesis vision of blessed interdependence, or more accurately, that we choose the process of finding our way into that vision even as it cuts against the grain of our experience in the Pharaonic regime of race.

10 | Economics

There are few contemporary discussions of Judaism and economics—however defined—that do not make reference to Deuteronomy 15 in the Bible, which begins: "Every seventh year you shall practice remission of debts," and goes on to declare, "There shall be no needy among you—since the Lord your God will bless you in the land that the Lord your God is giving you as a hereditary portion—if only you heed the Lord your God and take care to keep all this instruction that I enjoin upon you this day" (Deut. 15:4). There is no singular consensus in postbiblical Jewish tradition, classical or contemporary, about the meaning of these verses across time and space, but they have certainly established the idea of a relationship between questions of business practices, poverty, wages, and broad Jewish communal flourishing.

Each of the selections in this section represents an attempt to determine what, specifically, Judaism might have to do with these and related questions. If we begin with the descriptive observation that some people or communities are able to meet their basic material needs with ease while others struggle mightily, this does not, in itself, tell us anything about which questions or actions ought to follow from this observation. In analyzing the approaches each thinker takes to such issues, we may learn as much about their own assumptions and convictions as we do about the classical sources and themes of passages like Deuteronomy 15.

Jill Jacobs's book, *There Shall Be No Needy*, takes up the question of the relationship between Jewish texts, laws, and contemporary economic questions. She opens with what might be considered more existential concerns, like what it means to be a Jew in a world beset by poverty. Jacobs, notably, describes her own approach as "social justice," eschewing the language of "business" as an organizing principle. Her policy conclusions notably diverge from others in this section. For instance, she is a fierce advocate for living wage ordinances, emphasizing themes like "economic justice," taking as a given that common contemporary practices in wealth distribution, housing rights, and labor law are in need of serious correction that Jewish texts, laws, and tradition can provide.

Aaron Levine's selection opens not with a discussion of Judaism or ethical values, but with an overview of major concepts in modern economic theory. His particular focus is on welfare economics, the study of how the distribution of goods and resources affects a society's (if not a given individual's) wealth. Modern welfare economics, Levine notes, is largely consequentialist in its methods: a given economic action is worthwhile to the degree it results in an aggregate increase in wealth.

But Judaism, Levine argues, takes a qualitatively different approach. For an economic action to be justifiable from a Jewish perspective requires it to be subjected to the "moral code" of Jewish law. This process, which Levine fleshes out with various case studies from modern and ancient business practices as discussed in Jewish sources, is what Levine calls "Jewish business ethics" and "economic morality." Confident in the consistency and translatability of Jewish law across time and culture, Levine makes strong claims about the Jewish ethical character of many modern and contemporary business practices. In the selection below, Levine considers the question of living wage ordinances, which calculate the wage floor in a given setting according to the cost of living in that area, and argues the relevant classical Jewish concepts reveal that the living wage is not a requirement of Jewish law—and may in fact be prohibited.

Sam Brody's essay argues that there is deeper overlap between seemingly disparate approaches to economic questions than we might think. His argument proceeds from an analysis of several contemporary works in Judaism and economics (including books by Jacobs and Levine). He suggests, provocatively, that while contemporary Jewish economics-related ethical work may differ in its understanding of whether, or to what degree, some aspect of the economic market requires intervention, nearly all such work assumes that *the market* is a fundamental element of all such ethical consideration. Brody calls this uniting factor "neoliberalism," by which he means a twentieth-century theory of political economy in which the fixed presence of a relatively free market is the foundational assumption of any further economic theorizing (Jewish or otherwise). This unmarked assumption, Brody argues, dramatically circumscribes the kind of ethical reasoning that can take place. What would it look like, Brody asks, to imagine the role of Jewish ethics vis-à-vis economics in a more radical way?

JILL JACOBS

There Shall Be No Needy: Pursuing Social Justice through Jewish Law and Tradition

Jill Jacobs (b. 1975) is a Conservative rabbi and the founder of the nonprofit organization T'ruah: the Rabbinic Call for Human Rights. In her capacity as a rabbinic activist, she wrote the 2008 teshuva (legal statement) ratified by the Rabbinical Assembly of the Conservative movement that ruled that Jews in positions of economic power should pay their employees a fair wage and hire unionized workers.

From *There Shall Be No Needy: Pursuing Social Justice through Jewish Law and Tradition* (Nashville, TN: Jewish Lights Publishing, 2009), 10–12, 14, 16–22.

1. A Vision of Economic Justice

Many of the stories and laws of the biblical books of Genesis and Exodus offer the seeds of a vision for a just world.... While these stories and others offer a glimpse of justice or injustice in action, I would argue that the most important clues toward a Jewish vision of justice emerge from the laws given to the Jewish people as they prepare to enter the land of Israel and to establish an autonomous society there....

The most important evidence of a community's commitment to justice is not the actions of a few star individuals; nor is it the experience of oppression. Only upon gaining collective power does a community begin to demonstrate its approach to justice....

With this emphasis on communal power, I turn now to the biblical passage that, for me, best articulates a Jewish vision of economic and social justice.... Significantly, this book [Deuteronomy]—the last of the Torah—immediately precedes the Jewish people's entrance into the promised land of Israel. Moses's final instructions, then, may be read as an exhortation not to be corrupted by newfound power and wealth, but rather to use this new position to establish a just society....

> There shall be no needy among you—for Adonai will surely bless you in the land which Adonai your God gives you for an inheritance to possess it if you diligently listen to the voice of Adonai your God, and observe and do the commandment that I command you this day. For Adonai your God will bless you, as God promised you; and you shall lend unto many nations, but you shall not

borrow; and you shall rule over many nations, but they shall not rule over you. If there is among you a needy person, one of your brethren, within any of your gates, in your land which Adonai your God gives you, you shall not harden your heart, nor shut your hand from your needy brother; but you shall surely open your hand unto him, and shall surely lend him sufficient for his need in that which he wants. Be careful lest there be a hateful thing in your heart, and you say, "The seventh year, the sabbatical year, is coming" and you look cruelly on your brother, the poor person, and do not give him, for he will call out to God and this will be counted as a sin for you. Rather, you shall surely give him, and you shall not fear giving him, for on account of this, God will bless you in all that you do and in all that you desire. For the poor will never cease from the land. For this reason, God commands you saying, "You shall surely open your hand to your brother, to the poor and the needy in your land." (Deut. 15:4–11)

The overarching Jewish attitude toward the poor is best summed up by a single word of the biblical text: *achikha* (your brother). With this word, the Torah insists on the dignity of the poor, and it commands us to resist any temptation to view the poor as somehow different from ourselves....

In addition to challenging us to see the poor person as a member of our family, the word *achikha* also disabuses us of any pretense that we are somehow inherently different from the poor. Those of us who do not live in dire poverty often protect ourselves from any sense of vulnerability by finding ways to differentiate ourselves from the poor: they must be poor because they don't work hard, because they drink or take drugs, because they come from dysfunctional families, and so forth. Seeing each poor person as our sibling cuts through any attempts to separate ourselves from him or her....

A striking feature of the Deuteronomy passage is the apparent contradiction between verse four, "There shall be no needy among you," and verse eleven, "For the poor will never cease from the land." We expect the omnipotent God of the Torah to keep promises; we are therefore surprised to hear the Torah promise to eradicate poverty and then, almost in the same breath, admit that this promise will never be fulfilled....

A common debate among those involved in antipoverty work concerns the relative value of direct service addressing immediate needs and of advocacy or organizing addressing the need for systemic change. Advocates of direct service argue that the hungry need to be fed *today* and that the homeless need somewhere to sleep *tonight*. Those who prefer organizing or advocacy point out that soup kitchens and shelters will never make hunger and homelessness disappear, whereas structural change might wipe out these problems.

The Deuteronomic response to this debate is a refusal to take sides, or better, an insistence on both. Rather than advocate exclusively either for long-term systemic change or for short-term response to need, this passage articulates a vision that balances the pursuit of full economic justice with attention to immediate concerns. In this reading, the text in question becomes a charge to work for the structural changes that will eventually bring about the end of poverty while also meeting the pressing needs of those around us.

* * *

Significantly, alongside the promise of the eradication of poverty and the warning against ignoring the poor appears a mention of *sh'mitah* (the sabbatical year). During this year, debts are forgiven and no crops are planted. As a result, the gap between the rich and the poor necessarily closes, as landowners cease agricultural production while the poor free themselves from debt. Therefore verse nine above warns against refusal to lend to the poor as the *sh'mitah* year approaches, although the lender risks not getting his money back....

It is no coincidence that the laws of *tzedakah* [gifts to the poor] are deeply connected to the acquisition of land. Precisely at the moment at which the Jewish people, for the first time since before their enslavement in Egypt, are about to take hold of property, God chooses to remind the people of their obligation to eradicate poverty. The wilderness acts as the great economic equalizer. During their forty years of wandering, the Jewish people can own only what they can carry with them. While individuals may possess gold, silver, and rich linens, the wealth of each person is necessarily limited by the nomadic nature of the community. Once established in the land, however, some people will necessarily begin to acquire more land and wealth than others, and the wealthy may come to believe that they deserve their newfound fortune. Throughout the biblical discussion of the *sh'mitah* year, God constantly reminds the reader that "the land is mine" and that the land can literally throw up a community that ignores the received laws about how to live responsibly here.[60] Conscious of the human potential for greed, the Torah chooses the first moment of property ownership to remind the people that wealth ultimately belongs to God, and that human beings are simply sojourners in the land....

60. See, for example, Leviticus 25:23 and ff.

The Torah conspicuously does not mandate a full redistribution of land every fifty years. If, as some have argued, the Torah were a fully socialist document, we might expect a biblical demand to divide the land equally among all residents. On the other hand, if, as others have suggested, the Torah advocated an unrestricted free-market economy, the periodic redistribution of land would be nonsensical. Rather, the Torah—as well as later Jewish law—favors a checked market system that permits the ethical acquisition of wealth, with measures aimed at ensuring that the market does not allow the poorest members of society to end up with close to nothing. . . .

In the course of offering a vision of a perfected world and mandating human participation in achieving this vision, this passage also lays out a series of principles that will underlie virtually all Jewish economic law. These principles are:

1. The world, and everything in it, belongs to God; human beings come upon wealth only by chance and do not necessarily "deserve" the wealth in their possession.

2. The fates of the wealthy and the poor are inextricably linked.

3. Corrective measures are necessary to prevent some people from becoming exceedingly rich at the expense of others. Jewish law does not propose a full redistribution of wealth, but rather, institutes controls against the gap between the rich and the poor becoming too wide.

4. Even the poorest member of society possesses inherent dignity, and each member of the community is responsible for preserving the dignity of others.

5. The responsibility for poverty relief is an obligation, not a choice.

6. Strategies for poverty relief must balance short-term and long-term needs.

7. The eradication of poverty is an essential part of bringing about a perfected world, and each person has an obligation to work toward the creation of this world.

AARON LEVINE
Economic Morality and Jewish Law

Aaron Levine (1946–2011) was a professor of economics at Yeshiva University, as well as an ordained Orthodox rabbi. His many published works dealt with the relationship between modern economic theory and Jewish law, and questions of ethical conduct in modern business practices.

From *Economic Morality and Jewish Law* (New York: Oxford University Press, 2012), 8, 15, 191–214.

Welfare economics adopts what philosophers would label a consequentialist approach to morality. Under that approach, what matters is not means or intentions, but rather outcomes. Specifically, for welfare economics, the measure for evaluating the worthiness of an economic action is whether the action would increase society's wealth in the long run. If the action promotes wealth maximization, it is worthy, even if the increase in wealth makes some people economically worse off. What matters therefore is how the action affects the aggregate level of income, regardless of whether the distribution of income among the members of society will change. . . .

In sharp contrast to welfare economics, Jewish law espouses what philosophers would call a deontological ethical system. Under that system, the moral rightness or wrongness of an action depends on its intrinsic qualities, and not, as in consequentialism, on the nature of its consequences. For Jewish law, it is all a matter of discovering the rule that applies to the situation at hand. The measure of the worthiness of an economic action is whether the action satisfies Jewish law's moral code, which prohibits the infliction of harm on one's fellow even if the harmful action would maximize society's wealth in the long run. . . .

Chapter 7: The Living Wage and Jewish Law

To afford the working poor a decent standard of living, many local governments have enacted living wage ordinances (LWOs).[61] First adopted in Des Moines, Iowa, in 1988, LWOs have been enacted in over one hundred localities to date. . . .

Our purpose here will be to analyze the living wage from the standpoint of

---

61. [Living wage ordinances mandate that employers pay their employees a wage indexed to the cost of living (for housing, food, clothing, transportation, and other necessities) in that region.]

both welfare economics and Jewish law. Since the living wage is essentially an anti-poverty measure, it relates to economic morality on two levels. The first is whether requiring employers to pay their workers a living wage is a legitimate interference with market forces. The second issue is whether the living wage accomplishes its anti-poverty objective. Resolution of the latter issue entails identification of all the consequences that are likely to proceed from this policy initiative.

* * *

Standard economic theory demonstrates that despite the noble intent behind minimum wage legislation, this legislation sets into motion various distortions in the low end of the labor market. These distortions are so severe that the very people the legislation is designed to help actually become worse off. Insofar as proponents of the living wage aim to have government set the minimum wage at a level much higher than the federal minimum wage, the arguments against the minimum wage apply with even greater force to the living wage....

Studies have shown that when government requires firms to pay a higher money wage, employers will respond by reducing pensions, health insurance, and on-the-job training for their workers, if possible. Reducing fringe benefits means that the real wage employers pay rises by less than the money wage. Another negative side effect is that the imbalance between supply and demand created by the minimum wage allows employers to be more selective about whom they hire. When employers are faced with a glut of applicants, they can more easily discriminate on the basis of gender, race, age, or religion. One more negative consideration is that minimum wage legislation targets the individual worker. But if the goal of this legislation is to alleviate poverty for the working poor, the unit that anti-poverty programs should target is the poor family rather than the individual worker. This is so because most people who are paid a low wage rate are members of families that are not poor, and most people in poor families who work are paid more than the minimum wage....

We will consider whether Jewish law requires an employer to pay his workers a living wage from the standpoint of both labor law and charity law.... In Jewish law, the key moral principle in determining fairness of price in a commercial setting is the law of *ona'ah*.[62] The issue of the living wage therefore turns on the application of the law of *ona'ah* to the labor market.[63]

   62. "When you make a sale to your fellow or when you buy from the hand of your fellow, do not victimize one another" (Lev. 25:14).
   63. [*Ona'ah* refers to laws around fair pricing for goods and services. It is generally

The law of *ona'ah* gives validity to a plaintiff's complaint that a better marketplace opportunity was available to him at the time he entered into a particular transaction. In the terminology of economists, the *ona'ah* complaint would be called an opportunity cost claim. The plaintiff does not lose his right to transact at the market norm unless we can be certain that he waived this right at the time he entered into the transaction.

Before applying the law of *ona'ah* to the labor market, we note that halakha classifies an employee as either a day laborer (*po'el*) or a piece-worker (*kabbelan*). What distinguishes the *po'el* from the *kabbelan* is the provision for fixed working hours in the labor contract. While the *po'el's* labor contract obligates him to perform work at specified hours over a given period of time, no such clause is included in the *kabbelan's* contract. Given the controlling nature of the fixed-hours factor, an employee is considered a *kabbelan* if he is not required to work fixed hours, even if his employment agreement requires him to complete a project by a specified date....

The law of *ona'ah* as it applies to the labor market shows that labor law does not require an employer to pay his workers a living wage. This is so because the *ona'ah* claim, as mentioned earlier, is essentially an opportunity cost claim. In the context of the labor market, a worker's claim of underpayment is therefore valid only if the same job was reasonably available to him at the time he entered into his employment agreement. A *po'el* demonstrates this by showing that his own employer pays a higher wage to other workers for the same job, or that another local employer would have hired him for the same job at a higher wage. A worker who cannot command a living wage in the marketplace cannot claim a living wage based on *ona'ah*. Moreover, given that the restitution procedure does not apply to the *po'el* labor market, even a worker who commands a living wage in the marketplace is not entitled to any judicially mandated wage adjustment because of his *ona'ah* claim....

In a paper that was given recognition by the rabbinical membership organization of the Conservative Jewish movement, Rabbi Jill Jacobs proposed that Jewish law requires an employer to pay his workers a living wage.[64] She adduces a number of sources to prove her contention. Let's examine these sources.

---

understood to refer both to overcharging a buyer and to purchasing something for less than the buyer knows it to be worth.]

64. Rabbi Jill Jacobs, "Work, Workers, and the Jewish Owner" (responsum adopted by the Committee on Jewish Law and Standards of the Rabbinical Assembly on May 28, 2008, with thirteen members in favor, one opposed, and three abstaining). The resolution specifically said that "Jews should 'strive' to hire unionized workers and pay a living wage."

One source is the formulation of the biblical prohibition against withholding a worker's wages and Nahmanides's comment on this prohibition. In the rabbinic literature, this prohibition is commonly referred to as *lo talin*:

> You must not withhold the wages of a poor or destitute (*evyon*) hired worker, [regardless of whether he is] one of your brothers, one of your converts in your land, [or a resident alien] within your cities. You must give him his wages on the day they are due, and not let the sun set upon him, for he is poor, and he endangers his life [to work for you]. Do not cause him to cry out to God against you, for then [the punishment for] this sin will be upon you [more quickly]. (Deut. 24:14–15)

Commenting on the Torah's formulation of the prohibition against withholding the wages of the poor and destitute worker, Nahmanides remarks:

> For he is poor, like the majority of hired laborers, and he depends on the wages to buy food by which to live.... If he does not collect the wages right away as he is leaving work, he will go home, and his wages will remain with you until the morning, and he will die of hunger that night.[65]

According to R. Jacobs, Nahmanides's comment that a person who does not receive his wages on time will "die of hunger that night" assumes that a person who *does* receive payment on time will be able to provide sufficiently for himself and his family and will not die of hunger. This inference leads R. Jacobs to find support for the notion that Jewish labor law requires an employer to pay a living wage.

[However,] Nahmanides never meant to read into Deuteronomy 24:14–15 that *every* violation of *lo talin* in connection with the *evyon* worker will cause the *evyon*'s death. Indeed, the instances where nonpayment actually causes the worker to perish should be rare. The instinct of self-preservation alone would tell the unpaid worker not to allow himself to sink into paralysis and perish, but instead to do something to relieve his hunger and even resort to begging, if necessary....

If Jewish labor law does not require an employer to pay a living wage, perhaps Jewish charity law does. Consider that Maimonides regards preventing someone from falling into the throes of poverty as the highest level of charitable giving. One of his examples of this type of charitable giving is to provide a needy person with a job....

65. Nahmanides to Deuteronomy 24:14–15.

Hiring someone in need when more qualified candidates are available has limits. Most fundamentally, out of fear that over-generosity in charitable giving may subject the donor to a risk of falling into poverty himself, the sages decreed that one should not give charity in excess of 20 percent of one's net worth.[66] Putting the viability of one's source of livelihood at risk is an example of this prohibition.

Let's show how hiring a person based on need can put a business at risk. Suppose the needy individual does not have the requisite skills for the job but can be trained. If labor costs are a significant component of cost for the employer, the higher labor cost the employer incurs by hiring the needy candidate puts the employer at a competitive disadvantage. The law of *ona'ah* tells the employer that, other things equal, he may not pass on his differential cost to his customers by raising prices, except through upfront disclosure. To get customers to accommodate him and at the same time dispel their suspicions that he is either lying or inefficient, the employer would have to say: "My costs are higher because I hired a needy person who is unqualified for the job." . . .

Moreover, from a practical standpoint, introduction of the living wage disrupts the entire pay structure of the employer. This is so because the unit of support in Jewish law, as we shall explain in the next section, is not the individual, but rather the household. Accordingly, a teenager who is member of a household that is not poor is not entitled to a subsidy. At the other extreme, if the wage earner is a head of a household and the household is poor, the wage subsidy should be geared to the number of dependents the head of the household must support. Paying market-driven wages to workers who are not poor while paying workers who are heads of a poor household wages according to household need is very disruptive. This system may have the effect of dragging down the morale and productivity of the labor force because of the resentment it generates. . . .

The thrust of the above discussion is not that employers have no ethical duty to their poor workers other than to pay them a competitive wage for the type of work they perform. An employer's interaction with his workforce makes his indigent workers priority candidates for some of his charity funds. Giving these workers small bonuses before holidays, gifts to mark new additions to their families, and special consideration in the event of illness, is therefore appropriate. These gestures are not only good business, but also charity on the highest level.

66. *Ketubot* 50a.

SAMUEL BRODY

Jewish Economic Ethics in the Neoliberal Era, 1980–2016

Samuel Brody (b. 1983) is an associate professor of religious studies at the University of Kansas. His work deals with modern Jewish thought, classical Jewish texts, and the relationship between religion and politics.

From "Jewish Economic Ethics in the Neoliberal Era, 1980–2016," *Journal of Jewish Ethics* 7, nos. 1–2 (2021): 39–62.

This essay considers the emergence, over the last four decades, of a distinct genre of Jewish writing in English about economics....

"Business ethics" seeks to bring contemporary business practices into conversation with religious and philosophical wisdom traditions by analyzing textual sources that offer solutions for individuals who confront ethical dilemmas while engaged in business. Contemporary academic economics provides frameworks for the discussion, with the well-known Econ 101 warnings against "market distortions" such as wage floors and rent control setting parameters for moral reflection.... Jewish "social justice" literature, by contrast, has much less recourse to academic economics. It is heavy on ethical discourse, presented theologically as deriving from Jewish sources and as culminating in practical policy prescriptions. The emphasis is no longer on the individual distinguishing between legitimate profit-seeking and unethical behavior, but rather on how society should deal with systemic problems like homelessness, mass incarceration, and health care....

Despite their frequent political disagreements, both subgenres are characterized by formal features that may be taken as signs of their neoliberal times. They typically open with brief philosophical-theological overviews of the connection between Judaism and economic matters, emphasizing that despite perceptions to the contrary, the latter fall within the former's purview. Then they undertake serial, chapter-by-chapter consideration of discrete economic topics from the standpoint of biblical and rabbinic sources, measuring contemporary economic theory, law, and practice in the United States and the state of Israel against the sources. The aim is relatively concrete policy proposals, directed at audiences assumed to seek guidance from Judaism, and formulated to bring contemporary economic practice into line with Jewish values and/or halakha. My argument is that it is this structure itself, rather than the specific content of the policy discussions, that unites the subgenres and marks them as products of the neoliberal era.

Neoliberalism is a contested term. One popular view holds that it is little more than a resurgence of nineteenth-century *laissez-faire*, favoring privatization, deregulation, free trade, and austerity.... Another view argues that neoliberalism is anything but *laissez-faire*, since under neoliberalism a strong state applies "the model of the market ... to all domains and activities—even where money is not at issue—and configures human beings exhaustively as market actors, always, only and everywhere as *Homo economicus*."[67] ... A third view posits that "the impression that there exists a single coherent 'market mentality' seeping into every pore turns out to be a big part of the problem," since "there is no such thing as 'the market' as a monolithic entity."[68] On this account, neoliberalism is no simple matter of imperialist economic logic, and religious orientation is no guarantee against infiltration by neoliberal thought patterns. In fact, such infiltration would begin with the acceptance of the premise that the "market" exists as a kind of free-standing natural entity, into which governments may "intervene" or not.

In my view, this third interpretation helps us to see that while "business ethics" and "social justice" literature disagree regarding the degree of change required to bring the operation of contemporary American and Israeli capitalism into line with Judaism, they agree that Judaism stands outside and above "the economy," in a position to command it, as long as the rules of economics are respected....

As they begin, many of these works describe an uphill struggle simply to convince readers that Judaism and economics ought to be discussed together at all. ... Tamari opens with puzzlement at how both Jews and non-Jews treat Jewish economic behavior, "as though the Jew has been living an economic existence divorced completely from his religious and cultural milieu."[69] ... Similarly, Jacobs begins with what she calls "a search for an integrated Judaism."[70] ...

It is in this mood of striving to be all-encompassing that each writer then

---

67. [Wendy Brown, *Undoing the Demos: Neoliberalism's Stealth Revolution* (Princeton, NJ: Princeton University Press, 2015), 31.]

68. [Philip Mirowski, *Never Let a Serious Crisis Go to Waste: How Neoliberalism Survived the Financial Meltdown* (London: Verso, 2014), 90–91, 101.]

69. [Meir Tamari, *With All Your Possessions: Jewish Ethics and Economic Life* (New York: Maggid Books, 2014), xiii.]

70. Jacobs, "Work, Workers, and the Jewish Owner," 1–8.

addresses the fundamentals of political economy: the organization of production, the medium of exchange, the distribution of commodities, etc. These statements are as expansive as they are brief. Tamari, for example, as a professional economist personally committed to an Orthodox interpretation of Jewish history and practice, denies that "Judaism" is a plural entity; it is possessed of a single teaching, located in its authoritative textual tradition, and it is important to him that this tradition be understood as totally unique and as "differing radically" from all other religious or secular systems....

There is a contradiction, however, between Tamari's desire for a unique Jewish "economic system" and his practical commitments. He starts by saying, "There is no particular economic system preferred by Judaism nor does it have an economic philosophy. However, any system chosen is subject to the restraints and guidance that Judaism's permitted or forbidden acts mandate." ... Yet we soon find Tamari citing the second-century rabbinic text *Pirkei Avot* to the effect that "[on]e who says, 'mine is yours and yours is mine,' this is the mark of the ignoramus." Tamari's reading indicates, "Such an individual may imagine a well-meaning utopia, perhaps, but one contrary to human nature and therefore impossible and often, as the experience of socialism and communism has shown, giving rise to different but equally immoral evils." From one sentence of the *Tannaim*, Tamari adduces the entire "experience" of communism in many countries, understanding it to demonstrate the impossibility of eradicating the human desire for wealth and gain. He makes a similar move to oppose unregulated capitalism, highlighting a nearby sentence of *Avot* ("One who says 'mine is mine and yours is yours,' this is a median merit, many say this is the characteristic of the people of Sodom"). Here, however, he is careful to stress that this critique applies only to "unlimited" private property, or opposition to all public regulation of markets. Thus, we are left to wonder which economic systems or economic philosophies we are "choosing between."... The economic ecumenicism with which Tamari began quickly leads to a moderately regulated market capitalism as the only option for Jewish economic philosophy.

Jacobs similarly argues that "Judaism does not dictate a clear-cut answer to every—or even any—social and economic issue." She nonetheless believes that classical rabbinic sources can be marshalled in support of "a specifically Jewish approach to economic and social issues while offering perspectives that might not emerge out of an analysis either of text alone or of social policy alone." For Jacobs, as for Tamari, this means that Judaism cannot map perfectly onto either well-known political-economic extreme:

If, as some have argued, the Torah were a fully socialist document, we might expect a biblical demand to divide the land equally among all residents. On the other hand, if, as others have suggested, the Torah advocated an unrestricted free-market economy, the periodic redistribution of land would be nonsensical. Rather, the Torah—as well as later Jewish law—favors a checked market system that permits the ethical acquisition of wealth, with measures aimed at ensuring that the market does not allow the poorest members of society to end up with close to nothing.[71]

For Jacobs, too, Judaism's uniqueness dovetails with a regulated capitalism. The differences between Tamari and Jacobs, as between the larger subgenres of business ethics and social justice literature, are about the nature and limits of the regulation—in which areas of the economy, and to what ends....

These broad ideological statements aligning Judaism with regulated capitalism stand in contrast to the bulk of the texts that follow, which consist of discrete considerations of specific economic topics from the standpoint of Torah, Talmud, responsa, and codes, moving chapter by chapter through unsystematic agendas revealing of each author's priorities. Topic selection in each subgenre reflects a combination of these priorities with the perceived capacities of the sources to sustain argument on each question....

The same rabbinic sources appear repeatedly as central points of contention. A key example is B. T. *Bava Batra* 8b, which says, "The people of the city are permitted to regulate weights, prices, and the wages of workers. They also have the right to punish those who do not carry out their regulations."[72] For Tamari, this text is evidence that "associations of workers, whether hired employees or operating as independent contractors, were already permitted in Talmudic times." ... The ultimate implication is that contemporary trade unions appear to be a familiar, long-recognized phenomenon in Jewish law, with rights to make regulations for their members and to penalize noncompliance....

For Jacobs, the very existence of a straightforward Talmudic permission to "the people of the city" to set workers' wages, as well as prices and measures, constitutes "an explicit break with the controlled free-market system that some other texts describe. In granting individual communities the authority to determine wages, the rabbis indicate an understanding of the failures of a free-market

---

71. Jacobs, "Work, Workers, and the Jewish Owner," 2, 4–5, 19–20.
72. Translation of Tamari, *With All Your Possessions*, 161....

system. While certain economic conditions might enable such a system to succeed, other conditions will make this system unworkable. To maintain stability, the local authority must have the power to adjust wage rates as necessary."[73] ...

Bava Batra 8b illustrates how the tradition is read by both subgenres. It stands out because it seems to offer a general principle with legal impact, and it pertains to central economic concepts like prices (including, therefore, wages and rents). The business ethicists urge restraint in the application of its permissive edict, while the social justice writers seize upon it as a tool. In neither case, however, is the source treated historically as potential evidence about premodern economies that differ substantially from our own ... the unquestioned assumption that "labor markets" exist in this Talmudic text, and that the question is the "regulation" of such markets, deserves further scrutiny.

73. Jacobs, "Work, Workers, and the Jewish Owner," 118–19. ...

11 | Zionism

The modern state of Israel came into existence in 1948, on a day since celebrated by Jewish Israelis as Yom Ha'atzmaut, Independence Day, and mourned by Palestinians as Nakba, Catastrophe. Today, nearly 50 percent of the world's Jews live in Israel or the surrounding territories. But the fierce debates about the ethics of Zionism and Jewish political power extend well beyond the contested boundaries of the state. In these debates, questions of ethics and politics are deeply intertwined.

Seventy-five years later, the amount of ethical and political analysis surrounding Israel, its significance, and its trajectory is virtually endless. And yet the fundamental questions of 1948 are as prominent as they have ever been: What are the ethical demands of political Zionism, the movement for a Jewish state in the Middle East? Under what circumstances (if, indeed, any at all) might the creation of the Jewish state be justified, given its consequences for the existing Palestinian population of the land in question? Is it possible for past and current injustices to be rectified — and if so, how? What kinds of coexistence are possible? What alternative futures for the region can we imagine? What are the features of a thriving democracy? What makes a modern nation-state "Jewish"? And what sorts of ethical analyses are sufficient to effectively consider these questions at all?

Chaim Gans's and Ruth Gavison's selections are animated by two such questions: Was the means by which the state came into existence just? And, inasmuch as the state exists, what is necessary for it to be just? Despite their differences, Gans and Gavison are methodologically similar: Both consider their queries in light of Jewish history and modern theories of justice, without reliance on the classical Jewish sources that have been so present for most other thinkers in this volume. Both appeal chiefly to standards of modern international law and (secular) theories of statehood in their reasoning. Such methodological similarities allow their distinctive conclusions to stand out; similarly located thinkers may still come to quite divergent answers. Gans presents a critique of the Israeli Law of Return, which accords to Jews worldwide the right to Israeli citizenship, while Gavison's essay sketches out an argument for the establishment and maintenance of a Jewish state. It should be noted that Gans's selection is excerpted from a full book, and thus represents only a small fraction of his arguments as a whole. However, as his references throughout the work make clear, he is very much in conversation with Gavison.

Julie Cooper's work is distinguished from Gans's and Gavison's not simply, or chiefly, by her conclusions, but by the questions she takes to be fundamental. Her main conversation partners are three contemporary thinkers: Daniel and Jonathan Boyarin, and Judith Butler, here grouped together as advocates of "diasporism," a rejection of the ethnonationalism and exclusionism that, they argue, are the unacceptable but inevitable outcomes of a specifically Jewish state. Cooper's critical response suggests that a better historical and political account of antisemitism is necessary for diasporist proposals to effectively address the experiences and commitments that gave rise to the Zionist movement. Only then, she argues, can ethicists and political theorists effectively defend diasporist alternatives to a Jewish state (though, readers will note, Cooper argues that the language of "ethics" is itself insufficient to the task).

CHAIM GANS
A Just Zionism: On the Morality of the Jewish State

Chaim Gans (b. 1948) is an Israeli political philosopher and a professor emeritus of law at Tel Aviv University, widely recognized as an authority on theories of nationalism and political justice. Gans's research considers and critiques the defenses of Jewish settlement and sovereignty in the modern Israeli state.

From *A Just Zionism: On the Morality of the Jewish State* (New York: Oxford University Press, 2008), 111–12, 116, 121–22, 125–27, 129, 131–33, 137–38.

5. *Jewish Hegemony in Immigration and Other Domains*

For reasons stemming from Israel's interpretation of the general notion of the right to self-determination, the practices of many other nation-states around the world, the lessons learned from the persecution of the Jews and from the history of the Jewish-Arab conflict, Israel interprets the Jews' right to self-determination as conferring the Jewish people "ownership" over the state, or at least as entitling the Jewish people to hegemony therein. . . .

These issues have always been critical to Zionism, both in terms of how it viewed the relationship between Jewish self-determination in the land of Israel and the Jewish diaspora and in terms of how it thought Jewish self-determination in Israel would impact the fate of the land's indigenous Arab population. The Zionist movement aspired to establish a national home for the Jews in the land of Israel. Given the fact that most Jews were spread all over the world, Jewish immigration to Israel was essential to achieving this goal. Facilitating Jewish immigration to the land of Israel thus constituted the core of Zionist ideology, together with the tenet that this land is the only location for realizing Jewish self-determination. However, just as the Zionist movement was divided with respect to the institutional form of self-determination—whether the Jews would have a spiritual center, a substatist political unit, or a state in the land of Israel—and what the size of the territory for the Jewish national home should be, it was also divided over the demographic objectives of the Jewish return to the land of Israel and the dimensions of this return. . . .

Irrespective of whether the appropriate demographic objective of Zionism is the existence of a Jewish presence in Israel in numbers sufficient to allow its members to live in the framework of their culture, or the existence of a Jewish majority, the important normative issues regarding these demographic objectives pertain primarily to the legitimate means for the realization of these goals.

Israel's principal means for realizing these objectives thus far have been its Law of Return and its Citizenship Law. These laws grant every Jew anywhere in the world the right to immigrate to Israel and become a citizen of the state of Israel.[74] ... The right that the Law of Return grants to every individual Jew to immigrate to Israel was of great symbolic value at the time of its enactment, which was not long after World War II and the establishment of the state of Israel. This symbolic value presumably still holds sway. However, I will argue that the present-day reality in Israel requires immigration policies that are less ethnocentric and more universal. ...

I would like to argue now that national priorities in immigration could be derived from the right to national self-determination and that anyone recognizing this right for the reasons justifying it from the liberal perspective must also be committed to recognizing priorities in immigration for members of national groups.

One justification for the right to self-determination that also justifies granting priorities in immigration to members of a national group desiring to immigrate to their homeland is the interest that members of national groups have in adhering to their cultures, flourishing within the frameworks of their cultures, and sustaining them for generations. Another justification for self-determination, which at the same time also justifies nationality-based priorities in immigration, is that members of groups with a history of persecution might wish for their culture to thrive, since it provides a source of self-respect and since a community of their own may help them to protect themselves. If these interests do indeed justify the continued existence and the self-rule of national groups, then they certainly justify granting priorities in immigration to members of these groups. ...

The third justification that I wish to suggest for nationality-based priorities in immigration derives from the fact that such priorities serve the interests of all members of the group, and not only the immigrants themselves, in maintaining the framework of their culture and in its self-rule, regardless of whether they are living in the diaspora or in the country where the group has realized its self-determination. For example, regardless of whether they happen to be living in Turkey or in Germany, Turks may have an interest in maintaining the con-

---

74. The Law of Return ... was amended in 1970 to apply not only to Jews but also to non-Jewish spouses of Jews, or children or grandchildren of Jews and their spouses. The Citizenship Law, 5712/1952, allows those who have immigrated to Israel under the Law of Return to receive citizenship almost automatically.

tinuous existence of their group and in realizing its self-determination in their homeland. The same could be said to apply to Algerians, regardless of whether they are living in Algeria or in France, or to Jews, irrespective of whether they are living in Israel or anywhere else in the world. If this interest justifies the right to self-determination, it would seem that, subject to moral constraints, it must also justify auxiliary rights to carry out the necessary actions required to maintain that self-determination....

To sum up, the justifications for nationality-based preferences in immigration are not limited to considerations of diachronic justice and the need to remedy the wrongs of the past but also include considerations of synchronic justice and the need to fulfill fundamental and enduring human interests. One must reject the claim that the incompatibility of the Law of Return with the liberal ideals of neutrality and equality renders it unjust. Nonetheless, this does not mean that the Law of Return and Israel's other immigration and citizenship policies are just, for indeed they are not, as I will demonstrate in the next section of this chapter.

* * *

The Law of Return grants every Jew from anywhere in the world the right to immigrate to Israel. The Citizenship Law allows those who have immigrated to Israel under the Law of Return to receive citizenship almost automatically. According to the Citizenship Law, there are almost no other ways to attain Israeli citizenship. The fact that the Law of Return is the only law that addresses the issue of immigration to Israel means there is virtually no way for non-Jews to immigrate to Israel. In effect, Israel is open to all Jews and closed to all non-Jews. The nationality-based priorities in immigration to Israel are thus very different from nationality-based immigration priorities practiced in some other countries.... Most countries that grant special rights regarding immigration and naturalization to members of their main ethnocultural group—such as Finland, Germany, and Greece—do not do so by granting an individual right to all members of their diasporas to immigrate, and they certainly do not limit immigration and naturalization solely to members of their own ethnocultural group....

As noted earlier, both the unrestricted admission of Jews and the complete exclusion of non-Jews are problematic. With regard to the former, state authorities should at least have some discretion in making decisions regarding immigration policies. Any decisions made by the authorities should express their primary responsibility toward the country's citizens and their current needs. In granting categorical immigration rights to a large group of potential immigrants, the Law of Return does not leave the state the option of considering whether the country's citizens' current interests really allow for any immigration or how many immigrants should be admitted. This is problematic, both in itself and also because it implies that the immigration interests of a group of people from outside the country have absolute priority over the interests of the citizens of the country. This means that the ordinary interests of the country's citizens do not count vis-à-vis those of members of the diaspora group in immigrating....

The guiding principles presented below assume that ethnocultural considerations are only one factor shaping the general principles that ought to guide immigration policies. These principles are intended as a framework for striking a balance between the needs of the ethnocultural groups enjoying self-determination within particular countries and the general needs, which are not necessarily ethnocultural, both of the potential immigrants and of the citizens of these countries.... (1) When states attempt to determine immigration policies, the nationality-based motivation of potential immigrants should have considerable weight. States should allot a portion of their immigration quotas to those immigrants who, for nationalist reasons, wish to live where their nation enjoys self-determination; (2) national groups may admit the number of members into their homelands that is required in order for them to maintain their self-determination; and (3) states have a duty to take in refugees and persecuted members of specific national groups that have a right to self-determination within their specific states and also to grant priority to members of these groups within all of the other categories that make up their immigration quotas....

Unlike Israel's Law of Return and its immigration and naturalization policies, these three guiding principles for nationality-based priorities in immigration do not automatically include all Jews and exclude all non-Jews. The Law of Return and the immigration and naturalization arrangements in Israel reflect an ethnocentric view of the right to Jewish self-determination and the Jewish nation-state. It reflects the position that the country is, first and foremost, a tool in the hands of the Jewish ethnocultural group. This position is very prevalent among the Jewish majority in Israel and perhaps also among many non-Israeli Jews. According to this interpretation of Jewish self-determination, all interests that non-Jews might have, including ethnocultural interests, as well as any interests that Jews might have other than their ethnocultural interests (for example, their interest in improving their standard of living, or any individual's interest in pursuing a particular professional career), that might conflict with the Jewish interest in self-determination are not taken into account at all. Such an approach is not prevalent in any other country in the world that Israel should want to emulate and is unacceptable in moral terms. Also, in view of the fact that the Jewish people have lived in the diaspora for most of their history, Israel has its own special reasons for not endorsing this approach. . . .

On a symbolic and emotional level, Jewish history provides significant reasons for not waiving the declaration in the Law of Return that "Every Jew has the right to immigrate to Israel." However, I doubt whether these reasons provide a sufficient justification for preferential immigration practices guided by the principle of "all Jews and only Jews." . . . The principles I have proposed also include the principle that, in the places where national groups have realized their self-determination, they are entitled to admit the number of members of their national diasporas required to maintain their right to national self-determination. This principle serves to respond to the well-founded demographic concerns of the Jews living in Israel.

RUTH GAVISON

Reflections on the Meaning and Justification of "Jewish" in the Expression "A Jewish and Democratic State"

Ruth Gavison (1945–2020) was a professor of law at the Hebrew University of Jerusalem and a 2011 recipient of the Israel Prize, considered the state's highest cultural honor. Her work was concerned with legal and political theories of human rights and democracy, and the tensions inherent in Israel's aspiration to be considered both a Jewish and a democratic state.

From "Reflections on the Meaning and Justification of 'Jewish' in the Expression 'A Jewish and Democratic State,'" in *The Israeli Nation-State: Political, Constitutional, and Cultural Challenges*, eds. Fania Oz-Salzberger and Yedidia Stern (Boston: Academic Studies Press, 2014), 135–63.

In November 1947, the General Assembly of the United Nations debated the report of the commission that had been formed to address the question of Palestine-Eretz Yisrael, and recommended that two states should be founded in the territory between the Mediterranean Sea and the Jordan River: a Jewish state and an Arab state. The lines of partition were set mainly on the basis of demographic concentrations. The resolution stated that both states would be democratic and that both of them would not infringe the civil or political rights of those members of the other group, who should remain in their respective territories....

The Jewish leadership accepted the partition resolution, and the night of the UN vote was a night of celebration in the Yishuv. The Arab and Palestinian leadership rejected the resolution, claiming that it infringed on the right of Arabs and Palestinians to self-determination in the whole of the territory. But the Arab refusal led to the Jewish state being founded in 1948, while the territory allotted for the establishment of an Arab-Palestinian state was divided, at first, between Israel, Jordan, and Egypt, and then in 1967 was occupied in its entirety by Israel. About two-thirds of the Palestinian residents of what became the state of Israel in 1948 left and became refugees. Those who remained in Israel enjoy civil and political rights. Within the areas that fell under the control of Arab states, not one Jew remained.

The Declaration of Independence of May 1948 stresses the duality of the state's commitment to being the nation-state of the Jews, on the one hand, and its democratic character and commitment to the human rights of all its inhabitants, without distinction of ethnicity or religion, on the other. This duality received an explicit constitutional grounding in a series of laws, culminating in the Basic Laws of 1992. Israel is defined in these laws as a "Jewish and democratic state," and a vast majority in the country would like to continue that way. Moreover, this majority believes that there is no contradiction between Israel's character as the nation-state of the Jewish people and its commitment to democracy and to the defense of the human rights of all its residents....

The case for justifying a Jewish nation-state in (part of) Eretz Yisrael is based on the universal right to national self-determination, which is recognized in international law and international human rights law....

Supporting a right for state-level self-determination requires us to recall the reasons that lie at the foundation of the right for self-determination, and to determine if it is possible to secure effective self-rule for the group in question without granting them control of state institutions. The right to self-determination is the quintessential collective right, and is not reducible to individual rights. It is intended to guarantee for significant groups (or "all-encompassing groups") the possibility of sustaining themselves by ensuring the physical and cultural security of their members, as well as the possibility of passing their culture onto subsequent generations.

Jews lived for hundreds and thousands of years with no state. Nonetheless, they enjoyed various degrees of cultural self-determination in many diverse societies, and their separate existence was the product of both the choice of the Jews themselves and the preferences of the peoples with whom they dwelled. However, the fact that the Jews were a minority within other peoples led to great vulnerability, and over the course of time they suffered repeatedly from persecution, deportations, massacres, discrimination, exclusion, and pressures to convert, occasionally leading to forced conversion....

Zionism developed in the context of the combination of these two types of Jewish vulnerability. It became clear that a group that is a small minority everywhere cannot hope to generate for itself either physical security or security of identity. Zionism was intended to do two things: to concentrate Jews in one location so that they would constitute a large portion, or even the majority, in that place, and—as a result of this demographic dominance—to enable the Jews to live a complete Jewish existence, in a place where they did not depend upon the goodwill of other peoples, who would always see them as different and foreign. The idea of Zionism was that only such self-determination would, in the long run, make possible the preservation of a strong Jewish community that is a prerequisite for the complete, secure, and stable Jewish existence of its members.

It was no coincidence that the United Nations resolution on the foundation of a Jewish state came so soon after the scope of the Holocaust became known, and after it had become clear how helpless the Jews had been in those countries, where the governments of the day either encouraged or did not punish those who persecuted and harmed the Jews. Similarly, the establishment of the state of Israel appeared necessary in light of the fact that the nations of the developed world had not hastened to take in those fleeing the menace of the Nazi regime and also had not been overly eager to take in the displaced survivors in Europe, who could not (or did not wish to) return to the places from which they had been sent to be murdered....

The second element of the right to state-level self-determination for Jews in Eretz Yisrael pertains to the living conditions of Jews within Eretz Yisrael itself. If Jews had been able to immigrate freely to Eretz Yisrael and live there a complete and secure Jewish existence, it would have been possible to make do with sub-state self-determination for Jews in Eretz Yisrael, under the political rule of the Arab majority. This vision would have made it possible to avoid partition. Indeed, the vision of one state has accompanied the Zionist enterprise from its inception. The Arab residents of Palestine-Eretz Yisrael demanded it from the

Mandate authorities and from the international community up until the partition resolution, and vehemently rejected propositions for partition.... The Jews, for their part, refused to give up their dream for a national home in the entirety of western Eretz Yisrael. The agreement of the Jewish leadership to the principle of partition did not stem from a concession on the ideological level. It stemmed from the realization that, in the demographic conditions that prevailed at the time, the Jews would not be able to be a stable majority in the whole of Eretz Yisrael, and that in order to establish a Jewish state they would have to agree to its establishment in those areas where there was such a majority and in those where it would be possible to stabilize one by means of immigration (*aliyah*).

Even in the UN Special Committee on Palestine (UNSCOP), there was a minority recommendation that one state should be founded in Palestine-Eretz Yisrael on the basis of a federation of national communities. Fortunately for the Jews, the Arabs rejected the plan, and thus paved the way for the adoption of the partition resolution in 1947 ("fortunately" because the majority of the UN committee had determined that this solution did indeed address the needs of the Jews living in Eretz Yisrael at that time, but clearly would limit Jewish *aliyah* in the future). In this situation, the establishment of one state would not have satisfied the will of those Jews who were not yet residents of Eretz Yisrael to live in a state in which Jews could exercise effective self-determination. According to this proposal, the demographic statistics would have caused the Jews, in the best case, to be a recognized national minority possessing some extent of autonomy in the Arab state of Palestine.... The vision of Brit Shalom—the vision of a binational state—would have given way fairly quickly to the vision of Palestine as an Arab state with a sizable Jewish minority.

The vision of one state, in which Jews and Arabs live side by side and each group develops its own historical connections to the common homeland in its own way, is easier to justify than the idea of two states for two peoples. The Peel Commission recommended partition, more than seventy years ago, because it had reached the conclusion that this vision was not viable due to the significant cultural differences between the groups, and because of the enmity and emotionally charged history between them....

What was true in 1938 was also true in 1947, and unfortunately appears to be true today as well. Moreover, it is not clear if there is any process on both sides of accepting the necessity of coexistence within a single political entity or any move toward a readiness, resulting from that acceptance, to build common institutions or to make fundamental decisions with regard to managing the affairs of the single state that would be established. Thus the present reality establishes the right of Jews to self-determination specifically on the state level, at least as long as the deep conflict over the future of the region continues....

There are today more than six million Jews living in the state of Israel (and in the Judea and Samaria territories). Most of them have no other country to which they can go; Israel is their only home. They enjoy here an independent Jewish-Hebrew cultural existence, such as they could not have in any other place in the world. These Jews are without a doubt a collective with a right of self-determination in the place of dwelling. Removing them from their homes, or even bringing about a situation in which they are subject to the mercy of people with whom they have a long history of mutual enmity and suspicion, would constitute a serious violation of their rights.

These facts do not necessarily justify Jewish control of all the territory from the Mediterranean to the Jordan River, wherein dwell millions of Palestinians who are not citizens of the state. However, the Jewish collective does have a right to self-determination and self-defense, which it realizes—and which it is entitled to continue realizing—in the framework of the state of Israel.

The large majority of the Israeli public not only wishes for the continued existence of the state of Israel, but also for its continued attachment to the realization of the self-determination of the Jewish people. In this case, democracy requires that the will of the majority be respected, subject to the obligation to protect the rights of the minority. Thus, the state's Jewishness at the moment is not a component in conflict with democracy, but rather a characteristic required by it.

JULIE COOPER

A Diasporic Critique of Diasporism:
The Question of Jewish Political Agency

Julie Cooper (b. 1972) is a senior lecturer in political science at Tel Aviv University. Her research centers on modern political thought and theory, Jewish political thought, and secularization.

From "A Diasporic Critique of Diasporism: The Question of Jewish Political Agency," *Political Theory* 43, no. 1 (2015): 80–110.

In recent years, as the prospects for a negotiated two-state solution to the Israeli-Palestinian conflict have dwindled, American Jewish scholars have increasingly invoked the concept of diaspora to counter a purported Jewish consensus regarding Zionism. In diasporic Jewish traditions, these scholars find resources for contesting Israeli state violence, and, more important, for challenging the notion, which they impute to Zionism itself, that Judaism and Zionism are coextensive. The most prominent exponents of this stance, such as Judith Butler and Daniel Boyarin, advocate one-state and/or binational solutions to the Israeli-Palestinian conflict.[75] These scholars not only share a political critique of the state of Israel, they also share a political investment in what I call the ethics of particular identity. . . .

I call this project a "diasporic critique of diasporism," then, because the standpoint from which I engage the work of Butler and the Boyarins is not Zionist.[76] My goal is neither to discredit, nor rebut, these theorists' controversial public declarations regarding Israel/Palestine (e.g., support for the Boycott, Divestment, and

---

75. Daniel Boyarin is a signatory of "The One State Declaration." See http://electronicintifada.net/content/one-state-declaration/793. For Judith Butler's binationalism, see *Parting Ways: Jewishness and the Critique of Zionism* (New York: Columbia University Press, 2012), 4, 208, 216. For Jonathan Boyarin's position, see *Storm from Paradise: The Politics of Jewish Memory* (Minneapolis: University of Minnesota Press, 1992), 126.

76. "Diasporism" is not my coinage, nor is it a label that Butler and the Boyarins adopt. Indeed, Butler and the Boyarins would likely refuse much of what "diasporism" conventionally connotes. By invoking "diasporism," I do not mean to imply that Butler and the Boyarins proffer anything resembling an ideology, nor do I mean to suggest that they constitute a unified camp or movement. Yet Butler and the Boyarins share a political investment in modes of Jewish identity derived from diasporic traditions. Thus, I use the term "diasporism" to capture an influential strand within Jewish thought that makes reservations about Zionism the occasion for rethinking Jewish identity. . . .

Sanctions [BDS] movement).[77] Moreover, although I contend that Butler and the Boyarins misdiagnose Zionism's animating impulses, my primary goal in exposing these misdiagnoses is not to rehabilitate Zionism but to foreground liabilities of investing political energy in theories of identity formation. Finally, the vantage from which I engage these texts qualifies as diasporic because I do not presume that a nation-state is the default political option, given modern Jewish history. . . .

Butler and the Boyarins invest political energy in these projects because they understand Zionism as more than a political movement for the establishment of a Jewish state. Zionism also, on their view, advances a philosophically naive and morally reprehensible theory of Jewish identity. If Zionism's political failings are inextricably bound up with its theoretical failings, then one can gain traction against Zionism, Butler and the Boyarins suggest, by defining "Jewishness" otherwise. If, however, the demand for a Jewish state rests not on a philosophical mistake about the boundaries of the self, but on a historical, political, and economic analysis of antisemitism, then Butler and the Boyarins attack the wrong target. Moreover, in a theoretical framework that places a premium on articulations of "Jewishness," diaspora loses much of its traditional resonance as a condition that demands distinctive modes of political mobilization. In texts by Butler and the Boyarins, diaspora's appeal derives primarily from the resources it affords for constructing a philosophically compelling theory of the Jewish *self* or *collective*—rather than the resources it affords for constructing institutions appropriate to a nonterritorial Jewish *polity*.

My central argument . . . is that diasporic thinkers should redirect their energies from theorizing the Jewish self toward defending the ability of polities other than the nation-state to ensure Jewish political empowerment. Given the diverse sources from which Zionism derives ideological energy, critics of Zionism must engage politically on multiple fronts. . . . When it comes to enlisting support for such projects, however, the approaches of Butler and the Boyarins are less politically robust, because they neglect the singular political predicaments of modern Jews. More than a theory about what it means to be Jewish, political Zionism is a theory about the nation-state's ability to vanquish antisemitism. The recogni-

---

77. See "Judith Butler's Remarks to Brooklyn College on BDS," http://www.thenation.com/article/172752/judith-butlers-remarks-brooklyn-college-bds; "Academic Freedom and the ASA's Boycott of Israel: A Response to Michelle Goldberg," http://www.thenation.com/article/177512/academic-freedom-and-asas-boycott-israel-response-michelle-goldberg.

tion that emancipation did not deliver on the promise of full enfranchisement is the impetus for political Zionism. The admission of Jewish individuals to equal rights did not eliminate European antisemitism. Rather, emancipation created new forms of antisemitism. If modern Jews remain subject to forms of discrimination that demand a political response, they are without traditional foundations for Jewish solidarity—for emancipation sought to transform Judaism from a theologico-political membership into an individual, private faith. Thus, the admission of Jewish individuals to equal citizenship required the development of new idioms in which to confront political crises. Political Zionism not only diagnoses the political predicament of the modern Jew, it offers him or her a solution—namely, citizenship in a Jewish nation-state.

To contest this solution, diasporic thinkers must grapple with political Zionism's diagnosis of the Jews' vulnerability as a stateless people. Yet, in their preoccupation with the ethics of particular identity, Butler and the Boyarins neglect the political insights that propelled political Zionism. By developing ethically resonant visions of "Jewishness," Butler and the Boyarins may inspire Jews who have long felt muzzled to criticize Israeli policy. Yet the relevant debate to pursue, in this expanded conversational arena, is whether, at this juncture, Jews need a nation-state—not what "Jewishness" means.... Butler and the Boyarins approach the polity through excurses on the attainment or grounding of identity, confident that adoption of diasporic identities will incline Jews toward a determinate political stance. As the case of Zionism reveals, however, ethical principles provide little guidance regarding forms of polity adequate to current circumstances—let alone how to mobilize for their establishment.... I engage Butler and the Boyarins to move diasporic thinking beyond debates about identity—what does "Jewish" mean?—toward analysis of modern Jews' political predicaments. The pressing question for diasporic thinkers, I submit, is how to envision political agency in polities other than the nation-state....

At first glance, it is scarcely surprising that Butler and the Boyarins critique Zionism by elaborating alternative conceptions of "what it is to 'be' a Jew." After all, the conviction, shared by some American Jews, that support for Israel is a sine qua non of Jewish identity could inspire reluctance to criticize Israeli policy (let alone repudiate Zionism). If the "present time" is one "in which Jewish orthodoxy has been redefined as including the unquestioning support for a political entity, the state of Israel, and all of its martial adventures," one might argue, Butler and the Boyarins have no choice but to respond in kind, engaging Zionism on the terrain of identity. Admittedly, claims to orthodoxy, authenticity, and loyalty animate vocal strands of American Zionism. Yet the blackmail of authenticity does not exhaust Zionist argument, canonical or contemporary. Upon reflection, then, one wonders why the ethics of particular identity has become the default idiom for scholarly opposition to Zionism. If Butler hopes to "envision a new polity after Zionism," why does she proceed by elaborating an ethic of dispossession—instead of outlining the institutional contours of . . . such a polity?[78] The conviction that Zionism is amenable to this analysis reveals diasporic thinkers' acquiescence to a transformation in modern Jews' self-conception. In order for identity to emerge as the point of contention in the debate with Zionism, Judaism first had to become "Jewishness." . . .

As an empirical matter, it may be the case that, for twenty-first-century American Jews, the Jewish question surrounds the meaning of "Jewishness," rather than the terms of Jewish enfranchisement. This fact is cause for celebration, because it reflects the unparalleled success of Jewish integration in the United States. Yet it would be naive to imagine that the ascendance of "Jewishness" comes without cost. When Butler and the Boyarins contest Zionism on the terrain of identity, they tacitly accept the transformation of Judaism into "Jewishness" as a fait accompli. Indeed, they embrace the inward, affective turn, of which "Jewishness" is a prime symptom, as the precondition for a pluralization of Jewish identities—which pluralization provides fodder for the critique of Zionist hegemony. As [Hannah] Arendt warns, however, confining one's critical horizon to "Jewishness" can hinder political thinking. When the meaning of "Jewishness" becomes a paramount concern, one is liable to forget that political Zionism stakes its claim on a defense of the nation-state. For Butler, the critical project is establishing the conditions of possibility for a figure like Arendt—a Jewish critic of Zionism "whose political views made many people doubt the authenticity of her Jewishness."[79] To establish the conditions of possibility for a figure like Arendt is not, however, to grapple with the questions Arendt posed about the difficulty of sustaining political consciousness. As Arendt acknowledges, Zionism's ideological success derives, in part, from its claim to offer the definitive solution to the political predicaments of modern Jews.[80] Butler and the

---

78. Butler, *Parting Ways*, 33.

79. Butler, "Is Judaism Zionism?," in *The Power of Religion in the Public Sphere*, ed. Eduardo Mendieta and Jonathan Vanantwerpen (New York: Columbia University Press, 2011), 77. See also Butler, *Parting Ways*, 122.

80. See Arendt, *The Origins of Totalitarianism* (San Diego: Harcourt Brace, 1979) 79n61, 120; and Hannah Arendt, "The Jewish State: Fifty Years After, Where Have Herzl's Politics

Boyarins neglect to mount a direct rebuttal of Zionism's political claims because they trust that elaborating on an ethically compelling vision of "Jewishness" will yield the desired political stance....

To derive generalizable ethical principles (applicable to Jews) is not, however, to examine how *this* dispersed people can exercise political agency and confront political challenges. A compelling critique of Zionism, I would argue, must offer historically informed rejoinders to Zionism's diagnosis of the Jews' vulnerability as a stateless people.... The proper object of diasporic critique, I would argue, is not solidarity, belonging, or communitarianism, but the poverty of political imagination when it comes to envisioning political agency beyond the nation-state....

I have engaged texts by Butler and the Boyarins from a diasporic standpoint to restore neglected modes of political thinking to scholarly debate about Zionism. Elaborating diasporic visions of "Jewishness" is insufficient to challenge political Zionism's ideological hegemony. Critics must also counter the Zionist brief for state sovereignty with an alternative vision of Jewish empowerment—and, to elaborate such a vision, diasporic thinkers must restore analysis of Jewish political predicaments to a place of prominence....

The question of how Jews can exercise political agency in a world of sovereign states remains a live question—and it is the crucial question, I would argue, in the debate with political Zionism. If allegiance to Zionism derives not from a philosophical mistake about the self, but from the conviction that a Jewish state is required to combat antisemitism and achieve self-determination, then one can mount a forceful challenge by offering an alternative vision for political agency. Conversely, Jews who feel a non-paradoxical sense for national belonging—or nurture organic attachments to the land of Israel—might still be convinced, through political argument, that Israel's current regime is neither just nor necessary for the maintenance of Jewish peoplehood....

Appreciating limitations of Butler's and the Boyarins' respective rejoinders to Zionism should inspire reservations about the robustness of ethical approaches to conflicts over sovereignty, territory, and enfranchisement.... I have critiqued Butler and the Boyarins from a diasporic standpoint to expose the falsity of these conclusions. Once we detach arguments about the polity from ethical arguments about the self, new trajectories for non-Zionist thought open

---

Led?" in *The Jewish Writings*, eds. Jerome Kohn and Ron H. Feldman (New York: Schocken Books, 2007), 375–87.

up—specifically, trajectories that affirm Jewish self-rule. When understood in institutional terms, self-rule and shared rule are not mutually exclusive. It is possible to devise egalitarian arrangements, in Israel/Palestine, that honor desires for self-determination. Admittedly, retaining a political conception of Jewish peoplehood may not appeal to Butler and the Boyarins. I raise this prospect less to convince Butler and the Boyarins to embrace such a conception, than to persuade readers who remain invested in autonomy that one can resist the nation-state imperative without abandoning aspirations to self-rule. In other words, I address this point to readers reluctant to abandon the nation-state in the absence of alternative vehicles for Jewish self-rule. To engage such readers, and thereby expand the constituency for non-Zionist politics, diasporic thinkers must demonstrate that the nation-state is not the sole polity that facilitates self-rule. Having suspended debates about identity, authenticity, and ethics, one can challenge political Zionism in the name of an alternative vision of self-determination.

12 | State Power and Violence

The nation-state is not only one of the most embedded institutions in our lives today, but it is also, by nearly all accounts, one of the most distinctively *modern*. It derives from a theory of collective power that emerged from older forms of European religious and imperial governance. The 1648 treaties signed at Westphalia are often described as the foundation of modern statecraft and of the idea of state sovereignty: each bounded territory has the right to determine its own political order and conduct warfare on its own behalf.

It is unsurprising, then, that many of the selections in this section refer to or intervene in modern debates about the intentions or limitations of modern state power. The chief issues considered here are some of the most contentious in modern statecraft, international relations, and geopolitical conflict: the ethics of warfare, capital punishment, and torture. But in this volume on Jewish ethics, the modern state is only one of the political institutions of concern. Almost as prominent in some of these selections are other governing structures extending far further into the past. The earliest, perhaps, is the covenantal relationship between God and the Israelites, as introduced in the biblical book of Genesis and dramatically affirmed at Mt. Sinai in the book of Exodus. These events, unlike the treaties of Westphalia, are little attested outside the powerful biblical account. But whatever their historicity, these narratives are undeniably stories of political governance; the relationship between God and the chosen Israelites is defined by a profound power disparity, an extensive set of commandments and promises, and an array of punishments should the Israelites transgress.

These commandments, of course, form the basis of halakha and postbiblical Jewish legal reasoning, and are central to some of the following selections. In his essay, Geoffrey Levey appeals to relevant biblical commandments and narratives of warfare, as well as classical rabbinic and medieval debates about the permissibility of waging war, arguing that the tradition imposes useful limitations both on the absolute ability of a Jewish governmental entity to compel citizens to fight *and* on the absolute ability of an individual to refuse military service. Although Levey makes clear that his focus is on Jewish state-like entities and not on issues of individual Jews in non-Jewish states, he also argues that this "theory" of war may provide a useful corrective to modern Western understandings of the relationship between individual citizens and the state.

In his essay on Jewish ethics in war, Michael Broyde similarly appeals to biblical and rabbinic injunctions, and assumes that this set of ethical questions are addressable chiefly with reference to halakha. The selection below focuses on what Broyde calls "battlefield ethics": What constitutes correct Jewish conduct in declaring and waging war? In his introduction (not excerpted), Broyde notes that he finds this question of most interest to Israeli soldiers, for whom the concept of a "Jewish war" is most immediately practical. Broyde lays out the conditions for ethical actions taken in self-defense, but argues that in fact many combat situations permit actions well beyond what is permitted in other settings.

Melissa Weintraub's passionate argument against the Jewish ethical value of torture as a tool of a war critiques a number of claims—including one by Broyde—regarding what is permissible in war, even in service of saving Jewish lives. Weintraub also invokes a number of Jewish themes and legal principles, although she speaks more frequently of "the sources" or "the tradition" in her argument. The institution of the covenant, rooted in obligation, is never absent from this discussion.

For other thinkers, another premodern political institution is no less important: the Israelite commonwealth established in the Bible after the people settled in the promised land. God's extreme displeasure toward the Israelites' demand for a human monarch is famously described in 1 Samuel 8, and much of the books of Samuel and the Kings are an account of the ups and downs of the monarchy. Similarly, the massive political institution of the Roman Empire hovers over Beth Berkowitz's selection. This is so not only because halakha developed during the time of the empire, but also because the empire stands as a comparative (or competing) system of political governance. Berkowitz's work on capital punishment in classical rabbinic literature argues that the rabbis used the theoretical institution of capital punishment to construct their own authority as well as create a specifically Jewish governmental culture as an alternative to Rome. The excerpt below (though only a very small portion of Berkowitz's larger work) captures her claim that the fraught rabbinic discussions about methods of execution mark the rabbis' resistance to Roman governance. These ancient arguments have had profound influence in contemporary Jewish death penalty debates.

Finally, Nadav S. Berman, in his essay on Autonomous Weapons Systems (AWS), explains that AWS are "robots of various forms that have the technical capacity, by means of advanced technologies, such as AI, GPS, and facial recognition, to approach targets, identify them, and then harm or destroy them without human involvement." Though these systems could bypass some current ethical quandaries about human conduct in war, they present a host of new, difficult issues about technology and humanity. Berman argues that evaluating AWS requires us to activate our "faculty of moral imagination," which is best done through narratives, and appreciating the theme of "dehumanization" so central to debates about robotic war technologies. Berman thus appeals to two biblical narratives of the Israelite monarchy—questionable and dehumanizing acts by King Saul and King David—to assess the ethics of autonomous weapons.

GEOFFREY BRAHM LEVEY

Judaism and the Obligation to Die for the State

Geoffrey Brahm Levey (b. 1950) is an associate professor in the School of Social Sciences at the University of New South Wales in Australia. He has written prolifically on political theory, Jewish studies, and sociology.

From "Judaism and the Obligation to Die for the State," *AJS Review* 12, no. 2 (Autumn 1987): 175–203.

Dying on the state's behalf, and at its request, is a matter that one might expect to be of obvious concern to the Jews throughout their history.... Yet the obligation to die for the state is not a question that enjoys special treatment or ready resolution in Jewish sources.... Still, it would be wrong to conclude that Judaism and the Jewish tradition lack a coherent position on there being (or not being) an obligation to die for the state....

In classic Western treatments, the question of there being an obligation to die for the state typically turns upon a particular political theory.... In Judaism one's obligations to the social contract, like one's obligations generally, are determined not according to political relations or some elaborated theory of the state but according to laws understood as divine commandments, or mitzvot. It is true that these commandments became binding for the Jews after they entered into a bilateral covenant with God, a founding act of consent resembling at least one of the ways Western theorists attempt to ground political obligation....

But ... there is one difference unequivocally separating the Jewish and Western theoretical approaches to the issue of obligations to the body politic. The agents to whom consent is respectively rendered by the people in social contracts and in the biblical covenants are of completely different orders....

The Bible contains numerous references to the nature of the expectation associated with the call to risk one's life in the service of communal goals. Especially in the premonarchic period, the common feature of biblical wars is their sacred character. God marches along with the Israelites and is considered by Israel to be not only sovereign, but guardian....

But the effect of the sacred quality of biblical wars with respect to a duty to participate is very much a two-edged sword. The fact that God is both the legitimator of Israel's wars and its guardian in battle meant that participation had to be infused with the requisite faith....

This same emphasis on faith and consideration for the "fearful" is repeated and extended in Deuteronomy 20.... The chapter opens with a series of restatements of the need for having faith in God.

> When thou goest to battle against thy enemies, and seest horses, and chariots, and a people more than thou, be not afraid of them: for the Lord thy God is with thee, which brought thee up out of the land of Egypt... (Deut. 20:1)

Next is specified a number of conditions of exemption from battle.... The final exemption, explicitly referring to the "fearful," seems to take on extra force for having been preceded by other legitimate conditions of military exemption where any simple "crisis of faith" is *not* the issue.

> And the officers shall speak further unto the people, and they shall say, "What man is there that is fearful and fainthearted? Let him go and return unto his house, lest his brethren's heart faint as well as his heart." (Deut. 20:8)

The Bible, then, displays a central tension over the question of there being a duty on the part of the Israelites to risk their own lives in battle on behalf of their people. On the one hand, the sacred quality of Israel's mission and military pursuits suggests a responsibility of "equality of sacrifice" devolving upon each individual. On the other, this very same sacred quality requires that the duty to fight be undertaken with "proper" faith or not be undertaken at all....

On the face of it, the advent of the monarchy seems to confound this picture of "ultimate voluntarism" before any duty to risk one's life for the commonwealth.... The basis for the monarch being accorded these powers is found in a controversial passage in 1 Samuel:

> And Samuel told all the words of the Lord unto the people that asked of him a king. And he said, "This will be the manner of the king that shall reign over you: He will take your sons, and appoint them for himself, for his chariots, and to be his horsemen; and some shall run before his chariots."... (1 Sam. 8:10–11)

What ethical significance one attaches to these proffered royal prerogatives has tended to depend upon whether they are understood as divine dispensations ... or rather, and only, as dire prophetic warnings of the sort of despotism a monarchy invites. Each interpretation has its notable protagonists. It is perhaps reasonable, therefore, to see the merit in a third (although not necessarily exclusive) alternative: the Bible reveals a basic ambivalence toward the institution of the monarchy....

The crucial consideration is therefore not the kind or degree of legitimacy that the Bible accords to the kingship. It is that the king, though he may obtain certain prerogatives ... is nevertheless bound to abide by God's laws. ...

The king of Israel remains God's agent, as do indeed all the people of Israel. It follows that even in the monarchic period respect must be accorded the Deuteronomic provisions exempting certain "classes" of individuals elaborated earlier. ...

The idea that the will to fight precedes the duty to do so is a radical one. Just how radical can be seen by reference to a contemporary political theorist. Michael Walzer has argued that "there is a crucially important sense in which the obligation to die can only be stated in the first person singular."[81] Moreover, Walzer insists that this is so even though it "comes dangerously near to suggesting that a man is obligated to die only if he feels or thinks himself obligated."[82] ... As the text stands, if the Bible advances any obligations to die for the state, they are "loose" obligations indeed.

* * *

The significance of the Deuteronomic exemptions was not lost on the rabbis of the classical period. ... The Mishnah records that Rabbi Jose the Galilean understood the fourth exemption to refer to those fearful of having sinned and of having not yet repented.[83] ... Rabbi Akiba, however, insists upon a literal interpretation of the fourth exemption: it refers to the coward, those "unable to stand in the battle-ranks and see a drawn sword."[84] ...

An alternative, and more cogent, explanation is suggested by Rabbi Akiba himself. In another formulation, [he] maintains that the mention in [the] fourth exemption of *yareh*, or "fearful," refers to the coward, while the additional reference, *rakh halevav*, or "fainthearted," is to the compassionate. He who is "hero among heroes, powerful among the most powerful, but who at the same time is merciful—let him return."[85] ... Whatever the case, the inclusiveness of this formulation of the exemption effectively dismisses the need for determining genu-

81. [Michael Walzer (b. 1935) is an American theorist of political ethics, nationalism, and tolerance.]

82. Michael Walzer, "The Obligation to Die for the State," in *Obligations: Essays on Disobedience, War, and Citizenship* (Cambridge, MA: Harvard University Press, 1970), 97, 98.

83. *Sotah* 44a.

84. *Sotah* 44a.

85. Tosefta, *Sotah* 7:14.

ine cowardice. Indeed, it seems to recognize the difficulty in determining the real motivations of those not wanting to fight as against their stated reasons for not wanting to do so. Both the cowardly (or those fearful for their own lives) *and* the compassionate (or those fearful for the lives of others) are thus exempted. Such an argument, it may be noted, is even more radical than that of Hobbes. In his theory, only the genuinely cowardly—men of "feminine courage"—are esteemed to flee from fighting "without injustice."[86] As Rabbi Akiba appreciated, the fourth exemption is far more accommodating. It provides wide, almost open, opportunity to exempt oneself from duty on the battlefield.

But if the rabbinic interpreters recognized this, they were also moved to constrain its effects. This was done chiefly in the classification of biblical wars. The rabbis asked to which wars the exemptions applied. Except for one response where the terms are differently employed (entailing a peripheral dispute), the sages replied: "To discretionary wars [*milhamot reshut*], but in wars commanded by the Torah [*milhamot mitzvah*] all go forth, even a bridegroom from his chamber and a bride from her canopy."[87] This interpretation has stood as the more authoritative....

Compared with that of the classic Western thinkers, the Jewish approach to the question of the obligation to die for the state undoubtedly appears complicated and involved. Most of the complexities, however, reduce to a few simple principles, and these are what lend the Jewish approach its coherence and importance....

It is perhaps not too bold to claim that the Jewish approach to the issue of the obligation to fight suggests a certain "theory," what might be called a theory of "graded ultimate obligation." At the general level are the gradations in obligation that Judaism posits *between* categories of war. These "commanded" wars, in which the legal and conventional pressures upon the individual to fight are extremely compelling, to "discretionary" wars, where, because of the process by which the so-called military exemptions take effect, each individual determines for himself whether he will assume an obligation to fight....

Judaism, then, effectively grades the obligation to fight from its strongest to its weakest conditions. So whether or not there is an obligation to die for the state is a question not susceptible of decisive resolution in the sense of being either (and always) one way or the other: it is a question whose answer must depend

---

86. Thomas Hobbes, *Leviathan* (New York: Penguin, 1982), chap. 21, p. 115.
87. *Sotah* 44b.

on the context in which the problem presents itself. And the lines of division here do not, or do not only, fall between just and unjust wars. They also, and chiefly, fall between different kinds of just wars. The overall effect is to preserve the individual's freedom to protect his life and property in all but the most critical war situations....

In this fashion does Judaism overcome the dilemma plaguing Western theories of the obligation to die? Against those liberal theorists who assert that the state exists for the sake of individual purposes, Judaism asserts that individuals can, at critical times, be rightly asked to subordinate their personal lives to the shared life and values of the community. And against those theorists who argue that, because the state represents a shared life and set of values, the individual owes his life to it, Judaism asserts that, in all but the most critical war situations, the individual has his own life to lead and his own choices to make. By not assuming the superiority of the individual or of the collective in terms of the state's foundation or purpose, Judaism is, consistently, able to safeguard the "lives" of both. The state gives way to the freedom of the individual, as the freedom of the individual gives way to the survival of the state.

MICHAEL BROYDE

Just Wars, Just Battles, and Just Conduct in Jewish Law: Jewish Law Is Not a Suicide Pact!

Michael Broyde (b. 1964) is a legal scholar and professor at the Emory University School of Law as well as an ordained Orthodox rabbi. Much of his work considers the relationship between law and religion, as well as questions in Jewish law and ethics.

From "Just Wars, Just Battles, and Just Conduct in Jewish Law: Jewish Law Is Not a Suicide Pact!" in War and Peace in the Jewish Tradition, *eds. Lawrence Schiffman and Joel B. Wolowelsky (New York: The Michael Scharf Publication Trust of the Yeshiva University Press, 2004), 1–43.*

This article reviews Jewish law's attitude to an area of modern social behavior that "law" as an institution has shied away from regulating, and which "ethics" as a discipline has failed to successfully regulate: war. In this area, as in many others, the legal and the ethical are freely combined in the Jewish tradition. Unlike Jewish law's rules concerning "regular" war, regulations concerning those biblical wars as those against Amalek and the Seven Nations ... were designed to be used solely in the initial period of Jewish conquest of the land of Israel or solely in circumstances where God's direct divine commandment to the Jewish nation was clear. Thus, "Jewish law" as used in this article refers to that time period when direct visible divine direction in and interaction with the world has ceased.... Normative Jewish law confines itself to a discussion of what to do when the active divine presence is no longer in the world, and thus normative rules are in effect....

The initial question that needs to be addressed when discussing battlefield ethics is whether the rules for these situations differ from all other applications of Jewish ethics, or if "battlefield ethics" are merely an application of the general rules of Jewish ethics to the combat situation.... The Jewish tradition divides "armed conflict" into three different categories: obligatory war, permissible war, and societal applications of the "pursuer" rationale. Each of these situations comes with different licenses.... Battlefield ethics based on the pursuer model are simply a generic application of the [general] field of Jewish ethics relating to stopping one who is an evildoer from harming (killing) an innocent person. ... The touchstone rules of self-defense according to Jewish law are fourfold: Even when self-defense is mandatory or permissible and one may kill a person or group of people who are seeking to kill one who is innocent, one may not:

1. Kill an innocent third party to save a life;
2. Compel a person to risk his or her life to save the life of another;
3. Kill the pursuer after his or her evil act is over as a form of punishment.
4. Use more force than minimally needed.

These are generic rules of Jewish law derived from different Talmudic sources and methodologically unrelated to "war" as an institution. Thus, the application of the rules of this type of "armed conflict" would resemble an activity by a police force rather than an activity by an army. Only the most genteel of modern armies can function in accordance with these rules.

On the other hand, both the situation of obligatory war and authorized [permissible] war are not merely a further extrapolation of the principles of "self-defense" or "pursuer." There are ethical liberalities (and strictures) associated with the battlefield setting that have unique ethical and legal rules unrelated to other fields of Jewish law or ethics. They permit the killing of a fellow human being in situations where that action—but for the permissibility of war—would be murder.... Nearly all of the preliminary requirements to a permissible war are designed to remove noncombatants, civilians, and others who do not wish to fight from the battlefield.

* * *

Two basic texts form Jewish law's understanding of the duties society must undertake before a battle may be fought. The biblical text states:

> When you approach a city to do battle with it, you shall call to it in peace. And if they respond in peace and they open the city to you, all the people in the city shall pay taxes to you and be subservient. And if they do not make peace with you, you shall wage war with them and you may besiege them. (Deut. 20:10–12)

Although unstated in the text, it is apparent that while one need not engage in negotiations over the legitimacy of one's goals, one must explain what one is seeking through this military action and what military goals are (and are not) sought.[88] . . .

Maimonides . . . states:

> One does not wage war with anyone in the world until one seeks peace with him. This is true both of authorized and obligatory wars, as it says [in the Torah], "When you approach a city to wage war, you shall [first] call to it in peace." If they respond positively and accept the seven Noahide commandments, one may not kill any of them and they shall pay tribute.[89] . . .

The obligation to seek peace in the manner outlined above applies to battles between armies when no civilian population is involved. Jewish law requires an additional series of overtures for peace and surrender in situations where the military activity involves attacking cities populated by civilians. . . .

Maimonides codifies a number of specific rules of military ethics, all based on Talmudic sources:

> When one surrounds a city to lay siege to it, it is prohibited to surround it from four sides; only three sides are permissible. One must leave a place for inhabitants to flee for all those who wish to abscond to save their life.[90]

---

  88. See, e.g., Numbers 21:21–24, where the Jewish people clearly promised to limit their goals in return for a peaceful passage through the lands belonging to Sihon and the Amorites.
  89. Maimonides, *Hilkhot Melakhim* 6:1.
  90. *Hilkhot Melakhim* 6:7.

Essentially Jewish law completely rejects the notion of a "siege" as that term is understood by military tacticians and contemporary articulators of international law.... Secular law and morals allow the use of the civilians as pawns in the siege. *The Jewish tradition prohibited that and mandated that noncombatants who wished to flee must be allowed to flee the scene of the battle.* (I would add, however, that I do not understand Maimonides's words literally. It is not surrounding the city on all four sides that is prohibited—rather, it is the preventing of the *outflow of civilians or soldiers* who are seeking to flee. Of course, Jewish law would allow one to stop the *inflow of supplies* to a besieged city through this fourth side.)

This approach solves another difficult problem according to Jewish law: the role of the "innocent" civilian in combat. Since the Jewish tradition accepts that civilians (and soldiers who are surrendering) are always entitled to flee from the scene of the battle, it would logically follow that all who remain voluntarily are classified as combatants, since the opportunity to leave is continuously present. ... Essentially, the Jewish tradition feels that innocent civilians should do their very best to remove themselves from the battlefield, and those who remain are not so innocent. If one voluntarily stays in a city that is under siege, one assumes the mantle of a combatant.[91] ...

The unintentional and undesired slaying of innocent civilians who involuntarily remain behind seems to this author to be the one "killing" activity that is permissible in Jewish law in war situations that would not be permissible in the pursuer/self-defense situations. Just like Jewish law permits one to send one's own soldiers out to combat (without their consent) to perhaps be killed, Jewish law would allow the unintentional killing of innocent civilians as a necessary (but undesired) by-product of the moral license of war.

In many ways, this provides guidance into the ethical issues associated with a modern airplane- (and long range artillery-) based war. Air warfare greatly expands the "kill zone" of combat and . . . tends to inevitably result in the death of civilians. The tactical aims of air warfare appear to be fourfold: to destroy specific enemy military targets, to destroy the economic base of the enemy's war-making capacity, to randomly terrorize civilian populations, and to retaliate for other atrocities by the enemy to one's own home base and thus deter such conduct in the future by the enemy.

> 91. Although I have seen no modern Jewish law authorities who state this, I would apply this rule in modern combat situations to all civilians who remain voluntarily in the locale of the war in a way that facilitates combat.

The first of these goals is within the ambit of that which is permissible, since civilian deaths are unintentional. The same would appear to be true about the second, providing that the targets are genuine economic targets related to the economic base needed to wage the war and the death of civilians are not directly desired. It would appear that the third goal is not legitimate absent the designation of "compulsory" or "obligatory" war. The final goal . . . could perhaps provide some sort of justification for certain types of conduct in combat that would otherwise be prohibited, although its detailed analysis in Jewish law is beyond the scope of this paper.

MELISSA WEINTRAUB
Does Torah Permit Torture?

Melissa Weintraub (b. 1975) is co-founder and CEO of Resetting the Table, an organization dedicated to countering political polarization in the United States. She also founded Encounter, an organization dedicated to strengthening Jewish leadership on the Israeli-Palestinian conflict. She received rabbinic ordination from the Jewish Theological Seminary.

From "Does Torah Permit Torture?," *The Review of Faith & International Affairs* (Summer 2007): 3–8.

Guantanamo, circa 2002: Men are in dog leashes, being forced to perform dog tricks and wear lacy lingerie on their heads. Female interrogators—dressed in skimpy miniskirts—are straddling the laps of traditional Muslim men, rubbing their breasts against their backs, and wiping feigned menstrual blood on their faces. Some detainees are being subjected to dogs to scare them, others bombarded with painfully bright lights and loud violent music, left naked in isolation, hooded, spat on, urinated on, exposed to extreme cold to the point of induced hypothermia, and deprived of food and sleep.[92]

Torture joins slavery as the practice most unanimously condemned in international law as well as the domestic laws of most nations, including the United States. . . . May torture—or its milder cognates—ever be deemed permissible?

---

92. See, e.g., "Detainees Accuse Female Interrogators: Pentagon Inquiry Is Said to Confirm Muslims' Accounts of Sexual Tactics at Guantánamo," *Washington Post*, February 10, 2005, A01. . . .

Is torture an unseemly but necessary component of the state's right and responsibility to protect its citizens from terror?

In this essay I will interrogate torture's rationales from the perspective of Jewish ethics in order to argue for an absolute proscription against torture. My essay will pivot on two principles in Jewish law, twin commandments granted trumping priority relative to many other religious obligations, namely: (1) the imperative to honor the dignity of the human person, viewed as imbued with God's image; and (2) the kindred, and at times conflicting obligation to defend human life at great cost....

The most fundamental assumption of Jewish ethics is that there is something intrinsically and ineradicably sacred about the human person, the human body and spirit as such. The ontological fact of our collective creation in God's image enjoins us to moral behavior—commands us to work actively to honor the lives and dignity of other human beings. This idea originates in the first chapter of the Book of Genesis, in the idea that the human being is created *b'tzelem Elohim*, in the Image of God.

On the basis of this assumption, Judaism formulates a prohibition against violations of human dignity....

Human dignity is arguably the foundational and aspirational ideal of Jewish law. The rabbis grant human dignity the power to displace other religious commandments (*kvod habriyot docheh lo taaseh*). The injunction to avoid humiliating or contemptuous behavior takes legal precedence over all other rabbinic verdicts.[93] ...

What are some of the practical implications of this lofty principle?

1. *We are not to debase the human body.* ...
2. *We are not to shame others through demeaning speech, threats, or insults.* ... Shaming, teaches the Talmud, constitutes an irreparable wrong ... because it permanently injures another's personhood rather than his replaceable property.[94] ...

The Israeli Supreme Court extends these halakhic concepts to contemporary, concrete cases involving the rights and dignity of prisoners.... The Israeli High Court has determined in several landmark decisions that prisoners must be provided with all of their basic human needs and treated as civilized people:

93. See B. T. *Berakhot* 19b, *Shabbat* 81a–b, and *Megillah* 3b....
94. B. T. *Bava Metzia* 58b–59a.

Just as the [Talmudic] rabbis were bold enough to waive all prohibitions instituted by them where necessary to preserve human dignity, [our law] should be cautious in sacrificing human dignity on the altar of any other requirement whatsoever.[95]...

Torture cannot be repudiated on grounds of human dignity without reckoning with the other and still weightier moral and legal override of Jewish tradition....

Surely, goes the Jewish counter-argument, lost lives would hurt more than the bending of our other principles? Even were the law to take into account the dignity of the interrogated as *absolute*, might we not also be compelled to *suspend* this noble ideal in favor of the greater moral imperative of protecting innocent life?[96]

The sanctity of human life is perhaps Judaism's most preoccupying value. Life, the tradition teaches, is *kinyan hakadosh baruch hu*, the property of God rather than of human beings....

Jewish law recognizes not only a *right* to self-defense, but a positive *duty* to protect endangered life, elevating the 'Good Samaritan' principle to the status of a legal requirement.[97]...

Given the overwhelming sanctity of life, however, the rabbis recognize the enormous danger of providing a legal override to the prohibition against force, and so place stringent limitations on the application of the right to self-defense and duty of other-defense.

1. *Force must be the minimum necessary to thwart a grave harm*....

2. *Force must be a spontaneous reaction to a situation of present danger, not a premeditated act of preemption or revenge*.... One may cause harm in self/other-defense only in a moment of unavoidable urgency, when life is in immediate danger.[98]

---

95. Justice Haim Cohn, *Katlan et al. v. The Prison Service et. al.* (1980), 34(3) PD 294 at 305–7. Cited and translated in Nahum Rakover, *Modern Applications of Jewish Law* (Jerusalem: Library of Jewish Law, 1992), 199–202.

96. See Michael Broyde, "Jewish Law and Torture," *Jewish Week*, July 7, 2006.

97. See M. *Sanhedrin* 8:7; B. T. *Sanhedrin* 73ff; *Shulchan Aruch, Choshen Mishpat* 425:1–2. Rashi and Tosafot, ad. loc. *Sanhedrin* 73a and Maimonides, Mishneh Torah, *Hilkhot Rotzeah* 1:6....

98. See, e.g., Rambam, Mishneh Torah, *Hilkhot Gneiva* 9:7–10; Resp. Maharam bar Barukh cited in Mordekhai, *Baba Kamma* 196; and Rashi, ad. loc., Exod. 22:1.

3. *One must be reasonably certain that a threat is real, and force necessary to repel it.* . . .

Jewish law requires that violence be used in self/other-defense only as an expression of unavoidable urgency, when life is in immediate peril. Such a standard would allow the killing of a suicide bomber strapped with explosives, or return of enemy fire in battle. It would not permit deliberate, routine, premeditated violence in the cool, calculated conditions of the interrogation room in which a subject is at one's mercy and poses no immediate threat to life.

But, what about a true ticking bomb case, one might ask? The ticking bomb scenario presents . . . the following hypothetical: a captured fanatic has hidden an explosive in the heart of a major metropolis, set to go off within hours . . . and the nonviolent devices of their most expert interrogators have not yielded enough information to locate and disable the bomb. . . .

These circumstances are unlikely even within the realm of the thought experiment in which they seem exclusively to reside. . . .

In Algeria, during the French occupation, in Israel and the occupied territories, and now in Iraq and Afghanistan, defense of torture under supposed ticking bomb conditions has invariably opened the door to the routinization of torture. Once advanced preparation and legal authorization for the ticking bomb exception occurred, torture became entrenched as an administrative practice and customary procedure for interrogation and governance . . . as an ongoing and somewhat indiscriminate regime of cruel and dehumanizing treatment.

BETH BERKOWITZ

Execution and Invention: Death Penalty Discourse in Early Rabbinic and Christian Cultures

Beth Berkowitz (b. 1970) is the Ingeborg Rennert Chair of Jewish studies at Barnard College. Her research and teaching focus on classical rabbinic literature and its social impact, as well as Jewish difference, animal studies, and biblical interpretation.

From *Execution and Invention: Death Penalty Discourse in Early Rabbinic and Christian Cultures* (New York: Oxford University Press, 2006), 153–54, 159–65, 179.

Chapter 6: Paradoxes of Power:
"The Way That the Kingdom Does It"

A criminal condemned to death in the Roman Empire might, among other penalties, end up either decapitated, exposed to wild beasts, crucified, burned alive, or condemned to be a gladiator, depending on his or her social status and on the nature of the crime....

Philo, Josephus, and the rabbis describe Roman capital punishments being inflicted on Jews.... The rabbis tell stories of being martyred at the hands of Rome and also legislate for the scenario of Jews fighting in the arena. There is also the famous story of the execution of the Jew named Jesus. That Roman execution was a serious concern for late antique Jews is plentifully evidenced.

That being said, we can ask: Did the Jewish experience of Roman execution shape the rabbis' own laws of execution?... I will show that the discourse of rabbinic execution was engaged with Roman execution in both hidden and manifest ways. In one rabbinic text, the rabbis break into a dispute over whether they may borrow the Roman method of decapitation....

I borrow this approach from James Scott, whose postcolonial theory will be threaded through these interpretations.... While it may often appear that colonized peoples obediently submit to imperial authority, these writers uncover the appropriation and resistance that is often embedded within postures of submission, what Scott calls a "hidden transcript."[99] By looking at rabbinic law

---

99. See James C. Scott, *Domination and the Arts of Resistance: Hidden Transcripts* (New Haven: Yale University Press, 1990), 70–107.

as a "hidden transcript," hidden from Rome but also hidden from many other Jews, I will show that in their laws of execution, the rabbis attempt to reverse the conditions of Roman power and relative Jewish powerlessness, representing themselves as the agents of penal power. Moreover, the rabbis reverse the terms of power, shaping their executions both to resemble Roman executions but also to be their opposite....

The convergence of rabbinic execution with Roman execution becomes explicit in the death penalty of decapitation, the third of the four rabbinic death penalties.... Mishnah *Sanhedrin* 7:3 offers a dispute between Rabbi Judah and the sages about how the penalty of decapitation should be carried out. Which method of decapitation constitutes a "disgrace" (*nivul*) is at the heart of their argument:

> The commandment of those to be decapitated: They would chop off his head with a sword the way that the kingdom (*malkhut*) does. Rabbi Judah says: This is a disgrace. Rather, they should lay his head down on the block and cut it with an axe. They said to him: There is no execution more disgraceful than that.

According to the sages, decapitation is to be done with a sword, like Roman decapitation (as the sages conceive it). Declaring the sages' method to be a disgrace, Rabbi Judah proposes a different method that uses the tools of the butcher: The criminal is laid down onto the chopping block and his head cut with an axe. The sages respond in kind to Rabbi Judah's method, calling it more disgraceful than their own....

The main textual ambiguity of this mishnah has to do with the sages' description of decapitation, "the way that the kingdom does": To which kingdom do the sages refer? ... The entire phrase is used just one other time in tannaitic sources, in *Sifre* Deuteronomy, where it almost certainly refers to a Roman method of execution:

> Is it possible that they hang him alive the way that kingdom does? The Torah teaches: "[If a man is guilty of a capital offense] and is put to death, and you impale him on a stake..." (Deut. 21:22)

Hanging as a means of death, the practice of the "kingdom," is shown to be excluded by the Torah. "The way that the kingdom does" functions as a reference to a non-Jewish method of execution, likely Roman crucifixion....

Not only the referent but also the function of the phrase is ambiguous. "The way that the kingdom does" may be functioning as mere description, a handy tool of familiar reference, or as a statement of derivation, to indicate that the rabbis borrowed Rome's distinctive method....

Homi Bhabha's[100] writing on mimicry and James Scott's work on hidden transcripts and particularly strategies of reversal help to make sense of this nod to Rome. The sages seem to be mimicking Rome.... While some scholars do acknowledge that the sages seem to be borrowing Roman decapitation, others assert either the irrelevance or ambiguity of the key phrase in the Mishnah, "the way that the kingdom does."...

But the sages have good reason to borrow from Rome, if only to describe their form of decapitation. Under the Roman penal system, decapitation was a relatively honorable way to die, reserved generally for the upper-class condemned....

Does this emulation of Roman execution suggest that the rabbis have perversely internalized the images of Roman power to which they were subject? This model of a subordinate group's relationship to the dominant culture has been described by such terms as false consciousness, hegemony, and naturalization.[101] But Bhabha's notion of mimicry allows us to understand such instances in a more complex way, as a potentially subversive strategy.... The rabbinic mimicry at work here disrupts Roman authority by displacing it, as Bhabha continues: "I want to turn to this process by which the look of surveillance returns as the displacing gaze of the disciplined..." The sages of the Mishnah effect such a displacement, borrowing Rome's sword for their own executions, representing a reversal of the axes of power. The Mishnah creates an executioner that looks like the Roman one but with a rabbinic face. Rather than understanding rabbinic decapitation either as an unexamined borrowing from Rome or as totally unrelated to it... we can understand it as something more, as an appropriation of power.

Such a reversal frequently characterizes the "hidden transcripts" of dominated groups, according to Scott.... Scott makes this distinction between the public and the private transcript in order to explain why subordinate groups so often seem to embrace their servile status.... In their private life, however, "every subordinate group creates, out of its ordeal, a 'hidden transcript' that represents a critique of power spoken behind the back of the dominant."[102]

---

100. [Homi Bhabha (b. 1949) is a theorist of postcolonialism at Harvard University.]

101. See James C. Scott, *Domination and the Arts of Resistance: Hidden Transcripts* (New Haven, CT: Yale University Press, 1990), 70–107.

102. Scott, *Domination*, xii.

One strategy of critique is reversal. Scott brings the example of Aggy, an American woman slave in the antebellum South. Mary Livermore, a white governess from New England, describes Aggy's reaction after the master has just given Aggy's daughter a beating in Aggy's presence. After the master leaves the kitchen, Aggy turns to Mary and vents her fury: "Thar's a day a-comin'! Thar's a day a-comin'! ... I hear the rumblin ob de chariots! I see de flashin ob de guns! White folks blood is a runnin on the ground like a ribber, an de dead's heaped up dat high!" ... Aggy's speech and that of the sages share something: each of them draws on the cultural materials of the powerful in order to empower themselves. Just as Aggy adapts the apocalyptic language of American Christianity, so do the sages adapt the form of Roman execution, each in an effort to adapt the language of power and, in so doing, to challenge it.

The toseftan parallel to this Mishnah deals with the dangers of mimicry, however, asking: Is it possible that a reversal can leave everything exactly the same? The Tosefta expresses anxiety about whether rabbinic mimicry of Romans can leave the rabbis looking too much like them:

> Rabbi Judah says: Behold it says, "And love your fellow as yourself" (Lev. 19:18)—choose for him a nice execution. How do they do this for him? One lays his head on the block and cuts it off with an axe. They said to him: There is no execution more disgraceful than this. He said to them: Of course there is no execution more disgraceful than this, but rather, [one must do it this way] because of "nor shall you follow their laws." (Lev. 18:3)[103]

The dispute between the sages and Rabbi Judah, as it is represented here, proves to be not only about the problem of bodily dignity but also about the problem of following "their laws," prohibited by Leviticus 18:3. In Rabbi Judah's view as the Tosefta represents it, the sages are not cleverly constructing rabbinic power out of the cultural materials of Rome ... they are forgetting what it means to be a rabbi in the first place! ... The real reason (according to the *Tosefta*) for Rabbi Judah's disapproval of the sword is not, as we might have thought from the Mishnah, that it violates the dignity of the criminal, but, rather, that it compromises Jewish uniqueness. In this toseftan expansion, Rabbi Judah is willing to surrender human dignity if it preserves the boundaries of Judaism....

103. B. T. *Sanhedrin* 9:11 (Moshe S. Zuckermandel, Tosefta: *Al Pi Kitve Yad Erfurt u-Viyenah* [Jerusalem: Wahrmann, 1963], 429–30). This is the reading of the Vienna manuscript and the first printed edition of the Tosefta (as well as the *baraita* in both Talmuds)....

Rabbi Judah worries that in the sages' resistance to Rome they will ultimately come to resemble them. The reversal of power will really be no reversal, since the executioner will look exactly the same....

In the argument between Rabbi Judah and the sages, as it appears in the Mishnah and in various *baraitot*, is found both the drive toward resistance but also anxiety about the effects of resistance. These opposing forces represent a dilemma posed by the conditions of imperial domination, a dilemma whose terms might look something like this:

> *If rabbinic power is to look nothing like Roman power, then it is not power.*
> *If rabbinic power is to look too much like Roman power, then it is not rabbinic.*

The sages embrace the first horn of this dilemma, Rabbi Judah the second. But then each is laid bare to a critique from the other side. It is this problem with which the rabbis are contending: How do they assert their authority when they have so little of it within the status system of imperial Rome? ...

In their resistance to Rome—either through wholesale rejection or through subversive mimicry—the rabbis speak not only for themselves, but they try to speak for the entire Jewish population of the Roman Empire.... They creatively address problems of Jewish identity: how to be an oppressed minority and survive, maintaining commitment to the Bible and to Jewish observance in a pagan world. They capture the struggle for self-determination that characterizes colonized groups: the struggle to assert distinctiveness but also to co-opt sameness, to shun the colonizer, and also to mimic him.... The rabbinic laws of criminal execution, in their resistance to Rome and in their disputes about the best way to resist, display the charisma of the rabbis, in whose conversations the rabbis hoped the Jews of the Roman Empire would be able to recognize their own concerns.

NADAV S. BERMAN

Jewish Law, Techno-Ethics, and Autonomous Weapon Systems: Ethical-Halakhic Perspectives

Nadav S. Berman (b. 1978) is a research fellow in the faculty of law at the University of Haifa. His research deals with Jewish philosophy and thought, particularly pragmatism, Jewish–Christian relations, and the ethics of technology.

From "Jewish Law, Techno-Ethics, and Autonomous Weapon Systems: Ethical-Halakhic Perspectives," *Jewish Law Association Studies*, XXIX: The Impact of Technology, Science, and Knowledge, eds. Elisha S. Ancselovits, Elliot N. Dorff, and Amos Israel-Vleeschhouwer (Forest Hills, NY: Jewish Law Association, 2020), 91–124.

Jewish law and its research are hardly keeping pace with the acceleration of technological advancement and with emerging ethical technological dilemmas (or *techno*-ethics, as distinguished from bioethics).... This discourse gap is especially significant in the case of Autonomous Weapon Systems.... The objective of the present article is to help to fill in that lacuna, and to examine the halakhic-moral status of AWS, by clarifying the humane foundations of the philosophy of technology (that can, in its turn, be enriched by Judaism, or by Jewish law and values)....

AWS are robots of various forms that have the technical capacity, by means of advanced technologies, such as AI, GPS, and facial recognition, to approach targets, identify them, and then harm or destroy them without human involvement.... At first glance, this may not seem qualitatively different than the ancient development of the bow and arrow. Both allowed the distancing of the weapon from the combatant and opened the door for indiscriminate shooting. To consider modern weapons, armies already use land and naval mines, hand grenades, canons, and bombs.... The difference is that AWS, as AI-based inventions, possess a proactive capacity to "decide" whom to kill anytime and anywhere....

It may thus come as a surprise, in the modern intellectual atmosphere, to propose that ... universal concerns about AWS may have some roots in biblical sources. Nonetheless, early Jewish texts do provide a grounding for these concerns, and ethical principles that may instruct us concerning new conditions. The first of these ethical principles is createdness in the image of God (or *imago*

Dei). Its main ramification in the present case is the prohibition of unjustified killing. Based on the biblical narrative of createdness in the image of God (Gen. 1:27), M. *Sanhedrin* 4:5 aptly states that the unnecessary killing of one human being is equal to the destruction of the entirety of humanity. An additional relevant biblical principle is responsibility, which has tremendous ramifications for the present study: "Neither shalt thou stand idly by the blood of thy neighbor, I am the Lord" (Lev. 19:16); "Do what is right and good" (Deut. 6:18); and "Justice, justice shalt thou pursue, that thou mayest live" (Deut. 16:20). In addition, biblical narrative expresses legal teachings. In other words, although the Bible lacks a *systematic* treatise of war ethics (and of many other topics), it contains a relevant ethical orientation....

The theoretical disputes about the morality of AWS, as revisited above, are not enough to conceive the high socio-ethical stakes of AWS. We take it for granted nowadays that we constantly see human beings, talk to them, and often care about them. But that might change radically if human agency and interpersonal trust are fully replaced with mediating machines, and if we will ignore the inherent quest of many political rulers to bypass human agency, or to be "liberated" from their democratic dependency upon it. To appreciate these stakes properly, there is a need to reclaim the scope of halakhic reasoning—to include the faculty of moral imagination, which is a profound aggadic implement. Put differently, narratives may help figure out profound ethical implications that would otherwise be latent. This can be illustrated regarding AWS through two stories in the biblical book of Samuel, (1) the killing of the priests of Nob by King Saul, and (2) the killing of Uriah the Hittite by King David. These cases shed light on the dangers of dehumanization in the public-political sphere, a risk that AWS might intensify.

* * *

In the first case, of the killing of the priests of Nob (1 Sam. 22), King Saul is presented as a paranoid ruler who suspects everyone. He orders his immediate guardians to kill Aḥimelekh and the priests, but they refuse.... Saul, however, finds an alternative—Do'eg the Edomite... Do'eg's willingness to kill the priests of Nob manifests the complex nature of delegation in Jewish law.... It manifests the critical role played by the messenger/executor himself.... The messenger carries a direct responsibility, not only the sender. The problem in the case of AWS, however, is that *there is no* distinct or identifiable sender (this, in other words, is the "problem of the many hands"). The autonomous messenger seemingly "devours" by itself, and responsibility cannot be clearly assigned to any specific person or moral entity.... [It] makes no sense to punish a robot (in any foreseen future), since it has no personality and no embodied subjectivity.

A primary lesson from Saul's story is that one of the most important features of a moral soldier is his (or her) moral ability to say "no—that is an illegal command and I will not, I cannot, obey it."[104] Military commands may or may not be immoral, but being able to refuse—as in Saul's guardians—is necessary in order to consider a soldier an ethical agent.... The ethical concern could be termed, in the context of AI military ethics, as the *Conscientious Objection Versus Commandability* ... problem: the inherent concern about AWS is that the possibility for conscientious objection—which is of profound halakhic significance—is in deep tension with the *commandability* attempted by the programmers of the AWS. It is hard to imagine that such an algorithmic component—an option of a "conscientious objection"—would, and in fact even *could*, be programmed. ... Human ethical behavior cannot, in any foreseen future, be duplicated in non-living creatures, "smart" as those might be.... As long as this specific problem ... is not adequately settled by programmers and ethicists, it would be hard to assign halakhic legitimacy to AWS, or to killer robots.

The story of the killing the priests of Nob is instructive about the ethical role of human agency, which at the same time is telling about the importance of conscientious objection. Both moral requirements—moral agency and refutability—cast a shadow over the ethicality of AWS.

* * *

A second biblical case that is instructive for examining AWS (and techno-ethics more broadly) is the murder of Uriah the Hittite by King David, for the latter to acquire Bathsheba as his own wife (2 Sam. 11). In this case, there is a similar abuse of political power. However, the abuse of power is here camouflaged, rather than made explicit as in Saul's murder of Nob's priests.... King David's agency-manipulation is instructive for reflecting on the ethical problems of AWS. It leads to David's final letter to Joab, comforting him by asserting that *ki khazoh vekhazeh tokhal haḥerev*: "The sword devours sometimes one way and

---

104. This possibility of refusal is an internal and integral part of the IDF ethics. On the 1994 "Ethical Code," see A. Kasher, *Military Ethics* [Hebrew] (Tel Aviv, 1996), 231–38. On the later 2000 Ru'ab Tsahal document, see the IDF website (www.idf.il). It is questionable if AWS are permissible by this important ethical code....

sometimes another" (2 Sam. 11:25).... The singularity of biblical narrative, here as elsewhere, is in the moral critique of its human figures. In the "poor man's lamb" parable (2 Sam. 12:7), Nathan the prophet and the biblical narrator make it clear that David is *personally* responsible for Uriah's death. The hiddenness of the production of the power chain does not eliminate David's culpability for the crime that he performed. This carries a lesson in regard to the targeting of *enemy* combatants by AWS too. On the one hand, war *is* the place where you defeat your enemy by sophistication and deception. On the other hand, the reader of 2 Samuel 11 is reminded that remoteness from the battlefield does not excuse one from responsibility for the chain of events that one has set in motion.

Which halakhic-ethical conclusion could be made about AWS, based on this second biblical episode? ... [A] complete outsourcing of military activity to robots will practically put humans (and human agency) "out of the loop." It is noteworthy in this regard that both Saul and David are indeed taking human agency seriously, even if they try to bypass and manipulate it.... For in an age of "asymmetrical wars," and facing the shrinking gap between the *civilian* realm and the *military* battlefield (in Israel this is especially felt), AWS might bear devastating consequences....

Technology plays a central role in Israeli (and global) economy, culture, and self-esteem. Many Israelis have ethical sensitivities regarding various techno-ethical issues, and care about their traditional ethical commitments, but there still is a relative rabbinic silence regarding AWS, even though AI scholars and ethicists worldwide have deep concerns about it. The aim of this article was to point out the relevance of Jewish tradition for the debate over AWS by recalling some established ethical halakhic values and norms, and by invoking and provoking the reader's ethical-political imagination.

Addressing AWS requires an interdisciplinary discussion of the kind that I tried to provide here. For AWS are a product of technology, but cannot be treated properly on a purely naturalistic basis if Jewish law and ethics were to be our métier. By arguing that it is inherently problematic to grant machines the legitimacy to make decisions on matters of life and death, contemporary ethicists echo the imperative of human agency required by Genesis 9:6.

13 | Environment

Conventional Jewish environmental concepts and ethics emerge from the creation stories found at the beginning of the Torah. The first story theorizes God created the natural world nearly *ex nihilo* and granted humanity the right to rule and master that world with impunity (see Gen. 1:26 and 28). The second creation story posits a more restrained relationship between humanity and the rest of creation; here, humans are to serve and guard God's handiwork (see Gen. 2:5 and 15) and abide by rules that circumscribe human activity—specifically consumption—lest they face severe consequences (Gen. 2:16–18). Such sources gave rise to anthropocentric ethics, a way of thinking about the natural world that situates human interests at the core when tough decisions need to be made. When studied deeply, principles like *bal tashchit* (do not wantonly destroy, built upon the laws of warfare as found in Deut. 20) and *tza'ar ba'alei chayim*[105] (do not cause unnecessary suffering to sentient creatures, a principle drawn from Deut. 22 and elsewhere) similarly encourage thinking about environmental issues from a human-centered vantage point. Another standard Jewish environmental ethic is more theocentric. This perspective draws from the prophets (e.g., Isa. 6:3) and writings (e.g., Prov. 16:4; Pss. 8:2–10 and 24:1) to frame that the natural world and its components exist within a godly context: they are God's and thus must be respected and protected. And here and there within the Torah, one also finds biocentric approaches that focus on protecting life's diversity and well-being (e.g., Lev. 19:19; Deut. 22:10).

Since the 1970s, concern about the environment—inclusive of terrestrial, aquatic, and atmospheric issues—has grown substantially. This increasing awareness of human-generated impacts on the land, sea, and air, through such activities as industry, infrastructure, agriculture, urbanization, and power generation, has revealed complex webs of interdependence and mutual vulnerabilities. Climate change in all its manifestations is perhaps the most multifaceted challenge facing civilization. Given their complexities, it should not be surprising that no singular approach to thinking about them suffices.

As the following selections demonstrate, ways of thinking about environmental

---

105. *For more on bal tashchit*, see the piece by Tanhum Yoreh in part 1, section 6; for more on *tza'ar ba'alei chayim*, see Aaron Gross in part 3, section 14.

issues diverge among contemporary Jewish ethicists. A minority follow the attitude articulated by rabbinic scholar Steven Schwarzschild[106] in the early 1980s that Jews are urban creatures all but disconnected from the natural world, and that what happens to the world "out there" matters relatively little and Jews ought not disturb themselves regarding it.[107] Generally, this dismissive attitude emerges from anthropological reflection on where Jews predominantly live and the kinds of work and concerns Jews engage in.

Unlike Schwarzschild, Michael Wyschogrod's piece here operates in a register closer to meta-ethics. He describes two major concepts—*lower ecology*, which worries about the deleterious consequences technology and modern civilization more generally have for humanity, and *upper ecology*, which insists on the holiness of nature. Urbanization, evolutionary thinking, and the doctrine of creation collide in fascinating ways when investigated through these concepts.

Other scholars, like Tanhum Yoreh (see part 1, section 6), hew more closely to Judaic texts and principles to enunciate both a descriptive account of Jewish action vis-à-vis the natural world and a prescription for what Jews today and tomorrow can and should do. In his piece below, Ariel Evan Mayse takes a similar approach and draws on rabbinic law—specifically *Nezikin*, or tort law—as a foundation for "constructing a progressive ethical voice on issues of environmental degradation."[108] The laws he studies pertain to damages caused by inanimate forces and objects coming into contact with stationary objects and damages due to proximity to inherently polluting businesses. When viewed together, these laws advocate collective stewardship, not just individual guardianship, of the environment.

As if echoing Schwarzschild's methods of observing where Jews live, Adrienne Krone, in her piece here, uses anthropology and sociology to describe and analyze the growth of what she calls the Jewish community farming movement, a subset of Jewish environmentalism. Such studies reveal deeply rooted Judaic interest in thinking carefully about land use, agricultural practices, animal husbandry, constructions of time, and justice. The major aim of the Jewish farming movement, Krone says, is to "reconnect them to Judaism, the earth, and its creatures."[109] The

---

106. Rabbi Steven Schwarzschild was a twentieth-century German-American theologian and philosopher who worked primarily on interfaith dialogue, ethics, and pacifism.

107. Steven Schwarzschild, "The Unnatural Jew," *Environmental Ethics*, 6 (Winter 1984): 347–62.

108. Ariel Evan Mayse, "Where Heaven and Earth Kiss: Jewish Law, Moral Reflection, and Environmental Ethics," *Journal of Jewish Ethics* 5, no. 1 (2019): 69.

109. Adrienne Krone, "Ecological Ethics in the Jewish Community Farming Movement,"

work Krone studies and her own work, too, illustrate what Hava Tirosh-Samuelson calls environmental pragmatism that eschews focusing on meta-ethical questions at the expense of real-world application.[110]

In her selection here, Hava Tirosh-Samuelson admits that it is difficult to align Jewish normative environmental ethics with academic environmental ethics, as the former is framed in covenantal theology. Tirosh-Samuelson uses the tools of intellectual history to show that the environmental laws and rules in the Jewish corpus raise no tension between deontology or duty and virtue. They command actions that cultivate character traits "conducive to the right action toward the environment."[111]

If for Krone Jewish environmentalism is a restorative effort to reconnect Jews to the close-to-nature foundations of Judaism, for Wyschogrod the movement occasions profound ambivalence. In his view, nature is no longer sacralized as it once was, and making it so again would be as untenable as continuing to damage the world in the ways civilization today does. Tirosh-Samuelson is more optimistic, since Jewish environmentalists are ready to "tell ourselves narratives that fuse scientific data and religious values . . . those that see humanity as part of the web of life, recognizing that human flourishing depends on the ability of other forms of life to flourish, as well."[112] For Mayse, profound wisdom awaits extraction from the Judaic legal tradition—itself intertwined with aggadic sources—that can empower contemporary Jews, individually and collectively, to address the increasingly urgent and complicated environmental issues facing humanity and the world at large.

in *Feasting and Fasting: The History and Ethics of Jewish Food*, eds. Aaron S. Gross, Jody Myers, and Jordan D. Rosenblum (New York: New York University Press, 2019), 275.

110. Hava Tirosh-Samuelson, *Religion and Environment: The Case of Judaism* (Telford, PA: Pandora Press, 2020), 43.

111. Tirosh-Samuelson, *Religion and Environment*, 91.

112. Tirosh-Samuelson, *Religion and Environment*, 262.

MICHAEL WYSCHOGROD

Judaism and the Sanctification of Nature

Michael Wyschogrod (1928–2015) was a Modern Orthodox theologian and philosopher of religion. He was born in Germany and his family fled the Nazis to America in 1939, where he eventually studied Talmud with Rabbi Joseph B. Soloveitchik at Yeshiva University concurrently while earning multiple degrees in philosophy and Christian theology at City College and Columbia University. He was concerned about Jewish-Christian relations and much of his scholarship challenged long-standing presumptions held by these traditions, such as the rejection of incarnation by Judaism and supersessionism by Christianity.

From "Judaism and the Sanctification of Nature," *The Melton Journal* 24 (Spring 1991): 5–7.

Let me begin my presentation with two concepts that I call the *lower* and the *upper ecologies*. *Lower ecology* is the attitude that claims that the development of technology in our culture has had consequences that are no longer acceptable. Technology has had a profound impact on our planet. Some of its effects are still not known about or even suspected. However, the record is clear. Problems we have not known about in the past have often later turned into severe dilemmas....

* * *

This is what I call the *lower ecology*, because it involves protecting human beings against the damage of technology. This lower ecology, interestingly enough, is already clearly found in the Bible, as in the famous biblical passage, "When you wage war against a city and you have to besiege it a long time in order to capture it, you must not destroy its trees, wielding the axe against them. You may eat of them, but you must not cut them down. Are trees of the field human to withdraw before you into the besieged city" (Deut. 20:19). The reason given by the Bible for this injunction is that man lives from the trees and it is thus not within man's rights, even in the context of war, to destroy them. This is the famous biblical commandment *bal tashchit*, which was later expanded by the rabbis to include all wasteful destruction of useful things, whether natural or man-made. Thus the purposeless destruction of objects that are potentially useful to man is made into a sin. However, what must be understood in this context is that it is the welfare of human beings that is the main concern. We must not do things that hurt human beings. Any action that will directly or indirectly hurt them is forbidden. This is the lower ecology, which is centered on human beings. It is clearly not being sufficiently cultivated, with the net result that human beings all over the world suffer needlessly.

* * *

The essence of *upper ecology* is a conviction about the holiness of nature. Upper ecology takes the human being out of the center of nature and puts nature itself there instead. Human beings are part of nature and, therefore, their attitude toward nature must be appropriate to that which is holy.

There is also an area in which both lower and upper ecology overlap. In that sense, upper ecology cooperates with lower ecology. There is also the conviction among followers of upper ecology that an attitude of nonsanctity toward nature is harmful to man. But this overlap ought not to be exaggerated, because for lower ecology, nature per se is not sacred. What *is* sacred, if anything, is the human being. And it is only when the violation of nature hurts human beings that action is called for. As such, for lower ecology nature is a means toward human welfare.

For upper ecology, it is nature that is holy. Upper ecology is "nature religion," primarily a religious attitude toward nature. The difference between lower and upper ecology emerges in its most dramatic form when the interests of nature and of human beings are in conflict. In relationship to the divine, upper ecology usually expresses itself as polytheism, the theological view that there are many gods. These gods dwell within the forces of nature and are symbols of these forces. Greek or Hindu polytheism is animated by experiencing the powers of nature as sacred and then personifying them in the form of gods. However, this personification should not be of ultimate seriousness, because, from the point of view of polytheistic religion, it is really the natural forces themselves that are divine....

Now let us look at the other side. Is nature holy? This is the most difficult question, since it is the desacralization of nature that makes science possible. This is best exemplified in the field of medicine. It was really only in the seventeenth and eighteenth centuries that the dissection of human beings began. Prior to that the human body, the dead body, was considered too sacred to investigate. Therefore, knowledge about the organs of the human body was very limited. But it is not only the human body that is at stake here, but all of nature. In order for science to gain control of nature, the gods dwelling in nature too have to be expelled. And when the gods were expelled, nature became an object of study rather than of worship. Thus, when you no longer worship something, you can put it under the knife, or under the microscope, and obtain objective knowledge about it. You do not do that to the sacred.

Notice how, even in our own day, that which remains sacred, namely the human body, is still handled with a great deal of deference; and when the potential for conflict exists between the demands of knowledge and the demands of the holy, as long as you are dealing with the living human body, the holy generally, though not always, wins. At times when the needs of medical experimentation prevail, you can see how the experimenter's urge to know pushes the sanctity of the human body out of the way. This happens even more so with the animal body, because the animal body has less of that sanctity. Thus, we have large scale animal experimentation, with all the violations committed in that context. One is caught in a very difficult dilemma: the tension between the sanctity of nature and the human right to rule over and manipulate nature.

I think that the root of this conflict is in the doctrine of creation. It makes a tremendous difference whether the paradigm of the holy is God, and the sanctity of nature is a reflection of nature's having been created by God, or whether the paradigm of the holy is nature itself as an uncreated entity. Uncreated nature is the deepest source of the sanctity of nature. The moment the doctrine of creation emerges, nature is no longer self-sufficient, no longer eternal, no longer perpetual, no longer all-engulfing. Nature is derived from an act of creation, and this act of creation confers upon it some of the sanctity of the Creator, but it does not confer upon nature an independent sanctity. Thus, the Creator can dispose of nature and destroy it. In my opinion, that is the symbolism of the flood. The very fact that there is a Master over nature undermines its essential and independent sanctity. . . .

However, human beings also have dimensions and characteristics that are deeply discontinuous with nature. The very fact that the human being knows about her death, that she anticipates her death, constitutes a profound break with nature. Perhaps even more important, however, is the relationship of the human being to the moral dimension. Human beings do not follow their natural needs. An animal, when hungry and when there is food available, eats. An animal, when sexually aroused and a partner is available, copulates. But a human being has many reasons to do these things or not to do them. The human being can resist every natural force. There is no instinct to which a human being cannot say no, be it hunger, sex, or life itself. Only the human being can commit suicide. Only the human being conducts hunger strikes. Only the human being, for whatever reason, can declare celibacy superior to the married state. There is no natural drive to which the human being cannot say, has not said, and will not say no. Indeed, this is the greatest glory of the human being and his greatest danger, because people can put dignity or self-respect or whatever other idea above life and in the process bring about the end of human existence on this planet. This is something animals cannot and will not do, because the urge to live is rooted in the nature of life, rooted in the nature of the biological; to that extent, the human being can totally reject the biological.

ARIEL EVAN MAYSE

Where Heaven and Earth Kiss: Jewish Law, Moral Reflection, and Environmental Ethics

Ariel Evan Mayse (b. 1985) received rabbinic ordination from Beit Midrash Har'el in Israel the same year he completed a PhD in Jewish studies at Harvard University. Now faculty of religious studies at Stanford University, Mayse works on early Hasidic literature, modern mysticism, the relation between spirituality and law, and comparative religious ethics. His research in contemporary ecological questions will be encapsulated in his forthcoming As a Deep River Rises: Judaism, Ecology, and Environmental Ethics.

From "Where Heaven and Earth Kiss: Jewish Law, Moral Reflection, and Environmental Ethics," *Journal of Jewish Ethics* 5, no. 1 (2019): 68–110.

Global climate change and the impending environmental disaster represent one of the greatest moral and existential crises of our day. Seeking to grapple with this unprecedented challenge, Jewish scholars, philosophers, and activists have produced excellent work on ecology and environmental ethics across the past decades. These books and essays, which are constructive and programmatic as well as descriptive, address a wide range of core issues regarding our relationship to the natural world. These include far-reaching theological meditations, as well as specific reflections on ethical food production and consumption, the biblical prohibition against wanton destruction (*bal tashchit*) as a paradigm for environmental sustainability, and the question of responsible investing—whether or not mutual funds that include destructive, immoral or corrosive industries should be permitted by Jewish law.

The present article engages with many of these questions from a somewhat different perspective, examining the intricacies rabbinic law (halakha) with an eye to contemporary questions of environmental pollution. I aim to demonstrate that thinkers and activists should draw upon the categories of Jewish tort law (*Nezikin*) for constructing a progressive ethical voice on issues of environmental degradation. Science has shown us that global pollution and the overconsumption of resources *damage* our world and its inhabitants, altering our fragile ecosystem in ways that destroy property, injure human beings and animal life, and harm our common inheritance. We see humanity's capacity to fundamentally transform this world, and our feckless behavior may threaten the sustainability of higher life on this planet as we know it. I am arguing that the legal traditions of Judaism, interpreted together with our legacy of spiritual, theological and philosophical reflection, will help us formulate a response to this imminent crisis....

I should say that examining Talmudic law with an eye to environmental ethics is not necessarily an obvious pursuit. Reading the passages about rampaging oxen, haystack fires, and murderous pits, subjects that seem quite removed from our immediate situation, does not necessarily present itself as an opportunity for sophisticated moral reasoning or ethical reflection. The approach to study favored in most Talmudic institutions in which these tractates are studied remains the highly conceptual and formalistic mode of analysis—called *lomdus* or *lamdanut*—that emerged in Lithuania *yeshivot* and made popular in America by the influential Joseph B. Soloveitchik.[113] Building upon the work of scholars like David Hartman, Eliezer Berkovits,[114] and Emmanuel Levinas,[115] I have argued that Talmud and the literature of halakha must be studied as an opportunity for ethical reasoning, spiritual development, and ultimately moral action in the world. Seeing the Talmud with these eyes allows the student to confront deepest questions of existential and moral meaning. Such a lens transforms the rabbinic texts from abstract sophistry into a religious quest, a personal journey of self-formation through which one comes to reflect upon the critical moral and philosophical questions of our present day....

Mobilizing Talmudic tort law in addressing the environmental crisis demands that we infuse our reading of these legal sources with our tradition's store of

---

113. [On Rabbi Joseph B. Soloveitchik, see part 1, section 3, footnote 32.]

114. [Rabbi David Hartman was an American-Israeli philosopher and supporter of religious pluralism. Rabbi Eliezer Berkovits was an Austrian-Hungarian-American theologian and philosopher of religion and modernity, especially for Orthodox Judaism.]

115. [For more on Levinas, see part 1, section 4.]

sacred narratives, expansively defined as the theological reflections and moral reasoning from the Hebrew Bible up to modern philosophy.

Reintegrating halakha and aggadah into a complementary framework entails the close examination of the nonlegal material included in a given Talmudic unit. It also means expanding the scope of one's discussion of a particular rabbinic ruling to encompass the aggadah found throughout the entirety of classical rabbinic literature, invoking such passages to complement—and challenge—one's reading of legal precept....

These legal sources—read through the lens of aggadah—offer a different prescriptive vocabulary for the mandates of environmental activism from the heart of Jewish literature.

Rabbinic literature describes the laws of damages as critical to a stable society. Human beings flourish only when their lives and property are protected from harm. Peering beyond this utilitarian or instrumentalist approach, the Talmud refers to the Mishnaic Order of *Nezikin* as the "Order of Redemption" (*Seder Yeshu'ot*).[116] A community that lives in accordance with the moral principles and legal precepts, claim the rabbis, will be closer to God's vision. Secular law has dealt with these issues to some degree, but I firmly believe that the ethical voice of Jewish law should demand a *higher* standard of moral conduct than that prescribed in secular civil law. As a religious voice of obligation and responsibility, halakha must always be a force of courage, compassion, and integrity in striving to create a better world.

Our tradition teaches that we become partners with God as we formulate the halakha and seek to construct the world in light of its values. "A judge whose verdict accords with truth in the deepest sense is likened to a partner of the blessed Holy One in the works of creation."[117] Such judgment sustains the world and fashions a society infused with God's values. Our ongoing partnership with God, manifest in the inheritance of the earth, is insoluble. "The earth is all of one piece," declares the Talmud,[118] and Maimonides rules that "if a piece of land cannot be divided, no partner may force the others to reclaim his stake."[119] Our partnership with the divine is unbreakable, but it therefore demands that we take an active role in ensuring the continuation of life on this world.

---

116. B. T. *Shabbat* 31a; and *Be-Midbar Rabbah* 13:15.
117. B. T. *Shabbat* 10a; and *Mekhilta, yitro*, no. 2.
118. See B. T. *Bava Batra* 67a.
119. Mishneh Torah, *Hilkhot Shekhenim* 1:1 and 4.

ADRIENNE KRONE

Ecological Ethics in the Jewish Community Farming Movement

Adrienne Krone (b. 1982) read for a PhD at Duke University and now serves as the director of Jewish life at Allegheny College. Her work in religious and Jewish studies focuses on such topics as agriculture and food, food justice, environment, and animals. She is completing an historical and ethnographic study of the contemporary Jewish community farming movement in North America.

From "Ecological Ethics in the Jewish Community Farming Movement," in *Feasting and Fasting: The History and Ethics of Jewish Food*, eds. Aaron S. Gross, Jody Myers, and Jordan D. Rosenblum (New York: New York University Press, 2019), 273–86.

When I describe my research project, which focuses on Eden Village Camp and other organizations like it that together compose the Jewish community farming movement, a common response is some form of the question "Jews farm?"—often accompanied by a giggle. This response speaks to the real and perceived distance between most modern Jews and their agrarian ancestors. It surprises many Jews to learn that agriculture is central to many Jewish practices and holidays and a constant point of reference in Judaism's sacred texts. Jewish community farming organizations have a mission to educate people about the Jewish agricultural past while ensuring that there is also an agricultural Jewish present and future....

Coastal Roots is a community farm inspired by the Jewish tradition of agriculture. Eden Village Camp, Coastal Roots Farm, and other Jewish community farming movement organizations are united by a shared commitment to engage Jews in nondenominational settings to reconnect them to Judaism, the earth, and its creatures through the revitalization of Jewish agricultural laws and traditions....

The farms employ different approaches to "Jewish agriculture." The farms offer a diverse array of holiday celebrations and observe the agricultural laws to varying degrees. What binds these organizations together as a movement is their dedication to a set of values that undergirds the laws and holidays. At Shoresh Jewish Environmental programs, located in Toronto, Canada, these values guide their agricultural work around the city. On a sunny day in late June 2016, hundreds of people gathered in Erin, Ontario, for the grand opening of

Bela Farm, a Shoresh project. During her opening remarks, Risa Alyson Cooper, executive director of Shoresh, explained that at Bela Farm, they "are manifesting a 114-acre center for sustainable, land-based Judaism."[120] After her remarks and some more singing, we marched out onto that land led by a band, singing as we went. We walked by beds of garlic and soon entered a protected forest area. Then the band stopped playing so we could walk quietly through the apiary, where the Bela beehives live. We headed past nine hives accompanied by the quiet hum of thousands of bees buzzing away as they went about their work. This was not a traditional holiday but rather a celebration of the "land-based Judaism" that Risa described, which highlights an ecologically oriented interpretation of three traditional Jewish laws.

The first traditional law is *tza'ar ba'alei chayim*, which translates literally to "the suffering of living creatures" and is understood by rabbinic Jewish traditions as a prohibition on unnecessarily causing animal suffering. *Tza'ar ba'alei chayim* is often discussed in contemporary Jewish conversations around the ethics of contemporary animal agriculture and meat consumption as such. That conversation happens on Jewish community farms too, but on farms this traditional commandment is also understood as an ethical value applicable to animal husbandry. The animal husbandry work at Shoresh is focused on bees and other pollinators. Sabrina, the director of engagement, picked up an interest in beekeeping as a fellow at another Jewish farm, Adamah, and brought it with her back to Toronto, where she began to learn from a local master beekeeper. At Shoresh, Sabrina has set up a clear approach to protecting pollinators that gives high priority to the health of the bees and the restoration of native pollinator populations. First, the staff has worked hard to ensure the bees are fed a plentiful and diverse diet. At Bela Farm, they have set aside twenty acres as a bee sanctuary filled with indigenous wildflowers, but all Shoresh garden projects regardless of size always include a bee habitat. Second, they keep bees for honey, which they sell to the Jewish community. The honey harvest coincides nicely with Rosh Hashanah, a celebration that often includes honey, so Shoresh uses the sale of their honey to educate the community about the ecological, agricultural, and ultimately religious importance of pollinators. Third, they experiment with alternative materials and locations to see where and how the bees will thrive at the highest level. For example, Shoresh has used the common Langstroth hives

---

120. "Bela Farm Grand Opening," Shoresh website, accessed November 18, 2016, http://shoresh.ca.

for the majority of their work. These hives are composed of stacked boxes with removable frames. Sabrina learned from a fellow beekeeper that there was another type of hive that may provide the bees with a structure that is closer to what they would encounter in trees. In 2018, Sabrina began to experiment with these Warre hives, which are boxes with removable bars that are designed so that bees can build their own comb. Sabrina and the staff at Shoresh frequently revisit and revise their practices to ensure that the bees suffer as little as possible.

A second traditional law, *bal tashchit*, meaning "you shall not destroy," is based on Deuteronomy 20:19–20, which prohibits Jews from cutting down trees that bear fruit during times of war. This traditional commandment has been widely interpreted as an ecological value by Jewish environmentalism, including those active on Jewish community farms. In keeping with this value, Shoresh staff use and reuse materials in creative ways. I attended a honey harvest event in September 2017, and during a bottling break, Risa showed me their wax melters. These melters were made up of a quirky collection of buckets, Tupperware containers, pieces of metal mesh, and plastic sheeting. These makeshift melters ensure that nothing from the honey harvest is wasted. Next to the wax melters, there is a small hut that houses a compost toilet. Even human waste is not wasted at Shoresh.

The final traditional law that animates the work on Jewish community farms is *tzedakah*, which translates as "justice" or "righteousness" and is interpreted by many contemporary Jews as representing values related to social justice. All the Jewish community farms interpret this value and center it in their work. At Shoresh, in addition to their work with pollinators, they are also reforesting twenty acres of their land with native trees and planting twenty acres of perennial native fruit and nut trees, berry bushes, and native wildflowers. Shoresh donates all the food they grow at their gardens in and around Toronto. They also offer garden programming with social service organizations like Jewish Family and Child and Baycrest, a geriatric center. The values that are embedded at Shoresh around animal husbandry, resource conservation, and justice similarly inform the work at other Jewish community farming organizations.

HAVA TIROSH-SAMUELSON

Religion and Environment: The Case of Judaism

Hava Tirosh-Samuelson (b. 1950), an Israeli-born scholar of religious studies, is the director of Jewish studies at Arizona State University. A prolific writer in the field of Jewish intellectual history, she examines such topics as premodern Jewish philosophy and mysticism, interreligious relations in the Middle Ages, feminism, religion, science, bioethics, and Judaism and ecology. Editor of Brill's ongoing Library of Contemporary Jewish Philosophers, *among other projects, she brings an interdisciplinary approach to find connections, especially between religion and science.*

From *Religion and Environment: The Case of Judaism* (Telford, PA: Pandora Press, 2020), 90–92, 260–61.

Editor's Preface

Let me sum up the first lecture by saying the following: Judaism is a religious tradition whose law is believed to be divinely revealed. Normative Judaism specifies what one is expected to do in all aspects of life, including interaction with the natural world. Jews who define themselves in religious terms (be they Orthodox, Conservative, Reconstructionist, or Reform Jews) can find deep and rich insights within the Jewish tradition that support conservationist practices conducive to sustainability. The Judaic approach to nature revolves around the value of responsibility and follows from the belief that the earth ultimately belongs to God and that humans have been given the task of protecting it by following certain guiding principles. In Jewish normative ethics, there is a close connection between ethics and nature: when human beings conduct themselves in accord with God's will, the earth is fertile, but when they sin toward each other and toward God, the earth loses its fecundity, and consequently human beings suffer and their life loses vitality.

Jewish environmental ethics is characterized by the following features:

1. it focuses on human obligations, or duties, toward the natural world, rather than on the intrinsic rights of nature;

2. it focuses on action in specific situations and particular circumstances;

3. it highlights a long-term perspective and concerns itself with future generations, namely with sustainability of human practices;

4. it emphasizes the common good over private interest and aligns social justice and environmental well-being.

It is difficult to fit Jewish normative ethics into the academic environmental ethics. Jewish normative ethics is framed within a religious narrative of covenantal theology. Jewish normative ethics is neither anthropocentric nor biocentric, but theocentric, because it sees the world to belong first and foremost to God rather than to humans, although humans were given the task of caring for the created world. The human task is not understood as managerial "control and command" but rather as attentive "stewardship" or "caregiving," analogous to the loving work of the gardener. Although Jewish normative ethics is framed legally, in Jewish law there is no tension between duties and virtues: the divine commands that specify action also facilitate the cultivation of character traits conducive to the right action toward the environment. Jewish eco-justice (or eco-kosher) links right conduct toward humans with the appropriate treatment of soil, vegetation, and animals. Finally, Jewish normative ethics does not exhibit the radical break between theory and practice, because the Jewish sacred narrative shapes rules, attitudes, and acts in regard to a specific locale—the land of Israel—and under very specific circumstances. Jewish normative ethics thus touches various issues debated by environmental philosophers, but it frames them differently.

One does not have to be an observant Jew or even Jewish to endorse this ethics of responsibility.... Three Jewish philosophers ...—Buber,[121] Jonas,[122] and Levinas[123]—have inspired profound thinking about the human relationship to nature, even though only one of them was, technically speaking, an environmental philosopher. Already in the 1920s, long before the environmental crisis was recognized, Buber made it possible for us to think about nature as a moral subject. By recognizing the possibility of personal (i.e., subject-subject) relations with nature, he moved beyond the Kantian view of indirect duties toward nature.[124] When the scope of the environmental crisis was first recognized, Jonas courageously and creatively addressed it by articulating a philosophy of nature that challenged the philosophic assumption that "ought" cannot be derived

121. [On Martin Buber, see part 1, section 2, footnote 24.]

122. [Hans Jonas was a German-American Jewish philosopher specializing in religion and environmental ethics.]

123. [See part 1, section 4, for information about Emmanuel Levinas.]

124. [According to Kant, humans have duties to nonhuman creatures and by extension to the environment in general, though not for their own sake; it is for the sake of the (human) self, for how well one treats an animal, for instance, that will eventually shape how one treats oneself and other humans. Hence, "indirect duties."]

from "is." By insisting on the subjectivity of Being, Jonas grounded ethics in ontology, and conversely, endowed ontology with ethical meaning. In his philosophy, responsibility for the future of all biological life is the collective responsibility of humanity. Even more demanding was Levinas's radical understanding of responsibility, according to which to be human is to be infinitely responsible to the vulnerable other. When Levinas's ethics is applied to nature, it offers an eco-phenomenology that makes each and every human being personally responsible. The Jewish ethics of responsibility is a profound and compelling response to the environmental crisis....

[In previous lectures I discussed] the Anthropocene, an age in which massive ecological crisis is taking place, evident in climate change; extreme weather events; desertification; loss of biodiversity; retreat of glaciers; rising sea levels; loss of fisheries and forests; acidification of oceans; pollution of air, water, and soil; and numerous other manifestations of environmental degradation. These lectures have argued that world religions matter most to our attempt to address the ecological crisis because the overwhelming majority of people in the world conceptualize reality in religious categories. Human beings understand themselves, their societies, and their daily lives through sacred narratives and symbolic rituals that point beyond themselves to an ultimate reality. Within religious worldviews, human beings organize their lives and find meaning, purpose, and hope as they face an unknown future. Religion provides the moral lens through which we evaluate every aspect of our lives and decide what is right and wrong, what is permitted and forbidden, and what is desirable and undesirable. Religion expresses human existential and emotional needs and frames what we care most about, namely, our ultimate concern. Because this concern frames our understanding of ultimate reality (to which we commonly refer as "God"), people are willing to sacrifice their lives for what they consider ultimate reality. For this reason, religion, more than any other aspect of human life, is the force that mobilizes people to action. Since the challenges for the survival of humankind today are planetary in scope, religion offers the most comprehensive perspective within which to frame our global challenges and respond to them....

To address the challenges of the Anthropocene, we need narratives of care: care about the physical well-being of the world, care about the spiritual well-being of humans, care about the future of our children and their descendants, care about all those who are different from us but who, like us, suffer from the harms of climate change, be it extreme droughts, destructive fires, or devastating floods. Caring for the earth and its inhabitants is not narrow anthropocentrism, or speciesism, because it recognizes the interdependence and interconnectedness of humanity with the entire web of life and the physical conditions that give rise to life. But ethics of care does place the responsibility for the well-being of the world on human beings, and responsibility always entails recognition of limits. World religions have offered us the richest treasure of narratives of care, which we need to reinterpret in light of contemporary science, and Judaism, beginning with the Bible, offers the most influential narrative of earth care. If we care for the earth in our sacred narratives and in our deeds, we will ensure that our home will remain inhabitable for generations to come.

III | Constructions of the Human

> *God formed the Human from the soil's humus,*
> *blowing into its nostrils the breath of life: the Human*
> *became a living being.* Genesis 2:7

Introduction

It's not a foregone conclusion what "human" means. Fundamental "human" questions have animated Jewish deliberation across the ages. Are humans different from all other creatures? If so, what makes them different? Are such differences ontological and impermeable? Could Judaism endorse the ancient idea of the *scala naturae*, a great chain of being, that posits all created entities—from the elements to the most revered angels and demigods—exist along a tiered hierarchy, with humans above all other animals yet just shy of the angelic realm? Then again, perhaps differences are just apparent, maybe even malleable. Does it matter, and why? Furthermore, how should such differences be managed? Who or what is the more valuable and why? And what about the differences that subdivide humanity, differences of culture and differences of biology? Though Judaism embraces the conviction that all humans share in the divine image (*b'tzelem Elohim*, as expressed in Gen. 1:27), the tradition also acknowledges that humanity comprises multiplicities. How shall these differences be explained?

As will become abundantly clear in the following selections, there is no singular metric by which humans are to be assessed, categorized, or evaluated, much less how tensions and conflicts among these groups are to be managed. Nor does consensus exist regarding methodology, the ways to think through such issues. Thinking about what distinguishes humans from other beings, and humans from one another, inevitably leads to ethics.

One of the earliest observations regards human specialness in the created world. Texts like the Bible and Talmud offer competing theories about how and why humans are special. The first section here, on animals, addresses some of these concerns, specifically those that distinguish humankind from all other animated creatures. Thinking about animals helps our thinking about humans. The second section attends to issues of gender and sexuality, issues that often generate anxiety and joy. Desire and the erotic intermingle with meditations on the role of women and trans and intersex identities in Judaism. Recent insights about genes, genetic codes, and genetic testing animate the third section. The fourth section turns our attention to disability, inclusion, and voice. The final section looks at race, an admittedly modern and hotly debated construct, as well as racism and antisemitism.

Taken altogether, the pieces in this part assert the idea that humans are special. Yet they also raise serious concerns about how and why that is the case. They insist that human specialness requires clarification and justification, not unquestioning acceptance. In short, the "human" continues to be a contested issue of significant ethical import.

14 | Animals

Humans exist in a diverse menagerie. That the earliest biblical creation stories acknowledge this fact suggests that, as Claude Lévi-Strauss[1] quipped in *Totemism*, animals are "good to think." How we think about animals profoundly impacts how we comport and think of ourselves. Some traditional Jewish sources—like the Decalogue itself (Deut. 5:13–15)—do insist that animals are morally significant and warrant careful attention and care. Interpretations of the Hebrew Bible have also undeniably contributed to some enduring claims about human specialness; consider, for instance, the passages in Genesis (1:26–27) that describe the first humans being made "in the image of God" and command them to dominate and subdue the world.

But not all of those ideas or practices elevate humans at the expense of other creatures. Premodern Jewish textual sources do not often interrogate these foundational and hierarchical notions (though some do). Contemporary animal studies—a field that has emerged with gusto in the last several decades—engage these earlier sources to better understand both mainstream attitudes and practices as well as countertraditions that might suggest different orientations toward animals and ourselves. Animal studies also raises critical questions about Jewish communal attitudes, strictures, and practices that objectify, commodify, and oppress. Much current scholarship in this arena challenges the common tendency to forge and reinforce mutually exclusive binaries between human and animal, and the valuation of one category over others. Such research also argues for the necessity of thinking about species alongside other issues of justice like racism, classism, sexism, and disability.

Attention to animals in contemporary Jewish ethics has expanded beyond classic debates over the uses of nonhuman animals in agriculture, food, clothing, and science, where animals are more imagined than meaningfully considered on their own terms. If these discussions constitute "animal ethics," many contemporary Jewish ethicists delve more into "ethics of animals," whereby they interrogate the category of the animal and its role in formulating notions of the human

---

1. Claude Lévi-Strauss was a professor of anthropology and ethnology at the Collège de France 1959–1982.

and self. The selections in this section represent two such contributions to this emerging genre.

For example, in his celebrated 2016 monograph, *The Question of the Animal and Religion: Theoretical Stakes, Practical Implications*, Aaron S. Gross investigates what preceded and followed the release in 2004 of raw footage of abuses of animals on the killing floor of the largest kosher slaughterhouse, Agriprocessors. Some Jews defended or dismissed the unnecessary suffering endured by these animals, while others viewed it as violating not just halakha but also foundational Jewish values. Gross offers what might be understood as a post-structuralist[2] approach to "both expose the absent presence of animals in the history of the study of religion and clear a space for their future"[3]—that is, his is a descriptive and prescriptive project relevant for both the academy (the study of religion and ethics) and the community (regarding the practice of eating animals and the kashrut industry generally).

Rafael Rachel Neis's contribution, "'All That Is in the Settlement': Humans, Likeness, and Species in the Rabbinic Bestiary," advances the agenda of challenging conventional conceptual binaries and dichotomies. Neis, a scholar of classical rabbinic literature, combines close readings with feminist science studies, critical animal studies, critical race theory, and disability studies. Neis uses these tools to appreciate rabbinic knowledge-making in regard to likeness, difference, and similarity in discussions of (human) reproduction of species. What they find is that animals—and even humans—do not easily align with any one classic category (e.g., wild/domestic, pure/impure, human/animal). If such taxonomies ultimately are blurry at best, easy claims about human specialness are called into question as well.

---

2. Post-structuralism is a broad philosophical movement that challenges the purported stability and objectivity of ideas and ways of thinking championed by more conventional structuralism; common in this movement is the challenge to mutually exclusive binaries.

3. Aaron S. Gross, *The Question of the Animal and Religion: Theoretical Stakes, Practical Implications* (New York: Columbia University Press, 2015), 7.

AARON S. GROSS

The Question of the Animal and Religion: Theoretical Stakes, Practical Implications

Aaron S. Gross (b. 1972) is a historian of religions at the University of San Diego, specializing in Judaism and Buddhism and issues of oppression. An expert on animal ethics and food studies, he serves in leadership roles in the American Academy of Religion's Animals and Religions group, in the Society of Jewish Ethics, and is the founder and CEO of the nonprofit Farm Forward.

From *The Question of the Animal and Religion: Theoretical Stakes, Practical Implications* (New York: Columbia University Press, 2015), 148–51, 184–89.

6. Sacrificing Animals and Being a Mensch

It is not that kosher practitioners—or anyone eating animals—first form a view of the world around them and then begin to eat in a certain way in response to it. Before we eat animals, we are already, as the (Jewish) novelist Jonathan Safran Foer has expressed it, "eating animals"—that is, we are animals defined in part by how we eat. We are eating before we are ourselves—we are born into the world eating, constituted by eating....

How we eat animals may even help determine ... whether we will apprehend the world as divided between subjects and objects, culture and nature, humans and animals in the first place. It helps determine whether we imagine humans as coming to know the world "by virtue of first [having] removed themselves from it"[4] (the path of science and its promise of ever expanding objective knowledge) or whether, more along the lines Ingold[5] calls forth, we imagine humans "knowing" the world "through the very processes of living and making their ways in it."[6]

There is ample precedent for the idea that dietary practices contain multiple layers of meaning in Jewish studies. For example, Gillian Feely-Harnik's[7] important study of the meaning of food in early Judaism and Christianity opens

---

4. Tim Ingold, "The Man in the Machine and the Self-Builder," *Interdisciplinary Science Review*, 35, nos. 3–4 (2010): 361.

5. [Tim Ingold is a professor emeritus of social anthropology at the University of Aberdeen, UK.]

6. Ingold, "The Man in the Machine."

7. [Gillian Feely-Harnik is a professor emerita of anthropology at the University of Michigan.]

with the helpful observation that food provides "a powerfully concentrated 'language' for debating moral-legal issues and transforming social relations."[8] Jordan Rosenblum's[9] studies of food in the earliest strata of rabbinic Judaism, the tannaitic Judaism of the first two centuries (Tannaim refers to the rabbis of this period), similarly show how culinary regulations are wielded to address commensal concerns in general, and commensal concerns about women specifically, thus constructing social and gender relations. Rosenblum's analysis of the Babylonian Talmud's tractate *Hullin* 1:1 further brings us the important insight that in the ancient rules surrounding animal slaughter the distinction between Jew and gentile is linked to a distinction between the human and the ape—between man and animal. Rosenblum explains, "In order for slaughter to be tannaitically valid for Jewish ingestion, the butcher must be a Jew. Butchery—a cultural practice that separates humans from animals—is now marked by the Tannaim as a distinctly Jewish practice. Gentile slaughter is . . . equated with slaughter by an ape. . . . The gentile's slaughter is likened to the action of an animal; it is a natural, not human, act."[10] Jonathan Brumberg-Kraus[11]—who gives animal food considerable attention—has similarly argued that rabbinic dietary practices related to the consumption of meat encode a larger system of meaning that elevates "rational, imaginative humans over brute animals, men over women, Torah scholars over those unschooled in Torah, and ethnic/kinship ties over ties based on shared faith or shared charismatic experiences."[12]

The pairing together of views toward "those unschooled in Torah" and animals that Brumberg-Kraus alludes to is part of a larger trope in rabbinic texts in which non-Jews and animals are imaginatively linked. For example, one of the more persistent tropes regarding the status of non-Jews in Talmudic literature

---

8. Gillian Feely-Harnik, *The Lord's Table: Eucharist and Passover in Early Christianity, Symbol and Culture* (Philadelphia: University of Pennsylvania Press, 1981), xiii–xvi.

9. [Jordan Rosenblum is a professor of religious studies at the University of Wisconsin-Madison.]

10. Jordan Rosenblum, *Food and Identity in Early Rabbinic Judaism* (New York: Cambridge University Press, 2010), 79–80.

11. [Jonathan Brumberg-Kraus is a professor of religion at Wheaton College in Massachusetts.]

12. Jonathan Brumberg-Kraus, "Meals as Midrash: A Survey of Ancient Meals in Jewish Studies Scholarship," in *Food and Judaism*, eds. Leonard Greenspoon, Ronald Simkins, and Gerald Sharpiro (Omaha, NE: Creighton University Press, 2004), 310.

links the uniqueness of Israel among the nations with the uniqueness of humans among animals. Elliot Wolfson[13] has documented this phenomenon with some care.[14] A pervasive rabbinic trope that Wolfson finds persistent in later kabbalistic texts denies the full humanity of *certain* non-Jews: as it appears, for instance, in *Bava Metzia* 114a, "You are called 'adam,' but idolaters are not called 'adam.'" The borders between human and animal, Jew and non-Jew, the faithful and the idolatrous, eater and eaten are porous, interpenetrating and mutually constituting. Still today the production, certification, and consumption of meat from kosher animals remains an ever evolving symbolic "language" that shapes Jewish attitudes not only toward animal others but non-Jewish human others.

The consumption of animals, whether regulated by kashrut or not, lies at the intersection of multiple tectonic plates of meaning: human/animal, ruler/ruled, Jew/gentile, male/female, and so on. It is a paradigmatic example of what Pierre Bourdieu[15] has called "enacted belief, instilled by the childhood learning that treats the body as a living memory pad, an automaton that 'leads the mind unconsciously along with it.'"[16] Such symbolically invested activities function as "a repository for the most precious values. . . . Practical sense, social necessity turned into nature, converted into motor schemes and body automatism, is what causes practices, in and through what makes them obscure to the eyes of their producers, to be sensible, that is, informed by a common sense. It is because agents never know completely what they are doing that what they do has more sense than they know."[17] . . .

I wish to suggest three reasons that the structure of the humane subject, whatever it is called, deserves our attention in and perhaps outside of Jewish traditions.

First, attention to the structure of the humane subject helps clarify how Jewish

---

13. [Elliot Wolfson is a professor of mysticism, Judaism, and philosophy at the University of California, Santa Barbara.]

14. Elliot Wolfson, *Venturing Beyond: Law and Morality in Kabbalistic Mysticism* (Oxford: Oxford University Press, 2006), 40.

15. [Pierre Bourdieu was a twentieth-century French sociologist specializing in theories of aesthetics, education, and sociology, primarily at the School for Advanced Studies in the Social Sciences in Paris.]

16. Pierre Bourdieu, *Logic of Practice*, trans. Richard Nice (Stanford, CA: Stanford University Press, 1990), 68.

17. Bourdieu, *Logic of Practice*, 69.

texts and dietary practices can function in tandem to construct and perpetuate particular visions of the human and ethics, thus allowing better understanding of the meaning-making functions of these religious activities. It is widely acknowledged in Jewish studies and food studies that *food practices* reveal social dynamics, but the important role that animal lives play in this process is often forgotten. The animal is often the hidden generator that produces the meanings that are passed along in kosher practice, and the analytic of the humane subject helps make this visible. Second, attention to these constructions of the humane subject highlights how addressing questions about the kind of being we are inevitably is bound up with ethical questions and, conversely, how confronting ethical dilemmas often raises questions about subjectivity and identity. All are torsions in the same knot. The question of being and the question of being ethical are coprimordial. The third point, which is also of special interest to animal studies, relates to the manner in which attention to the humane subject exposes the intimate interconnections between our constructions of gender, race, animality, and otherness—something this book has only begun to trace, but that the analysis presented here invites. In sum, first point: animals, especially those we eat, are integral to human self-imagination; second point: ethics and subjectivity are coimagined and coprimordial aspects of self; third point: the question of the animal is also inherently a question about gender, race, and otherness (not to mention technology, the machine, modernity, and so on)....

If we find there are profound limits to our ability to change the deeper structures of sexism and racism, this study suggests that it is because we sometimes focus on the tip of an iceberg. The broader religious structuring of the human relationship with the rest of creation—a relationship worked out today vividly in the question of animal food—constrains our ability to reimagine gender and race, us and them. If we actively defend something like the present articulation of the human/animal binary, we constrain our ability to rethink the other binaries to which it is linked. Trimming back the relatively small part of a weed that is above ground will not eliminate it if one is simultaneously fertilizing its roots.

Perhaps we should "no longer... seek new—more effective or more authentic—articulations" of the human in contrast to "the animal" and instead confront what Agamben[18] characterizes as "the central emptiness, the hiatus that within man—separates man and animal, and to risk ourselves in this emptiness: the

---

18. [Giorgio Agamben is an Italian philosopher focusing on totalitarianism and Foucault's notion of biopolitics.]

suspension of the suspension, Shabbat of both animal and man."[19] What would happen if we entered this darkness that stands before an infinitely deferred dawn, a darkness that precedes the division of the world into human and animal?

What would it mean if we paused, put to rest, or let go of the categories animal and human? As Calarco[20] maintains, "any genuine encounter with what we call animals will occur only from within the space of this surrender."[21] The question of eating animals—both whether we should and, if so, how—matters and matters profoundly in and of itself because animals matter in and of themselves. The question of eating animals also matters because it simultaneously shapes the gendered and racialized world in which we live in pragmatic, macroeconomic, and symbolic ways. In the depths of the religious dimension of existence, who we are is bound to who *they* are: who animals are.

It is not a matter of doing away with differences and taxonomies, as if that were even possible, but rather a matter of taking diversely differing differentiations into account within experiential fields and "a world of life forms, and of doing that without reducing this differentiated and multiple difference."[22] I do not suggest that we pay less attention to the differences between the "vast heterogeneity of presences,"[23] with whom we share the substrate of life, but rather more—enough attention so that the hierarchical binaries human and animal, male and female, white and black, civilized and primitive, and us and them fade before the demands of the undeniable that proceeds them all; the "possibility of giving vent to a surge of compassion, even if it is then misunderstood, repressed or denied, held at bay."[24]

Impossible though it may be, the final hope of this book is to return to the clearing that precedes the animal. If we are patient, if we can slip past the gears of the anthropological machine, if we can sacrifice sacrifice, we may sense our-

---

19. Giorgio Agamben, *The Open: Man and Animal*, trans. Kevin Attell (Stanford, CA: Stanford University Press, 2004), 92.

20. [Matthew Calarco is a professor of continental philosophy and animal and environmental philosophy at the California State University, Fullerton.]

21. Matthew Calarco, *Zoographies: The Question of the Animal from Heidegger to Derrida* (New York: Columbia University Press, 2008), 4.

22. Jacques Derrida, *The Animal That Therefore I Am*, ed. Marie-Louise Mallet, trans. David Wills (New York: Fordham University Press, 2008), 126.

23. Donna Haraway, *When Species Meet, Posthumanities* (Minneapolis: University of Minnesota Press, 2008), 74.

24. Derrida, *The Animal That Therefore I Am*, 28.

selves seen by others we cannot yet name. In this surrender, the phenomena we name religion in the academy and in the public square will not look the same and the face of the religious actor may no longer be a human face.

RAFAEL RACHEL NEIS

"All That Is in the Settlement": Humans, Likeness, and Species in the Rabbinic Bestiary

Rafael Rachel Neis is a scholar, writer, educator, and artist who teaches history and Judaic studies at the University of Michigan. Through interdisciplinary and multimedia investigations of ritual, gender, and classification, they focus on rabbinic movement cultures of the first centuries CE and how those interacted with surrounding communities.

From "'All That Is in the Settlement': Humans, Likeness, and Species in the Rabbinic Bestiary," *Journal of Jewish Ethics* 5, no. 1 (2019): 1–39.

Likeness served as a key indicator of relatedness in reproductive contexts. This is most repeatedly and explicitly evinced in rabbinic sources about humans, rather than animals. One might say that likeness as a key to humanness and its reproduction is instantiated in Genesis, where the human is created uniquely "in the image and likeness of God" (Gen. 1:26–27) and then blessed with fertility. This is reiterated in Genesis 5:1–2, in the "generations of *adam*," along with its dual-sexed implications, "in the image of God, he made him, male and female, he created them, and he called their name *adam*." We are then informed that Adam, "bore in his image, according to his likeness, and he called his name Seth" (Gen. 5:3), linking the notion of likeness not only to the first *adam* (or to humanity in general) but to its subsequent reproduction. After Seth's birth Adam lived another "eight hundred years and he bore sons and daughters" (Gen. 5:4), dying at the grand age of nine hundred and thirty (Gen. 5:5). This structure repeats with Seth, and named male firstborns all the way to Noah, but henceforth without the qualifier that the successive "begettings" are "in his image, according to his likeness." While a later rabbinic tradition capitalizes on this absence to infer that the divine image vanished "in the days of Enosh,"[25] most trade on the

25. Genesis Rabbah 23:6.

presumption that the image of God transferred to "the first *adam*" continued on as a signature feature of humans.[26] On this basis, early and later rabbinic sources link human reproduction with mimesis and mechanisms of image-making and artistry, and of course with the divine.[27] Put simply, physical resemblance was often understood as a materialization of affinity and kinship.

If likeness was thought to be a key to reproductive or *vertical* relationships, it or its construed opposite—difference—also served as a way to sort *across* kinds, in other words, *horizontal* classification. Perceptions of difference were important in making sense of the tumbling morass of living beings, allowing ancient people to recognize the ways in which creaturely life appeared to fall into certain patterns, or cluster in particular ways. The rabbis, like the natural historians Aristotle and Pliny, lumped and split creaturely life according to an assortment of shared and non-shared features or groupings. These features, which included bodily characteristics, reproductive and gestational modes, habitat, and locomotion, allowed distinctions between land animals, sea creatures, and creatures of the skies to be registered. Assessing the varied bodies of creaturely life via signs (*simanim*), form (*tsurah*), and physical resemblance (*dimyon*), the rabbis sorted them into species (*minim*) of various registers—pure/impure, wild/domesticated animals, birds, fish and locusts, creeping and crawling creatures, etc.—and along other vectors of difference.[28] ...

So far, we have argued that in antiquity—as in the present—looks could be deceiving. Creatures with similar appearances could nonetheless be considered different species. A creature that lives with humans can be "wild"; those in the wild can be considered domesticated. Some creatures confuse: bird-like they do not fly. We see that others seem to cross categories: they may look reptilian but are dubbed wild animals, and yet, for the purpose of corpse impurity be

---

26. See also Genesis 9:1–7.

27. See M. *Avot* 3:14; M. *Sanhedrin* 4:5; T. *Yevamot* 8:7 (note how B. T. *Yevamot* 64a converts a generalized imperative to reproduce into a Jewish one). Some sources more specifically link the image and its making with paternal similitude or patrilineal genealogies, e.g., Mekhilta deRabbi Ishmael Shira, 8; Leviticus Rabbah 32:12; *Bava Batra* 58a (par B. T. *Bava Metzia* 84a); B. T. *Bava Metzia* 78a. Others work with a "three partners" approach (mother, father, God), e.g., B. T. *Niddah* 31a in which God supplies *qlaster panim* (facial features).

28. These rabbinic species groupings included: small livestock and larger cattle; fish and locusts; creeping things and crawling things; bipeds and quadrupeds; those that reproduce and multiply (sexual generation) versus those that do not; those that are vertebrates versus those that are not; those that live on dry land versus those that live in water.

treated as reptiles. They may be classified as a wild animal, and yet, be treated as a human for the purposes of corpse impurity. It is this last creature, the *adne hasadeh*, that concerns us: What was the *adne hasadeh* and what impact did its existence have on rabbinic zoology?

The *adne hasadeh* are literally "humans of the field" (where *adan* is *adam*).[29] ...

The rabbis not only acknowledged likeness across kinds, including humans. They also had an entire theory that explained them. This is the theory of territorial doubles embedded in this zoological mini-tractate in Mishnah and *Tosefta Kilayim*. The theory itself bears repetition:

> Every [creature] that there is in the settlement (*yishuv*) there is in the wilderness (*midbar*), whereas many [creatures] that are in the wilderness do not exist in the settlement.
>
> Every [creature] that is on dry land (*yabashah*) there is in the sea (*yam*), whereas many [creatures] that are in the sea are not on dry land. But there is no marten of the sea (*huldat hayam*).[30] (T. *Kilayim* 5:10)

This striking idea of territorial doubles serves as explanation and undergirding principle for the phenomena of likeness and difference that pepper tractate *Kilayim*, the *Sifre*, and rabbinic zoology broadly speaking. Before delving into the substance of this theory, it is worth dwelling again on how it serves as linchpin in the broader Tosefta passage, as well as key to its parallel Mishnah passage. These main elements involve: the principle of generation (T. *Kilayim* 5:9); the collection of creatures that resemble others, straddle classifications, or are otherwise exotic or unusual (T. *Kilayim* 5:7–8; M. *Kilayim* 8:5–6); and the particular concerns with the *adam* (the *adne hasadeh*, the role of the human in enforcing *kilayim*[31] but itself not counting as a species, and the inclusion of the human in the generation principle)....

---

29. Rashi on Job 5:23 comments on *adne hasadeh*, "they are a species of human (*min adam*)," identifying the verse's *hayat hasadeh* as the *adne hasadeh*, which he glosses (in French) as *garou* (werewolf).

30. See Y. *Shabbat* 14:1, 14c, and B. T. *Hullin* 127a. These only contain the second component of the principle of territorial doubles (i.e., dry land and sea). The version in Y. *Shabbat* specifies *species* in its formulation: "Everything that exists on dry land exists in the sea, but there are many species [מינים] in the sea which are not on land, and there is no mole in the sea."

31. [A biblically based proscription of mixing seeds, certain fabrics, grafting, crossbreeding animals, and creating teams of different draft animals.]

The classical rabbis also worked with a concept of the human as a creature in God's image. Echoed by Levinas,[32] the concept grounds the killing of the human as a form of deicide and, in some views, a distinctively human obligation to propagate.[33] It also figures into the very mechanisms that perpetuate human reproduction. Sometimes the resemblance-based reproductive implications of *b'tzelem Elohim*[34] could make for gendered, genealogical, and ethno-religious exclusions about who exactly bears this distinctive image. This could reinforce human exceptionalism when taken with the general idea that like produces like species, especially when paired with the rabbinic principle of generation in T. *Kilayim* 5:9 that foreclosed the success of interspecies reproduction (or genuine hybridity). Yet, even within such contexts, the rabbis also contemplated "mimetic dissemblance," including species dissemblance (Neis 2017, 2018).[35] In other words, they understood that two parents of the same species could produce offspring that looks like other kinds. Notably, the rabbis included the human amid such phenomena. Thus, M. *Niddah* 3:1–2 (and parallels) envision women expelling a variety of uterine entities including those that look like a range of nonhuman materials and creatures. M. *Niddah* 3:2 describes a woman expelling a creature "like a kind of wild animal, domesticated animal, or bird." In this respect, nonhuman animality could enter into the heart of the human generative process....

Moves like Rabbi Haninah's[36] trouble the very frames that allow clusters of characteristics to coagulate into species determinations. As we have seen in the case of tannaitic zoological inquiries, the ostensible effort is to know and uphold distinctions between *minim* (kinds). And yet, as Trevor Murphy[37] has shown for Pliny's *Natural History*, the "insistent pursuit of the similarities between

32. [See part 1, section 4 for a selection by Emmanuel Levinas.]
33. See B. T. *Yevamot* 8:7 and Mekhilta de-Rabbi Ishmael, *Bahodesh* 8.
34. [Image of God; from Gen. 1:26–27.]
35. Rachel Neis, "Reproduction of Species: Humans, Animals, and Species Nonconformity in Early Rabbinic Science Reproduction of Species," *Jewish Studies Quarterly* 24, no. 4 (2017): 308–309; Rachel Neis, "Directing the Heart: Corporeal Language and the Anatomy of Ritual Space," in *Placing Ancient Texts, the Ritual and Rhetorical Use of Space*, eds. Mika Ahuvia and Alexander Kocar (Tübingen: Mohr Siebeck, 2018), 131–65.
36. [Rabbi Haninah bar Hama was a second-third century Palestinian amora, or rabbinic sage. He taught in T. *Niddah* 4.7 that "the eyeballs of an animal resemble human eyeballs," which is the "move" Neis references.]
37. [Trevor Murphy is a professor of ancient Greek and Roman studies at the University of California, Berkeley.]

different things . . . continually threatens to disrupt the integral coherence of those classes."[38] Seemingly hard binaries like the *adam* versus "all of them" (nonhumans) or *ḥayah/behemah* are undermined via the continual search for resemblance. The horizontal zoological approach we have studied has the potential to soften the supremely presumptuous dichotomy of the human versus "the animal" (the singular collective noun flattens nonhuman diversity and plurality[39]). But this project that is at the heart of T. *Kilayim* betrays a paradoxical movement. On the one hand, the rabbis attempted to sharply delineate genealogical continuities within species and to shore up the distinctions between them via a combination of prohibition and natural philosophy (theory of generation restricting hybridization). On the other hand, the rabbis in their recognition of similarities across kinds, simultaneously opened up the concept of the double in parallel realms, and indeed, of an excess of noncorresponding life-forms in the wilderness and water. Thus, whereas human distinctiveness is preserved by prohibition and by generative limitations, paradoxically *Kilayim*'s theory of doubles opens up a specter on another front: the human is not the *only* human after all. This contradiction offers opportunities for critically reengaging with the problems and limitations of the *imago dei*, its attendant and explicit speciesism, and its historically and exegetically generated sexisms, racisms, and ableisms.

It turns out, then, that one way that the rabbis blur the edges of the *b'tzelem Elohim* is via the very concepts of likeness and difference to which it is indebted. Likeness—that search for resemblance that draws entities together—is itself a moving target.

---

38. Trevor Murphy, *Pliny the Elder's Natural History: The Empire in the Encyclopedia*. (Oxford: Oxford University Press, 2004), 45.

39. Jacques Derrida, *The Animal That Therefore I Am*, ed. Marie-Louise Mallet, trans. David Wills (New York: Fordham University Press, 2008).

15 | Gender and Sexuality

Divergent views of gender and sexuality are as old as the Torah, as evidenced in its two creation stories. In the first story, humankind comprises two gender types (male and female) that are concomitantly created, and they are immediately equally blessed by God (*Elohim*) with the primordial task of procreation. In this worldview, genders are binary, and sexuality's primary purpose is to bring about offspring. End of story. In the second creation story, God (*Adonai Elohim*) discovers that the individual man God had created lacks a companion, considers this bad, and so sets about to forge such a one. All sorts of species are presented to the man as possible companions but none of them piques the man's interest. So, God pulls from the man biological resources to build another creature—now more like the man—and this one surprisingly suffices; the man calls this entity "woman." Neither the man nor the woman are described as male or female, which suggests they may be more alike than different.

An etiological observation then interrupts the narrative: "Hence a man leaves his father and mother and clings to his wife, so that they become one flesh" (Gen. 2:24). The author of this verse is apparently aware of certain roles and relations (father, mother, wife—itself suggestive of marriage) that in the prior story were unintelligible. And while this author indicates that intimacy (if that is what "clinging" means) is something partners share, procreation could occur (hence the reference to parents) but it is not necessarily intimacy's central purpose (unless one reads this verse both (a) eisegetically, that "one flesh" refers to offspring, and (b) prescriptively, instead of descriptively, that this verse articulates what should transpire). This peculiar verse aside, this second story offers more expansive and fluid ideas about partnership and sexuality than are expressed in the first story. Here, even God cannot predetermine who or what is a rightful companion for an individual, and sexual intimacy between humans need not be constrained to procreative intentions.

Such stories provide many things for us to consider: language (words themselves like "female," "father," etc.), institutions (like marriage), purposes (procreation, companionship), and behaviors (clinging/intimacy), to name a few. For millennia Jews have wrestled with these sources, ideas, and resources. The rise of feminisms in the last half century or so has reinvigorated Jewish consideration of these themes, though there is no singular way this renewed attention has unfolded. As probably may have been predicted, some in the field of modern Jewish ethics balked at these developments and reinforced conventional notions and practices that championed, for the most part, androcentric interests, gender binarism, and procreation's primacy, among other issues. Other scholars embraced the challenges feminisms raised and used their various tools to interrogate long-standing assumptions, rules, and rituals.[40] In short, there can be no singular or simple story about how feminisms, with their diverse attentions to gender and sexuality issues, intersect with modern Jewish ethics.

The pieces here do more theoretical work than pragmatic. Consider, for example, Daniel Boyarin's 1995 essay on desire. It starts with a classic Judaic source extolling licit heterosexual desire and sex within the confines of marriage. Through careful analysis of a sampling of rabbinic sources, Boyarin argues that rabbinic ideas about desire do not align as comfortably with a dualist view in which persons wrestle with two distinct desires (one good, the other evil) as they do with a dialectical one wherein desire is understood to be both good and evil, especially when it comes to sexuality. He moves on to analyze the rabbinic wont to metaphorize sex with references to food (e.g., "setting the table"). Just as eating fulfills several purposes simultaneously with bodily nourishment being one of them, sex also has multiple valuable purposes, with procreation being probably the most privileged among them.

By contrast, Tamar Ross's 2004 book, *Expanding the Palace of Torah: Orthodoxy and Feminism*, digs into the ways feminisms challenge Orthodox Judaism. Hers is more than a reflection on halakha and how women figure in Jewish law. Ross presents an extended historical review of how different "waves" of feminisms challenge conventional halakhic structures, theologies, and meta-ethics. The aim is to maintain the commitment to divine revelation while seeking "to break down the usual distinction between naturalistic, historic processes and claims of transcen-

---

40. See, for example, two early Jewish feminists elsewhere in this volume: Judith Plaskow, *Standing Again at Sinai* (part 1, section 2) and Rachel Adler, *Engendering Judaism* (part 1, section 3). For a more recent voice exploring difference and similarity, see Rafael Rachel Neis, "'All That Is in the Settlement': Humans, Likeness, and Species in the Rabbinic Bestiary" (part 3, section 14). For a feminist interrogation of Jewish marriage, see Gail Labovitz, *Marriage and Metaphor: Constructions of Gender in Rabbinic Literature* (part 2, section 7). For a reevaluation of Jewish ethics with regard to procreation, see Rebecca Epstein-Levi, "Person-Shaped Holes: Childfree Jews, Jewish Ethics, and Communal Continuity" (part 2, section 7).

dence."[41] This leads Ross to present a "cumulativist view of revelation," in which Jewish women are empowered to view themselves embedded therein.

Laura Levitt's 2009 selection juxtaposes two prominent feminist scholars, Audre Lorde (1934–1992), a Black lesbian poet and philosopher, and Judith Plaskow,[42] to explore dimensions of the erotic turn to the other. Levitt celebrates Plaskow's call for respect, responsibility, and honesty as a way to open up the possibility of non-heterosexual eroticism and intimacy. Yet simultaneously, Levitt critiques Plaskow for embracing a liberal view of marriage, complete with its asymmetries of power, as the metric against which lesbian and gay relationships are to be evaluated. Levitt calls for a "vision of the erotic that does not already presume a single erotic ideal even for (Jewish) feminists."[43]

Finally, the 2023 selection by Max Strassfeld pushes the conversation forward, challenging the social categories of sex and gender by closely analyzing trans and intersex identities in classic Judaic sources. In one part of his work, Strassfeld considers how the Leviticus prohibition of "lying with a man" applies to an *androginos*, an individual with several sexual organs, to show that "penetrability, gender, and body itself are remapped."[44] Such a lens disaggregates bodies from rules, roles, and expectations thereof, and resists the scholarly habit of conflating contemporary categories of sex and gender with ancient ones.

---

41. Tamar Ross, *Expanding the Palace of Torah: Orthodoxy and Feminism* (Waltham, MA: Brandeis University Press, 2004), xx.

42. For more on Plaskow, see part 1, section 2.

43. Laura Levitt, "Love the One You're with," in *The Passionate Torah: Sex and Judaism*, ed. Danya Ruttenberg (New York: New York University Press, 2009), 256.

44. Max Strassfeld, *Trans Talmud: Androgynes and Eunuchs in Rabbinic Literature* (Oakland: University of California Press, 2023), 104.

DANIEL BOYARIN

Dialectics of Desire: "The Evil Instinct Is Very Good"

Daniel Boyarin (b. 1946) is a professor emeritus at the University of California, Berkeley. Trained as a scholar of rabbinic literature at the Jewish Theological Seminary, he invigorated Jewish studies when he brought concepts and methodologies of critical theory to bear on rabbinic texts in works exploring intertextuality and gender in the early 1990s. A prodigious scholar of books integrating religious studies, psychoanalysis, and cultural studies, he interrogates theological, conceptual, and behavioral borders in his work, ranging over such topics as early Christianity, modern masculinities, and diasporic alternatives to Zionism.

From "Dialectics of Desire: 'The Evil Instinct Is Very Good,'" in *Carnal Israel: Reading Sex in Talmudic Culture* (Berkeley: University of California Press, 1995), 61–76.

The first half of the story is an etiological myth,[45] which explains why the Jews of rabbinic times are no longer attracted to the worship of idols. Upon returning from the Babylonian exile, the Jews prayed to God to have the desire for such worship removed from them, and their prayers were answered favorably. They were able to capture the Desire for idolatry and to execute him. In the second half of the story, the Jews attempt to rid themselves similarly of desire for sexual transgression, i.e., adultery and incest. They capture the personified Desire, but Desire himself warns them that he is necessary to the continuation of the world. Prudently, instead of executing him they imprison him for three days, only to discover that there are no eggs in the world. Eggs are, of course, the ultimate symbol of generation and regeneration. Realizing that nothing can be done about the situation, for halfway prayers are not answered, they blind him and let him go. The blinding avails to reduce the desire for incest with one's closest relatives—but no more.

The crucial sentence in the story is that halfway prayers are not answered. It is this which gives us the central clue to the rabbinic psychology and their concept of Evil Desire. In order for there to be desire and thus sexuality at all, they are saying, there must also be the possibility of illicit desire. Desire is one, and killing off desire for illicit sex will also kill off the desire for licit sex, which is necessary

45. [The story is quoted from Bavli *Yoma* 69b about returnees from Babylonian exile.]

for the continuation of life. Unlike the desire for idolatry, which serves no useful purpose other than testing resistance, the desire for sex is itself productive and vital—but it has destructive and negative concomitants. These concomitants need to be controlled, and can be, but only with difficulty. Desire itself is referred to as the "Evil Desire" because of this admixture of destructiveness and lawlessness that it necessarily carries, not because licit sexual desire and expression are evil in any way according to the rabbis. This interpretation gives us important clues for the understanding of several seemingly mysterious rabbinic dicta....

I wish to suggest that there were two partially conflicting psychologies within rabbinic culture. One was more straightforwardly dualistic, considering the human will to be composed of good and evil instincts at war with each other; the other psychology, the one to which I have been relating up until now, regarded the human being as having a singly monistic nature, which is, however, dialectical in structure.[46] ...

Once again, my hypothesis here is that those rabbinic texts that speak of the Evil Desire as being necessary and even good represent a dialectical anthropological tradition that stands in opposition to an alternative dualist one, and that this oppositional dialectical tradition holds that good and evil are inextricably bound up in the human being and especially in sexuality. There is a strong tendency in the dialectical tradition to dispense with the term "Evil Desire" entirely and refer to that entity simply as "Desire," as in the legend from the Babylonian Talmud with which this section was begun. Because that legend is perhaps the most openly thematized representation of the impossibility of separating the evil from the good in sexuality, its language provides confirmation of my suggestion that texts that refer only to Desire hold to the dialectical and not the dualistic ideology....

One of the most pervasive metaphors for sex in Talmudic literature associates it with food. A close reading of this metaphorical field will provide important clues to the rabbinic discourse of sexuality in general, in contrast to that of other cultural formations, in which sexuality was figured in the semantic field of elimination. For example, wives in the Talmudic texts to be discussed below describe their and their husbands' sexual practice as "setting the table" and "turning it over," and the Talmud itself produces a comparison between sexuality and food —either of which one may "cook" however one pleases, provided only that it is

---

46. Note that by "dualist" here I do *not* mean the dualism of body and soul or matter and spirit.

kosher to begin with. This metaphorical association is very productive in the culture, producing (or supporting) normative determinations of various types . . .

Let us think about the functions of eating in our culture. I think we all assume that its primary purpose has to do with the continuation of the vitality of the body, though we also recognize other very important functions and values for eating, including pleasure in good food, social binding from sharing food and eating together, and even ritual purposes in many groups from particular acts of eating. All of these are understood, however, as being subordinated to and generated by the primary function of eating, the continuation of life in the body. We consider absurd if not repelling such cultural practices as that of those Romans who reportedly caused themselves to vomit so that they could eat again. I think that for the rabbis, sexuality was conceived of in an analogous fashion. It was clear to them that the primary purpose for the existence of sexuality was the continuation of creation—in many senses: first and foremost, procreation. However, there were also well-understood and valorized secondary purposes for sexuality: pleasure, intimacy, and corporeal well-being. When the rabbis speak of pleasure and intimacy as leading to the conception of desirable children, then, they are simply integrating various realms of erotic life into one harmonious whole. When for whatever reason sex could not be procreative, its other purposes remained valid and valorized, for as we have seen, in this culture's normative determinations, sex was permitted and indeed encouraged with pregnant and sterile wives. And when pregnancy was contraindicated for medical reasons, contraception was permitted for the pleasure and health of the body. Sexuality was primarily oriented toward the needs of the body, and the central need of the body was to continue its life, through eating and ultimately through reproducing. . . .

In fine, then, what I am suggesting is that rabbinic Judaism was marked by a double discourse on human good and evil. The first was a moral psychology in which a fully formed Evil Instinct contested with a Good Instinct within the breast of each human being. The goal was, of course, for the Good Instinct to defeat the Evil Instinct. There is a tendency—but only that—for the Evil Instinct to be identified with sexuality in this anthropology, although some texts seem only to identify illicit sexuality with the Evil Instinct. In contrast to this, there is another ideology in which humans are made of only one kind of Desire. Although sometimes this tradition uses the term "Evil Desire," it uses it in paradoxical ways that subvert its association with evil per se and make it refer to the destructive aspects that are inseparable from sexuality along with its creative aspects. At times, in this tradition, we find even the disappearance of the modifier "evil," and we are left with Desire alone, Desire that leads human beings both to enormous feats of creativity and love and to enormous deeds of destruction and violence as well. "To the extent that a person is superior to his or her fellows, to that extent will his or her Desire be greater also."[47] Although the second (dialectical) tradition uses the language of the dualist tradition, it does so only to subvert it. For this tradition, the use of the term *yetzer hara* does not by any means mark desire as evil but only denotes a recognition of the potential for evil that resides within all sexuality and desire.

Procreation, then, is not the "purpose" or the justification or excuse for sexuality but its very essence in rabbinic thought. Just as, for them, the very essence of eating is to continue the life of the body, so the very essence of sexuality is to continue the life of the collective body. In neither case, however, are other values and purposes excluded or even marginalized. But there is a strong construction of desire as problematic and ineluctably dangerous as well. In this reading of desire, then, rabbinic culture fits neither with medieval Christian theological notions of the sinfulness of all concupiscence, nor with modern conceptions of the innocence of all desire, but somewhere else, all its own.

TAMAR ROSS

Expanding the Palace of Torah: Orthodoxy and Feminism

Tamar Ross (b. 1938) taught Jewish philosophy, with a special focus on religious feminist philosophy, at Bar-Ilan University in Israel. An advocate of "Expanding the Palace of Torah," which sees feminism as innate to Judaism, and cumulative revelation, she writes broadly on Judaism, gender, and modern Jewish thought and has served in leadership roles for the Jewish Orthodox Feminist Alliance.

From *Expanding the Palace of Torah: Orthodoxy and Feminism* (Waltham, MA: Brandeis University Press, 2004), 210–12.

10. *The Word of God Contextualized*

Feminists may look askance at considering patriarchy a manifestation of divine providence or a gradual unfolding of the divine being. By the same token, however, we may also consider the emergence of feminism as a new revelation

47. [See Bavli *Sukkah* 52a.]

of the divine will; we may see a newly evolving appreciation of the importance, integrity, and value of female spirituality in our time as a rare religious privilege. The cumulative understanding of revelation allows us to view the phenomenon of feminism itself—even if it appears to stem from sources outside of Judaism—as a gift from God. In this sense, assimilating feminism into Judaism is no different than the imbibing of Aristotelianism by Maimonidean rationalism or the absorption of certain ideas from Gnosticism and the Neoplatonic tradition by the Kabbalah, among other examples. What we are now beginning to know is being bestowed upon us. We are the beneficiaries of what has gone before us, as we grope toward a new light reaching out to us from God. Listening to feminist claims with sympathy and understanding need not be thought of as a deep violation of Jewish tradition. Instead, it should be regarded as a spiritual undertaking of the first order (an *avodat kodesh*, or holy task).

If feminism is indeed thrust upon us today in a manner that cannot be avoided or ignored, this constraint is not a problem but an agenda to be addressed and incorporated positively into Jewish religious life. A cumulativist view of revelation permits us to entertain the thought that some feminist understandings reflect more refined moral sensibilities that ought to accrue to the original religious model and even alter its meaning. At the same time, such accretions do not violate in any way the formal status of that model as an immutable element of our foundational canon. For men, regarding feminism as the manifestation of higher moral sensibilities, instead of as a necessary evil or as pandering to the spirit of the times, may mean voluntarily ceding the privileges of hierarchy for the sake of greater equality and justice. For women, it represents the taking on of greater active participation and responsibility in the religious life, instead of merely enjoying vicarious merit through the accomplishments of the menfolk. Patriarchy, in this scheme, is not an eternally fixed and ideal social form, but rather something necessary for its time, which can now be recognized as a stepping-stone, the residual traces of which continue to function as a necessary prism for the achievement of greater moral sensibilities.

In sum, the importance of a cumulativist understanding of God's revelation, as communicated in a gradual manner via natural historical process, is twofold. First, it allows for the very possibility of divine communication, despite the inevitability of cultural bias. It also provides a way of accommodating feminist claims to hearing a new message free of that bias, without undermining the authority of the original. In seeing the initial core divine message as scaffolding to build upon, the understanding of revelation as accumulating embodies one of the most important contributions that historic religion can offer to the feminist enterprise.

Valuing the past is a central feature of the religious sensibility. It comes to teach us that there is a powerful spirituality in uniting with that which went before. Tradition is the special way our parents and grandparents spoke and sang to God. And while a good measure of nostalgia is no doubt present whenever an old tune is sung, it is not only nostalgia that makes us sing. Maintaining the practices of the past allows us not only to unite with our immediate community, but also with all our coreligionists all over the world. It connects us to those no longer with us—and even to those as yet unborn: according to *midrash* (*Shemot Rabbah* 28), they also participated in the revelation at Sinai. It adds the weight of precedent and continuity to the authority and legitimacy of our current endeavors. It allows us to incorporate valuable sources of inspiration from the past in fleshing out the empty spaces of our here and now. It affords us a bond with something larger than ourselves, and establishes our contemporary way of doing things as the realization of an ancient dream, rather than merely a passing whim. It expresses the insight that no human being can create ex nihilo, and that there is no neutral territory we can escape to in developing our present and our future. Abandoning tradition is tantamount to abandoning language itself.

At its deepest level, the feminist critique would most likely take this hymn to the past as evidence of my profound assumption of male categories of thought. Indeed, feminist theologian Daphne Hampson[48] regards seeking meaning in continuity with a past history, beyond the here and now, as a narrowly male way of experiencing the spiritual dimension of reality. In her eyes, theologies of revelation or of history do not place human beings at the center of the stage. In a theology of revelation, truth is not found within; it must be revealed precisely because it is other than the self. And in a theology of history, "the problem is not that the self has to base itself on that which is other than itself, but rather that there is little concentration on the individual self at all." As opposed to feminism's fundamental concern for the individual, and the transformation of individual lives, "the person knows salvation only as he or she is caught up in a greater whole which will be redeemed, and that scarcely in that person's lifetime!"[49]

I disagree. It is precisely traditionalist religion and a cumulativist merging with

---

48. [Daphne Hampson is a professor of theology at the University of Oxford.]
49. Daphne Hampson, *After Christianity* (London: SCM Press, 1996), 281–82.

history that is consonant with the uniquely feminine view of self as enmeshed in a web of relationships. Through tradition women may approach life in a manner that sees the greater significance of the passing moment not because they seek to transcend it, but because they see in it the reflection of other moments, and do not view the present as something discontinuous and atomized all on its own. Especially when traditionalism is linked with the concepts of process theology, it is precisely the emphasis on the interconnectedness of all reality that resonates to female sensibilities, potentially avoiding the dualism that has plagued so many conceptions of monotheism and its concomitant tendency to dichotomized thinking. Such traditionalism teaches that there is no basis for drawing strict boundaries between differing moral conceptions and separating them from the past in which they are grounded.

LAURA LEVITT

Love the One You're with

Laura Levitt (b. 1960) is a scholar of religion, Jewish studies, and gender at Temple University. An expert on material culture, trauma, and loss, she also works on feminism, sexual misconduct, the Holocaust, and story-telling. She has held leadership roles in the Association for Jewish Studies and the American Academy of Religion, among other academic and community organizations.

From "Love the One You're with," in *The Passionate Torah: Sex and Judaism,* ed. Danya Ruttenberg (New York: New York University Press, 2009), 245–58.

Plaskow[50] argues that her mutual vision of the erotic sharply contrasts with "the structures of marriage as Judaism defines them."[51] Although these arrangements still define Jewish women as subordinate to Jewish men, she focuses on their failure to recognize "the possibility of loving same-sex relationships."[52] Plaskow points out: "A first concrete task, then, of the feminist reconstruction of

50. [See part 1, section 2 for more information about and a selection by Judith Plaskow.]
51. Judith Plaskow, "Towards a New Theology of Sexuality," in *Twice Blessed: On Being Lesbian, Gay, and Jewish*, eds. Christie Balka and Andy Rose (Boston: Beacon Press, 1989), 144. In this account, Plaskow, like many other liberal theologians who build on the work of Buber imagining a relational covenant, does not directly refer to the rabbinic marriage contract, or *ketubah*, in her account of what becomes a marital covenant.
52. Plaskow, "Towards a New Theology of Sexuality," 144.

Jewish attitudes toward sexuality is a radical transformation of the institutional, legal framework within which sexual relations are supposed to take place."[53] Besides advocating lesbian and gay relationships, she also calls for a reaffirmation of consent as a criterion for her liberal feminist position. As Plaskow explains,

> In the modern West, it is generally assumed that such a decision [mutual consent] constitutes a central meaning of marriage, but this assumption is contradicted by a religious (and secular) legal system that outlaws homosexual marriage and institutionalizes inequality in its basic definition of marriage and divorce.

In this way, Plaskow opens up the legal definition of marriage to include gay and lesbian relationships without altering the structure of liberalism's legal framework. For her, marriage continues to be about consent, which she uses as an answer to patriarchy as well. Marriage, she contends, will not be about the acquisition of women by their husbands or the sanctification of potential disorder through the firm establishment of women in the patriarchal family, but about the decision of two adults to make their lives together, lives that include the sharing of sexuality.

This is where Plaskow's argument begins to break down, because she cannot fully distinguish between the modern Western legal tradition and her feminist alternative. She cannot account for the fact that the patriarchal family is not just a rabbinic problem; therefore, even her efforts to affirm lesbian and gay relationships are based on a liberal premise of inclusion. Lesbian and gay relationships are affirmed in their likeness to liberal marriage, not in their queerness....

For me, Lorde's[54] construction of the erotic also offers a new perspective on relationships and selves in their complexity, over and against the sexual contract and other forms of individual and social oppression. Among these, Lorde includes resignation, despair, self-effacement, depression, and self-denial. In this way she acknowledges how she has internalized and sustained various histories of oppression within herself, even as she works against them. In these ways her text speaks to me and is a reminder of how the erotic is powerful and liberating without having to contain its powers within an overarching framework. This

---

53. Plaskow, "Towards a New Theology of Sexuality," 145.

54. [Audre Lorde was a twentieth-century Black scholar, poet, and civil rights activist who worked on a range of topics, including oppression, feminism, sexuality, and disability.]

contingency is what is inviting about Lorde's work. In other words, the contingent nature of Lorde's notion of the erotic opens it up to different possibilities. In this case, the possibilities it opens are Plaskow's two different interpretations of the theology of sexuality.[55] The specificity of Lorde's account, as opposed to its all-inclusiveness, makes it highly appealing to me. I do not have to share Lorde's position to learn from her; I can apply her approach to my own situation, and this may even lead to contradictory results.

Lorde's notion of the erotic is at the heart of Plaskow's theology of sexuality, giving shape and texture to some of Plaskow's most powerful accounts of community, relation, and belonging. In these moments, Lorde offers an alternative to Plaskow's normative vision of liberal inclusion. I have focused on Plaskow's reading of Lorde because I see it as a promising site of contradiction within Plaskow's text. Through reading Lorde, Plaskow begins to push at the seams of her own liberal feminist stance. What I have tried to demonstrate is that these are, indeed, liberating moments. Within Plaskow's understanding of Lorde, she offers a more contingent feminist notion of erotic community that challenges her liberal theological vision. It is this partial vision that I carry with me out of Plaskow's text as an alternative to her liberal feminist position....

By returning to my reading against the grain of Plaskow's text and thinking again about the relationship between the *Vayikra Rabbah* passage[56] and Lorde's essay, I want to build a bridge from Lorde through Plaskow to Brettschneider.[57]

---

55. Lorde herself writes about these connections in "Age, Race, Class, and Sex: Women Redefining Difference," in *Out There: Marginalization and Contemporary Cultures*, eds. Russell Ferguson, Martha Gever, Trinh T. Minh-ha, and Cornel West (Cambridge, MA: MIT Press, 1990), 281–88. She writes: "Black women and white women are not the same. For example, it is easy for Black women to be used by the power structure against Black men, not because they are men, but because they are Black. Therefore, for Black women, it is necessary at all times to separate the needs of the oppressor from our own legitimate conflicts within our communities. This same problem does not exist for white women. Black women and men have shared racist oppression and still share it, although in different ways. Out of that shared oppression we have developed joint defenses and joint vulnerabilities to each other that are not duplicated in the white community, with the exception of the relationship between Jewish women and Jewish men" (284).

56. ["David said before God, 'My father Jesse did not intend to sire me, but intended only his own pleasure. You know that this is so because after the parents satisfied themselves, *he turned his face away and she turned her face away* and You joined the drops'" (Levitt's emphasis). *Vayikra Rabbah* 14.5, ed. Margoles, 2:308.]

57. [Marla Brettschneider is a professor of gender, women's studies, and political science at the University of New Hampshire.]

Maintaining Plaskow's criteria of respect, responsibility, and honesty, I want to more fully appreciate those rare and powerful moments when we can and do love the ones we are with. Building on the work of Martin Buber,[58] Brettschneider explicitly challenges the institutions of marriage and monogamy. As she explains,

> In the expectations and promises of monogamous marriage the present is lost, and relation becomes an object with a pretense to the future as real. For Buber this is a stultifying of the present. It is not the aliveness promised by the ideological vision, but instead "cessation, suspension, a breaking off and cutting clear and hardening, absence of relation and of being present."[59]

We are no longer able to connect to ones we are with. To do that means embracing a vision of the erotic that does not already presume a single normative erotic ideal even for (Jewish) feminists.

MAX STRASSFELD

Trans Talmud: Androgynes and Eunuchs in Rabbinic Literature

Max Strassfeld (b. 1976) is a scholar of rabbinic literature, transgender studies, and Jewish studies at the University of Southern California. His most recent monograph explores how Talmudic discussions about eunuchs and androgynes in halakha not only establish the rabbinic boundaries of normative masculinity but also reflect tensions around law and gender that invite a reevaluation of gender in Judaism and of transgender history more generally. He serves on the board for the Association for Jewish Studies.

From *Trans Talmud: Androgynes and Eunuchs in Rabbinic Literature* (Oakland: University of California Press, 2023), 183–88.

Conclusion: Re-Reading the Rabbis (Again)

In rabbinic literature, the drama of regulating unruly embodiment plays out over and against the bodies of androgynes and eunuchs.[60] Eunuchs and

---

58. [For more on Buber, see part 1, section 2, footnote 24.]

59. Marla Brettschneider, *The Family Flamboyant: Race Politics, Queer Families, Jewish Lives* (Albany: State University of New York Press, 2006), 133. The passage from Martin Buber cited here is from Martin Buber, *I and Thou* (New York: Collier Books, 1958), 13.

60. [Androgynes are persons with male and female characteristics, inclusive of biological sex, gender identity, and expression. Eunuchs are persons incapable of reproduction,

androgynes experience the vicissitudes of reproductive failures, uneven and idiosyncratic bodily development through time, the vulnerable penetrability of the body, and the uncertainties of sex changes. In response to these "failures," the rabbis subject eunuchs and androgynes to heightened levels of bodily surveillance, including genital scrutiny. This fascination with the bodies of eunuchs and androgynes elides the ways that it is not just eunuchs and androgynes that are subject to penetrability, reproductive failures, and stubborn idiosyncratic development. I have argued, therefore, that in the sources I have analyzed in this book, the rabbis displace the fragility and changeability of all bodies onto androgynes and eunuchs. And yet, the very attempts to define what makes androgynes and eunuchs unique point to the changeability of bodies and to the way all bodies may refuse to develop in accordance with normative gendered expectations.

Transing rabbinic literature has not, for me, located a gender-subversive core at the heart of rabbinic discourse. The rabbinic sources that I analyze in this book are often invested in shaping the entanglement of sex, sexuality, and embodiment, and are embedded within a (perhaps imaginary, but no less violent) disciplinary system. And yet, sometimes these stories also seem to offer an implicit critique of the feasibility or even desirability of the regulation of gender. Take, for example, the story of the androgyne with which I began [my] book and which I discussed at length in chapter 3:

> Rabbi [Yehudah HaNasi] relayed [the following story]: "When I went to learn rabbinic teachings with Rabbi Elazar ben Shamua, his students banded together against me like the [famously aggressive] roosters of Beit Bukiya.[61] They allowed me to learn only one teaching (and it was this]: "Rabbi Eliezer says that [in the case of the] androgyne: [the man who penetrates the androgyne anally] is liable for [the penalty of] stoning [for transgressing the prohibition against sex with a man, just] as [he would be if he had anal sex with a non-androgyne] male." (B. T. *Yevamot* 84a)

This is the story of Rabbi Yehudah HaNasi, who goes to learn from a teacher. Students block Rabbi Yehudah HaNasi's access to their teacher. Because of the

---

due in part to congenital or somatic reasons (like surgical castration). Strassfeld elaborates on the various terms in *Trans Talmud: Androgynes and Eunuchs in Rabbinic Literature* (Oakland: University of California Press, 2023), 6–9, 237–41.]

61. Beit Bukiya is a place-name.

interference of the students, Rabbi Yehudah HaNasi manages to learn only one teaching. This teaching is that a man who has anal sex with an androgyne transgresses the biblical prohibition against "lying with a man."

There are certainly ways to read this story as a critique of heteronormative gender. The penetrable body of the androgyne subverts the hypermasculine territorial boundary erected by the students. In that reading, the permeability of the androgyne is a metaphor for the potential for cross-fertilization when boundaries are transgressed. In other words, it is possible to interpret this story as a criticism, not just of aggressive masculinity but also of the value of maintaining strict dichotomies and boundaries. The story's critique focuses on scholarly boundaries; but through the inclusion of the body of the androgyne, that critique can be extended to other dichotomies, including the gender binary. In the debate over which kinds of penetrative sex with an androgyne constitute "lying with a man," the very sex of the androgyne seems to shift and morph....

Similarly, when the rabbis explore the instability of sex and gender, they set themselves up as interpreters of sexed materiality. The endless rabbinic debates shaping and reshaping the connection among genitals, sex, gender, and sexuality scrutinize and define eunuch and androgyne bodies. In turn, the rabbinic definitional and regulatory interests in sexed embodiment bring eunuchs and androgynes into the realm of halakha and therefore into rabbinic jurisdiction. It is the very fact that the rabbis do not invest in either stable sex, or in a clear binary, that enables them to become interpreters of sex.

When the rabbis absorb eunuchs and androgynes into halakha, then, they position themselves as experts on sex, with the ability to interpret bodies and assign roles, rituals, and obligations on the basis of that interpretation. When, for example, the rabbis rename the anus of the androgyne as the "masculine orifice," they are mapping the body. Renaming can often function as a powerful tool of trans resignification. I was not born with the name "Max," for example. Trans people rename body parts to match our embodied self-knowledge as well. And yet, in this case, renaming is a type of mapping that colonizes the territory it describes.

At the same time, while the mutability of sex enables rabbinic halakhic expertise, it also has paradoxical effects. Even as the rabbis position themselves as interpreters of sex through their close scrutiny of the ways in which sex can change (either through time or owing to transformations of the body), this very mutability also makes eunuchs and androgynes difficult to regulate. When the rabbis discuss in lengthy and intimate detail the ways in which sex changes for androgynes and eunuchs, the changeability of bodies is precisely what makes it so difficult to definitively "know" a person's sex. For example... if the disambiguating surgery practiced on the *tumtum*[62] does not wholly demonstrate their capacity for reproduction, then there are limits to our ability to determine masculine reproductivity from the scrutiny of sexed bodies.... The way in which changes to genitalia, and the consequent halakhic judgment of some genitals as kosher, are connected to a social system of access to women. Because sexed embodiment can change at any time, this kind of genital surveillance, which is linked to social consequences, speaks to the ultimate impossibility of definitively determining which men are fit for which kind of marriages. The very same emphasis on mutability, then, simultaneously undermines the possibilities for stable knowledge about sex/gender. In many of the sources I have analyzed in this book, there are visible cracks in the rabbis' ability to definitively identify and assign sex/gender....

I have nevertheless been cautious throughout this book about trumpeting the subversive potential of eunuchs and androgynes. This is, in part, because it is almost impossible for me to know the cost of that subversion to the people who inhabited those categories at the time. The mutability of sex and gender has, at different historical times and in diverse places, led to classifying certain bodies as incoherent. As we know from more recent history, the repercussions of gendered incoherency can sometimes be deadly. Violence (whether rhetorical or material) underlies many of the rabbinic sources. Subversion, then, may be bought at too high a price when we lack an ability to account adequately for harm. In this respect, I remain stubbornly attached to the "bad" literal reading of the materiality of sex, of bodies that existed in the world, and what it might have meant to them to navigate contested and changing terrain.

My research on eunuchs and androgynes poses a series of larger questions that are ultimately beyond the scope of this [work]: Since bodies change through time, and bodily functions are not entirely within our control, are there limits to the rabbis' ability to regulate the body? How do the rabbis address this seemingly endless variability of bodies within the structure of halakha without sacrificing the idea that halakha is flexible enough to address every situation? There is an

---

62. [*Earlier in the book, Strassfeld defines Tumtum as* "a person with a flap of skin covering their genitals. If the flap of skin were to be removed, the *tumtum*'s sex would be revealed. The *tumtum* is conceptually linked to the *androginos*; while the *androginos* has a surplus of visible genitalia, the *tumtum* has a dearth." Strassfeld, *Trans Talmud*, 9.]

inherent tension in the way that bodies exceed the strictures of halakha, in parallel to the way that bodies exceed their own boundaries: the rabbis extensively contemplate bodies that leak or bleed, become "damaged," lose bodily integrity, or challenge orderly taxonomies. Texts that address gender, sexuality, ethnicity, and disability tend to foreground these questions. Perhaps the rabbis invoke these categories to grapple with the regulation of the body and the limits of the halakhic enterprise itself....

The idea of "Jewish law" as a unified entity is a fiction, and rulings often draw on centuries of different layers of debate, codes, and responsa, alongside medical and scientific knowledge, among other sources. Still, even as "Jewish law" is not synonymous with rabbinic literature, it is my hope that the analysis in this book undermines simple and straightforward narratives about halakha and sex change. While the rabbinic sources are not radical from a contemporary trans and queer perspective, they incorporate eunuchs and androgynes into halakhic discussion, and they do so at length. In most cases, this extensive engagement with eunuchs and androgynes cannot be explained by any formal relationship with the Hebrew Bible. The rabbis chose to situate nonbinary people at the heart of rabbinic discussions of sex and gender. At the same time, when they discuss eunuchs and androgynes, the rabbis embed the mutability of sex within those conversations. Sexed mutability is inscribed from the very earliest layers of the sources. These rabbinic sources should complicate any easy appeal to a (singular) position of halakha on sex changes.

At the very least, rabbinic sources make laughable any appeal to a "Judeo-Christian" consensus on transsexuality. The Christian evangelical citation of Genesis as a prooftext for binary gender disregards the rest of the Hebrew Bible and the various categories of sex and gender that circulate biblically. But it also completely ignores any development in Judaism after the advent of Christianity. Given the rich and complex late antique discussions of eunuchs and androgynes in rabbinic literature that are roughly contemporaneous with the Christian Bible, ignoring all postbiblical Jewish texts is nonsensical. Of course, Focus on the Family[63] and its ilk are not trying to construct careful scholarly and philological genealogies of sexed changes within Judaism (or Christianity,

---

63. [Focus on the Family "is a global Christian ministry dedicated to helping families thrive. We provide help and resources for couples to build healthy marriages that reflect God's design, and for parents to raise their children according to morals and values grounded in biblical principles." https://www.focusonthefamily.com/about.]

for that matter). Still, this book arises out of a context in which Jewish ideas about sex and gender are both imagined and enlisted in the service of Christian evangelical aims. These deeply theological statements purport to represent Jewish opposition to trans theology as self-evident. In turn, this betrays a deeply supercessionist understanding of Judaism while simultaneously staking a claim for Christianity's ability to speak authoritatively for Jewish ethics and values. On occasion, contemporary Jewish thinkers similarly assume a Jewish antagonism to trans theology in the absence of any specific arguments or interpretations of texts. These ungrounded statements can be understood as colluding with a Christian evangelical agenda.

Similarly, within Jewish communities there is a persistent message that trans and intersex bodies are a question to be adjudicated, even when some halakhic decisions rule in favor of trans or intersex "inclusion." It should not surprise us, then, that trans and intersex Jewish activists have increasingly turned to biblical and rabbinic sources to interpret the tradition directly. As such, Jewish activists, rabbis, and artists have responded in turn, drawing on androgynes and eunuchs to provide proof of existence. In the face of the current drive to argue that trans and intersex people generally, and trans and intersex Jews specifically, should not exist, activists turn to the past to write themselves into history.

Genes

The well-known maxim of Ecclesiastes, "there's nothing new under the sun," suggests that whatever appears to be brand new might be a novel answer to a well-worn question. As Ecclesiastes continues: "Sometimes there is a new phenomenon of which they say, 'Look, this one is new'—it occurred long since, in ages that went by before us" (Eccles. 1:10). Similarly, a contemporary technology may certainly be innovative, yet address long-standing issues or concerns. In this regard, genetic technologies are no exception. The dramatic advances of recent years through pioneering genetic technologies nonetheless address enduring anxieties and challenges. For example, while genetically modified food crops (GMOs) are often developed for aesthetics or sustainability concerns, they address an ancient human concern about securing stable nourishment. More recently, CRISPR-cas-9 technologies facilitate manipulation of DNA in viruses, organs, and even organisms like humans. Since Covid-19, mRNA vaccines are increasingly de rigueur, yet they too are just another device in the proverbial biomedical toolbox to keep humans healthy. And though genetic modification of the human genome is no longer some utopian dream, the application of these tools raises serious ethical concerns about the nature of human nature. Where are the boundaries of and what are the characteristics of the human—and what would it mean were we to conscientiously manipulate them by meddling with the human genome? The answers to such questions are as ethically troublesome as determining who gets to make those answers. Some of these questions are addressed in the selections here.

Paul Root Wolpe's 1997 selection, "If I Am Only My Genes, What Am I? Genetic Essentialism and a Jewish Response," reflects on recent trends that constitute what has been dubbed the Genetic Age. Modern genetics offers "a biologized portrait of human behavior, personality, and physicality—in short, a portrait of a genetic sense of selfhood." Such genetic essentialism carries within it the tantalizing opportunity to view ourselves as a text awaiting professional decoding. It also enables us to pathologize ourselves and thereby "relieve us of the burden of working to gain self-knowledge." Better genes, not insights or communal support, will solve our problems. Instead of offering "an exercise of Jewish bioethics" that privileges texts, Wolpe attends to these observations through "an exercise in the bioethics of Jews" that looks to Jewish historical and bodily experiences. Diaspora, embodiment, and eugenics serve for him as experiences that justify being "wary of the temptation of the possible." In his view, we are emphatically *not* only our genes.

A dozen years after the human genome was completely sequenced in 2003, Robert Gibbs analogized gene therapy to repairing a Torah scroll. In his selection, "Mending the Code," he aims to show "a parallel kind of reasoning about the limits of mending" — that only certain kinds of errors and tears warrant intervention. He makes this argument through iterative close readings of three pieces from the Talmudic tractate *Menachot* that address the importance and limits of repairing mistakes and ruptures in a Torah scroll. Do mistakes disqualify a Torah scroll? What makes a column perfect — one without mistakes or one with correctable mistakes? What if a word (a name of God, in particular) is missing: Where, if anywhere, should it go and how? And what kinds of tears may be repaired, and which not? If the analogy between textual repair and genetic therapy holds, Gibbs argues that limits to mending and ways of reasoning toward those limits warrant careful consideration.

During the surge of the Black Lives Matter movement, concerns about race animated Jewish ethical conversations of all sorts, including Sarah Imhoff's investigation of "how ideas about race can structure Jewishness." She begins her selection by referencing recent advertisements for DNA testing companies that imply a genetic basis of Jewishness. These fall into the trap of racialist thinking, a kind of logic that posits heritable characteristics and traits shared exclusively by certain groups or races. Imhoff demonstrates that there are significant costs to racialist conceptualizations of Jewishness, which exclude large swaths of people who identify as Jewish as well as include many who do not. A more compelling method that may be less fixed, knowable, and certain is one that relies more on performance, as intimated by the biblical story of those "standing with us" at the moment of revelation in Exodus 20.

These selections articulate serious disquiet among Jewish ethicists about the power, meaning, and limitations of genetic technologies and genetic ways of knowing. Yet theirs is not a call to stop advancing these technologies or ways of knowing. Rather, they demonstrate that novel technologies touch on ancient concerns. They offer diverse critiques — sociological, textual, racial — that enrich collective deliberation about the means and ends of the Genetic Age.

PAUL ROOT WOLPE

If I Am Only My Genes, What Am I?
Genetic Essentialism and a Jewish Response

Paul Root Wolpe (b. 1957) holds appointments in medicine, pediatrics, psychiatry, neuroscience and biological behavior, and sociology at Emory University. A bioethicist and futurist, he focuses on the social, religious, ethical, and ideological impact of medicine and technology on the human condition. Most recently he was director of Emory's Center for Ethics. He was a senior bioethicist for NASA and has held leadership positions in the American Society for Bioethics and Humanities, among other organizations.

From "If I Am Only My Genes, What Am I? Genetic Essentialism and a Jewish Response," *Kennedy Institute of Ethics Journal* 7, no. 3 (1997): 213–30.

We have begun the process of changing our perceptions of who we are and who we will become on the basis of such genetic information. While the average person resists it, we see more and more the cultural drift toward genetic essentialism, the idea that our lives and our behaviors are simply the inevitable reflection of our genotypes. Even good and evil have been given over to our genes. We used to say a man had a black or evil soul; now we speak of his evil as being in his genes. Genes have become the metaphorical locus of our fate—our personalities, our successes, our kindness and goodness are no longer products of a life mastered, but prizes in the genetic lottery. In fact, if we get good enough at this, we will be able to design into our descendants all the traits we value. A trip to the gene store, and we can have children who are kind, generous, and self-reliant—and we will take blue eyes and 160 IQ while we are here, thank you....

Of course, being able to replicate human beings has its down side as well. Jean Bethke Elshtain[64] (1997) complains in *The New Republic* that if the wrong people get hold of genetic technologies, we might be confronted by an "army of Hitlers;" nor is Elshtain the only one to have made that analogy. It is the ultimate irony that Hitler, the man who institutionalized the idea of genetic essentialism and took it to its final solution, has become the poster child of those arguing against it. People who talk about cloning an "army of Hitlers" little realize that by arguing that a cloned Hitler would be a Hitler, sharing his traits of hatred

---

64. [Jean Bethke Elshtain was an American political philosopher and ethicist and a professor at the University of Chicago Divinity School.]

and control, they are affirming and reinforcing the very genetic essentialism in which Hitler so deeply believed and that he used to slaughter millions.

How simple and yet terrifying it will be if it turns out that all that we are, this self that we have spent so many centuries glorifying and elevating above the mundane, is reducible to our accidental biological legacy; if the true divine text is not the one engraved by the finger of God in stone on Sinai, but the one that has been here all along written into millions of base-pairs in our cells; the voice of God not in sound and fury but the barest microscopic whisper. This is not a Jewish (or Christian) view of the soul. But it is a seductive one. From the Jewish perspective, however, such a cultural attitude is a kind of idolatry; for what is idolatry, but a worship of the representations of power instead of the ultimate power?

* * *

We have created a sense of self written into the letters of our personal genotypes and have invested that vision of the self with all the power and prestige of modern science. It matters little that science itself is wary of such reductionism; as David Cox, a Stanford geneticist, has stated:

> From the molecular genetics point of view, it's absolutely clear that we're demolishing the arguments of genetic determinism. But the facts have never got in the way of people who wanted to use genetics in a deterministic way in our society.[65]

Science could not foist such a profound reinterpretation of the self onto a society without a cultural predisposition to accept it. Certainly it is true that there is a long history of eugenic thinking in the Western world and that modern genetics to some degree taps into a Western tendency to periodically use biological and racial categorizations to explain social and political realities. Yet the anthropologist Mary Douglas[66] has written: "The human body is always treated as an image of society and . . . there can be no natural way of considering the body that does not involve at the same time a social dimension."[67] So, too, with the genetic self; there is something uniquely powerful about modern genetic es-

---

65. [Quoted in Arthur Allen, "Policing the Gene Machine: Can Anyone Control the Human Genome Project?," *Lingua Franca* (March 1997): 34.]

66. [Mary Douglas was a British structural anthropologist who taught at University of College London.]

67. Mary Douglas, *Natural Symbols* (New York: Pantheon Books, 1970), 70.

sentialism, for it taps into a powerful cultural trend that has nothing to do with eugenics....

We live in the age of hermeneutics and the metaphor of society as a text. Virtually all modern intellectual traditions, from sociology to philosophy to legal studies, have been profoundly influenced by the idea that all human interaction is a type of text and all text is subject to the disciplines of literary analysis and criticism. Science has always been profoundly influenced by the intellectual currents in the culture in which it is embedded, and the "rhetorical turn" in intellectual fashion, as it has been called, is no exception.

Today we see the process of textual decoding as the path to truth. Is it any wonder then that our particular understanding of the human organism should be reduced to a decipherable biological text? That we have relinquished the Bible to a new set of sacred letters, which, when rearranged in the right way, when interpreted by our revered experts, when manipulated through complex rituals of micropipette, polymerase chain reaction, and delivery vector, will create the perfect life, the perfect personality, the perfect society?...

What cultural question, then, does the genetic self solve?...

Finally, after setting the genetic stage and painting a portrait of the modern, genetic self, let us turn to Jewish experience and tradition to see what it can add to the discussion. Judaism has an enormous body of literature on a number of bioethical issues, and rabbis and scholars already have begun the task of creating religious responses to modern genetics based on Talmudic law and textual interpretation. Here, however, I will focus on a single problem—the Jewish response to genetic selfhood—and will look to Jewish historical experience, not texts, for insights. In other words, rather than an exercise in Jewish bioethics, the following discussion might be seen as an exercise in the bioethics of Jews.

Judaism has a long history of making problematic the idea of selfhood. In fact, one of the most famous sayings in all of Jewish tradition is explicitly about the nature of the self and is paraphrased in the title to this article. It is the saying of the sage Hillel: "If I am not for myself, who will be for me? And if I am only for myself, what am I? And if not now, when?" [Pirkei Avot 1.14] Hillel underscores the centrality of the idea of self in Judaism by asking, "If I am not for myself, who will be for me?" We are each responsible for the maintenance and development of selfhood. But he goes on: "And if I am only for myself, what am I?" In Jewish thought, the self is not defined in isolation, but in relation to a community. The genetic self does not fulfill Hillel's dictum; a genetic self can only be for itself.

Hillel began the long discussion of selfhood that Jews have brought with them through their travels in the diaspora. But it was their diaspora experiences that sharpened and defined Hillel's dictum and imbued Jewish experience with a singular perspective on the self. Three examples may suffice to show the fruitfulness of this kind of inquiry.

* * *

The Jews, as a diaspora people, have always had the problem of establishing an identity in the context of the culture in which they lived. Much of Jewish history is a struggle to live in some dynamic tension between the expectations of society and the expectations of being Jewish....

Jews have always understood that identity is chosen, is to some degree the product of moral choice. The great American Hollywood myth, the individual triumphing over odds and holding on to principle in face of the pressures of a hostile world or great challenge was in no small degree a Jewish invention. The absolution the genetic self offers for the responsibility for one's behavior is anathema to Jewish thinking and to Jewish experience.

* * *

The second reason that Jews have something unique to say about genetic selfhood is that Judaism has, since the earliest days of the Talmud, been preoccupied with the conflict inherent in our being divine yet embodied creatures....

Judaism never has been naive about embodiment and never has denied the basic physical nature of the human being or its needs. Sexuality never has been denigrated in Judaism, is not the result of a "fall," and sexual pleasure, within the confines of marriage, is extolled. Similarly, there is no true ascetic tradition in Judaism, no celibacy, no abstention from alcohol. There are strict controls around these things, but little value is placed on renunciation. Judaism thus recognizes the ongoing tension between our corporeality and our divinity, and much of Jewish tradition is dedicated to managing that tension through ritual. The genetic self, however, can speak only to our embodiment, and undermines the delicate balance that the tension between corporeality and divinity always presents to humanity....

The third reason Jews must contribute to any discussion of the genetic self is their unique history as the victims of biological and eugenic categorizations. The Jewish cosmogonic myth, the Jewish myth of origin, was the first fundamentally anti-racist myth, postulating a common ancestor for all humanity. The Talmud states, "for the sake of peace among creatures, the descent of all men is traced back to one individual, so that one may not say to his neighbor, my father is greater than yours" (*Sanhedrin* 4:5). The irony, of course, is that Jews so often have been the victims of precisely the opposite thinking. . . .

Therein lies the great danger of modern eugenic manipulation, a point too seldom commented upon, a sociological point about the dangers of misunderstanding the meaning of living in a particular historical moment in a particular society. Imagine what would have happened had genetic engineering techniques been available in the 1850s, 1900s, or, for that matter, in the 1950s. Imagine for a moment the traits that those societies would have chosen to splice in and weed out of their offspring, thus molding future generations. Physiological traits were said to determine personality in the 1850s—imagine if you could weed those traits out of Jews and others. Women in the early twentieth century were supposed to be delicate and to faint at the sight of blood; why not select for those desirable traits? Teenagers in the 1950s were often portrayed as too promiscuous, suffering from rampant hormones that had to be controlled and in constant danger of masturbating or getting themselves or their partners "into trouble." How convenient it might have been had the genetic means been available to suppress sexual desire until the twenties, or to delay puberty.

What kind of manipulation might we do to our own children to mold them into the models operative in our historical moment? What are the values that *we* will choose to engineer into our offspring, values that later generations will see as misguided, parochial, or even evil? We give our children Ritalin now to fit them into a society that demands a kind of conformity that they cannot achieve. What happens if those very traits are desirable in a society of the future? We run the risk of reifying our parochial social conventions into the genetic legacy of our ancestors. We always bring our moral beliefs to our science. . . .

We are in the process of a fundamental change in the nature of the self. The problem is not the cloning of an army of Hitlers, and the solution is not the Luddite reaction against technology. Rather, we must monitor the slow, fundamental change in our conceptions of ourselves and our place in the world. We must be wary of the temptation of the possible, and we must draw from the deep fount of accumulated human wisdom to temper and judge developments that can so profoundly alter the nature of our existence.

ROBERT GIBBS

Mending the Code

Robert Gibbs (b. 1958) is a scholar of philosophy and religion at the University of Toronto. His work on the borderlines of law and ethics draws on his expertise in continental philosophy and modern Jewish thought. His most recent enterprise delves into unpublished materials about the collaboration of Franz Rosenzweig and Martin Buber translating the Bible.

From "Mending the Code," in *Jews and Genes: The Genetic Future in Contemporary Jewish Thought*, eds. Elliot N. Dorff and Laurie Zoloth (Philadelphia: Jewish Publication Society, 2015), 342–74.

Perhaps the greatest challenge the new genetics represents is the need to reconceive not only scientific practices but also biological ones. While we are used to thinking of medicine as a therapy that cures or manages disease, that attempts to restore our bodies to their normal or healthful condition, gene therapy intervenes at a deeper level in our bodies: it alters the genetic code. The idea that our bodies are governed by a code, by strings of DNA, is a fundamental change in paradigm. The code itself must be copied and recopied, and its governance depends on a translating mechanism, whereby our cells take instruction and become able to do their healthy functions. Therapy then becomes a way of fixing a code or even fixing the translating mechanisms. But biological evolution now gains a different possibility, because the selection of one trait or one capacity, even one chemical or one propensity, now seems to appear on the horizon. Evolution will be augmented by interventions at the level of the code. We require serious thinking about how writing, copying, translating, and reading work in order to grasp the new logic of genetics.

I hope in these pages to bring old light to our new problems by a somewhat awkward analogy. I wish to offer the basic analogy that gene therapy may be compared with repairing a Torah scroll. The Torah scroll is also a code that governs life (albeit not at a molecular and cellular level), and it also is copied meticulously. I am *not* saying that the human genome is predicted or contained or even within the bounds of imagination of those who have copied the Torah scroll for centuries. But what I hope to show is a parallel kind of reasoning about the limits of mending. And I will emphasize the reasoning about limits as the key for this chapter. Besides the pleasant shock of thinking about the scroll and the genetic code in one frame, reflection on repair here has a distinctive feature: the "rules" about repair are themselves a matter of dispute. Moreover, the dispute about these rulings shows us a great deal about how a code works and indeed some ways we will want to think about repairing codes....

For Jews, the Torah "is a tree of life for them that grasp it" (Prov. 3:18). It is the center of the cult (now that there is no Temple with its sacrifices). All of Jewish religious thought and normative practice are bound up with the Torah. Through its interpretation it guides Jews in how to live. Some Jews are more tightly bound to the Torah text, others more loosely. The Torah also requires a series of processes in order to function as the code for Jewish life.

First, the scroll itself is copied by scribes. Parchment and ink must be prepared, and the scribe, too, is trained and prepared. The text is copied with great care. There are many regulations for the scribes. These regulations are not included within the scroll but arise from later strata of interpretation and custom.

Second, the scroll is read aloud. It is proclaimed in synagogues in a lectionary cycle (in some synagogues the scroll is read in a one-year cycle, in others a three-year cycle). This practice is linked to the book of Ezra, but there are some presages of the practice in the Torah itself.

Third, the scroll does appear in book form and is studied as such by many Jews. It is not clear whether the transcription of the contents of the scroll into another form is parallel to RNA transcription, but it is true that the second function (the proclamation of the text) does depend on a scroll proper.

But fourth, and most importantly, there is a body of interpretation of the Torah, starting at the time of its redaction and continuing through the rabbinic sages, including those of the Mishnah (approximately 220 CE) and the Talmud (sixth century CE), and leading through medieval interpreters and on to the current day. Much of Jewish traditional study is devoted to these later interpretations, and indeed the Torah itself is largely read through the lens of later interpretive traditions....

What is relevant, however, is the need to maintain the accuracy of the text and to repair a faulty text. When a text becomes worn out or turns out to be disfigured or filled with mistakes, it no longer can function as the governing code for the community. A mistake in the Torah scroll would be copied into other scrolls and would also lead to faulty interpretations/translations into the practices of life. A faulty scroll is then hidden away in a safe room or buried in the ground like a corpse. The analogy of the scroll with a human body is complex and recurs in part to recognize that the scroll has the dignity and authority of a human teacher, that it has life within it. Most holy of all are the words that are names of

God, and these must be hidden away or buried even when they appear in texts other than the Torah that are defaced or defective. . . .

The conflict in the first part [of B. T. *Menachot* 29b] focuses on how many mistakes disqualify a scroll. A column holds about forty lines, or about one thousand characters. We can mend the scroll, replacing a defective or incorrect letter with its proper letter, but only to the limit of a few mistakes per column. What is noteworthy about the argument is that the quarrel is about two or three versus three or four. The two choices are very near each other, and the contrasts that are missing are, on the one hand, the choice of ten or twenty-five mistakes that can be repaired and, on the other hand, the choice of no mistakes at all — a possibility that becomes clear [in the middle of that section of B. T. *Menachot* 29b].

This dispute presumes that any given text will have some errors. Indeed, if the text were immaculate, if there were a total accuracy to be expected, we would find an argument between zero or one error versus three or four. This particular argument is thus bad news for the fundamentalist, literalist vision of the Torah scroll. In copying the scroll, we aim for accuracy, but we tolerate a small margin of error (two or three out of a thousand). Because both sides tolerate a small number of errors, there is no requirement of perfection, and, indeed, the implication is that there is a small amount of imperfection to be expected in replication. Moreover, this means that some measure of variation is not only inevitable but, religiously speaking, tolerable. The community can function with a Torah scroll with a small margin of error.

What, then, is the argument? Rab[68] takes a stricter line. Not that the earlier ruling is so lenient, but still, he positions himself as more strict. He seems more worried about errors being tolerated, but his position still cannot insist on inerrancy. The thrust of the text, of course, is that he was wrong. The older standard position seems to be a quite strict requirement, no more than three in a thousand. This differs from the "fundamentalist" position of inerrancy (zero), and it also is a choice that is more tolerant than a respectable position (Rab's). We learn, thus, that even a strict requirement can be situated against a stricter one and so seems to be more generous. . . .

Rather than explore this first argument further, let me now merely nod in the

---

68. [Rab, also known as Abba bar Aivu or Abba Arikhah, was a second-century Babylonian sage who straddled the Tannaim (sages whose teachings are found in the Mishnah or other early teachings) and the Amoraim (successor sages who discussed and interpreted the work and positions of earlier scholars, among other things).]

direction of gene therapy. Mutation is inevitable and, to our surprise, is even positive, *sometimes*. Most errors in replication of genetic code are irrelevant, and our bodies can tolerate these few errors. Some, of course, are much worse than others, but in general, our bodies do not require absolute accuracy, just very high accuracy (of the order of 2.5 mutations in 10 million). Given that there are errors, we might be able to repair them to restore the text to a condition of perfection. We also may be able to tolerate some lingering errors. But there seems to be a limit to how much we may fix, or how much we should be willing to fix....

The second text deals with a different kind of error, but the stakes are much the same. The question is this: Would this mistake disqualify a scroll? But the specific problem seems to be this: In the midst of copying, what happens if a person leaves out one of the names of God? For of all the words that make a text holy, a specific set of names of God are those that impart the character of holiness. The most important name, the Tetragrammaton (YHWH), hereinafter referred to as "the Name," is not even pronounced, and often it is only written by an abbreviation, but it also is the proper name of God and as such cannot be erased either. If it were lacking, there would be a fundamental flaw in the text....

The problem is how to repair the text: how to insert the Name of God that is missing. So we start with an opinion ascribed to R. Judah, according to whom the scribe should (1) scrape off the word he wrote in the place of the Name, (2) give that place to the Name, and (3) insert the word that occupied that place above the line. We then hear five other opinions on correcting the error: (1) the Name itself may be inserted above the line, (2) the wrong word can be wiped off and the Name put in its place, (3) the Name written above the line must not be abbreviated, (4) the Name can only be inserted above the line, and (5) none of these options. Ultimately, almost in frustration with this wealth of choices, the answer is ["He must remove the whole sheet and hide it away," B. T. *Menachot* 30a]: the scribe must hide away the section of the scroll on which the error occurred....

Now when we can discern a fault in the code, particularly an omission, perhaps of something that is vital in the processes of our living, if we could repair that bit of code, we would need to consider the kinds of repairs that are desirable (and also possible). Some might take R. Meir's position, that an error in the code should not be repaired. Others might hold that the therapy requires a strict replacement of correct code in the same location as the faulty code. And others might be willing to flood a nucleus with loose correct code and take the risk that it might trigger other effects but that it also might serve to generate the proper transcribed RNA. Even if the goal is strictly to replace a defective piece of code, there might be a sense that it can be done during replication (while we still can wipe away the error) or that it should be done with a completed replication. The risks of above the line and of scraping and wiping away are different, as are different modes of replacing faulty code with correct code. Mending here revolves around the different interventions that we choose to make to replace the missing name.

* * *

The third and final text I will interpret is specifically about sewing and about tears. Compared to paper, parchment is not easy to tear, but it does tear through normal use (particularly after repeated rolling and rerolling of the scroll). Hence, there is again a question of limit....

At the deepest level the parallel with the genetic code lies here: that the sheer chemical materiality of the base pairs and chains of pairs is not foreign to the function of the code. Fully embodied, the chemicals are not mere things, but they are signs, a code that can be replicated, transcribed, and translated into the orders for the functioning of the proteins in the cell. A tear in the Torah scroll is like a mistake or a damaged gene in the DNA code. We might think we can only sew up little tears (very little tears), but it is also possible to mend the "new" ones as best we can, not just the sequence itself but also the structure upon which the relevant code rides. Perhaps this is about the large part of the DNA that is copied reliably but is largely irrelevant in the functioning of the cells. Still, those large zones carry the part that does signify, and they require copying, and possibly mending, too.

The challenge for a chapter like this, of course, is that we are trading only with analogies that are in principle not suited for collapsing. The rules for mending a Torah scroll are not in themselves binding in our reflections on what the new genetics can do for us in gene therapy. And they should not be binding. But a careful reading of these three texts has shown a series of reflections that are parallel to those we share in viewing the promise of gene therapy. If Jewish bioethics is not simply a task in setting limits, in giving rules for government or science to follow, then it might find a further task in exploring this more fundamental question, about how codes work and what sorts of repairs make sense, of how to limit the repairs and how to gauge the risks.

SARAH IMHOFF

Racial Standing: How American Jews Imagine Community, and Why That Matters

Sarah Imhoff (b. 1981), professor of religious studies at Indiana University, focuses on issues of the body and religion. Questions of race, gender, and ability animate her scholarship of religious meaning. She is founding co-editor of the journal American Religion.

From "Racial Standing: How American Jews Imagine Community, and Why That Matters," in *Judaism, Race, and Ethics: Conversations and Questions*, ed. Jonathan K. Crane (University Park: Pennsylvania State University Press, 2020), 217–36.

In this chapter, I take a rather unorthodox path to analyzing Jews and race: I begin with internet advertisements and end at Mount Sinai. The route that connects the ads to the Israelites at the mountain is an epistemology of Jewishness, and the questions that propel the journey are: How do we know who is Jewish? How should we know? And what are the consequences of these ways of knowing? In particular, I look at how ideas about race can structure Jewishness —often invisibly, always with consequences. After the devastating effects of the racist constructions of the Third Reich and the Shoah, "race" talk as it related to the Jewish community receded. In US American contexts, talk about "Jews and race" came to refer to how Jews interacted with Blacks, or, more recently, how Jews inhabited their whiteness.[69] But just because Jews today rarely explicitly invoke the idea of a "Jewish race," this doesn't mean that race-based conceptions of Jewishness have also disappeared. Even though the language of "race" has fallen out of cultural favor, many of the ideas connected with it persist. I thus begin by discussing this racialist construction of Jewishness, then suggest its liabilities, and finally pose a categorically different means of answering the question "Who is a Jew?" ...

Racialist logics of Jewishness underwrite each of these examples, but there are different species of the genus "racialist conception of Jewishness." Though there are many, I will explore two of these species here: the genetic body and the apparent body. The genetic body encompasses discourses about DNA, "Jewish

---

69. The very phrase "how Jews inhabited their whiteness," of course, writes Jews of color out of the narrative of Jewishness.

diseases," and other kinds of gene talk, while the apparent body relies on visual cues on the surface of the body, such as skin color, hair texture, stature, and eye color. The two modes of conceptualizing Jewishness are by no means identical, but they do similar work: they create boundaries that seem clear but are in fact incoherent when applied to the social world in which we live. I have argued elsewhere that conversations about personal DNA testing and recently increased interest in claiming *anusim* (or "crypto-Jewish")[70] heritage demonstrate how racialist ideas undergird many cultural constructions of Jewishness. Whether they discuss the genetic body or the apparent body, it becomes clear that people use biological and geographical discourses—both components of the social construction of race—to claim Jewish identity. DNA studies and American crypto-Jews are only two manifestations of this biologized thinking about Jewish identity. "Gene talk" runs through discussions of Jewish genealogy, in both professional and amateur settings. And in political ones too: in 2013, Birthright Israel refused to accept nineteen-year-old (light-skinned, Russian) Masha Yakerson without a DNA test "proving" that she was Jewish.

This racialist logic of Jewishness is perhaps most clear in discussions of genetics, yet it also subtly pervades dominant popular contemporary understandings of Jewishness. While some racialist ideas of physical traits—such as comic celebrations of big noses or "Jewfros"—seem innocuous and superficial, others are more deeply embedded in the notion of what it means to be a Jew and have a Jewish body. The normative Jewish body, to take a nonexhaustive list, has light skin, hair that may be curly, and a certain sort of nose (not aquiline). Persons who do not conform to these norms are often perceived by others as non-Jews, regardless of whether they actually identify as Jewish. Blond-haired, blue-eyed Jews are often told they "don't look Jewish." And so are many Jews of color. . . .

These two species of racialist conceptions of Jewishness, those of the genetic and the apparent body, are not always separate, and they frequently intersect with each other. For instance, the reluctant inclusion of the Lemba[71] as "real Jews," Israeli attitudes toward Ethiopian Jews and Bene Israel (Indian Jews), and even to some extent ethnic inequality among Ashkenazim, Sephardim, and Mizrahim—all demonstrate the complicated relationships among Jewishness,

70. [*Anusim* means "coerced" or "the coerced ones." There are many terms for Jews who hid their heritage to "pass" in public: *converso*, *marrano*, *Cristão-Novo*, "crypto-Jew"—among others.]

71. [A tribe in southern Africa, the Lemba have many customs similar to Jewish ones, and some genetic evidence suggests biological connections to other Jewish communities.]

race, and DNA. Racialist constructions of Jewishness, then, are not merely vestiges of Nazism or antisemitism, and we see their subtle workings far beyond contemporary racist discourse.

In short, racialist thinking does not have neutral effects. So if implicitly racialist definitions of Jewishness exclude or devalue many people who identify as Jews, and if Jewish communities generally want to include and value Jews, then why do they persist? Part of the answer to why Jews of color in particular experience exclusion is the continuing racism across all strata of American culture. But American racism is not a sufficient explanation for all of the species of racialist conceptions of Jewishness. Even beyond skin color and other visible traits that seem to make race knowable, racialist logics structure ideas about Jewishness. Elsewhere, I have suggested that racialist discourse about Jewishness has gained such popularity and explanatory power because of its appeal to biomedical criteria for Jewishness: these criteria may be so attractive precisely because they seem to provide objective criteria for "who is a Jew" at a time when Jewish identity has become increasingly fluid and contested. For instance, a discourse in which genetic language and scientific authority produce Jewish bodies can seem to provide certainty instead of complexity or ambiguity when it comes to defining Jewish identity. Racialist definitions seem to offer fixity and predictability, which can be both calming and alluring.

In the end, of course, they cannot: genes for Tay-Sachs disease or linked to Cohen ancestors cannot make a person Jewish, nor can their absence make someone non-Jewish. These genetic markers, and other racialized traits such as skin color, do not always align with other norms of Jewishness, such as Passover observance, eating lox, or even having a Jewish mother. Tying Jewishness to genetics, for instance, might be done to ensure the certainty of who is a Jew on a case-by-case basis, but the resulting collection of people deemed Jewish would bear little relationship to the boundaries of any current community or theological ideas of the Jewish people. Nevertheless, the appearance of certainty holds appeal for many Jews and non-Jews who find the increasingly porous boundaries of Jewish identity destabilizing. . . .

Racialist conceptions of Jewishness reinforce the sense that identity is fixed and stable, rather than acknowledging that identification is an ongoing process subject to missteps. Rejecting the scholarly insistence that race is socially constructed, racialist ideas hold that there is something essential—often biological—and therefore immutable about how people identify themselves and are identified by others. When Jewishness is underwritten by racialist conceptions, then the idea of Jewishness seems more stable. But there are costs to such stability. Many of these costs are exacted from those who do not clearly conform to the norms of racialist senses of Jewishness, such as Jews of color, converts, and others who do not "look Jewish." ...

We cannot create genetic or bodily categories in a way that would include only self-identified Jews and not others, or in a way that would match any existing Jewish community. If we created a category of all people with the "Cohen gene," we would have a group with many Jewish men—but it would have no women at all, and it would likewise exclude the vast majority of Jewish men. If we created a category with people in the J haplogroup, it would have many Jews—but it would also have many non-Jewish Middle Easterners, and it would exclude converts, adoptees, and many of their descendants. If we looked only at people who have certain nose shapes and certain hair textures (and what, precisely, would they be?), we would exclude some people who consider themselves Jews and include others who do not consider themselves Jews. Any definition of Jewishness based on genetics or physical features would be exclusionary, falsely inclusionary, or both. And none would map neatly onto the way that Jewish communities define themselves. ...

Once articulated, the racialist logics of Jewishness raise a theological issue related to the social process of identification: they profoundly confuse the concept of the people of Israel. Peoplehood remains a central theological concept in Judaism, but it begs the question of who, precisely, is included in that people. Racialist logics suggest that the contours of peoplehood are fixed and knowable, that there is a clear "us" and a clear "them." But there are textual resources in Jewish tradition that suggest otherwise and conceive of Jewishness in a more open, perhaps even performative, fashion. ...

The goal of this performative notion of Jewishness is to reflect more accurately the ways people identify Jewishly in the world, which includes the normative dimension of greater inclusiveness for Jews of color, converts, and other Jews who experience marginalization. ...

Ancient Jewish interpreters returned to Deuteronomy 29 to think about communal identification. Two rabbinic texts, Midrash Tanhuma and Babylonian Talmud *Shevu'ot*, both read the Deuteronomy passage to say something not only about events in Moab but also about Sinai: they interpret it to say that all Israelites throughout time were actually present at Sinai. These texts read the event at Sinai as a moment that not only defines the historical community that was physically present but also the transhistorical community of the people of Israel throughout history. They draw the warrant for this reading from the ambiguity of the text: if Moses began Deuteronomy 29 by calling "all Israel" (29:1) together—and even reiterated that everyone, from the infants, to the workers, to the leaders, was present—then every Israelite was "standing with us." Who, then, could Deuteronomy 29:14 mean when it referred to those who were "not with us here this day"? Rabbinic readers of the biblical text interpreted this to mean all members of the community throughout history. They read themselves, and all future Jews, into the event at Sinai. . . .

The idea of the Jewish people is a theological one, and it cannot be reduced to the apparent body, to genetics, or to biological relation. Ancestry and progeny do feature prominently in biblical, Talmudic, and midrashic texts; in fact, this Talmudic passage from *Shevu'ot* explains the "oath of judges," which has implications for past and future generations if one breaks it. And yet even with this emphasis on descent, the revelation at Sinai—the seminal event of the Jewish people—defines Jewishness not by descent but by "with"-ness. The deciding factor is who is "with" the community at Sinai. The text specifically includes converts, both present and future. Presence and connection, not descent, signal communal belonging.

These Jewish texts do not, of course, fully espouse a theory of performativity. But they open the door for it. First, they emphasize the idea of "standing with" rather than an essentialized and predetermined idea of who was (and is) Jewish. Second, they do not locate all Jewish bodies at the defining moment of Jewishness. At first, the absence of bodies seems like it cannot fit with the performative notion of identification, because bodies and materiality are a crucial part of how people engage in the process of identification. However, because the bodies are not all predefined through the Sinai event, the text allows individual people to go through the process of identification in whichever cultural context their bodies come to inhabit. By *not* locating all Jewish bodies at Sinai, the text opens up the possibility for each person's body to inhabit his or her own historical and cultural space in the context of "local" norms, one of the fundamental aspects of identification.

17 | Disability

Recent decades have witnessed a sea change in Jewish ethical, legal, and cultural treatments of disability. While impairment and illness have always been a central part of human experience, Jewish sources have only rarely considered the perspective of disabled people, instead focusing on how the able-bodied or how society in general should treat those with disabilities. Within the past fifty years, the activism of disabled people who insist "nothing about us without us" has prompted scholars to reexamine attitudes about disability. New critical scholarship about disability has brought about significant shifts that are reflected in the field of Jewish ethics to varying degrees.

One important shift is the prominence of disability as a topic or theme. All of the pieces gathered in this section approach disability as a broad category of human experience, and this alone is a departure from Jewish discussions in earlier ages. While biblical and rabbinic texts are full of stories about people who are blind, deaf, and physically disabled—including prominent biblical figures and leading sages—traditional interpreters have not generally focused on disability as a theme. And while halakhic literature includes extensive discussions of how various disabilities condition individuals' status vis-à-vis ritual obligations and other religious laws, these writings generally provide disparate treatments of different kinds of disabilities—for example, focusing on the legal status of the deaf, or on how to categorize mental illness. In contrast, all the pieces gathered here address disability as a broad concept.

The four scholars represented here engage different methodologies in their examinations of disability ethics. Judith Z. Abrams offers a historical study of biblical and rabbinic attitudes about disability. For Abrams, it is self-evident that ancient Jewish attitudes fall short of contemporary values with regard to the dignity and inclusion of disabled people; she argues that the classical texts need to be understood as important historical background for later ethical developments. For example, she demonstrates that in the Torah, there is a strong association between disability and sin, a troubling attitude that is only partly mitigated in rabbinic literature. While Abrams's findings with regard to the content of classical Jewish attitudes run counter to contemporary disability ethics, her work is groundbreaking in that it addresses disability as a focus of scholarship and of ethical concern. She demonstrates the prominence of disability in classical Jewish narrative and law.

Like Abrams, Tzvi C. Marx focuses on classical Jewish texts, but his interest is constructive and presentist rather than historical. As an Orthodox scholar and thinker, Marx is committed to maximizing respect and opportunity for disabled Jews within the bounds of traditional halakha. While he acknowledges that some traditional Jewish texts and practices unfairly exclude disabled people, he argues that these tendencies are exceptions to the general tenor of Jewish tradition, which upholds dignity and compassion. Writing in an activist vein, he proposes mechanisms within the halakhic tradition for ameliorating the marginalization of disabled people.

While Marx and Abrams focus on classical Jewish texts and their interpretation, both Adrienne Asch and Julia Watts Belser center their scholarship on the experience of disabled people themselves. In different ways, they both express core insights of disability activists and of critical disability studies, conceiving of disability as a feature of human life rather than as a problem to be solved. Disability scholars and activists point out that many of the limitations that disabled people contend with are a function of societal failures to accommodate the full range of human diversity. It is this insight that animates Asch's intervention in the ethical debate over end of life decision-making, as she challenges the prevalent assumption that disability is inconsistent with quality of life. Asch argues that with better accommodations for disability—and better education about what those accommodations entail—those facing disability would be less inclined to choose to die. Unlike the other pieces in this section, Asch does not directly engage Jewish themes or sources. Her arguments are squarely focused on the impact of policies, procedures, and practices on patients, families, and society. Is Asch's work appropriately considered Jewish ethics? While there is nothing distinctively Jewish about her sources or methods, her insights and arguments helped shape the discourse within the subfield of Jewish bioethics, justifying her inclusion within this volume.[72]

Julia Watts Belser is a scholar of rabbinic literature whose work on disability engages biblical and rabbinic texts, but she is far less sanguine than Abrams and

---

72. For more on the ethics of decision-making at the end of life, see part 4, section 22. For more on quality of life, see Noam J. Zohar, "Is Enjoying Life a Good Thing? Quality-of-Life Questions for Jewish Normative Discourse," part 4, section 19.

Marx about the potential for Jewish textual sources to advance disability ethics. In the piece excerpted here, she takes issue with one of Abrams's readings of biblical narrative. Even as Belser exposes tendencies in Jewish sources and contemporary discourse to marginalize those with disability, her work in Jewish ethics includes creative, constructivist efforts to develop a more liberating and inclusive ethical discourse. One way she does this is by drawing on new resources. Here, she identifies disability dance as a medium that can more effectively express bodily experience and difference than the written word.

JUDITH Z. ABRAMS

Judaism and Disability: Portrayals in Ancient Texts from the Tanach through the Bavli

Rabbi Dr. Judith Zabarenko Abrams (1958–2014) was among the first generation of women ordained as Reform rabbis. Following her ordination, she pursued doctoral studies in rabbinic literature, focusing her dissertation research on disability. A public scholar, teacher, and writer, she pioneered the online teaching of Talmud through her website MAQOM. She wrote for both adults and children. Many of her books are dedicated to making Talmud study accessible and relevant to broad audiences.

From *Judaism and Disability: Portrayals in Ancient Texts from the Tanach through the Bavli* (Washington, DC: Gallaudet University Press, 1998), 84–88, 152–53.

Chapter 4: Disabilities, Atonement, and Individuals

In this chapter, we will examine narratives in which disabilities actually allow individuals to function more effectively than they could have done otherwise. This situation occurs often, though not always, because the disability atones for a sin or allows the individual to show how divine power trumps human power. The atonement that disabilities can bring in these stories, and the symmetry that atonement restores, is called in rabbinic literature *bamidah she'adam modeid ba, mod'din lo*—"With the measure that a person measures shall they mete [out] to him"—or, more colloquially, *midah k'neged midah*, simply "measure for measure." As the symmetry of heaven and earth was crucial in the Temple, so the symmetry of sin and punishment is operative here.

This principle is at work in our earliest sources. The life story of Jacob, son of Isaac, is one of great narrative and moral symmetry shaped by disabilities in some of its characters. Jacob is able to steal his twin brother's birthright because his father's eyes have grown dim (Gen. 27:1). Poor eyes will then almost immediately set Jacob up for a fall. After fleeing his angry brother, Esau, he comes to his uncle, Lavan. Jacob, looking at Lavan's daughters, disdains the elder because of her poor eyes: "And Leah's eyes were weak; but Rachel was of beautiful form and appearance" (Gen. 29:17). Having disregarded the rights of an elder sibling (his brother) once, Jacob now attempts to disregard them again, wanting to marry Rachel, the younger sister, before Leah. Lavan, Leah, and Rachel collude to marry off Jacob to Leah. When Jacob confronts Lavan, his uncle pointedly remarks, "It must not be done so in our place, to give the younger before the firstborn" (Gen. 29:26). As Jacob tricked his father and brother, exploiting the opportunity of his father's poor vision, so he is tricked in turn by a father and a sister because of his repugnance at Leah's poor eyes. Jacob himself is blinded by his lust for the birthright and for Rachel.

In another part of Jacob's story his punishment is likewise meted out "measure for measure." When Jacob is born, he emerges holding onto his brother's heel (in Hebrew, the word for "heel" is *akeiv*; this is the source of Jacob's name, *Ya'akov*). Just before he is about to meet his brother, Esau, after a long separation, Jacob struggles with an angel, probably Esau's representative spirit. This spirit wrestles with, wounds, and finally blesses Jacob, renaming him Israel (Gen. 32:25–31), reflecting symmetrically the struggle of the boys in Rebecca's womb and their blessing decreed by God (25:22–23). When Jacob fled from his brother, he ran fearfully into the setting sun. As the sun rises, Jacob greets Esau again after many years, limping and unafraid, with a new identity won fairly instead of stolen (32:32–33).

Jacob's disability is accompanied by a blessing. His flawed moral state has finally been made manifest in his physical state and he is, somehow, released from his sin of tricking his father and brother. At this point, he can assume a new name and a new role as patriarch of a family in the land of Israel. Israel, then, in its first incarnation is physically disabled. In this case the disability itself, by finally becoming physically manifest and fulfilling the narrative's demand for symmetry, allows Jacob to move forward as a character and a nation. In a sense, then, Jacob's disability actually heals him as it signifies that his competition with his brother at last is over: he has been appropriately punished for stealing the birthright and may move on with his life....

In a similar way, a disability actually helps Samson attain his goal of slaughtering as many Philistines as possible. In Samson's story, sight and sexuality blind the judge to what is right. Even Samson's name, *Shimshon* in Hebrew, hints at the importance of light, enlightenment, and sight in the story, for it is derived from the same root as the word "sun," *shemesh*. He follows his eyes, quite literally: "And Samson went to Gaza, and saw there a harlot, and went in unto her" (Judg. 16:1). Subsequently, the harlot Delilah harasses Samson until he finally tells her that his strength derives from his Nazirite vows, one of which is a prohibition against cutting his hair. She cuts his hair, and he loses his strength, is taken captive, and is blinded (16:21). Yet his blindness and presumed helplessness enable him to kill three thousand Philistines at the end of his life (16:27) — a great triumph over his enemies. Had he not been blinded, this opportunity would not have been his. Like Jacob's wounding, Samson's physical disability brings symmetry into the protagonist's life and actually enables him to act potently again. . . .

The Mishnah is well aware of the principle of symmetry established in the Tanach. Only two passages in the entire Mishnah (M. *Sotah* 1:8–9) speculate on the causes of disabilities and they both utilize the idea of *midah k'neged midah*, "measure for measure." . . . In both cases, sin leads to disability in that faculty with which the sin was committed. . . .

Chapter 6: Categorization, Disabilities, and Persons with Disabilities

. . . The Mishnah differs from the Tanach by consistently differentiating among disabilities, because, within its system, some disabilities are more disabling than others. Just as the priestly culture guarded its practitioners against dangerous contact with lethal holiness by barring blemished priests and those contaminated by ritual impurity from the cult, so rabbinic culture identifies those abilities that allowed a person to function within that culture and, hence, the corresponding disabilities that would make a person unable to participate. The sages developed an intellectual and spiritual system of Judaism that was cultivated in a communal, professional culture and transmitted with a great degree of orality. Thus, within this system one who could not communicate intellectual content orally was more disabled than any other individual.

Mental, hearing, and speaking disabilities compromised one's ability to participate in the sages' system. These sorts of disabilities are most often designated by the category *cheresh, shoteh v'katan*: the person with hearing and speaking disabilities, the person with mental disabilities or mental illness, and the minor. Such individuals suffer a common stigma, as their linked categorization serves as a "master status": no differentiation is made between, for example, a schizophrenic person and a normal one-year-old, or a deaf-mute person and one with an IQ of 40. All such persons are placed into a single discredited group; their performance of mitzvot is questioned and often discredited. However, as we will see, an individual may move from this category and become a full participant, if it can be proved that he has *da'at*, that is, has been impressed with the seal of his culture's *gnosis*[73] and can form a legally actionable intention and act on it legitimately.

In contrast, blindness and such physical disabilities as lameness or a malformation of the hands compromised participation only in certain, limited aspects.

---

73. [*Gnosis* is Greek for "knowledge."]

With regard to most activities, blind and physically disabled persons are not even considered to be liminal: though visibly marred, they can function satisfactorily. They are fully credited participants in the sages' system, except in those limited circumstances for which vision or mobility is absolutely necessary. . . .

In this way, the Mishnah innovatively considered disabilities and redefined perfection. Perfection no longer means "zero defects," as it did in the priestly literature (although traces of that attitude can still be found). Instead, perfection is identified with intellectual functioning and communicative abilities. In rabbinic literature, these concepts are often related to the term *da'at*. There is almost no action that one can validly perform in the Mishnah's system without *da'at*.

TZVI C. MARX
Disability in Jewish Law

Tzvi C. Marx (b. 1942) is an Orthodox rabbi and an international leader in Jewish education. Shortly after his birth in France, his family escaped the Nazis by fleeing to Switzerland. Following World War II, the family immigrated to New York City, where he grew up. He was ordained at Yeshiva University and then pursued his doctorate at the Catholic Theological University of Utrecht. He was director of education at the Hartman Institute in Jerusalem and founded the Folkertsma Institute of Talmud in Holland.

From *Disability in Jewish Law* (London: Routledge, 2002), 1–2, 17–19.

1. Introduction

Sensitivity to the disabled is a hallmark of contemporary culture in most Western countries. The compassion underlying the current awareness is hardly new to modern society, however, and permeates the monotheistic religions. It is at the heart of the Jewish tradition, and clearly reflected in the Jewish sources. The biblical foundations of the Judaic tradition manifest a sensitive, humane, and dignified attitude to all persons, regardless of individual differences. To a great extent, this attitude is expressed in the precepts, the divine commandments enjoining performance of or abstention from various acts, that constitute the structural framework of the tradition. Yet examination of the halakhic literature also reveals instances of apparent indifference, or even callousness, with respect to the disabled: laws and liturgical passages that appear to evince a dismissive, even derisive attitude toward individuals with disabilities. This inconsistency gives rise to a certain dissonance within the tradition, a dissonance that cannot be ignored by those who value its teachings. It is love and respect for the tradition, and recognition of its moral authority, that motivates this study and its methodology. While an adequate examination of the Jewish approach to disability may entail critique of specific laws, this critique should, I believe, be carried out on the basis of criteria internal to the halakhic culture, and not simply on the basis of contemporary sensibilities. Indeed, the principle that the criteria governing the process of halakhic self-scrutiny ought to be internal is itself internal.

Although this work is academic in nature, it is my hope that it will serve to enlighten readers, and among them, members of the rabbinate, by alerting them to the possibilities of inclusion on the basis of the classic sources of the law. The legitimacy of responsiveness to the marginalized, though clearly mandated by the tradition, will only come to the fore if those administering the law are sensitized to it. It is also my hope that this encounter will encourage the undertaking of observance by the non-obligated.

My study reads the tradition as conceiving of human existence as worthy in itself in the eyes of God: achievement is irrelevant to human worth. While I do not deny that halakhic culture is inherently precept-oriented, I argue that this orientation does not conflict with the tradition's broader ideals of compassion, helping, and responsibility. As these ideals are shared with other religions and societies, affirming their significance in the context of disability also highlights the universal elements in the tradition.

Excluding individuals from full participation in religious activities on the basis of physical or mental impairment is offensive to contemporary thinking. But the possible lack of correspondence with contemporary views is not what drives my interest in Jewish law on disability; rather, the source of my unease is the intra-traditional dissonance, the dissonance within the halakhic culture itself. It is the offense against Jewish ethical sensibilities that motivates my desire to clarify the position of the halakha. Biblical culture . . . is inclusive, and does not regard the individual as dependent on specific mental or physical endowments. Its heroes, the patriarchs and matriarchs of Israel—Isaac, who is blind; Jacob, who limps; the initially childless matriarchs Sarah, Rebecca and Rachel, and the speech-disabled Moses are no less esteemed because of disability. When the tradition admonishes us not to place obstacles before the blind, or curse the deaf, it clearly directs us, its adherents, to relate to the impaired among us with consideration. In general, the teaching of compassion for the disadvantaged members of the community—its orphans, widows, strangers or disabled—is a defining parameter of the culture. Overall, then, the aim of this book is to explore an internal ambivalence and to consider whether and how the law can better express the tradition's ethical mandate with respect to the disabled....

4. Disability as Reflected in the Tradition

... A society's treatment of its weakest members reveals its moral character. In a culture that proclaims human dignity as its central value, do the disabled have dignity? Modern ethics is clearly offended by the exclusion of any from full social participation and equal access to community life due to any personal circumstance, including disability. Is Jewish law receptive to this attempt to foster maximalization of human fulfilment?

Halakhic culture is characterized by unconditional affirmation of the value of every human life. However, because piety and religious status are measured by observance of the precepts, the mitzvot, it is also characterized by admiration for competence and mastery, both in the realm of conduct, and in that of learning. Impairment poses a difficult challenge to the halakhic culture, which —as its vocabulary of *mitzvah* and *maaseh*, commandment and action, attests —esteems mastery of the law, observance of the precepts, and forthright action. Clearly, the physically and mentally infirm are incapable of achieving such mastery. Must they incur further distancing and loss of self-esteem due to their exemption or disqualification from observance of certain precepts? Does Jewish law provide for the spiritual self-expression and self-respect of the disabled via precept-observance, or are the disabled excluded from the halakhic universe? If indeed a distancing tendency exists in Jewish law, is it inevitable—is the halakha innately dismissive of disabled individuals because of its character as an achievement-centered tradition? Can it broaden opportunities for inclusion and foster awareness of the needs of those with disabilities? In the application of the law, can allowances be made for individual differences in function?

Jewish tradition encompasses two attitudes to the disabled, one exclusionary, another, integrative. The former defines the person by his disability, recategorizing him outside the customary norms. The disabled individual is seen, not as an ordinary person, but as one who is "disabled," the qualifier "disabled" diminishing the "personhood." To illustrate this halakhic propensity, consider that the deaf-mute is exempted, and sometimes disqualified, from observance of the commandments....

The integrative attitude, on the other hand, views a disability as an element of a whole human being and keeps the disabling effect of the disability in proportion. It perceives the disabled individual as someone who needs help to overcome the limitations of his disability but is essentially like any other member of society....

The tension between the two tendencies is well illustrated in the continuation of the midrash quoted earlier. R. Tanhuma[74] contrasts the central significance of the disabled in Egypt with their devaluation at Sinai:

> When they came to the wilderness of Sinai, God said, "Is it consonant with the dignity of the Torah that I should give it to a generation of impaired people (ba'alei mumim)? If, on the other hand, I wait until others take their place, I will be delaying the giving of the law." What then did God do? He bade the angels come down to Israel and heal them.[75]

The dignity of Torah could not suffer the disabled, according to R. Tanhuma. Or differently put, redemption from Egypt could accommodate the disabled, but revelation could not.

There appears to be profound theoretical ambivalence underlying the law. It seems paradoxical that a tradition that entertains the notion that prophetic powers could devolve upon the cognitively less-capable restricts the religious obligations of the disabled. One might concede due cause for this caution with regard to precepts governing civil and criminal matters, since these depend upon interaction and accords between parties; hence, some minimal level of competence in undertaking mutual obligations is required. But what of the broad range of other religious actions with respect to which no others are involved? In what sense is a less competent person's ritual act, such as the waving of the *lulav* on the Festival of Tabernacles, offensive? ...

The question of why observance is primarily mandated for the whole-bodied and whole-minded, and the disabled individual appears to be relegated to halakhic liminality, remains. Evidently, there is something unsettling about disability in the halakhic culture, and a distinct reluctance to embrace inclusiveness. The dissonance between Judaism's unconditional affirmation of human life, and its discrimination against the disabled by partial, and in some cases, total, exclusion, exemption or disqualification from observance of many of its precepts,

---

74. [Tanhuma bar Aba was a fourth-century sage who figures prominently in midrashic literature.]

75. Numbers Rabbah 7:1.

does not sit easily. Indeed, it cries out for understanding, if not resolution; and if complete understanding is unattainable, for a better understanding of the problem.

ADRIENNE ASCH

Recognizing Death while Affirming Life: Can End of Life Reform Uphold a Disabled Person's Interest in Continued Life?

Adrienne Asch (1946–2013) was a bioethicist and pioneering scholar of disability studies. Initially trained as a social worker, she began her career as an advocate for those facing employment discrimination. After completing doctoral studies in social psychology at Columbia University, Professor Asch became a leading scholar of bioethics and disability, with a focus on reproduction and gender. Her scholarly interests were informed by her own experience as a blind woman.

From "Recognizing Death while Affirming Life: Can End of Life Reform Uphold a Disabled Person's Interest in Continued Life?" in *Improving End of Life Care: Why Has It Been So Difficult? Hastings Center Report Special Report* 35, no. 6 (2005): 31–36.

Early in 2005, a real-life drama and two acclaimed films engaged the nation in discussions of issues that had been a staple of the end of life field for over twenty-five years. Terri Schiavo's medical condition resembled that of Nancy Cruzan, whose family had succeeded in convincing the US Supreme Court to remove her feeding tube. Hollywood's *Million Dollar Baby* and Spain's *The Sea Inside* reminded many of the Broadway play and movie *Whose Life Is It Anyway?*, in which a sculptor, like the boxer and the diver of the contemporary films, chose death over life with disability. The powerful reactions to those motion pictures, the controversy over the Schiavo case, and, in Boston, a public dispute between a leading hospital and a patient's family over the withdrawal of life support, underscore our urgent need to reform how Americans deal with life-prolonging or life-ending decisions.

Sometimes the media, the public, and professionals in end of life treatment and policy frame the debate in terms of "quality of life" versus "sanctity of life," but this casting oversimplifies the story and neglects critiques from people who share many values espoused by the end of life movement but nonetheless oppose some views that pervade the field. A sensitive decision-making process and sound conclusions demand weighing several factors: what gives life meaning and value for a particular individual; what circumstances or setting would permit the ill, disabled, or dying patient to derive comfort and fulfillment in existing relationships, experiences, or activities; whether a presumed decision-maker should ever be replaced by another person in the patient's life; and whether any factors other than patient and family preferences should influence life-ending decisions.

* * *

In the years since the 1976 case of Karen Ann Quinlan,[76] much greater weight has been given, both in law and the culture at large, to informed consent; to the experiences, views, and needs of patients and families in the medical encounter; to respect for patient autonomy and family decision-making; and to the quality, not merely the preservation, of an individual's life. These beliefs have meshed well with the efforts of feminists and other marginalized groups to equalize the power relations between doctor and patient, and they have also supported twenty-first century cultural norms of self-fulfillment, self-determination, and control over one's destiny. These ideals should have promoted an alliance between end of life reform, the emerging scholarship of disability studies, and the movement for disability rights and equality. Unfortunately, many scholars and practicing health care professionals have failed to grasp crucial insights of disability scholars or activists. Despite the common cause of disability scholars and activists with those in the end of life movement around maximizing self-determination and giving more respect and authority to patients in their encounters with medicine, the end of life movement has sharply differed with disability theorists and activists in understanding how illness and impairment affect quality of life.

Thanks to the sustained efforts of scholars, clinicians, and grassroots citizen groups like Compassion in Dying, both clinical practice and case law recognize that ill or dying patients and their intimates often are concerned about their experiences and relationships during whatever time they have left to live, not merely with how long they might be maintained by medications, feeding tubes, and breathing machines. Disability activist and lobbying groups such as Not

---

76. [Karen Ann Quinlan was a young woman in a persistent vegetative state whose parents sued for the right to remove her from a ventilator. They won the case on appeal.]

Dead Yet or Americans Disabled for Attendant Programs Today (ADAPT) also espouse the goals of creating and maintaining opportunities for ill, disabled, or dying people to enjoy fulfilling, meaningful relationships, activities, and experiences for however much time they will live. Compassion in Dying and Not Dead Yet differ in their policy and practice goals for two reasons: they focus on different kinds of paradigm cases, and they have profoundly different understandings of how illness and disability affect life's meaning and rewards. The typical case for the misnamed "right to die" movement is an elderly man or woman in the final of an inevitably terminal illness, who will soon die regardless of how much medical treatment is invested in his or her last days or weeks. The case that fuels the disability rights movement is that of a relatively young person with a disability, who could live for several years with the condition, but who instead asks to die—as in *Million Dollar Baby*, and as in many real-life cases.

Although mainstream reformers have criticized the way professionals often dealt with patients and their families, the mainstream has too often accepted medicine's view that illness and disability inevitably diminish life's quality. In contrast, disability theorists and activists point to research demonstrating that people with physical, sensory, and cognitive impairments can and do obtain many satisfactions and rewards in their lives. When people with illness and disability report dissatisfaction and unhappiness, they link their distress not to physical pain or to reliance on medications, dialysis, or ventilators, but to those factors that also trouble nondisabled people—problematic relationships, fears about financial security, or difficulties in playing a valued work or other social role.

Disability theorists and activists endorse the growth of hospice, palliative care, pain relief, and greater attention to the psychological and social needs of patients and their loved ones; however, they argue that endorsing treatment withdrawal from people simply because their health or their capacities are impaired undermines the goals of human dignity, patient self-respect, and quality of life. Such goals are best achieved by helping people discover that changed health status and even impaired cognition need not rob life of its value. Respect for self-determination and human dignity entails a commitment to fostering the activities, experiences, and relationships that enrich an individual's life by finding techniques and resources to use those capacities that remain. In the case of Elizabeth Bouvia, a woman disabled by cerebral palsy and painful arthritis who sought aid in dying, the California Court of Appeals supported her request to end her life by focusing on her limitations, pointing to her physical immobility and her need for assistance with tasks like eating and toileting. Although the court described her as alert and "feisty," it also characterized her as "subject to the ignominy, embarrassment, humiliation, and dehumanizing aspects created by her helplessness." The 1996 court decision that supported physician-assisted suicide in *Washington v. Glucksberg* was filled with similar portrayals of life with impairment: it referred to people who are in a "childlike state" of helplessness, as exemplified by physical immobility or by their use of diapers to deal with incontinence.

The disability critics of the California court decision revealed an entirely different side to the Elizabeth Bouvia story. They focused on her remaining capacities and on the social and economic problems that contributed to her isolation and depression. Educational discrimination had prevented her from using her mind; she had been denied the full amount of personal assistance services that would have enabled her to stay in the community; and her depression, which stemmed from serious family problems, would have been immediately treated in a nondisabled person who had attempted suicide.

Many of the disability theorists and activists who protested the court decisions in the Bouvia case—and in the similar Michigan case of David Rivlin, who became quadriplegic and sought death rather than remaining in a nursing home—have very similar physical conditions but entirely different life circumstances. By recruiting paid or volunteer personal assistants, they live in their own homes by themselves or with family and friends. They are in the community, not in institutions. They hold jobs, engage in volunteer activities, visit friends, go out to dinner or the movies, and generally participate in ordinary family, civic, and social life. Wheelchairs do not confine: they liberate. Voice synthesizers aid communication for people who can no longer speak. Diapers or catheters are akin to eyeglasses. Using the services and skills of a personal assistant who helps them get into and out of bed, eat their meals, or travel to their next appointment is no more shameful or embarrassing than it is for a nondisabled person to work closely with an administrative assistant or to value the expertise of a mechanic, plumber, or the magician who restores data after a computer crash.

JULIA WATTS BELSER

Improv and the Angel: Disability Dance, Embodied Ethics, and Jewish Biblical Narrative

Julia Watts Belser (b. 1978) is a rabbi, activist, theologian, and professor of rabbinic literature at Georgetown University. Her scholarship brings Talmudic and biblical narratives into conversation with environmental ethics, queer theory, and disability studies. Her most recent book, Loving Our Own Bones: Disability Wisdom and the Spiritual Subversiveness of Knowing Ourselves Whole *(2024), won a National Jewish Book Award.*

From "Improv and the Angel: Disability Dance, Embodied Ethics, and Jewish Biblical Narrative," *Journal of Religious Ethics* 47, no. 3 (2019): 443–69.

Disability studies scholars have long recognized disability arts as a means to express the political, cultural, and sensory sensibilities forged through disability experience.... This article considers the affective and ethical import of disability dance, arguing that disability dance—like other art forms rooted in disability experience—can be a generative force for drawing forth disability ethics. Disability arts aim to upend conventional notions of normativity, to crack the chrysalis of shame that has so often been woven around the disabled body. Such art is not simply a political or cultural intervention, but an ethical one: a deliberate act of resacralizing bodies and minds that are all-too-often disdained and treated as disposable.

In this article, I examine the ethical insights expressed through "The Way You Look (at me) Tonight," a disability dance performance by Jess Curtis and Claire Cunningham,[77] using the performance to guide a queer/crip reading of the biblical narrative of Jacob wrestling with the angel (Gen. 32:23–33). "Crip" is a reclaimed term of kinship used to signal a bold, politicized embrace of disability, a way of refusing what Robert McRuer[78] calls "compulsory able-bodiedness."[79] I use the designation "queer/crip" to situate this reading within queer feminist disability circles as well as to underscore the theoretical and political affinities

---

77. [Cunningham is a performer and choreographer who uses crutches and is based in Glasgow, Scotland. Curtis was a dancer and choreographer based in California; he died in 2024.]

78. [Robert McRuer is a theorist in queer and disability studies.]

79. Robert McRuer, *Crip Theory: Cultural Signs of Queerness and Disability* (New York: New York University Press, 2006), 2.

between queer and crip analysis.... In forging a disability-sensitive ethics, I lift up the cultural production of disabled artists as a vital source of moral insight, one that showcases not only the narrative voices of disabled people but also the embodied sensibilities and kinesthetic knowledge borne out of lived experience of disability....

My work is deliberately, unabashedly constructive. While I tarry with "The Way You Look" and probe its nuances, my aim is not to offer an analysis of the performance itself. I take Jess and Claire's work as a hermeneutical invitation, refracting the questions "The Way You Look" raises about corporeality, intimacy, and perception through the prism of my own disciplines: disability studies, feminist ethics, queer religiosity, and ancient Jewish narrative. This project began out of my frustration with the limits of the conventional sources for disability theology and ethics, with my desire to shiver something new into the familiar constellations of biblical and rabbinic sources on disability. It emerged, in part, out of a need to name the persistent sacrality I experience in disability circles, the embodied ethics of mutuality and care I have come to know through disability community.... I situate disability dance as a potent site for revealing the interplay of affect and ethics, for articulating and inhabiting the political knowledge borne out of the experience of living as a dissident body....

Before I bring "The Way You Look" into conversation with Genesis 32, let me lay a foundation for a disability-informed reading of Jacob and the Angel. Jacob's struggle by night in Genesis 32 marks a pivotal point in a complex biblical saga, a moment when the biblical patriarch comes face to face with his past and grapples with the limits of his own character. In Judith Abrams's reading, disability lies at the very center of this tale, a way of reconciling a rivalry between twin brothers that began at the moment of their birth....

Genesis 32, Judith Abrams observes, links Jacob and the entire people of Israel indelibly with disability. Jacob's hip is strained in the struggle with a mysterious figure, first identified as a man and then as God, a physical trial that Abrams reads as a mirror image of Jacob's first wrestling match in his mother's womb.[80] But where the first struggle sets Jacob on a course of deceit and trickery, the second encounter frees him from the conflict that defined his psyche. In Abrams's reading, Jacob's "flawed moral state has finally been made manifest in his physical state." But when his disability becomes visible, it releases him "from the sin of tricking his father and brother," fulfilling the biblical narrator's need for

---

80. [See passage from Abrams above.]

symmetry and allowing the patriarch "to move forward as a character and a nation."

While my own disability hermeneutics call me to trouble Abrams's equation between physical disability and moral defect, I will ultimately upend this reading from an entirely different direction. Disability performance—and disability studies theory more broadly—suggest a radical rereading of the place of disability in Genesis 32. Rather than read Genesis 32 as the story of how the patriarch got his limp, an approach that focuses on Jacob's acquisition of impairment, I locate disability in the other body that dances on the banks of the river: the body of the angel. Over the course of this article, I will argue that Claire Cunningham's artistry on crutches shares cultural and kinesthetic qualities with the biblical angel, a figure who likewise provokes a transformative encounter with difference....

The turn to embrace disability difference is a hallmark of what many disabled artists and activists describe as "crip culture," a culture that celebrates and embraces the provocative power of the dissident, nonnormative body. The angel has largely been read in Western culture as a sublime figure whose embodiment is ethereal and insubstantial. By contrast, a crip reading of the angel demands attention to the visceral physicality of the angel as a body. It refuses the normalization of that body, centering attention on difference as an invitation and provocation to imagine differently. In considering the angel as a crip body, I focus on the wing as an emblem of difference—a marker that reveals the distinctive otherness of the angelic form....

In imagining the crip angel, I imagine an angel whose wings alter normative human anatomy and musculature—an angel who can actually, not merely miraculously, fly. The anatomical demands of a functional wing serve as a striking reminder of the way disability difference can change a body, the way disability sculpts new forms of physical expression. As a woman who wheels rather than walks through this world, I feel some kinship with the angel's strength. The particular athleticism that my own disability provokes—the way manual wheelchair use has strengthened my pectoral muscles and built up my shoulders—becomes a striking site of physical difference. My wheeler's body has a muscled chest. These arms are built to lift a body's weight. Think with me about the physicality of flight....

In the limping Jacob, I find a powerful reminder that disability is an essential part of the human experience.... Yet even as I celebrate the quotidian ordinariness of disability, the way it reveals a fundamental fleshy truth that lies at the heart of our shared creatureliness, I refuse to frame disability solely in these universalizing terms. Such language cannot fully encompass the experience of disability as difference, the way in which disability gives rise to the extraordinary. I imagine disability difference through the angel's body, through the spectacular peculiarity of the body that cannot be assimilated, that refuses the cover of the conventional. Consider, in Claire's artistry, the relationship between the crutch and the wing. Claire's crutches have become extensions of her body, material expressions of support that she has turned, through expertise and kinship, into sturdy, supple limbs. They are her primary dance partners, the medium through which her artistry emerges. They make possible a certain kind of movement —lift, height, suspension—all qualities I associate with flight. But we must be careful here. There is a popular imaginary that fantasizes flight as an escape *from* the body, a release from the contingency of the flesh: a flight from disability. Claire's work is precisely the opposite. The exquisite beauty of her movement becomes possible because of disability; her flight is born of skillful embrace of disability and the expertise it engenders.

"The Way You Look" allows the audience to experience the visible, in-breaking of queer/crip movement. In "Perch and Pounce," Claire moves at speed over and around Jess's body, using her crutches to lift and jump and pivot. When the score begins, Jess is low to the ground, his body mostly on the floor, his knees bent. Claire moves fluidly among the audience on stage, her steps fast and light, the music up-tempo and staccato. As she approaches Jess, she plants her crutches to either side of his legs, then levers her body up, lands her feet upon his knees. She lingers there for a moment, then spins off her perch, tucking herself into a curl, her body held horizontal by the crutches, one breath of perfect suspension before she sweeps her leg into a slow, deliberate curve that brings her feet back to the ground. She approaches again, spiraling her way through another portion of the audience. Jess shifts position, turning over onto elbows and knees, his head bowed to the ground, his back raised to meet her. Claire lands her toes into the small of his back, pushes off against his muscle and her crutches. She spins, circles, comes around again, her feet against his flank....

I recognize the sacred in these physical acts of attention, this profound receptivity to the tactile presence of another. In bringing Jess and Claire's work into conversation with Genesis 32, I illuminate queer/crip body knowledge in the biblical tale of Jacob and the angel, reading the angel as a wondrous and anomalous body whose presence reveals the brilliant in-breaking of disability difference. As Jacob grapples with the angel, he is drawn into a queer embrace:

a wrestling that brings him into kinesthetic contact with the numinous. The angel's touch leaves its mark upon his flesh. Against a traditional reading that figures Jacob's wound as an injury without lasting consequence, I imagine the limp as a generative source of insight. Jacob arrives whole in Shehem having integrated disability into his own sense of self. Rather than disavowing disability, Jacob allows himself to be changed by the angel's touch.

18 | Race

While early Judaism differentiated people in all manner of ways, color was not a valid criterion. Insiders were distinguished from outsiders, the righteous from the wayward, the pure from the impure. Such divisions drew boundaries between Jews and others as well as among Jews themselves. For millennia these and other differences have been defined, layered with value, and guarded through a variety of mechanisms.

What we today call race is a recent idea, invention, social construct. Racialized thinking arose in the early modern period, a mechanism for justifying hierarchies and access to resources. The impulse to devalue certain groups based on skin color or place of origin is inextricably tied to rise of the transatlantic slave trade. As Jonathan Schorsch[81] documents in *Jews and Blacks in the Early Modern World*, Jews not only participated in and benefited from that trade, but they also were inevitably impacted by the racialization on which it was based. It is thus fair to say that modern Jews have both been perpetrators of racialized thinking and its victims.

Especially during the modern period, racism melded with long-standing anti-Jewish sentiment to produce racialized views of Jews. Over time, these insidious perspectives influenced Jews themselves, who began to look upon themselves through racialized lenses. Questions about Jewish racial "purity," Jewish traits and uniqueness, Jewish hereditary diseases, and more animated late-nineteenth-century and early-twentieth-century Jewish thinkers, as documented in Mitchell B. Hart's[82] *Jews and Race: Writings on Identity and Difference, 1880–1940*. Later in the twentieth century, liberal American Jews joined with others to oppose Jim Crow laws and other systemic racist institutions and to call for new kinds of relationships across diverse communities. Current considerations of critical race theory have inspired some Jewish thinkers to weigh in on the importance of interrogating historiography and conventionally prominent Jewish self-understandings.

All this is to say that there is no singular way Jews or Jewish ethics approach issues of race. Lewis R. Gordon's short essay poses Afro-Jewish ethics as an

---

81. Jonathan Schorsch is a professor of Jewish studies at Columbia University.

82. Mitchell B. Hart is a professor of history and Jewish studies at the University of Florida.

interrogative, a perpetual challenge to prevailing assumptions. That Jews are and always have been white; that Jewish life, law, and lore either are Euromodernist or seek Euromodernist recognition; that mutually exclusive binary categories constitute Jewish ethical deliberation—all of these, Gordon argues, warrant careful scrutiny. Such investigations lead Gordon to three core themes to animate an Afro-Jewish ethics: what it means to be human, freedom and human dignity, and the search for justification in an unjust world. Pulling from sociology and anthropology as well as philosophy, theology, history, and futurity, Gordon's eclectic methodology demonstrates that interrogations can be both liberative and burdensome: "It involves taking responsibility not only for ethics but also, in doing so, for responsibility as well."[83]

Judith Kay wonders how white Jewish ethicists could address racism and antisemitism. Kay uses psychological and Marxist approaches to analyze how anti-Jewish prejudice intersects with socioeconomic difference to divide Jews from other historically marginalized groups. The combination of internalized oppression with externalized domination often reproduce divisions, particularly along racial lines. Jewish ethicists, especially those on college campuses, would do well to interrogate the ways in which oppression and domination operate in their own classes, conversations, research, and communal engagement.

Finally, Annalise E. Glauz-Todrank's essay investigates how popular thinking about race and religion apply to Jewish Americans, how Jewish Americans are simultaneously privileged and often marginalized, and how these are ethical concerns. In some profound ways, American Jews typically associated themselves with "religion" yet shied away from "race." Glauz-Todrank draws from critical race theory, civil rights law, and "religionization" to analyze the Supreme Court case *Shaare Tefila Congregation v. Cobb* (1987) and argue that it exemplifies a *Jewish critical race theory*. Secular law thus becomes another tool by which to understand and remedy race-based marginalization of Jews.

See also the section on genes (part 3, section 16).

---

83. Lewis R. Gordon, "Afro-Jewish Ethics?," in *Jewish Religious and Philosophical Ethics*, eds. Curtis Hutt, Halla Kim, and Berel Dov Lerner (New York: Routledge, 2018), 223.

LEWIS R. GORDON

Afro-Jewish Ethics?

Lewis R. Gordon (b. 1962) serves in the department of philosophy at the University of Connecticut. With specializations in Africana, continental, and social and political philosophies, he focuses his scholarship on education, aesthetics, film, literature, music, culture, race and racism, medicine, psychiatry, psychoanalysis, and decolonial theory. He holds leadership roles for the American Philosophical Association and the journal Philosophy and Global Affairs.

From "Afro-Jewish Ethics?," in *Jewish Religious and Philosophical Ethics*, eds. Curtis Hutt, Halla Kim, and Berel Dov Lerner (New York: Routledge, 2018), 213–28.

This reflection is on Afro-Jewish ethics, which I pose in the interrogative. I pose it as a question, since one would presume that Afro-Jewish ethics is simply Jewish ethics. Such a presumption would presume an intrinsic legitimacy to *Jewish* ethics as a category despite the concern that could emerge from critics who would ask, as well, whether Jewish ethics is simply, ultimately, *ethics*. If Jewish ethics could sustain the force of such criticism, why, then, should *Afro*-Jewish ethics not hold its own? The immediate response is that "Afro" is not an intrinsically ethical, moral, or religious category. As an ethnic or racial concept, it would particularize the ethical, moral, or religious ones it modifies. Those who know Judaism may pause for a moment, however, as "Jewish" isn't entirely free of ethnic significance. As well, given the unique treatment unleashed on people of African descent in the emergence of the Euromodern world, the term "Afro" hardly stands as one devoid of normative content. Afro-Jewish signification warrants, then, some reflection....

So, we begin with the Afro-Jewish question. The obvious question is this: Why is it a question at all? If the term refers to Blacks or African people who practice Judaism, the source of the mystery would be mysterious. There is a question, however, for the same reason there have historically been a "Black question" and a "Jewish question." Such people are, as W. E. B. Du Bois[84] observed more than a century ago, a "problem." Thus, wherever they go, problems emerge. The

---

84. [W. E. B. Du Bois was an American pan-Africanist social historian and civil rights activist and co-founded the National Association for the Advancement of Colored People.]

problem, ultimately, at least for the anti-Black racist and the antisemite is that they exist. There are, however, differences.

As problems, Black people face ironic and paradoxical situations where legitimacy is premised on their absence. Thus, to enter the room as a Black person in an anti-Black society is, in effect, to delegitimate the space. Blacks thus, Du Bois argued, had to develop two perspectives: the first is the anti-Black one in which the second . . . [is seen by] the self as loathsome. If this position is accepted, then the world is simple and Manichaean:[85] whites are good, legitimate, right; Blacks are bad, illegitimate, and wrong. This binary view also takes the form of white being universal and Black being particular, which appeals to the former as pure and without contradiction, and the latter as impure. A form of theodicy of thought follows, in which the infelicities of whiteness are placed outside for the sake of systemic integrity. The result is divestment of things negative to the outer realm and beyond, a sphere of, in other words, Blackness. As long as the two worlds don't interact, segregation preserves a strict order of fullness of being versus its absence. This order of contraries faces its challenge, however, in the lived reality of Blacks. As long as Blacks are locked out of equations of reality, it means the avowed reach of the universal is particular. If, that is, Blacks must take into account the point of view of whites, it makes Black perspectives farther in scope than white ones. If, that is, Blacks are part of reality and that is ignored, then whites who do so live in a very partial world, one that falls short of actual reality. This realization leads to questioning the sources of limits. Put differently, if Blacks could be otherwise, then the limitations imposed must not be intrinsic to Blacks but instead a function of a world that makes Blacks into problems instead of regarding them as people who face problems. Realization of the latter is what Paget Henry[86] calls *potentiated double consciousness*. That form of thought addresses the many sides and dimensions of reality; it faces not only the light but also the darkness through which light achieves distinction. Black people thus pose a fundamental ethical challenge to the modern world, to which, though indigenous, they face normative and political exclusion. Put differently, the ethics in the Euromodern world are animated by the paradox of being indigenous to a world that rejects Blacks. Interestingly enough, this was Jewish history. It's not

85. [Manichaeism, from a third-century Chinese tradition, views the world as a fundamental struggle between good and evil.]

86. [Paget Henry is a professor of critical theory and Caribbean studies at Brown University.]

that there isn't antisemitism. It's just that the conditions that led to the rejection of Blacks in the modern world offered opportunities for certain groups of Jews —those who could prove whiteness—to belong. There is thus a split between Jews also along lines of color....

Returning to the question of Afro-Jewish studies, then, it compels us to raise critical considerations through which an enriched understanding of Jewish people can emerge and the problems following from a form of methodological and disciplinary apartheid premised on erasure of its African. This conclusion is important for avoiding a variety of additional fallacies in the study and portrait of Afro-Jews.

The first, already mentioned, is the tendency to read "Afro-Jews" as "Blacks and Jews" instead of "Black Jews." The others are manifold. Here are a few: (1) the presumption that Afro-Jews must be "converts"; (2) Afro-Jews are a recent development in Jewish history; (3) Afro-Jews are basically African diasporic people seeking (white) Jewish "recognition"; and (4) Afro-Jews are not agents of history.

A detailed response to each of these would require separate study.... That there are whites who convert to Judaism should make it no surprise to find Asians, Blacks, Native Americans, and varieties of other racialized groups doing the same. A presumption of their being converts but whites not being so leads to the erroneous thesis of an original whiteness of Jews....

In terms of the second claim of Afro-Jews being historically recent, the answer is that history doesn't bear that out.... Basically, many historians impose whiteness on a multiracial population. In effect, their scholarship erases the historical diversity of Jews.... For our purposes, that diversity included people we would today call "Afro-Jews."

The recognition issue is, for the most part, an arrogant presumption of Afro-Jews either wanting or needing white Jewish acceptance or approval. It would be a good idea to consult Afro-Jews. There are Black people who wish to be white, but, if so, it's not a good stratagem to choose a historically hated group....

The last is a problem faced primarily by Black and many First Nation peoples across the globe. An outcome of colonialism is a set of presumptions whose consequence is the denial of the historical agency of such people. Things are *done* to such people, but they are, supposedly, never doers beyond reaction and, when romanticized, resistance. Doers, in historical terms, are conquerors and those to whom are attributed human status according to the prevailing philosophical anthropology. To understand this, consider the emergence of the notions "modern" and "primitive."...

We arrive, then, at three core themes at the heart of Afromodernity, which work their way into Afro-Jewish ethics: (1) what it means to be human or, simply, humanity; (2) freedom and human dignity; and (3) the search for justification in a world patently unjust and, for the most part, unreasonable. As we will see, they are also overlooked, elided, or disavowed dimensions of what ethics must be addressed in the Euromodern world....

Take, for example, the Jewish concept of election. Many non-Jews erroneously interpret this as a testimony of Jewish superiority of being "chosen." Yet what Judaism teaches is that election is an immense responsibility through which one may suffer affliction. Election is a terrible burden to bear, for what could be more heavy and terrifying than taking on the responsibility for the ethical face of reality? This is borne out in the opening verse of most Jewish prayers: *"Baruch atah Adonai, eloheynu melekh ha'olam . . ."* ("Praised are You, the Eternal One our G-d, Ruler of the Cosmos [the Universe or all reality] . . ."). G-d, in Judaism, is both being (creator) and just (ethics). Here, however, is the tricky part of Judaism, which often shocks many who see religion in terms of a supreme being: G-d, in Judaism, isn't ontological, although there are Jewish people who think such. G-d's namelessness and the injunction against images or idols, in short, G-d's invisibility is one ultimately anti-theological reason for this. Another emerges paradoxically from secular Jews who do not believe there is a god yet they believe *in* G-d. This twist makes sense if one understands that for such Jews, G-d *is ethics*. G-d emerges from our taking responsibility for ethical life. Returning to the three themes with which I closed the previous section, this is a radical idea since it involves taking responsibility not only for ethics but also, in doing so, for responsibility as well. That radical responsibility is G-d.

Afro-Jewish ethics, then, involves taking a position in a world in which there is no room for optimism (given radical anti-Black racism) or pessimism (since that would require a foreclosed future) but, instead, ethical *commitment*. Such radical responsibility brings to the fore the second element, the importance of freedom and human dignity. To act at all manifests that freedom, and to do so ethically requires transcending the self (through the burden of election) to the value of others (dignity). Such valuing also leads to a value of the self through realization of the self as other. This intersubjective element of Jewish life comes back in Afro-Jewish ethics in a relationship of we that reaches beyond in the concept of mitzvot. Though the word technically means a commandment, as in the 613 mitzvot, committing a mitzvah isn't limited to those. Properly done, it is not actually done for the self but for the sake of what ought to be done, which leads, interestingly enough, to an understanding of things greater than the self unaccounted for as life's experiences unfold. The best example of this is attending to the dead, as the recipient cannot give compensation. This mitzvah is expressed as *hesed shel emet* (true kindness). Scholars of African communal ethics such as the southern African concept of *ubuntu* would immediately see the connection in its message of "I am because you are." The "I" here is actually a relational "we," which makes the expression become, "We are because you are." The three elements of humanity, freedom, and justification come together, then, because they are ultimately symbiotic.

JUDITH KAY

Jews as Oppressed and Oppressor: Doing Ethics at the Intersections of Classism, Racism, and Antisemitism

Judith Kay (b. 1951), a scholar of religion, spirituality, and society, taught at the University of Puget Sound. Her scholarship investigates theories of oppression, virtue ethics, and intersectionality. She led race and pedagogy efforts at UPS for decades and has held leadership positions for the Justice Studies Association.

From "Jews as Oppressed and Oppressor: Doing Ethics at the Intersections of Classism, Racism, and Antisemitism," in *Judaism, Race, and Ethics: Conversations and Questions*, ed. Jonathan K. Crane (University Park: Pennsylvania State University Press, 2020), 66–104.

Antisemitism has surfaced consistently in ways that sidetrack or sink movements to end classism or racism. I argue that classism and racism depend on antisemitism to divide and conquer. These dynamics work effectively when gentiles are conditioned not to recognize or understand antisemitism and to isolate Jews from their fellow oppressed groups. I aim to expose these dynamics so that we all can do our part, from our social location, to forge alliances and clear our harbors of all oppressions. . . .

Without the external pressure of a grassroots movement to compel the study of antisemitism, academic liberationists proceeded to study racism, sexism, and other "isms." The distinctive structural dynamics of anti-Jewish oppression remained largely unexplored by gentile scholars. Such historical factors, plus the cultural denial of antisemitism, suggest that any deployment of gentile liberation theories by Jewish ethicists needs to be approached with suspicion.

Liberationists remind us that the liberatory intent of any analytic construct or practice is no guarantee of its accuracy, adequacy, or immunity to the ingress of oppressive ideas. They themselves are not immune to false consciousness given their social location within intersecting oppressions. One method that liberationist scholars use to help expose their own blinders is to strive for insight into how knowledge production is affected by social location. This chapter focuses on the social location of white, Ashkenazi Jews in the United States in predominantly white, gentile settings who work at the intersections of classism, racism, and antisemitism.

Two analytical tools prove particularly helpful in mapping the structural aspects of antisemitism: oppression and intersectionality.[87] Oppression is understood to be systemic and structured in institutions and social dynamics. Race theorists, for instance, have explicated the linked interdependent practices of racism constituting a structure of white supremacy. They understand racism as the systemic, structured, one-way targeting of groups for mistreatment (using skin color as a pretext) by whites who escape such targeting. I suggest that antisemitism deserves to be studied using this analytical tool of structural oppression, too. Oppression, of course, implants attitudes; both targeted and nontargeted groups internalize attitudes that condition them to accept their roles in the exploitive system. But combatting antisemitism should not only be focused on prejudice and hatred. Liberationists hope to change structures as well as habits of heart and mind. The path forward entails risk, resistance, and a commitment to forming effective coalitions with the shared goal of transformational structural change.

Although the tool of intersectionality needs refining for use by Jewish ethicists, it too will help map the structure of these interlocking sandbars (to continue the nautical metaphor with which I began). Womanist[88] sociologist Patricia Hill Collins views intersectionality as "an emerging field of critical inquiry and practice that examines how social inequalities are organized, endure, and change."[89] I suggest that although intersectionality was intended to prevent

---

87. [See part 2, section 9, footnote 57.]

88. [Womanism, coined by Alice Walker in 1982, is a type of feminism that focuses predominantly on the experiences and concerns of women of color, especially Black women.]

89. Patricia Hill Collins, "With My Mind Set on Freedom: Black Feminism, Intersectionality, and Social Justice," fifth annual Gittler Prize Lecture, Brandeis University, October 29, 2013, https://www.brandeis.edu/gittlerprize/videos/collinslecture.html.

our seeing single oppressions in isolation, it has not totally escaped the dualism of treating groups as either oppressed or oppressive. This binary poses perils for Jewish ethicists because it could fail to capture a key structural feature of antisemitism—namely, that Jews are simultaneously oppressed and oppressor. An intersectional analysis, combined with the analytic tool of oppression, will reveal the insufficiency of framing antisemitism as hatred....

A corrective begins by reconceiving antisemitism as a form of oppression—that is, as the systemic, structural, one-way mistreatment of Jews by non-Jews. This oppression cannot be understood apart from its intersections with classism. Let's attend to this intersectionality that has shaped anti-Jewish oppression from the early modern period to the present.

Anti-Jewish oppression has involved a particular dynamic of classism, which means that anti-Jewish oppression is difficult to map without an analysis of class oppression. Classism is the division of society into different groups hierarchically stratified on the basis of their relation to production. Slavery is one form of class society in which the enslavers own the bodies of those who work, their offspring, and the profits of their labor. Capitalism is a form of classism in which those involved in the direct production of goods and services constitute the working class. The small owning class consists of those who exploit workers by taking "the surplus produced ... and us[ing] it for their own material well-being" —in Karl Marx's[90] terms, those who either own the means of production or live off the inheritance of previous owners (unearned income). Within this conception of capitalism, the middle class is part of the working class—its members work for a living and provide services as social workers, doctors, lawyers, bankers, teachers, and managers—but these roles have the added function of funneling profits from the working class to the owning class....

Anti-Jewish oppression and classism combined to isolate Jews from peasants and, later, the working class (despite the fact that most Jews worked for a living). In the early modern period, ruling elites may have acted intentionally to allow the isolation and scapegoating of Jews. Once this structural dynamic was embedded in systems, institutions, and the minds of both gentiles and Jews, the oppression took on a life of its own. It no longer required intentionality.[91]

90. [Karl Marx was a nineteenth-century German philosopher and political theoretician whose *Communist Manifesto* critiqued capitalism through a historical materialistic lens that highlighted the role of classes and labor.]

91. Sociologists ... differentiate three levels of discrimination. Individual discrimination involves "an intention to harm," whereas a second form, institutional oppression,

Dominant elites benefited by obfuscating how Jews were oppressed and encouraged recognition only of Jews' exploitive role. Both this external oppression and Jews' consequent internalized oppression propelled many to seek temporary security as agents of gentile elites. The oppression set up Jews simultaneously as both oppressed and oppressor. . . .

To summarize, anti-Jewish oppression intersects with classism to set up some Jews to be targeted as middle agents of the oppressive society. Jews escape certain kinds of mistreatment, but their isolation and interstitial position keep them vulnerable to blame and isolation from potential allies. . . .

I have shown how the knowledge project of intersectionality can be useful to ethicists, if refined to avoid the binary that regards groups as either oppressed or oppressor. That binary portrays white Jews *solely* as oppressors because of their white privilege. This picture misses the key intersecting structural dynamics of antisemitism and classism—middle agency. Jewish flight into middle-agent roles after World War II is a function of anti-Jewish oppression as well as of white privilege. It is futile to ponder how much Jewish privilege is due to middle agency, how much is due to whiteness, and how much is due to internalized Jewish oppression. The important conclusion here is that a nonbinary intersectional analysis of structural dynamics reveals the inherent vulnerability of Jews' class position. . . .

If white Jewish ethicists accept an analysis of their own oppression that ignores or minimizes structural dynamics, they are in a weak position to notice the structural realities of racism. Jews would not be unique in studying racism as if it were only a social construct—prejudice, belief, discourse—without attention to material reality. Scholar of religion Jennifer Harvey argues that regarding race as a construct divorced from structural dynamics has at least two negative consequences. First, it has misled some whites into thinking that if they could disregard race—by becoming colorblind—they would cease participating in racism. This attitude is self-deceptive, Harvey argues, because not noticing race often reinforces the pattern of ignoring the material realities of structural white supremacy.[92]

---

has the same intentionality but is mediated by people who implement unjust policies by virtue of their roles in institutions. By contrast, structural discrimination, the third form, is "neutral in intent," yet its outcomes have a differential, negative effect on oppressed groups.

92. J. Harvey, *Whiteness and Morality: Pursuing Racial Justice Through Reparations and Sovereignty* (New York: Palgrave Macmillan, 2007), 26–27.

Analyses of oppression that refer only to attitudes have a second consequence, Harvey adds, of diverting oppressors' attention to their interior life in ways that blind them to their complicity in racist policies and practices.[93] White Jews can deceive themselves that if they do not practice open bigotry, then they are not entangled in racism. Gentiles can deceive themselves that if they lack feelings of Jew-hatred or superiority, they cannot be complicit in anti-Jewish oppression.[94] White Jews might be lulled into thinking that ending racism requires individual solutions alone, without collective action to seek material change. Harvey proposes white reparations for slavery and genocide as one such material change.[95] ...

Racism is an inadequate and misleading way to frame anti-Jewish oppression.[96] A slippage between these two different kinds of structural oppression permits gentiles to target white Jews as racist without recognizing antisemitism. Precision in Jewish ethicists' analyses will encourage further distinctions

---

93. Harvey, *Whiteness and Morality*, 41–43.

94. Gentiles can deceive themselves about their complicity in anti-Jewish oppression by denying that they feel any hatred. They might admit to a dislike of Jews, or even suggest that they like a few individual Jews, as if that rendered their passive or active complicity unoppressive. Adolf Eichmann may be the best-known and most striking example of the ability to deny responsibility based on a lack of negative emotion. He "'personally' never had anything whatever against Jews; on the contrary, he had plenty of 'private reasons' for not being a Jew hater," as Hannah Arendt tells us in her masterpiece *Eichmann in Jerusalem: A Report on the Banality of Evil*, rev. and enl. ed. (New York: Penguin Classics, 1994), 26. Eichmann's stepmother's family had married Jews and Jewesses; he once had a Jewish mistress, and a Jewish boyhood friend; he had also studied Jewish authors. "I myself had no hatred for Jews"; thus, he said, he should not be seen as antisemitic (Arendt, *Eichmann in Jerusalem*, 30). See also "Eichmann Claims He Had 'Many' Jewish Relatives; Says He Is No 'Jew-Hater,'" Jewish Telegraphic Agency Archive, April 21, 1961, https://www.jta.org/1961/04/21/archive/eichmann-claims-he-had-many-jewish-relatives-says-he-is-no-jew-hater.

95. Harvey, *Whiteness and Morality*, chap. 4.

96. Many will disagree with me. In his op-ed "Antisemitism Is Racism," English comedian David Baddiel writes, "Jews are, after all, the only entity, in terms of the racist stereotype that operates on two levels, low and high status—that can be imagined as vermin but also as moneyed and secretly in control. The moneyed and in-control thing undoubtedly still has some traction on the left (see France), and it's why Jews, at best, might not be considered to be really in need of the protections that anti-racism offers, and at worst might be the enemy" (*The Guardian*, December 2, 2014, https://www.theguardian.com/commentisfree/2014/dec/02/antisemitism-is-racism-malky-mackay-david-whelan-mario-balotelli).

between racism and anti-Jewish oppression, even when they interlock and their forms of mistreatment are similar....

A singular focus on identity, however, can lure scholars away from studying the structural dynamics of oppression and from engaging in collective struggles. Identity studies can falsely imply that rejecting or changing one's identity is sufficient for liberation. As Harvey observes, the study of white identity has limits—claiming or rejecting a white identity does not actually change the material relations of white supremacy.[97] Jewish intellectual historians have presented Jewish identity as a central issue emerging from Jewish emancipation. Ashkenazi Jews have puzzled over how to honor communal Jewish obligations while being citizens of democracies. Jewish identity is not irrelevant to Jewish ethics, but terror about the Holocaust—like any major trauma visited upon an oppressed group—makes debates over identity take on an urgency related to survival. The underlying fear is that settling on the wrong identity may have lethal consequences. Adding to this urgency, students of the Holocaust know full well that when essentialist, racialized forms of anti-Jewish oppression were operational, abandoning a Jewish identity did not guarantee survival. Jewish ethicists must steer a careful course when including analyses of identity in our ethical projects, because this can lead attention away from structural dynamics.

97. Harvey, *Whiteness and Morality*, 36.

ANNALISE E. GLAUZ-TODRANK

Jewish Critical Race Theory and Jewish "Religionization" in *Shaare Tefila Congregation v. Cobb*

Annalise E. Glauz-Todrank (b. 1978), a religion scholar at Wake Forest University, works at the intersection of race, law, and religion, with a special focus on Jewish identity in the modern period. She is particularly curious about how socially constructed categories become normalized, reinforce inequalities, and influence conceptions of the self and the other. She serves on the Law, Religion, and Culture committee for the American Academy of Religion.

From "Jewish Critical Race Theory and Jewish 'Religionization' in *Shaare Tefila Congregation v. Cobb*," in *Judaism, Race, and Ethics: Conversations and Questions*, ed. Jonathan K. Crane (University Park: Pennsylvania State University Press, 2020), 191–216.

This chapter addresses the perception of Jews and the legal protection of Jews. I situate Jews within the American racial and religious infrastructure. My aim is to explore the racial and religious dimensions of identity for Jewish Americans within the framework of critical race theory (CRT) and in most Jewish Americans' assimilation to religious norms, or what I call "religionization." Critical race theorists know that race is a multifaceted, multipurpose structure that changes over time, and that it serves the needs of the majority, whether those needs are economic, political, social, or all three. CRT also addresses the *ethical* problem of the American legal system, which values white Christian (Protestant) men more than it values other individuals. For example, the legal system uses the benchmark of a "reasonable man" who might make decisions in various contexts; it is fairly obvious that this man is straight, white, Christian, able-bodied, and so on. With this in mind, I focus on Jewish Americans through the lens of racial formation and religionization, which allows us to better think through the challenges they encounter, the experiences that affect them, and the particular issues they face as Jews. Furthermore, this approach provides an important perspective within CRT that allows us to interrogate sites or identifications where race is less apparent and even more abstracted from real life....

With these concepts in mind, let us examine *Shaare Tefila Congregation v. Cobb* (1987) to consider more closely how Jewish Americans appeal to, and yet resist, the term "race" within the context of a civil rights lawsuit. *Shaare Tefila* was the first legal case to assert that Jews are *not* a race yet *are treated* as one. The case was brought by a synagogue in Silver Spring, Maryland, in response to Ku Klux Klan and Nazi-related vandalism on the surface of their building, playground equipment, and a car. The case ended up in the US Supreme Court, after two lower courts dismissed the suit on the grounds that Jewish Americans were citing race-based protection, and the judges viewed Jews as white people. So the synagogue's lawyers constructed the argument that although Jewish Americans are not "a racially distinct group," they have been *viewed* as one, and that the men who desecrated their synagogue were motivated by racial prejudice....

"Race" was something that many Jewish Americans prior to the Shoah wanted to preserve, because, ironically, it enabled them to ensure that Jews, who were not people of color, had a minority presence among other "white" people. For instance, a majority of them intended to marry within the community. Whereas other "white ethnics" could marry among Christians, whether Protestant or Catholic, it was undesirable for Jews to marry Christians. In public settings, however, "white" Jewish Americans often had to suppress what was explicitly "Jewish" about themselves to conform to the beliefs and expectations of the dominant majority of white people.... Thus it was a hardship to Jewish Americans—who had for so long been a persecuted minority in other places—to claim to be "white" in the United States....

Critical race theory aims to develop new ways of thinking about and enacting the relationships between race and the law. These new conceptualizations are necessary because the language of the law and the usual forms of legal interpretation do not sufficiently protect people who are categorized and then alienated on the basis of race. The fundamental flaw in the legal system that critical race theorists address is its ongoing inability to protect people of color from the marginalization that they experience by being racialized in American society....

Critical race theorists identify existing problems in the legal system with the objective of changing how laws are written and interpreted. In order to make sense of the relationship between racialization and marginalization, they write about specific situations and legal cases that highlight the distinctive experiences of particular groups of people. They often focus on the lack of fit between a legal decision and discourses or characteristics that define, or that are employed to define, a given group.

Central to the formulation of most such arguments is the primary role that mainstream conversations play in informing the unequal treatment that occurs. In other words, the problems in question do not pertain to qualities *inherent* in a particular group of people but rather to *conceptions* of that group that are also usually grounded in a long social and economic history of oppression. Because of these histories of oppression and because the conceptions at stake are often assumed to be inherent or factual, the discourses that undergird the discrimination are deeply rooted and difficult, if not impossible, to eradicate. As Eduardo Bonilla-Silva[98] puts it, "although the racialization of peoples was socially invented and did not override previous forms of social distinction based on class or gender, it did not lead to imaginary relations but generated new forms of human association with definite status differences. After the process of attaching meaning to a 'people' is instituted, race becomes a *real* category of group association and identity" (emphasis added).[99] Thus racialization effectively "creates" social realities: it constrains groups of people on the basis of social perceptions that are seemingly ingrained. The development of this process over time has functioned to give racial categories every appearance of being real and apparent....

As noted above, two lower courts dismissed the congregation's claim that the synagogue had been the victim of a racist attack, on the basis that Jews are "white." First, federal district court judge Norman Ramsey rejected the congregation's argument and dismissed the case, and then the three judges on the Fourth Circuit Court of Appeals determined that "no racial discrimination was present," in part because congregants did not identify themselves as members of a separate race.[100]

In the court of appeals, however, the judges were divided, with the majority claiming that to gain civil rights protections, Jewish Americans had to assert that they *were* members of a separate race. Outlier judge J. Harvie Wilkinson III differentiated between the *embodiment* of race and the *discourses* that inform thinking on race. "Rather than allowing ignorance and misperception to provide their own defense," he wrote in his dissenting opinion, "I would find the erroneous but all too sincere view of the defendants that Jews constitute a separate race worthy of humiliation and degradation sufficient to bring the claim."[101] Nevertheless, the synagogue lost its appeal, and there the story would have ended had the US Supreme Court not agreed to hear the case in conjunction with another

---

98. [Eduardo Bonilla-Silva is a professor of sociology at Duke University.]
99. Eduardo Bonilla-Silva, *White Supremacy and Racism in the Post-Civil Rights Era* (Boulder, CO: Lynne Rienner Publishers, 2001), 40.
100. *Shaare Tefila Congregation v. Cobb*, 785 F.2d 523 (4th Cir. 1986).
101. *Shaare Tefila Congregation v. Cobb*, 538.

case, argued on the same legal basis in another appeals court, which had resulted in a different ruling.

In the Supreme Court, the justices grappled with the question "Can Jews claim race-based protection?" But instead of concluding immediately that Jews are white, as both of the lower courts had done, they considered Jewish American experiences of discrimination in historical context, noting that institutional restrictions on Jews in the past had significantly limited Jewish access to the social privileges held by whites. They also discussed the virulent racism against Jews in Nazi Germany and how vividly the graffiti evoked that history....

To fully accommodate Jewish Americans—however they choose to identify—a Jewish CRT that also accounts for "religionization" must account for Jewish history. Whether Jewish Americans identify themselves as secular, Reform, haredi, or something else, they must at least *consider* the Torah. Secular Jews, for instance, may acknowledge the Torah's existence or may be outright hostile toward it. But *all* Jews look to the Torah for their origins. Whether they actually study the Torah, it forms the basis of Jewish existence. Many Jews think of themselves as a continuation of the lengthy history that Israelites, and then Jews, have experienced since biblical times....

To adequately address Jewish history, Jewish critical race theory must not only take this history into account but also must consider how it affects Jewish American experience today. For instance, just as CRT draws on Black history in the United States to address how Blacks have responded to racism—and, more specifically, to Black narratives of slavery, theologies of liberation, "double consciousness," integrationism and nationalism, and the diasporic character of Black Americans[102]—Jewish CRT must emphasize not only the common history and traditions of Jews but the role of "religion" within them.[103] ...

    102. On Black narratives of slavery, see Frederick Douglass, *Narrative of the Life of Frederick Douglass* (Boston: Anti-Slavery Office, 1845), available at https://www.gutenberg.org/cache/epub/23/pg23-images.html; on theologies of liberation, see Cornell West, *Prophesy Deliverance!* (Louisville, KY: Westminster John Knox Press, 2002), 69–91; on "double consciousness," see W. E. B. Du Bois, *Souls of Black Folk* (1903), available at https://www.gutenberg.org/files/408/408-h/408-h.htm; on integrationism and nationalism, see Gary Peller, "Race Consciousness," *Duke Law Journal* (1990): 758–847; and on the Black diaspora, see Paul Gilroy, *Black Atlantic: Modernity and Double-Consciousness* (Cambridge, MA: Harvard University Press, 1995).

    103. I put "religion" in quotation marks because, like "race," its meaning changes over time, and because religion was not a separate component of identification in ancient Israelite times.

A Jewish critical race theory must recognize that being accepted as white by the white majority becomes a roadblock, for many Jewish Americans, to feeling accepted by people of color, an acceptance for which many of them may yearn. This acceptance as "white" also has implications for Jews of color, who can be marginalized by their own communities because these assumptions do not account for multiple identifications among Jews.

For most Jewish Americans, being situated squarely within "whiteness" means that they may be mocked behind their backs by white American non-Jews. It means that, depending on where one is in the United States, Jewish Americans may choose to display more or less of their Jewish identification. It means that however nice Christian Americans may appear to be to Jewish Americans on the surface, quite a number of them still believe that Jews killed Jesus. Many non-Jewish Americans think that they can identify Jews by their pointed noses, their hair, or even . . . their horns. Jewish Americans continue to conceal their synagogues architecturally, so that they do not attract attention, not wanting to expose them to vandalism or other forms of destruction and attack. A Jewish CRT must examine the fact that many Christians, and other non-Jews, have passed down religious dogma to their children that paints a negative picture of Jews, must look at how that dogma has been structurally reinforced, and must take account of how both things have, to some degree, incorporated Jewish racialization along the way. . . .

Investigating the concept of how Jewish Americans *experience* race allows Jewish studies scholars and critical race theorists to examine their complicated history outside the boundaries of the typical ways in which Americans think about race. Certainly, Jews were a considered a "race" in many contexts before they came to the United States. But even in the United States, Jews have dealt with racial forms of discrimination. Many Jewish Americans encounter, to varying degrees, injustice in a long history of past harms.

Thinking about how Jewish Americans identify and are identified racially as an *ethical* issue provides an entry point into discussion about the ways in which race, religion, gender, and ability, among other factors, affect their standing under the law. Relative privilege and marginalization accompany these and other categories, such that American norms have urged Jewish Americans to identify Judaism predominantly as a "religion" rather than as a "race." Considering this type of problem as an ethical one enables us to identify it as a social justice issue: CRT aims to correct the problem of racialized discord in the law, in which people's experiences do not match the legal arguments that are made for them, or in which no legal arguments account for those experiences. This is where we are now, perhaps: we have a race-based ruling in *Shaare Tefila Congregation v. Cobb* but very little legal theory—or little theory that accounts for legal issues—that can help us situate Jewish identification according to ideas about "racialization."

298 | CONSTRUCTIONS OF THE HUMAN

IV | Bioethics

> *Therefore, choose life so that you and your offspring would live...*   Deuteronomy 30:19

Introduction

The imperative to choose life has inspired Jews to take seriously the healing arts, *ars medica*. The classic rabbis built upon the biblical injunctions to heal injured parties (Exod. 21:19–20), to restore lost objects to people (Deut. 22:2), and to not stand idly by while someone's blood spills (Lev. 19:16)—among other sources—to insist that intervening to care for someone if not to cure them is more than permitted: it is an obligation (e.g., B. T. *Bava Kamma* 85a; B. T. *Sanhedrin* 73a). At the same time, being cavalier is a recipe for condemnation (M. *Kiddushin* 4.14; Rashi at B. T. *Kiddushin* 82a) and refraining from providing succor would be tantamount to murder (*Shulchan Aruch, Yoreh De'ah,* 336.1). Thus great care must be given about the very care one provides.

Concern about *ars medica* is found in every age and community. Jewish sources address both the practice of healing as well as the values that ought to guide that practice, though they rarely added much to extant medical knowledge and prowess until the modern era. For example, Jewish sources never questioned the humoral theory popularized by Galen and the Hippocratic tradition that understood human health as dependent upon the equilibrium of four vital fluids (blood, phlegm, yellow bile, and black bile). The advent of germ theory in the latter part of the nineteenth century disproved that idea: microbes (viruses, bacteria, etc.), not imbalanced humors, cause disease. This raises a serious challenge for contemporary Jews who yearn to plumb the Judaic textual tradition for guidance on pressing medical issues: since the classic sources operate with an unfounded assumption about the human body, how much weight should they be given?

Compounding this conceptual challenge is one regarding control. Perhaps Immanuel Jakobovits, then the chief rabbi of Great Britain, put it best in his 1959 *Jewish Medical Ethics*, one of the first books on this field: "Today the contest between science and religion is no longer a competitive search for the truth as in other former times. It is a struggle between excesses and controls, between the supremacy of man's creations and the supremacy of man himself.... Who will control the physician and the growing army of other scientists?"[1] Insofar as biomedical technologies advance at an increasingly frenetic pace, who should control those advancements, how, and why? Should it be scientists and physicians, ever eager to find the next cure or better intervention? Or should policy makers, public health officials, or industry? What role can and should religious sensibilities, like Jewish law and ethics, have in these discussions? Such questions understandably make the field of modern Jewish bioethics dynamic and diverse.

The sections in this part illustrate the breadth and depth of this rapidly expanding subfield of Jewish ethics. The first, section 19, opens with a large conversation about the interrelationship between Jewish norms like halakha and secular biomedical assumptions and practices. No consensus exists here, as some insist that halakha is normative whereas others view it and other Jewish sources as complementary to secular bioethics. Such disagreements illustrate that it is imprecise to say that there is *one and only one* Judaic position about any biomedical issue.

The following three sections address key moments in the human lifecycle. Section 20 attends to issues surrounding the generation of new human life as enabled by recent advancements of artificial reproductive technologies (ARTs). These novel methods both trouble conventional notions of procreation that involve sexual intimacy between men and women yet enable many to fulfill the biblical call to procreate who otherwise cannot. In section 21, we focus on abortion not because it is a prominent topic in classic Jewish sources but because it dominates contemporary conversations, especially in the United States. Here, disagreements among Jewish bioethicists emerge from their nuanced reading of similar sources, nuances that are often overshadowed in public debate. Reading carefully matters also when regarding end of life issues, as seen in section 22. Caring for the aged and the dying surface conflicts between duties, burdens, harms, and benefits. The topic of euthanasia is especially fraught and relevant, given the development of myriad ways to palliate pain and forestall death.

1. Immanuel Jakobovits, *Jewish Medical Ethics* (New York: Bloch Publishing Company, 1959), vii–viii.

Though this part on bioethics concludes the book, its intention is to demonstrate the unfolding nature of Jewish ethics. Novel knowledge and technologies empower humans to do incredible things, yet questions of who or what should control those powers, and why, remain.

19 | Medical Ethics

Medical ethics addresses the responsibilities of doctors and other health care professionals in their pursuits of patient care and research. Among the questions medical ethicists discuss are: How is one to balance benefit and risk when considering experimental or therapeutic treatments? How aggressive should one be in pursuing medical interventions? When is it appropriate to forgo treatment, and who should decide?

As a secular field of professional ethics, medical ethics is grounded in core principles that govern relationships among health care providers, patients, patient families, and the broader public. Jewish thinkers ground their approaches to quandaries in medical ethics in Jewish teachings, which sometimes accord with the prevailing secular principles and sometimes diverge from them. The pieces gathered in this section construct the relationship between Jewish ethics and the secular field of bioethics in a variety of ways as they draw on Jewish writings to illumine ethical questions and themes in the practice of medicine.

Some trace the field of medical ethics back to antiquity, when a doctor's oath attributed to the Greek physician Hippocrates articulated, among other things, the responsibility to "do no harm" and not to share secrets. The professionalization of medicine in the modern period led to the codification of medical ethics in the nineteenth century. Despite this long tradition, however, medical professionals perpetrated heinous abuses during the course of the twentieth century, most infamously, Nazi experiments on Jews and others during the Holocaust, and the Tuskegee Syphilis Study (1932–1972) in the United States, in which hundreds of Black patients seeking health care were denied effective treatment and were never informed that they were being used as research subjects.

Theories and practices of medical ethics today emerge out of efforts to reckon with this shameful history. The abuses of Nazi experimentation and of the Tuskegee study help explain the strong emphasis on informed consent and individual autonomy as cornerstones of modern bioethics. Four broad principles first articulated by Tom L. Beauchamp and James F. Childress in 1979[2] are considered foundational:

· Autonomy: a patient's right to make their own decisions and to be self-determining

---

2. Tom L. Beauchamp and James F. Childress, *Principles of Biomedical Ethics* (Oxford: Oxford University Press, 1979).

· Beneficence: duty to help the patient advance their own good and to act in a patient's best interest
· Nonmaleficence: duty to do no harm to the patient
· Justice: duty to be fair in how care is provided and in how resources are allocated

Within the field of bioethics, these principles are often promoted as universal guidelines that pertain across cultures. But as we will see, some Jewish ethicists present Jewish teachings as a complement to these principles, while others highlight the ways that Jewish teachings diverge.

The five selections gathered here address a range of topics in medical research and health care. While they are presented below in chronological order, they can be subdivided into two groups on the basis of methodology, not chronology. One group seeks to bring the insights of Jewish ethics into the secular field of bioethics, showing how Jewish ethics can contribute to its theories and methods. A second group draws on the sources of halakha to generate distinctly Jewish responses to questions and concepts that arise in secular frameworks.

The thinkers who belong to the first group—Benjamin Freedman, Toby Schonfeld, and Laurie Zoloth—do not share a single methodology in common. What unites them is an interest in bringing insights and concepts drawn from Jewish ethics into the field of bioethics. Their interest is not so much in answering discrete ethical questions but rather in refining and elaborating the theories and methods that ground the field.

Freedman draws on his professional experiences as a clinical ethics consultant in hospitals. He argues that on its own, the prevailing secular approach to bioethics falls short, because its emphasis on autonomy means that it focuses exclusively on who has the right to make medical decisions, rather than on how to make those decisions. He proposes that Jewish ethics offers a helpful complement to the secular approach because it is grounded in duties rather than rights. He shows how framing ethical questions in terms of the responsibilities that patients have to care for their own bodies and that doctors and relatives have to the patient can make a practical difference in the face of difficult medical decisions.[3] Like Freedman, Schonfeld looks to Jewish ethics to correct for what she sees as secular bioethicists' overemphasis on individual autonomy. She argues that Jewish ethics, like feminist ethics,

---

3. For more on the difference between a rights-based approach and a duties-based approach, see the piece by Robert Cover in part 1, section 3.

can serve the field by opening it up to diverse perspectives and by highlighting the importance of relationships when it comes to making medical decisions.

The selection by Zoloth is from the culminating chapter of a book in which she reflects on her experiences in clinical consultations at children's hospitals decades earlier. Zoloth identifies deep resonances between the practice of clinical hospital ethics consultations and the distinctive features of classical rabbinic discourse. Just as rabbinic discourse accommodates and even celebrates dissident voices and minority opinions, the ethics consultation allows for voices from the margins to unsettle dominant opinions, opening up new possibilities for ethical decision-making. For Zoloth, clinical cases can serve bioethics in much the same way that narratives serve Talmudic discourse, by grounding discussions of principles in particular experiences. Though she looks to the same classical Jewish texts that halakhic thinkers like Zohar and Weiner do, her interest is not in the texts' normative content, but rather in their capacity to expand and elaborate theories of ethical decision-making.

The second group includes pieces by Noam J. Zohar and Jason Weiner. These writers seek to provide normative Jewish answers to ethical questions. For them — as for other and earlier scholars devoted to this mode of reasoning, such as Moshe Feinstein, Moshe Tendler, Fred Rosner, Abraham S. Abraham, Abraham Steinberg, and J. David Bleich — Jewish ethics is largely coterminous with the sources and methods of halakha. When ethical questions arise that are not directly addressed by traditional sources, the halakhic approach entails scouring classical rabbinic texts, halakhic codes, and responsa for direct precedents or analogs that can yield principles that apply to the questions at hand.[4]

Zohar and Weiner, like many others in this arena, construct the relationship between halakha and secular bioethics in similar ways. Moving back and forth between the two discourses, they treat halakha as a realm apart, even as they endeavor to show that the halakhic sources are ultimately in accord with concepts and claims advanced in secular bioethics. Zohar here investigates the bioethical concept of "quality of life" and Weiner interrogates the limits of a health care professional's responsibility to serve; each demonstrates how halakha ultimately authorizes ideas that secular bioethics promote.

The selections gathered here focus on a variety of medical problems and settings. For further discussion of ethical decision-making at the end of life, see part 4, section 22. For discussions of reproductive ethics, see part 4, sections 20 and 21.

---

4. For more on the relationship between halakha and Jewish ethics, see part 1, sections 2 and 3.

BENJAMIN FREEDMAN

Duty and Healing: Foundations of a Jewish Bioethic

Benjamin Freedman (1951–1997) was a professor of medicine specializing in bioethics at McGill University. Alongside his academic work, he worked as a clinical ethicist at the Jewish General Hospital in Montreal. In the book Duty and Healing, *he sought to bring insights from his own practice and study of traditional Judaism into conversation with the ethical dilemmas he confronted alongside hospital patients. He initially shared these writings on the internet so that they would be widely accessible for free. The book was published posthumously after his untimely death from cancer.*

From *Duty and Healing: Foundations of a Jewish Bioethic* (New York: Routledge, 1999), 13, 31–33, 43–45, 48–49, 52–54.

This is a book about certain personal moral questions that arise in the provision of medical treatment, especially of hospital care, and about one approach to reasoning about them. The book can be thought of as a religious project, for in it I try to explore Jewish texts and precedents and show different ways in which they may illuminate these issues. I intend the book to be a bioethical project as well, one that takes seriously the real world in which doctors practice and patients are treated and that suggests ways of improving our common understanding and resolution of those moral questions that arise in a health care context. It does this by marking the distinction between an ethics whose foundational language is duty, as is true of the Jewish approach, and contrasting that with our common Western ethical approach, whose basis is rights.

While actively seeking another model for understanding bioethical questions, I am reacting at the same time to a philosophical and bioethical approach that, in some fundamental ways, often misconstrues the moral reality felt by doctors, patients, and family members who deal with these ethical issues and to a Jewish literature that sometimes adopts a reductive and parochial stance to issues, one that fails to mobilize the extremely rich resources of Jewish legal and moral reasoning deposited over many centuries of inquiry. . . .

Clinical ethical consultation is, in many respects, a practice done by, at, and for the margin. The practice of such consultations began very recently. Its practitioners come from a diverse group of backgrounds with highly disparate qualifications and are employed in a variety of settings with very different expectations. Even in those institutions where clinical ethics consultation has been most firmly and longest established, it remains highly unusual for a case to become the subject of a formal ethics consultation.

For these very reasons clinical ethics consultation deserves close examination. Consultants work around the edges of the health care team, with respect to cases that are themselves out of the ordinary. These cases, and the contribution to their resolution that can come from clinical ethics consultants, challenge us to reexamine our understanding of what kinds of ethical problems exist in health care, of how they arise, and of how they can be resolved. For this same reason, clinical ethics consultations provide a useful context for understanding some ways in which a Jewish approach may differ from our current bioethical approaches....

The consultation, requested by Dr. G, concerned his ninety-eight-year-old patient, Mrs. T, who had been admitted to the hospital with congestive heart failure and pneumonia. For a woman of her years, she had maintained remarkably good health, apart from urinary incontinence of many years' standing and more recent mild bowel incontinence. The precipitating cause of the consultation: Mrs. T's statement "I am just tired; let me die a natural death." She has repeated this desire to Dr. G for the last four days running.

The patient continues to be a very sharp and lucid woman, although she is blind and nearly deaf. To illustrate the kind of woman she is, Dr. G told me how she had traveled to Florida when she was well into her eighties in order to care for her daughter, who was dying of cancer.

Mrs. T maintains a close relationship with her family, including a son, daughter-in-law, and granddaughter. They come to visit frequently; until her admission they had been caring for Mrs. T well, enabling her to maintain her own apartment. Dr. G had not spoken to them about Mrs. T's desire, pending the opportunity to speak with me; he does not, therefore, know their feelings about this.

Dr. G, a family physician who is managing her hospital care, has been Mrs. T's primary physician for about twenty years. He feels terrible ambivalence about agreeing to her wish to withdraw treatment, and anguish is evident on his face as he asks: "Is this my decision to make or hers? Isn't she asking me to exercise more power than any human being should have?"...

In one sense, it is not surprising that the model of duty has received so little attention. The model of expert consultation trades upon a traditional and still-powerful professional hierarchy; that of rights, our common, largely procedural, approach to social ethics. By contrast, we have no public shared understanding of duties and personal morality. We indeed pride ourselves upon developing a legal system that entails personal morality apart from public discourse, as a private preserve.

Yet in another sense, this is very surprising indeed, for in my experience, at any rate, the claims and dilemmas of duty suffuse the consultative experience. Consultations within the clinical setting do not, after all, occur within a fully public setting; a consult is not a trial. In this respect, too, consultations occur at the margin: the borderline between the utterly private and the absolutely public. Within the normative universe of the consultation, I find, although the particulars may be in dispute, the claims of duty in general are deeply respected. The family has one view, the doctor another. At the same time, each recognizes the ethical basis of the other's stance.

Any theory of duty is ultimately substantive, not structural. To understand duty fully, a particular theory detailing duties must be provided, and the theory I shall use for that purpose in this book is duty as understood from Jewish sources. I shall describe a nonparochial Jewish understanding that has much to commend itself on its own merits to those with no commitment to the Jewish tradition per se. As we approach this substantive view, however, we need to get more clear about what grounding an ethics consultation in duty implies....

In their pure form, consultations begin with a question of duty. I have argued that Dr. G was not concerned with his rights, or with those of Mrs. T. My further claim that he was not asking for a consultation to clarify his own options and views may have been more opaque, for he did in a way want such clarification: not, however, because he wanted to know what he would think—in a calm, clarified, and reflective moment—was the right thing to do, but because he wanted to know what *was* the right thing to do, or better yet, *whether there was a right thing to do here*....

In a regime of duty, in fact, conflict is attenuated; were there to exist a shared understanding of duty, indeed, conflict would be—in principle!—obviated altogether. A remarkable Talmudic passage expresses this spirit. "Let he who comes from a court that has taken from him his cloak sing his song and go his way!" (B. T. *Sanhedrin* 7a)—"sing his song" at his relief that he is no longer in possession of property that does not belong to him.

In a regime of rights, every conflict is a zero-sum game: for every winner, there must be a loser. Each rights claimant is making a personal assertion of power; each comes before the court saying, "I should have my way." Within a shared regime of duty, on the other hand, even civil conflict is framed in court as an honest inquiry, raised by two persons, over what the law requires....

The model of duty thus helps to set the question, in ways that sometimes surprise the protagonists. What, after all, is a consultation about? What is "the question"? Within a model of rights, the question is inevitably narrowly construed as social ethics, hence, as the resolution of a defined conflict. The terms of discussion are set by the claims of those in conflict, and so innovative solutions tend to be ruled out of order. . . .

For the model of duty, by contrast, the first question is: What is to *be done*? and usually, in the clinical context: What is to be done for this patient? . . . The model of duty thus broadens its focus, and its consultations tend to deal with an ongoing treatment plan rather than simply with an isolated issue or conflict. This seems to me useful, even if the precipitating cause of a consultation is a perceived conflict, for ethical conflicts have both a history and an aftermath, one of which needs to be acknowledged, the other managed. . . .

The model of rights poses a larger, and more interesting, problem. Its presence in ethics consultation is the merest epiphenomenon of an approach that underlies the major portion of our legal and political institutions. The Subject of this model is an etiolated person, a possessor of bare rights, and this attenuated personum is self-willed in two ways. At the stage of the ethics consultation and thereafter, actors in this drama choose or decline to exercise their rights. Setting the stage for the consultation, moreover, the rights model understands persons as acquiring or losing rights on the basis of their free and uninhibited choices; the only kind of "duty" recognized within this model is that established by a freely chosen undertaking, upon the model of promising. This process extends back into the mythic past, to a point at which the very social rules establishing the structure of the rights model were themselves determined by choices of self-presentation, a decision to take certain acts as normatively binding. I cannot improve upon Robert Cover's[5] exposition:

> The story behind the term "rights" is the story of social contract. The myth postulates free and independent if highly vulnerable beings who voluntarily trade a portion of their autonomy for a measure of collective security. The myth makes the collective arrangement the product of individual choice and thus secondary to the individual. "Rights" are the fundamental category because it is the normative category which most nearly approximates that

---

5. [For a selection from American legal scholar Robert Cover (1943–1986), see part 1, section 3.]

which is the source of the legitimacy of everything else. Rights are traded for collective security.⁶

Not so—or, not simply so—for the model of duty. A duty can be acquired by voluntary choice, but its moral force is not exhausted by that choice.... As your life is shaped by forces, only some of which are subject to your influence, so is your moral life shaped.... Cover writes of Judaism, as a paradigmatic system of duty,

> The basic myth of Judaism is obligation or mitzvah. It, too, is intrinsically bound up in a myth—the myth of Sinai. Just as the myth of the social contract is essentially a myth of autonomy, so the myth of Sinai is essentially a myth of heteronomy. Sinai is a collective—indeed, a corporate—experience. The experience at Sinai is not chosen.⁷

NOAM J. ZOHAR

Is Enjoying Life a Good Thing? Quality-of-Life Questions for Jewish Normative Discourse

Noam Zohar (b. 1954) is a professor emeritus of philosophy at Bar Ilan University in Israel, where he founded the graduate program in bioethics. Zohar's publications and teaching span rabbinic literature and the philosophy of halakha, as well as moral and political philosophy, with an emphasis on applied ethics, particularly the ethics of war and bioethics. He has served on various public commissions, including a seven-year term as member of Israel's National Bioethics Council.

From "Is Enjoying Life a Good Thing? Quality-of-Life Questions for Jewish Normative Discourse," in *Quality of Life in Jewish Bioethics*, ed. Noam J. Zohar (Lanham, MD: Lexington Books, 2006), 19–31.

We have ... established that seeking to improve one's quality of life can be deemed permissible and perhaps even laudable (though this judgment may not be shared by the Jewish ascetic tradition), and that seeking the same for others is even to be deemed a mitzvah.⁸ Promoting quality of life is, then, a valuable

---

6. Robert Cover, "Obligation: A Jewish Jurisprudence of the Social Order," *Journal of Law and Religion* 5 (1988): 65–74, at 66.
7. Cover, "Obligation."
8. [See the full article for Zohar's establishment of these principles.]

pursuit; but just how valuable is it? One way of answering this question is by comparing that value to the value accorded, in the Jewish tradition, to preventing death—to "lifesaving," *pikuach nefesh*.

Preserving life—whether one's own or that of others—at least when in clear and present danger, comes under the heading of "lifesaving" and takes precedence over almost all other values and normative considerations. This is classically stated with relation to desecrating Shabbat—and is meant to apply *a fortiori* to virtually all prohibitions, equal or lesser in severity. Accordingly, when a medical procedure involves desecrating Shabbat, the prohibition is immediately and without question set aside, provided that the situation is defined as *pikuach nefesh*, that is, there is (even a slight) risk of a life being lost.

But what if there is no danger to life, but "merely" the danger of losing some bodily part or function? Here traditional teachings are in fact far from clear-cut. If we move down the scale and consider medical procedures aimed just at restoring comfort or removal of pain, it should be recognized that they have definitely not been seen, on the whole, as warranting Shabbat desecration. And remember—Shabbat is just the classical example; in principle, the same applies to any other Torah prohibition.

The lesser value attached, in traditional formal halakha, to quality of life per se, is thus expressed in the sixteenth-century classical code, Rabbi Joseph Caro's *Shulchan Aruch*.[9] The relevant section (OH 328) contains two clauses: Clause 9 addresses cases where there is a "way out," following Talmudic precedent—danger to a limb can often be defined as a threat to life itself. Clause 17 addresses cases where no such construal is plausible.

> (9) If a person has an ailment in his eyes [or even] in one eye, and there is fluid, or tears flowing because of the pain, or blood flowing etc. . . . Shabbat should be desecrated for him. [Based on B. T. *Avodah Zarah* 28b: "An inflamed eye may be treated on Shabbat, since eyesight is linked to the power of the heart."]

> (17): If a person falls ill without danger to life . . . Shabbat may not be desecrated on his behalf in a prohibition *de-orayta*,[10] even if he is at risk of losing an organ.

    9. [The *Shulchan Aruch* by Rabbi Joseph Caro (1488–1575) of Spain is widely considered to be the most important and authoritative code of Jewish practice.]

    10. [The term *de-orayta*, Aramaic for "of the Torah," refers to religious obligations that are understood to be rooted in Scripture, and therefore are the most serious and stringent imperatives.]

Is there room, in halakhic discourse, to give greater weight to quality of life in itself? An illuminating argument has been put toward by the nineteenth-century halakhist, Rabbi Shelomo Kluger (also known as Maharshak, 1785–1869):

> I was asked with regard to a person who suffered from the eye ailment called "Schwarzer Star" [amaurosis = partial or total loss of sight without pathology of the eye; caused by disease of the optic nerve or retina or brain (N.Z.)], may God spare us, and all the doctors despaired of finding a cure. However in one gentile town they propose to receive him in the gentile hospital, to provide him with healing so that his eyesight not be destroyed entirely—at this stage he is still capable of moving around on his own. He would be forced, however, to eat their nonkosher food. What is the law—may he do so or not?

First, Kluger admits that the law seems to plainly preclude overriding a Torah prohibition in order to save the patient's eyesight, since the case at hand cannot be construed as involving a risk of death. Nevertheless, he is able to produce an argument based on one of the several reasons offered by the Talmud to justify its basic ruling, that Shabbat observance must be set aside for lifesaving: "It is better to desecrate one Shabbat on his behalf, so that he will [be able to] observe many Shabbat days" (B. T. *Yoma* 85b). Kluger thus reasons:

> Since his blindness will prevent him from the study of Torah and from the [ritual] Torah reading—and the sages have stated that "Study is greater than practice"—therefore, if for the sake of practice it is better to desecrate one Shabbat on his behalf, so that he will [be able to] observe many Shabbat days, how much more so for the sake of study! It follows that in any case where the [loss of the] endangered limb will prevent the study of Torah, it is certainly permitted to "desecrate one Shabbat so that he will be able to observe many Shabbat days." This is particularly true regarding blindness, which will certainly prevent [him] from the study of Torah and will also prevent [him from observing] several [other] commandments. (Hokhmat Shelomo on *Shulchan Aruch, Orah Hayim* 328)

It is worth noting that Kluger hesitated to rely on this novel reasoning as a sufficient basis for his actual ruling. Still, these lines are an instructive record of a prominent halakhist's struggle to furnish formal grounding for the value of "quality of life." Through the value of the mitzvot, he seeks to endow the preservation of bodily function with the value of the religious practices that will remain possible.

For my part, I would propose another line of reasoning, aimed at giving formal recognition to preserving and promoting quality of life. As I emphasized toward the end of the previous section, caring for *another's* quality of life is a mitzvah—formally, it comes under Positive Commandment #206. "Love your fellow as yourself" (Lev. 19:18).[11] According to Rabbi Akiva,[12] this is the foundational mitzvah of the entire Torah. Hence, even if providing medical treatment aimed at quality-of-life goals does not have the same supreme priority as treatment aimed at lifesaving, it does not lack imperative force. If a conflict arises between this duty and another halakhic norm, its proper resolution will not necessarily be self-evident. The halakha—as might be expected of a millennia-old normative tradition—contains second-order rules to provide guidance where first-order norms conflict. Since we are dealing here with a positive commandment, it is appropriate to mention the Talmudic dictum that "a positive commandment overrides a negative commandment" (B. T. *Yevamot* 3b).

Let me make it clear that I am not advocating that our thinking about medical treatment be reduced to application of such formal definitions and rules. Rather, I mean to give expression—in the traditional halakhic medium—to the value of improving patients' quality of life, while recognizing the higher priority of saving patients' lives.

---

11. [The reference is to the list compiled by Maimonides in his *Sefer Ha-Mitzvot* (Book of the Commandments)].

12. [Rabbi Akiva was a renowned rabbi in the land of Israel during the period of the Mishnah, in the second century CE.]

TOBY SCHONFELD

Messages from the Margins:
Lessons from Feminist Bioethics

Toby Schonfeld (b. 1973) spent the first part of her career in academia before bringing her expertise in bioethics to public service. Much of Schonfeld's scholarship and leadership has focused on advancing the ethics of human subjects research. She serves on the Committee on Jewish Law and Standards (CJLS) of the Rabbinical Assembly, the rabbinic organization of the Conservative movement.

From "Messages from the Margins: Lessons from Feminist Bioethics," *Journal of Christian Ethics* 28, no. 1 (Spring/Summer 2008): 209–24.

Some of the same features that have enabled feminist approaches to bioethics to gain a foothold in mainstream bioethics discourse can also augment the acceptance of religious approaches to ethical problems in health care. It is a mischaracterization of religious approaches to assert that they have nothing to offer the general moral conversation. In this section, I describe how the same three features of feminist ethics can be seen in Jewish bioethics in particular, and argue by analogy that these features make religious approaches to bioethics worthy of consideration in the mainstream bioethics discourse.

* * *

Jewish bioethics is sometimes characterized as a rule-based system, with an appeal to precedent cases to specify the application of the rule. Scholars point to some of the fundamental principles that guide action in regard to health care, such as the sanctity of human life and the preservation of life and health, and argue that action follows from the application of these rules to a given situation. However, how these rules are applied to a particular situation matters. The fundamental principles in Jewish bioethics are derived from ancient texts that are then interpreted by contemporary authority figures. To be what Elliot Dorff[13] terms "intellectually honest," the individuals doing this interpretation and application must consider the "effects of historical and literary context on the meaning of texts" and recognize the "multitude of meanings that writings can often legitimately have."[14]

13. [See part 1, section 2, for a selection from Conservative rabbi and scholar Elliot Dorff.]
14. Elliot N. Dorff, *Matters of Life and Death* (Philadelphia: The Jewish Publication Society, 2003), 413.

This consideration and recognition point to a crucial element of decision-making in Jewish bioethics. If all that mattered in Jewish bioethics was adherence to a set of rules or principles, then any rational agent ought to be able to obtain a taxonomy of the principles and make moral decisions according to this set of guidelines. Yet virtually all the texts on Jewish bioethics include a caveat that reads something like this: "This work is not intended to replace a conversation with your rabbi, and you are encouraged to seek him out for discussion of your particular situation." This common statement speaks to an important priority within the context of Jewish bioethics and the process of decision-making. Rules and principles are important, as are reasonably similar precedent cases. But there is something more here.

Scholars warn against the substitution of a book for a conversation for an important reason: context matters. There is an implicit recognition of the fact that one's situation is unique, and that a decision about medical care affects more than just the patient. This particularity is also why the caveats do not say "you are encouraged to speak to *a* rabbi," but rather "*your* rabbi." The (sometimes faulty) assumption is that the patient has a relationship with his or her rabbi, whose insight into the person's social, emotional, and relational context will enable him or her to advise on a course of action....

This sensitivity to context is not unlike the appeal to a woman's situatedness that is seen in an ethic of care and other feminist approaches to bioethics. Furthermore, the relatively recent rise in popularity of narrative approaches to bioethics demonstrates the recognition in health care of the importance of understanding the particular features of a case rather than abstracting only a few features. As a result, demonstrating how religious approaches to bioethics attend to the context of a particular patient's story is one way to incorporate these views into the mainstream bioethics discourse.

* * *

Once it is established that the context of a patient is important for decision-making, then it should come as little surprise that the family is a crucial element in the process. The family is the fundamental unit of organization in Judaism. Families come together to form communities, and these communities act as extensions of the family in terms of caring for the members. Judaism fosters this notion by reinforcing the "cohesiveness and moral effectiveness of our families and communities" through "values, stories, rituals and laws."[15] Other

---

15. Dorff, *Matters of Life and Death*, 400.

scholars take this a step farther. Benjamin Freedman[16] argues that certain duties toward family members entail particular moral commitments with regard to health care....

Even for the most traditional Jews who subscribe to a system of prescribed roles within a family, the interdependence of the human condition is essential. Successful fulfillment of those roles depends on others successfully fulfilling their roles: mothers depend on fathers, who depend on children, and so on. This consideration of roles within a family and community is what helps to give rise to empowered decisions about issues in health care. How this decision will affect who I am in this community, as well as affect those who depend on me and on whom I depend, is just as important as ensuring that my decision conforms to other aspects of my faith tradition.

The recognition of the important role that the family plays in health care decision-making has come full circle—from a place where paternalism reigned and others made decisions on behalf of (often female) patients, to a position of radical autonomy for every individual patient, to a recognition that even an autonomous individual can properly consider how a particular decision will affect her family without compromising her interests. Jewish bioethics reflects this understanding by including familial considerations as part of the decision-making process.

* * *

Just as there is no one "feminist bioethics," there is also not one "Jewish bioethics." Though the methodology remains more or less constant, the weight placed on each component of the process (rules, precedent cases, and context) varies according to the source consulted for assistance with decision-making. Some maintain that this variety weakens an approach to moral decision-making; without a unified theoretical or practical basis to ground the process, no coherent system can be developed....

Far from being an impediment to policy creation, recognizing the existence of a plurality of views on a subject can encourage discourse between various stakeholders. Such discussions can enrich resultant policies by demonstrating respect for the views of the multiple constituencies that are often affected by these choices.

The charge may even be broader. As Cahill[17] states, religious voices in bio-

16. [See the selection by Canadian Jewish bioethicist Benjamin Freedman above.]
17. [Lisa Sowle Cahill is an American Christian ethicist who teaches at Boston College.]

ethics must "redefine the public sphere as a social arena in which multiple value traditions and their representatives join together in shaping the social relations and institutions in which all participate."[18] This is true not just of religious convictions, but also cultural, ideological, or moral commitments deeply held by individuals. Insights into important concepts may be revealed by approaches to particular cases, and it is only by engaging in discourse with stakeholders that respectful, and therefore useful, policies can be developed.

Yet what is most appealing, and important, about the pluralistic approaches to Jewish bioethics is that it empowers individuals to make choices informed by a wide array of authorities in the tradition. Because there is a pluralism of approaches to questions even within a particular movement, the individual patient is able to consider how a proposed treatment option may be viewed by various groups within Judaism. Such a plurality empowers individuals by demonstrating the range of acceptable action and encourages the patient to consider how his or her particular situation coincides with these choices. Because of the variety of perspectives on any given issue, Jewish bioethics offers a set of considerations that can be useful to any patient who desires to understand how a faith tradition views the options from which he or she has to choose. Appreciating the layered approaches to ethical questions in health care is an important lesson for mainstream bioethics.

---

18. Lisa Sowle Cahill, *Theological Bioethics* (Washington, DC: Georgetown University Press, 2005), 11–12.

JASON WEINER

Are There Limits to How Far One Must Go for Others? Toward a Theoretical Model for Health Care Providers

Jason Weiner (b. 1978) is a bioethics scholar and board-certified chaplain who serves as senior rabbi and director of spiritual care at Cedars-Sinai Medical Center in Los Angeles. An Orthodox rabbi with a doctorate in clinical bioethics, he conveys his approach to Jewish medical ethics in his book Care and Covenant: A Jewish Bioethic of Responsibility.

From "Are There Limits to How Far One Must Go for Others? Toward a Theoretical Model for Health Care Providers," *Journal of Jewish Ethics* 6, no. 1 (2020): 94–108.

Many people enter the health care profession out of a profound desire to help others in need. They frequently take upon themselves responsibility and burdens to care for others. Sometimes, whether due to chronic illness, severe pain, mental illness, contagious disease, or numerous other factors, patient demands can test the limits of a health care provider's skills and patience. Nevertheless, some seem to claim that no limits to health care providers' duties exist....

Is this statement indeed what Judaism requires? There must be limits to the extent that one is expected to go to on behalf of a patient. Must one spend all their surplus time and income for this cause or live an especially modest lifestyle in order to be able to achieve these ends? Personal danger, physical or emotional exhaustion, and difficult or noncompliant patients can be challenging aspects of contemporary health care. May one never take a break or ever say no to any patient's request for treatment?

This article will examine the basis for the duty to provide health care, and some potential limitations to that duty, from the perspective of classical Jewish sources and some contemporary Orthodox thinkers. The article will compare and contrast them with parallel discussions in the general bioethics literature, in order to suggest a focused and rigorous approach to this issue that arises out of applying classical interpretations of specific biblical verses to this issue. It will then suggest a unique approach based on the rabbinic laws of charity that can help articulate an optimal level of obligation, with a particular focus on some lessons learned during the Covid-19 pandemic....

The goal and justification for health care is not just to avoid causing harm, but the positive duty to take steps that aim to provide benefit to patients. In bioethics, this principle is known as "beneficence," or doing good. It is often traced directly to the Torah's commandment to love one's neighbor as one's self, and has played a central role in many ethical theories throughout history. The rabbis codified this principle as a matter of Jewish law, and "the great principle of the Torah,"[19] and it is a basis in Jewish law for the requirement to provide health care. Therefore, many argue that Judaism demands a higher level of beneficence than secular bioethics, or prioritizes it higher, because actively doing good for others is not just praiseworthy or seen as appropriate or going "above and beyond," but an ethical *obligation* in Judaism....

Although attempting to heal the sick is a commandment of the Torah, some debate is found in rabbinic literature as to which verse in the Torah commands it. One answer is that the verse "do not stand idly by . . ." (Lev. 19:16) obligates anyone who can help a patient who is enduring tremendous suffering or has a very serious illness to do whatever they can do for that individual. However, if the patient's illness is certainly not life threatening, the requirement to care for them is based on the verse that requires returning lost objects, "you shall give it back" (Deut. 22:2) (i.e., help to return their health to them), for which there is much more flexibility, because Jewish law does not always require returning every lost object. Although this verse includes an obligation to attempt to help someone regain their health, it does not require going to every extent possible, nor significant self-sacrifice or loss, in order to do so. For example, the Torah does not require enduring significant financial or personal loss in order to return a lost object, nor therefore is one required to support such a patient, though doing so would certainly be considered meritorious....

A limitation on how far one is required to go to fulfill Jewish law, and the parameters of its application, can be expounded from a different Jewish legal category based on a unique interpretation of another verse. Regarding the verse in the Torah, "Everything that you give me I will tithe to You" (Gen. 28:22), the rabbis decreed that "when one dispenses their money to charity, they should not dispense more than one-fifth" (B. T. *Ketubot* 50a). The reason for this limitation is that the Torah does not want one to spend all their money on one mitzvah, since that would leave them destitute and unable to perform any other meritorious acts. Rather, one is expected to carefully ration the way they distribute their resources, despite any of the Torah's obligations. The rabbis determined

---

19. *Sifre, Kedoshim* 2:4(12); *Shabbat* 31a.

that one fifth of one's wealth is the maximum that one may spend on fulfilling the requirements of any given positive commandment.

Some later rabbinic authorities have applied this principle to areas beyond financial concerns in a novel fashion. They argue that just as one is not required to spend a large sum to fulfill a commandment, neither are they expected to become physically ill in order to do so, because a person's financial well-being should not be more important to them than their physical well-being. Since most people would be willing to spend much more than a fifth of their financial resources to avoid severe pain and suffering, some rabbinic authorities argue that enduring tremendous physical pain or emotional suffering, or giving a large amount of one's time, would be tantamount to spending more than a fifth of one's resources, and is thus not required. This approach, therefore, becomes a strong basis for limiting the extent to which heroic endeavors are taken in order to fulfill a positive commandment such as providing health care....

Many health care providers have been conditioned not to consider their own safety or well-being when caring for their patients. However, caring for oneself and articulating limits to a health care provider's duties are not only vital, but also philosophically and ethically defensible. Although the two approaches examined begin with very different foundations and assumptions—bioethics are often based primarily on philosophy and logic, while Jewish approaches tend to be based on interpretations of specific biblical verses and Talmudic tradition—they both come to many very similar conclusions. Both rabbinic and bioethics thinkers have articulated high expectations of health care providers, as well as justifications for limiting those expectations when necessary. Both recognize that excessive demands may prevent people from entering the field, while both recognize that at times going above and beyond for one's patients is praiseworthy. Judaism seems to have slightly higher expectations of health care providers than many secular bioethicists (e.g., utilizing the language of general obligation, limiting the possibility of even taking breaks and regarding health care providers who do not provide care to be guilty of murder), but also offers very specific exemptions. The Jewish approaches examined also seem more focused on communal responsibilities than individual roles.

Within both traditions, even as limits on the duties of health care providers are articulated, the societal importance of the role of health care providers to care for the sick is maintained. The perspectives examined do not see health care providers merely as mechanics of the body, but as individuals who have taken upon themselves social and even divine expectations of responsibility to go out of their way for others. Bioethicists as well as the Jewish tradition demand that one who undergoes the training to care for people's health take on an obligation to do so that cannot be taken lightly. Yet, both perspectives recognize that human capabilities are limited and that a person cannot be expected to extend themselves unreasonably.

Although setting very high expectations can encourage people to strive to live up to them, if the expectations are too demanding, many will become disillusioned and less likely to carry out even minimal moral requirements. Determining the right balance is thus crucial. The one-fifth rule can help articulate an optimal level of obligation, as it demands real self-sacrifice, but also sets a clear and definite limit while granting subjective case-by-case calibration. As health care providers navigate the demands and struggles of providing care during crisis, such as the Covid-19 pandemic, approaches such as this one can help set proper limits and promote care provider well-being and longevity.

LAURIE ZOLOTH

Second Texts and Second Opinions: Essays toward a Jewish Bioethics

Laurie Zoloth (b. 1950) is the Margaret E. Burton Professor of Religion and Ethics at the University of Chicago Divinity School. She worked as a neonatal nurse in marginalized communities before embarking on a career in religious studies, focusing on Jewish ethics and bioethics. Her publications address such issues as genetic engineering, stem cell research, inequities in the health care system, and global climate change. She provides ethical counsel to many public agencies, including the NASA Advisory Council, the International Planetary Protection Committee, the National Recombinant DNA Advisory Board, and the executive committee of the International Society for Stem Cell Research.

From *Second Texts and Second Opinions: Essays toward a Jewish Bioethics* (Oxford: Oxford University Press, 2022), 232–53.

Chapter 11: Ordinary Talk about Ordinary Trouble: Witnessing

In this ... chapter, I want to consider three things: first, to suggest a theoretical construct for the work of clinical ethics; second, to explore how it is that we do bioethics in practice; and third, to demonstrate how uncertainty, complexity, and most of all, interruption, shape these cases. ...

We are discussing the options for care for a thirteen-month-old baby girl, Bonnie, whose own father has beaten her nearly, but not quite, to death, and then left her alone in a pool of her own blood. We do not know how long she lay there not breathing before the paramedics were called by a neighbor who heard the screaming and screaming and then heard it stop. She is, we are told, at three weeks after that terrible night, entering a persistent vegetative state, a profound coma from which she will never recover. Unstably weaned from her ventilator, she breathes unevenly, still fighting a case of pneumonia. Worse, an MRI shows the clear shadows and patterns of doom, and when I had visited her in the ICU, she was flaccid, her eyes drifting, open, lost. . . .

The entire first hour of the meeting is spent with one after another specialist describing the utter hopelessness of her condition. One of the many pediatric specialists, the trauma surgeon who saw her the night of her beating, urges that we withdraw all our treatment and allow her to die, makes the case with the text of his own life. "I cannot imagine allowing my own child to live like this," he tells us. "I do not think it is moral." When he speaks, there is a moment just after, when everyone with children imagines their own child, and the room is full of other children, for just one moment, and it is completely still. . . .

But we are interrupted. I have been told that the grandmother is "deeply in denial," but now it is her turn to speak. She holds a picture of the baby and tells us she expects her to "just wake up and get all better." This is seen as difficult for all, a lot of trouble, and there is much talk of psychotherapy for the resisting grandmother: "Perhaps we can get you some help?" But the grandmother is here, in the room, for this is a core part of the method of ethics that we practice. But the grandmother thinks that is ridiculous. She is worried that we are somehow morally blind. She says, carefully, as if to people who cannot understand the simplest of realities: "I am ready to raise her, I've has told [sic] the nurses, and I love her, whoever she will be. Whatever happens. Somehow it is wrong, just wrong to just watch and allow a child to die. With the help of God, I will take her home again, even if she is not worth that much to you." This is, after all, the woman who called Child Protective Services ten months ago to warn them about the volatile father, but whose perceptions were dismissed by that agency, because we suspect, they saw her as we did then, as an unstable witness.

The physical therapist has sat quietly, but now it is his turn. "She is getting better every day, this kid, breathing on her own and a bit stronger when I come to move her, I could swear. What if she survives, but we have not been aggressive enough? Then, if she lives anyway, won't she be worse off? Maybe we would limit how much she could recover? Why not act as if she could wake up?"

What is the right act? How should we think about this case? Let me turn to text about the possibility of life after terrible trouble.

Babylonian Talmud *Berakhot* 54b

There are four [classes of people] who have to offer thanksgiving: those who have crossed the sea, those who have traversed the wilderness, one who has recovered from an illness, and a prisoner who has been set free. They cried unto the Lord in their trouble. He brought them out of darkness and the shadow of death. Let them give thanks unto the Lord for His mercy. What blessing should he say? Rab Judah said: Blessed is He who bestows loving kindnesses. Abaye said: And he must utter his thanksgiving in the presence of ten, as it is written: "Let them exalt Him in the assembly of the people." Mar Zutra said: And two of them must be rabbis, as it says, "*And praise Him in the seat of the elders.*" R. Ashi demurred to this: You might as well say [he remarked], that all should be rabbis!—Is it written, "In the assembly of elders"? It is written, "In the assembly of the people"!—Let us say, then, in the presence of ten ordinary people and two rabbis [in addition]?

What is happening in this debate? Consider the problem of the text: when one has survived mortal danger, a special blessing is said but it must be said aloud and in public. One blesses God, that is clear, but by who is this blessing witnessed? After all, an individual can and ought mutter blessings all the time in private: when you see a rainbow, or the sea, or a blossoming tree. But this is a matter of far more import, of life and death. What is the community that will respond and reply "amen"? Amen, as in this is also true for me? Should the community of meaning, the people who are there when you emerge from the very worst catastrophe of your life, and reclaim your life, be the political leaders, the rabbis, or the priests? The text answers in the negative. No, the Talmud argues, what is needed is the presence of ten ordinary people. The rabbis can come, but the assembly of the people, the minyan, which constitutes the whole community, must be ordinary people. Experts may attend, but the ordinary people are the witness to the possibility of salvation.

What to make of this?

When we do the work of bioethics, meaning the talk that surrounds the reflection on the crossroads in the journey (across that sea or that wilderness) that each medical case represents, we can know that the talk is useful on a purely subjective level.... But we have not been as successful in thinking about why it is so, nor in developing a theory to justify this subjective experience. And because of this, we struggle as a discipline about the meaning, goals, and nature of the work, about how it is that we can teach what we do, how we can develop standards of bioethics, how to frame the work, and thus ourselves as well. We struggle with the kind of experts we should be....

The field of bioethics is, by definition, based in the presupposition that questioning, arguing, interruption, and response are the means by which we question the truth claims of medicine and health care policy. The field began with the premise that another voice, one of at least critique, if not dissension, was just what was needed in any arena in which the hegemonic expertise of medicine held sway. It began with the idea that ordinary people's voices were just what was needed when the expertise of medicine was not enough....

What, then, is the meaning and role for committees of the ten, of "ordinary people" coming to consensus in such a case? One of the most important roles, I think, is not only how to come to consensus, but how to listen to the ones opposed to consensus—to the interruption of the dissenting voice....

In general, the arguments against the search for consensus on clinical issues are powerful ones.... Hence, our theory would need to include the reality of conflict in conversation. What if the ordinary people did not respond as the expert would? Grandma is not convinced, and once you have brought her here, you need to listen. Isn't the subtext of the halakhic ruling precisely that? That even there, at the sharpest boundary between life and death, one does not stand in front of experts? Yet: how can clinical medicine proceed if we cannot agree? ...

Despite the richness of the Talmudic discourse, and the complex power of the interpretive community, there are not two, but several options for the end of the debate about a contended issue. The community can conclude with the majority (usually done); the community can ... decide with the minority, either at the time or in later arguments [during] the ongoing debate and follow the view of one who [is] in the minority, since all arguments are preserved in the record of the etiology of the law; and finally and most interestingly for our purposes, the discursive community can decide that the matter is not resolvable at this time, that all good arguments are made and then—*teyku* ("the matter stands"). ... There is a mechanism for allowing a non-consensus to proceed in policy matters, a sense that both sides in a dispute can be both honored and allowed to enact the practice in distinctive manners....

It is decided that we will wait a little after all and give the grandmother what we call "time to adjust." After all, in the opinion of most of the staff, the baby will die in any case within the week.

But it turns out that it is we who have to do the adjusting. Once again. A week later, I visit the ICU and find the baby's crib is turned up, empty. But it is not what I expect—she is not dead, and when I ask, I am told she is to be found in the rehabilitation floor. When I go there, she is in the arms of the physical therapist. She is teaching her how to wave hello, which the baby does, and the startled ethicist waves back. "Pretty remarkable," the therapist says, "considering that that committee nearly took her off life support."

I have gone to see the child with another member of the committee, a woman who is a "citizen-member" with a badly disabled daughter of her own. "That baby is far better than my girl," she tells me, as we stand in the hall. "Oh. What we almost did," she says, tears on her cheeks as she says this to me.

But the point, I would argue, is that we did not do the obvious thing, which would have been to go without question along the course of action that the staff was suggesting. The point of ordinary talk about terrible trouble is precisely that it allows for the entrance, as a significant voice, the interruption of the grandmother, to give a temporal attention to the possible correctness of her perceptions....

Developing a theory from our work allows us to remember the conversation by taking it out of the extraordinary, expertly rendered "speech" of medicine into the ordinary talk of our creaturely selves. When we ask for the details of each hour for the patient, it is asking for the embodied experience described, unclothed, naked under the gown of the patient, a linguistic role designed to cover up and medicalize the pain. We say that the lesions are closed when we cannot speak of the blood and the wounds and the tragedy of loss. This radical encounter is rendered possible only in the ordinariness of speech. The encounter of the conversation is the encounter of ethics: to hear the voice of the Other and to hear it as one's own is to cut against the significant hierarchies in the clinic, to draw attention to the nakedness of each of us, and to recall how no one's talk is the final word.

20 | Reproduction

Contemporary Jewish thinkers address ethical questions about assisted reproductive technologies (ART) against the background of a long-standing Jewish emphasis on procreation as both a blessing and a religious obligation. Many trace the religious mandate to procreate back to the first chapter of Genesis, where God's blessing to the newly created humans is to "be fruitful, and multiply, and fill up the earth" (Gen. 1:28). Classical rabbinic tradition interprets this charge in concrete legal terms, delineating the commandment to procreate as an obligation incumbent upon Jewish men that can be fulfilled through the birth of at least two children.

That Jewish women are a necessary accessory to the fulfillment of this commandment but are not themselves subject to it is a puzzle that Jewish legal thinkers have explained in a variety of ways: it might reflect the rabbis' presumption that infertility was primarily a female problem and that women should not be saddled with a religious obligation they could not necessarily fulfill. Across the Jewish tradition, a strong association between fecundity and human flourishing has persisted alongside an awareness of biological infertility. Until the recent advent of new contraceptive and reproductive technologies, procreation was a Jewish ethical obligation that people had limited agency in fulfilling. Medical advances over the course of the last century mean that people today may have far more control and choice over their reproductive lives than ever before, provided they have the means to access them. They can choose when and whether to have children, and they have an array of medical and nonmedical options for addressing infertility.

Among the pathways to parenthood that contemporary Jews can now pursue are a diversity of arrangements with varying degrees of medical intervention, including artificial insemination, in vitro fertilization (IVF), gamete donation, surrogate pregnancy, egg-freezing, and adoption. These strategies allow individuals and couples to overcome biological infertility, and enable new configurations of family, facilitating parenthood for single people and same-sex couples. This section focuses exclusively on ethical issues with regard to IVF and surrogate pregnancy.[20]

---

20. For discussion of Jewish values governing marriage and childrearing, see part 2, section 7, "Families." For discussion of genetics, see part 3, section 16, "Genes." For discus-

The essays in this section document a trajectory that moves from suspicion to embrace of reproductive technologies. The first, from 1983, offers a snapshot of Jewish ethical and religious concerns about IVF during a period when the science was still new and the practice was rare. Fred Rosner catalogs the many unresolved questions and concerns that Orthodox Jewish thinkers bring to their consideration of whether halakha could countenance IVF. (Rosner uses a colloquial term, "test tube babies," that was in wide use at the time but is discordant and considered pejorative today.) The long and sundry list of issues that Rosner raises juxtapose ethical considerations about the risk to and welfare of prospective parents and potential children with broad questions about the integrity of family and of the social fabric and also with technical halakhic questions about Jewish identity, ritual impurity, and illegitimacy. Rosner describes a lack of consensus among Orthodox rabbinic decisors about many of these issues, in large part due to the lack of precedents in classical halakhic literature.

Writing over a decade later, Conservative rabbi Elie Spitz makes a forceful argument that Jewish law should allow and even endorse the use of both ovum donors and gestational surrogates for those facing female infertility. By 1996, ovum donation and IVF are safe and well-established practices, and so Spitz need not address ethical concerns about health risks that loomed large for Rosner. Spitz agrees with Rosner that there is no legal precedent for ART in halakhic literature, yet he finds relevant lessons and values in biblical narratives and practices relating to infertility.

By 2010, when anthropologist Don Seeman examines Jewish ethical discourse with regard to ART, there has been a sea change in Jewish attitudes toward surrogacy and IVF. The state of Israel boasts more IVF clinics per capita than any other country, has laws on the books protecting surrogacy contracts, and offers full coverage of multiple rounds of IVF through national health insurance programs. What's more, these liberal policies were adopted with the support of Orthodox rabbinic authorities. Seeman seeks to account for the liberal tendencies of Jewish ethicists and halakhic decisors. In contrast to Spitz, who appeals to biblical narrative and broad principles in making his argument, Seeman argues that it is the distinctively legal focus of Jewish culture that enables Jewish thinkers to take

---

sion of sex ethics, see part 3, section 15, "Gender and Sexuality." For discussion of abortion, see part 4, section 20, "Abortion." See part 1, section 1, "Doing Jewish Ethics," for the work of Michal Raucher, a leading scholar of Jewish reproductive ethics. See part 1, section 4, "Covenant," for Mara Benjamin's discussion of childrearing as a theological model.

liberal positions.[21] He highlights the role of culture in shaping ethical discourse and the interpretation of authoritative texts.

One way to tell the story of how Jewish ethical discourse about ART develops is to trace an arc of increasing liberality among ethicists in tandem with the increased embrace of ART among doctors and patients. But there is another important methodological trajectory as well, as ethical thinkers shift away from textual argumentation and increasingly invoke the lived experience of intended parents, donors, and surrogates. At the earliest stage, Spitz does this by examining court cases. Scholars like Seeman and Michal Raucher (see part 1, section 1) do this by engaging ethnography, and both point out the frequent disconnect between ethicists' theoretical concerns and the reported experience of women involved in fertility treatments. The final and most recent selection in this section, by Sarah Zager, appeals not to ethnographic research, but to personal experience. Zager uses her own personal narrative of fertility treatments to theorize about the distinctive ethics of prospective parenthood, when care and responsibility are extended to those who do not as yet exist.

While these selections demonstrate changing evaluations and approaches to reproductive technologies among Jewish ethicists, they do not represent the full spectrum of attitudes and experiences of contemporary Jews. One important perspective that is missing is the experience of queer Jewish parents who have used IVF and other surrogacy to build their families; this is one area where Jewish ethics scholarship lags behind important developments in culture and society. Another area that has yet to receive sustained scholarly attention is the way adoption, fostering, and other nonmedical approaches to family-building are expanding notions of what reproduction means that move beyond genetics and biology.[22]

21. For other examinations of the relationship between halakha and Jewish ethics, see part 1, section 3.

22. For discussion and critique of locating Jewish identity in genes and biology, see the piece by Sarah Imhoff in part 3, section 16.

FRED ROSNER

In Vitro Fertilization and Surrogate Motherhood: The Jewish View

Fred Rosner (1935–2024) was a physician and Orthodox Jewish thinker who published widely on contemporary halakhic discussions of medical ethics. Born in Berlin, Germany, he went to the United Kingdom as a small child through the Kindertransport, and then immigrated to the United States after World War II, pursuing his studies at Yeshiva University and earning his MD with the first graduating class of the Albert Einstein College of Medicine in 1959. His medical specialty was hematology and he served as a professor of medicine at the Icahn School of Medicine at Mount Sinai. He chaired the Medical Ethics Committee of the State of New York.

From "In Vitro Fertilization and Surrogate Motherhood: The Jewish View," *Journal of Religion and Health* 22, no. 2 (Summer 1983): 139–60.

It is a cardinal principle in Judaism that life is of infinite value and that each moment of life is equal to seventy years thereof. In Jewish law, all biblical and rabbinic commandments are set aside for the overriding consideration of saving a life. It is, therefore, permitted and even mandated to desecrate the Sabbath to save the life of someone who may live for only a short while and certainly for a patient who may recover from illness or traumatic injuries.

A second fundamental principle of Judaism concerns the sanctity of human life. Man was created in the image of G-d, and, hence, human beings are holy and must be treated with dignity and respect, in life and after death. Our bodies are G-d given, and we are commanded to care for our physical and mental well-being and to preserve and hallow our health and our lives. Only G-d gives and takes life.

Are we tampering with life itself when we perform in vitro fertilization? Are we interfering with the divine plan for humanity? If G-d's will is for a man and/or woman to be infertile, who are we to undertake test tube fertilization and embryo reimplantation into the natural or genetic mother, or into a host or surrogate mother, to overcome the infertility problem?

Judaism teaches that nature was created by G-d for man to use to his advantage and benefit. Hence, animal experimentation is certainly permissible provided one minimizes the pain or discomfort to the animal. The production of hormones such as insulin from bacteria or in tissue culture or in animals by recombinant DNA technology for man's benefit also seems permissible. Gene therapy such as the replacement of the missing or defective gene in Tay-Sachs disease or hemophilia, if and when it becomes medically possible, may also be sanctioned in Jewish law. But is man permitted to alter humanhood and/or humanity by in vitro fertilization, by transfer from a woman inseminated with her husband's (or other) sperm of the embryo into another woman's womb or by artificial gestation in a test tube or glass womb, or by sex organ or gene transplants, or by genetic screening and/or counseling, and the like? . . .

In vitro fertilization, embryo transfer, host motherhood, and sex organ transplants in Jewish law have been subjects of several recent publications. In a situation in which the husband produces far too few sperm with each ejaculation to impregnate his wife or where a woman is unable to move the egg from the ovary into the uterus because of blocked fallopian tubes, the Sephardic chief rabbi of Israel, Ovadiah Yosef,[23] gave his qualified approval to the in vitro fertilization of the woman's egg with the husband's sperm and the reimplantation of the fertilized zygote or tiny embryo into the same woman's womb. The Ashkenazic chief rabbi, Shlomo Goren,[24] asserted that conception in this manner is morally repugnant but legally unobjectionable.

This situation represents a type of barrenness akin to physical illness and, therefore, justifies acts that entail a small amount of risk, such as procurement of eggs from the mother's ovary by laparoscopy, a minor surgical procedure.

There is certainly no question of adultery involved, since the sperm used is that of the husband. Sperm and egg procurement for this procedure is permissible because the aim is to fulfill the biblical commandment of procreation. The offspring is legitimate, and the parents thereby fulfill their obligation of having children. However, certain serious moral and Jewish legal problems relate to this type of test tube baby. If one uses sperm other than that of the husband, objections as discussed above under artificial insemination exist. Furthermore, if one obtains several eggs from the mother's ovary at one time and fertilizes all of them so as to select the best embryo for reimplantation, is one permitted to destroy the other fertilized eggs? Do they not constitute human seed and therefore should not be "cast away for naught"? Is one permitted to perform medical

23. [Rabbi Ovadiah Yosef (1920–2013) was Sephardic chief rabbi of Israel from 1973 to 1983.]

24. [Rabbi Shlomo Goren (1917–1994) was Ashkenazic chief rabbi of Israel from 1972 to 1983.]

research on the unused fertilized eggs? What is the status of other fertilized ova in the petri dish? Is the destruction of such fertilized ova tantamount to abortion? Is such a fertilized ovum regarded as "mere water" during the first forty days of its development?

There is no concept in Judaism of waste applied to tens of millions of superfluous sperm lost following normal coitus. Perhaps excess fertilized eggs might be implanted into nonovulating women. What, then, should be the approach if no woman is available for an additional implant and there has been more than one successful fertilization? If a fertilized ovum is "more than nothing," would Jewish law mandate in vitro procedures with only one ovum at a time? There may well be a Jewish legal and ethical distinction between a fertilized egg in a petri dish and a fertilized egg in a uterus. If there is no human fetal life outside the uterus, a superfluous fertilized ovum could be disposed of by any means, such as flushing down the drain. An alternative course of action would be to refrain from supplying nutrients to the ovum, thereby allowing it to perish. One can redefine the question in terms of whether or not an unfertilized egg may be deemed to be of ethical import as potential life. Since the vast majority of unfertilized sperm and eggs are never fertilized and do not constitute new life, only a fertilized ovum might be considered as potential life. If a fertilized ovum were equated with human life, Jewish law would require even the expenditure of substantial sums of money to transport a superfluous fertilized ovum great distances, if necessary, for implantation into a nonovulating woman.

The question of the possible independent existence of a zygote has legal import. Jewish law requires the desecration of the Sabbath to preserve the existence of an embryo in the mother's womb even less than forty days old. Is there Jewish legal distinction between a fertilized ovum reposing within the mother and a similar ovum lying in a petri dish?

The Committee on Medical Ethics of the Federation of Jewish Philanthropies of New York, chaired by Rabbi Moshe D. Tendler,[25] concluded that a fertilized egg not in the womb but in an environment—the petri dish or test tube—in which it can never attain viability, does not have humanhood and may be discarded or used for the advancement of scientific knowledge. It should also be stressed that even in the absence of Jewish legal or moral objections to in vitro fertilization using the husband's sperm, no woman is required to submit to this

---

25. [Rabbi Moshe D. Tendler (1926–2021) was an Orthodox rabbi, a professor of biology at Yeshiva University, and a leading Orthodox thinker on medical ethics.]

procedure. The obligations of women, whether by reason of the scriptural exhortation to populate the universe or by virtue of marital contract, are limited to bearing children by means of natural intercourse....

The explosion of medical knowledge and technology in the past decade have made in vitro fertilization, host mothers, sex organ transplants, genetic engineering, and their like a reality of the present and not a dream for the future. The potential risks, potential benefits, and ethical considerations of such advances in biomedical technology must be carefully considered. Tampering with the very essence of life and encroaching upon the Creator's domain are considerations worthy of extensive discussions from the Jewish standpoint. In the meanwhile, Jakobovits[26] expresses sentiments that one might take to heart:

> "Spare-part" surgery and "genetic engineering" may open a wonderful chapter in the history of healing. But without prior agreement on restraints and the strictest limitations, such mechanization of human life may also herald irretrievable disaster resulting from man's encroachment upon nature's preserves, from assessing human beings by their potential value as tool parts, sperm donors, or living incubators, and from replacing the matchless dignity of the human personality by test tubes, syringes, and soulless artificiality of computerized numbers.[27]

Man, as the delicately balanced fusion of body, mind, and soul, can never be the mere product of laboratory conditions and scientific ingenuity. To fulfill his destiny as a creative creature in the image of his Creator, he must be generated and reared out of the intimate love joining husband and wife together, out of identifiable parents who care for the development of their offspring, and out of a home that provides affectionate warmth and compassion.

---

26. [Rabbi Immanuel Jakobovits (1921–1991) was the chief rabbi of Britain from 1967 to 1991. See the introduction for discussion of his pioneering work in Jewish medical ethics. See part 4, section 21, for Rebecca Alpert's discussion and critique of his views.]

27. Immanuel Jakobovits, "Artificial Insemination," in *Jewish Medical Ethics* (New York: Bloch Publishers, 1975), 244–50, 261–66.

ELIE SPITZ

"Through Her I Too Shall Bear a Child": Birth Surrogates in Jewish Law

Elie Kaplan Spitz (b. 1954) is a Conservative rabbi who also trained as a lawyer. He served on the Rabbinical Assembly Committee of Law and Standards, the central halakhic decision-making body of the Conservative movement. He spent much of his career as rabbi of Congregation B'nai Israel in Orange County, California, and is the author of several books about Jewish spirituality.

From "'Through Her I Too Shall Bear a Child': Birth Surrogates in Jewish Law," The Journal of Religious Ethics 24, no. 1 (Spring 1996): 65–97.

When King Solomon judged who was the real mother of a baby, his criteria were clear (1 Kings 3:16–28). Today the issue is more complex. Judges and legislators grapple with defining motherhood itself. Thousands of children have been born during the past two decades to birth surrogates who did not intend to raise the child and who in some cases were not the genetic mother either. What does Judaism have to say about the ethics and acceptability of these new social arrangements? Is paid birth surrogacy kosher?

Jewish authorities are divided, in part along denominational lines, in regard to surrogacy. Among the Orthodox, ovum surrogacy is almost universally condemned. For example, Immanuel Jakobovits, the former chief rabbi of England, writes, "To use another woman as an incubator . . . for a fee . . . [is a] revolting degradation of maternity and an affront to human dignity"[28] . . . Nonetheless, the national bodies of the Conservative and Reform movements have accepted ovum surrogacy as a last resort for couples who are otherwise prevented from having children. Implicit in the split in outcomes is the greater weight given by opponents to traditional pro-creation and traditional family structure. . . .

The rabbis who have written on surrogacy have done so from a theoretical vantage point and have largely concluded that surrogacy is unacceptable. Jewish law is worth reexamining in light of the positive track record of surrogacy to date, the growing use of surrogacy, and the fact that surrogacy has successfully allowed the blessing of children for so many seeking parents.

* * *

---

28. Jakobovits, "Artificial Insemination," 264–65.

Jewish law has no direct precedent for surrogacy. Until recently the possibility of gestational surrogacy was restricted to the realm of science fiction. Similarly, ovum surrogacy was not performed. Early rabbis, however, possessed a prescient imagination and were able to envision embryo transfer. Targum Yonathan[29] says that Dinah was conceived by Rachel and transferred to the womb of Leah and that Joseph was conceived by Leah and transferred to the womb of Rachel. Such speculation, however, has no legal significance since the commentator derived no legal lesson from this legend, and, in the rabbi's account, neither mother intended or even knew that the embryo transfer had occurred.

* * *

Surrogacy is a matter of legal first impression in Jewish law, as in American law. The analysis of jurists to date, both in the US courts and in the writing of the rabbis, has largely tried to analyze it within previously existing categories. Yet, ovum surrogacy is something new, a constellation of five factors: artificial insemination; payment of fees to a biological mother; agreement by a biological mother to relinquish rights; legitimation by a biological father; adoption by his wife. Gestational surrogacy, in which the birth mother has no genetic link to the newborn, is totally new. To define surrogacy by means of partial analogies to existing laws is a distortion of the issue and a disservice to halakha (Jewish law). Whether surrogacy is worthy of halakhic support should come down to a balancing test that includes moral, financial, communal, and personal costs. Since there is no direct legal precedent for surrogacy in Jewish law, a place to begin such an analysis is with underlying values found in Judaism that touch on surrogacy.

* * *

Children are among God's chief blessings. Indeed, procreation is the first command in the Torah: "Be fruitful and multiply and fill up the earth" (Gen. 1:28). So important are offspring that the Mishnah contains a debate between Hillel and Shammai as to the number (they each say two) and genders of children (males for Shammai, one of each for Hillel) needed to fulfill the biblical mandate. Nonetheless, the Tosafot[30] criticized those who fulfill only the minimum requirement (Bava Batra 60b, s.v. din hu).

29. [Targum Yonathan is an ancient Jewish translation of the Bible into Aramaic that includes expansive midrashic commentary.]
30. [Tosafot is a collection of medieval commentaries on the Talmud.]

Abundance of offspring is a recurring promise to the patriarchs—your descendants shall be "like the stars in the heavens and sands of the sea" (Gen. 15:5, 22:17, 26:4; Exod. 32:13; Deut. 1:10, 10:22, 28:62)....

Despite God's promise of progeny, each of the patriarchs had wives who confronted infertility. Reflective of the pain of these couples are Rachel's words to Jacob: "Give me children lest I die!" In response, "Jacob was incensed at Rachel, and said, 'Can I take the place of God, who has denied you fruit of the womb?'" (Gen. 30:1–2). Jacob's anger reveals both his frustration and limitation. There was no medical knowledge in his day that could have solved Rachel's or Jacob's infertility. An infertile couple had only prayer and the possibility of the aid of a third party—which we will see was Rachel's request of her husband.

To deal with the problem of infertility, the Torah does provide for third-party intervention. Interestingly, there is such a possibility for both female and male infertility: the *shifkhah* and the *yibum*,[31] respectively. These two responses of last resort are not the direct equivalent of modern-day surrogacy or artificial insemination by a donor, but they are worth examining closely to uncover shared underlying values.

* * *

Unable to conceive, Rachel said to Jacob: "Here is my handmaid Bilhah, come unto her, and she shall give birth on my knees and I will be built up through her" (Gen. 30:3). Rachel's use of Bilhah, her *shifkhah* (handmaid), as her surrogate conforms to precedent both among the patriarchs and in the society in which she lived. Sarah, too, resorted to a *shifkhah*. "Look, the Lord has kept me from bearing," Sarah said to Abraham. "Consort with my handmaid, Hagar; perhaps I shall have a child through her" (Gen. 16:2). Abraham consented and Hagar gave birth to Yishmael. Later on, when Leah (Rachel's sister) was unable to continue to bear children, she asked Jacob to consort with her handmaid, Zilpah (Gen. 30:9).

The handmaids were subservient to the matriarchs. Their rights were limited. Hence, when Sarah was displeased with Hagar, who at this point was pregnant by Abraham, Abraham said to Sarah: "Behold, your *shifkhah* is in your hands, do with her that which is good in your hand" (Gen. 16:6). Subsequently, Sarah

---

31. [*Yibum* refers to levirate marriage, the ancient Jewish practice of requiring a widow who does not have children to marry the brother of her deceased husband and thereby provide the deceased with offspring. It is not discussed within the section of the article excerpted here.]

was so harsh that Hagar ran away (Gen. 15:6). Consistent with the matriarchs' primacy in the marriage, when children were born to Bilhah and Zilpah, it was Rachel and Leah who gave the children their names (see Gen. 30:6 and 30:8 for Rachel's naming of Dan and Naftali; see Gen. 30:10 and 30:13 for Leah's naming of Gad and Asher). When Rachel said, "she shall give birth on my knees," she used language similar to that found in descriptions of the formal act of adoption in contemporaneous Hittite documents. The children born to the handmaids were considered Jacob's sons and were included among the twelve tribes along with the natural sons of Leah and Rachel. Yet, Zilpah and Bilhah were never referred to in the Torah as Jacob's wives nor would later generations refer to them as matriarchs....

Despite the second-class status of the *shifkhah* in the Torah, she also had certain privileges that are absent in modern surrogacy arrangements. The *shifkhah* was part of the patriarch's family and apparently helped raise her own children. Some critics of surrogacy have pointed to the case of Hagar as a warning. To quote Arlene Agus,[32] "Despite many circumstances—the status and rights offered Hagar, the absence of payment, the shared custody arrangement—the arrangement failed. Perhaps there is a lesson to be learned here."[33] However, holding out Hagar and Sarah's relationship as typical overlooks the apparent success of Rachel and Leah with their handmaids. Moreover, modern surrogacy offers the advantage of simplifying the family arrangement so that two women do not need to compete for the affection of the same man.

Indeed, the most obvious difference between the *shifkhah* and the modern surrogate is that the *shifkhah* existed in a polygamous context. It was then socially acceptable for a man to conceive children with a woman in addition to his primary wife. With Rabbenu Gershon's[34] mandate in the tenth century, monogamy was required, a restriction that some critics construe as a prohibition of surrogacy today.

Yet, there is a fundamental difference between procreation in the past and today. In the ancient world, the only way a man had children with a woman was through sexual intercourse. Today, children may be born outside the marriage

32. [In 1971, Arlene Agus co-founded Ezrat Nashim, the first American feminist organization. She serves as adviser to the Jewish Heritage Initiative of Jewish Child Care Association and is a teacher at the Skirball Center for Adult Jewish Learning.]

33. Arlene Agus, "Surrogacy," *Lilith* 19 (Spring 1988): 31.

34. [Rabbenu Gershom ben Judah (960–1040) was a rabbinic authority of the Ashkenazic realm who banned polygamy.]

without violating the sacred, sexual intimacy of marriage. A broad spectrum of halakhic authorities have therefore concluded that artificial insemination by a donor should not be considered an act of adultery. Because of the division between sex and procreation and even between gestation and providing the ovum, modern surrogacy is not easily dismissed by reference to the category of monogamy alone.

Despite some differences between the *shifkhah* and the contemporary surrogate, there are significant shared values to glean from the Bible's acceptance of a third party to procreation. First, the use of a third party is a permitted last resort to assure genetic continuity for the husband. Although the patriarchs and matriarchs could have adopted a child, a legal category in the ancient world too, they chose the option of using a *shifkhah*. Second, although children were born to the *shifkhah*, the Torah recognized the maternal role of the "intended mother" and gave her rights. The offspring were adopted by the matriarchs and named by them. Third, although the *shifkhah* was not recognized as a "wife," her offspring were treated as descendants of the patriarch, which entailed full inheritance rights.

DON SEEMAN

Ethnography, Exegesis, and Jewish Ethical Reflection: The New Reproductive Technologies in Israel

Don Seeman (b. 1968) is a professor of religion and of Jewish studies at Emory University. As an anthropologist, his research and teaching focus on Jewish religious experience in diverse forms, including Ethiopian-Israeli life, medieval Jewish theology, and Hasidism. He also serves as rabbi of an Orthodox congregation.

From "Ethnography, Exegesis, and Jewish Ethical Reflection: The New Reproductive Technologies in Israel," in *Kin, Gene, Community: Reproductive Technologies among Jewish Israelis*, eds. Daphna Birenbaum-Carmeli and Yoram S. Carmeli (New York: Berghahn Books, 2010), 340–62.

The state of Israel has emerged as a leader in the use and development of new reproductive technologies. It is well-known, for example, that Israel boasts more IVF clinics per capita than any other country in the world, and is one of the only nations to make this technology available at public expense to women without regard to their marital status or sexual orientation. More surprising perhaps is that Israel, where determinations of personal status and the legality of reproductive technologies are subject to veto by state-authorized religious authorities, specifically legalized donor insemination at least a decade before the militantly secular Republic of France.... The tendency of scholars who study Israel to assume a self-explanatory rift between religious-conservative and secular-scientific worldviews must obviously be reexamined. One of the primary arguments of this chapter is that we need a more nuanced analysis of the ways in which ethical reflection upon new medical technology grows out of culturally grounded interpretive practices.

The French comparison is instructive here because of the way in which an avowedly secular yet deeply metaphysical discourse on the "laws of nature" has helped to inform contemporary decisions about social and public health policy. In France, judgments about the propriety of reproductive technology were made not primarily by recourse to sacred texts but to foundational documents of modern secularism like the 1789 Declaration of the Rights of Man, which encodes a complex web of ideas about the "natural" and the "good." This secularized version of natural law theory did not invoke revelation, but it did invoke ideas about the natural "rights and dignity of man" in order to call into question practices like IVF treatment for postmenopausal women or postmortem sperm collection that seemed to stretch the definition of what could be considered "natural."... Ultimately, French policy makers limited the legal practice of IVF to sterile, heterosexual couples of childbearing years—"natural" parents in other words, whose inability to bear children could be conceived as *extrinsic* to their social position or cultural identity.

Concerns of this type have been relatively peripheral to the Israeli Jewish context, but they echo the concerns of modern Catholic writers, who continue to view most forms of artificial reproductive technology with suspicion or hostility as counter to nature....

Bioethical deliberation cannot be severed from the broader hermeneutical concerns that shape other styles of reading and forms of thought, including religious worldviews.... My goal in this chapter is simply to outline some of the distinctive hermeneutic strategies that have helped to define Jewish and Israeli approaches to the new reproductive technologies, and to differentiate them from their Christian and Western-secular counterparts. At the same time, I will argue as an anthropologist that our understanding of these textual strategies and traditions ought to be complicated by calling ethnographic attention to the situated character of human experience in real-world settings of possibility and constraint....

Every one of the matriarchs in Genesis struggles with barrenness, which comes to define the very architecture of biblical narrative. Women's movement across the thresholds of tents comes to signify a literary enactment of the problematic quest for motherhood, and contributes to a uniquely biblical idiom of the relationship between gender, fecundity, and national identity. This is very far from the concern with nature and natural reproduction that has characterized many modern responses to assisted reproduction. Sarah's miraculous conception in old age ("Sarah had stopped having the periods of women" [Gen. 18:11]) betrays no hint of the ethical conflict surrounding postmenopausal reproduction that continues to bedevil some modern policy makers. Nor is Sarah the last of the biblical women to reproduce in unexpected ways. Jacob's wife Rachel has trouble conceiving and prays bitterly for death if God refuses to give her a child (Gen. 30). She resorts to pharmacological measures through fertility-enhancing "mandrakes" (a kind of plant) and competes with her sister Leah over who can produce the most sons for their common husband through surrogacy involving each of the two women's female servants: "She [Rachel] said [to Jacob], 'Here is my maidservant Bilhah; come in to her and she will give birth upon my knees *so that I also may be built up through her*" (Gen. 30:3) [emphasis added].

The fact that servant-surrogacy seems to be an assumed element of the biblical kinship system need not deflect modern thinkers—even religious ones—from raising the whole knot of thorny ethical problems raised by surrogacy in its different settings. The text can be read to raise important and highly relevant contemporary questions about the ways in which surrogacy in some contexts may be said, for example, to put poor women's reproductive capacities at the disposal of rich women along clearly established lines of social and economic power. But we must also acknowledge that this is very far from the text's primary and explicit concern with the possibilities for reproductive success on the part of its protagonists, and with the ambiguity and instability in local kin relations that surrogacy can sometimes introduce. Classical midrashic literature is filled with allusions not just to tensions between the families of Rachel and Leah but also to tensions and hierarchies pitting the sons of the wives against the sons of the concubines among Jacob's progeny, without thereby implying that servant-surrogacy was in any way ethically problematic. Though we may sometimes read biblical texts for contemporary edification, this should not come at the expense of imposing foreign or anachronistic modern concerns upon them....

One of the ways to avoid an exaggerated belief in our own era's incommensurability is to insist upon shifting from a discourse of ethical, religious, and reproductive *norms* in the language of academic bioethics, to a discourse of cultural, religious, and reproductive *strategies*, in the manner of anthropologists. Strategies differ, but they are rarely incommensurate inasmuch as human beings pursue similar (though culturally inflected) goals in different settings. Surrogacy is a strategy for replacing the womb of a woman who is recognized as the mother of a child in social terms with the womb of a woman who can bear the child in biological terms. Technologies available to accomplish this goal vary, as do the social institutions that make it possible, but modern technological surrogacy and the servant-surrogacy of the Hebrew Bible are at least comparable, as are the levirate and today's controversial postmortem collection and delivery of sperm cells. It should be very clear that this is not an argument for the foundational authority of biblical texts or the assertion of seamless cultural and religious continuity between ancient and modern Israel. On the contrary, by insisting on the importance of speaking through and about classical texts on reproductive strategies I am arguing that these ought at least to be appreciated as "other countries heard from," that can help us to expand the scope of our moral imagination. Investigation into the lives of other societies and their literature provides a necessary counterpoint to that which is assumed to be natural and necessary in our own. While advocates and opponents of new reproductive technologies both seem prepared to believe that this technology stands ready to unhinge traditional families and kinship structures, or even to bring about "the end of the body" as we know it my experience as an anthropologist as well as a Judaics scholar has conditioned me to treat such claims with caution. Reproductive strategies have *always* been diverse, and so have the textual hermeneutic strategies that some societies have deployed to make sense of them.

* * *

An American Orthodox rabbi with a reputation for expertise in matters of reproductive ethics and Jewish law recently surprised his Christian colleagues at a multifaith academic roundtable when he openly resisted their suggestion that the discussion of religion and reproduction should start with consideration of texts from Genesis. Many Christian and some Jewish writers have, after all, sought strong support in the opening chapters of Genesis for what has come to be known as "traditional marriage"—monogamous, heterosexual, and procreative—in the language of the American culture wars. There is no reason to deny that Jewish Orthodoxy today also holds up this kind of marriage as an ideal, but the halakhic or Jewish legal grounding for claims about permitted and forbidden reproductive practices begins not with Genesis but Leviticus, whose largely nonnarrative focus on rules of consanguinity and rules of purity constitutes the main corpus of biblical kinship norms that underlie later Jewish family law. This simple fact is one of the reasons that Jewish law experts (*poskim*) have tended to be so much more favorably inclined toward artificial reproductive technologies than many of their Christian counterparts, just as the state of Israel has been more supportive than many other Western states. The discrepancy between dominant Jewish and Christian approaches derives not just from a formal normative dispute, but also from an interpretive stylistic one. . . .

The reason for this disconnect is that Jewish law tends to derive not from the open-ended narrative analysis favored by many Christian ethical writers, but from a more formal and abstract notion of discrete and bounded legal prohibitions (i.e., "Do not uncover the nakedness of your brother's wife" [Lev. 18:16]), that constitute a negative *limit* for human behavior rather than a simulacra of some positive ethical ideal. This is why the discussion of artificial reproductive technologies for Jewish writers tends to start with Leviticus rather than Genesis, and also why implications for kinship relations tend to loom so much larger than the kinds of abstract concerns evinced by the Catholic Church. Yet this is also one of the reasons that Jewish legal decisors have tended to be so much more permissive than Catholics and some Protestants with respect to artificial reproductive technologies. Halakha presents itself as a species of positive law that has been revealed, transmitted and elaborated in legal discourse over an extended period; it is relatively difficult to impose new prohibitions on the basis of subjective literary readings of sacred texts. Although some rabbinic writers have expressed discomfort with particular aspects of new reproductive technologies, they typically require a more definite legal basis to rule them definitively impermissible. What this really means is that it is *precisely the legalistic emphasis on discrete prohibitions that has given Jewish bioethical deliberation so much more flexibility* than that derived from narrative-based "foundational anthropology" approaches.

SARAH ZAGAR

Water Wears Away Stone:
Caring for Those We Can Only Imagine

Sarah Zager (b. 1990) is a scholar of modern Jewish thought. She teaches in the religion department of St. Olaf College in Minnesota. Her research interests include ethical theories, feminist thought, and how Jewish discourse can contribute to contemporary philosophical debates.

From "Water Wears Away Stone: Caring for Those We Can Only Imagine," *Nashim: A Journal of Jewish Women's Studies and Gender Issues* 37 (2020): 116–31.

In this autoethnographic essay, I explore the confluence of my experience with early infertility and my scholarly work in both Jewish studies and feminist thought. I argue that, while feminist theorists' efforts to emphasize the political importance of "care work" and particular caregiving relationships contribute significantly to the field, they also risk ignoring some of the disorderly, unpredictable, and painful ways that this "situatedness" can arise....

Some of the most trenchant critical work in philosophy has come from theorists who demand that the philosophical tradition be reshaped in ways that account for their own experiences. Rather than hoping that their experiences can somehow be worn away by philosophical thinking, these theorists demand that our thinking conform to the contours of what it is like to live life in our particular bodies, even if these bodies have tended to be ignored by the philosophical tradition.

The classical texts of liberal political theory often imagine the citizen as a full-formed adult with no connection to his (and I really mean his) family of origin. Ties to fathers, brothers, and grandfathers, to home life, and to religious and ethnic identity, are understood to cloud the citizen's ability to form communal bonds in the public sphere with people who do not share the same roots. To be keepers of the public good, these texts argue, we first have to stop being our brothers' keepers; by extension, this means that people who are the "keepers" of sons and husbands and aging parents are ill-suited to tending to the "commonweal." Their lives are best kept "in private." In a passage widely repudiated by feminist critics, the political philosopher Thomas Hobbes[35] argues that the

---

35. [Thomas Hobbes (1588–1679) was an English philosopher.]

best way to think about politics is to imagine human beings "as if but even now sprung out of the earth, and suddenly (like Mushroomes [sic]) come to full maturity, without all kind of engagement to each other."[36]

In the past several decades, feminist scholars have emphasized what is lost when we imagine ourselves as "sprung out of the earth" into "full maturity" in this way: we—women in particular, but men too, once they look carefully at their own lives—are who we are because of our relationships with the particular people whom we love and who cared for us. Political theorist Seyla Benhabib[37] describes this as a contrast between an older model where "individuals are grown up before they have been born; in which boys are men before they have been children; a world where neither mother, nor sister, nor wife exist," and a new one that puts the personal relationships of mothers, sisters, wives, and other caregivers, people Benhabib calls "situated selves," at the center of political life.[38] The dependents cared for by these situated selves are not born immediately into "full maturity," with the capability to take care of themselves on their own. They need to be breastfed and diapered, then spoon-fed and toilet trained, and taught to drive and to cook dinner for themselves, and eventually to help care for others. Thus, to pretend that we are not "our brothers' keepers" is to misunderstand what is really going on; all of us need to be "kept" in some way or other. . . .

But just as I began to spend more time with texts both ancient and modern that suggested that human beings do not simply spring up immediately into adulthood, fully formed and without worrying loyalties to some brother or other who demands "keeping," I found myself thrust into a kind of "situatedness" that neither the rabbis nor the care ethicists could fully recognize.

"Sarah is only twenty-seven," the older man on the end tells the rest of the row of assembled white coats. "But she seems to have an extremely low ovarian reserve. We are going to see if we can get something with egg freezing so she can use them later. I don't know. But this is an interesting case." . . .

For care ethicists, one of the main theoretical payoffs of focusing on "situated selves" is that it moves us away from the assumption that ethics is a system of

---

36. Thomas Hobbes, *De Cive: The English Version Entitled in the First Edition Philosophical Rudiments Concerning Government and Society*, ed. Howard Warrender (Oxford: Clarendon Press, n.d.), 117.

37. [Seyla Benhabib (b. 1950) is an American philosopher.]

38. Seyla Benhabib, *Situating the Self: Gender, Community, and Postmodernism in Contemporary Ethics* (Hoboken, NJ: John Wiley & Sons, 2013), 157.

"universal" obligations that I have to all other people, regardless of my relationship to them. There is something ethically important, [Virginia] Held[39] argues, in responding to *my* child's needs, simply because she is *mine*:

> What a parent may value in her child may well not be what makes this child like every other, but the very particularity of the child and of the relationship that exists between them, such that she is the mother of this child and this particular person is her child.[40]

This model didn't make sense of my experiences. I wasn't caring for any particular person because she was *my* child; *my* child didn't exist yet. For the moment, at least, my sense of situatedness and my experience of care came not from attending to one specific child's particular physical and emotional needs, but from the experience of having imagined and wanted—desperately, desperately wanted, in a way I guess I knew but certainly hadn't yet felt before I began treatment—to be able to create my own little subpart of the web of other situated selves.... It's not really about the physical, intimate form of care for another person, or, to use Held's language, "attending to and meeting the needs of particular others."[41] Instead, it's about care for a hypothetical being whose presence I hope for.... That being doesn't talk back; it doesn't have the particular characteristics or features that are so important to philosophers like Held....

This being doesn't demand specific things of me of its own accord. It's not a situated self, and it may never see enough daylight to become one, but it is making me into one....

---

39. [Virginia Held (b. 1929) is an American philosopher who developed a feminist approach to ethics known as "ethics of care." For another piece that draws on this approach, see Mara Benjamin in part 1, section 4.]

40. Virginia Held, *The Ethics of Care* (Oxford: Oxford University Press, 2006), 93.

41. Held, *The Ethics of Care*, 10.

21 | Abortion

In contemporary political debates about access to abortion, there are some persistent questions: "Under what circumstances is a decision to terminate a pregnancy justified?" "Who should be allowed to make such a decision?" "Does a fetus have rights?" "When does life begin?" Though these questions loom large in American politics today, they get scant attention in traditional Jewish sources. The Torah, Mishnah, and Talmud do not address abortion directly, and this means that modern thinkers seeking Jewish answers from classical Jewish sources have had to extrapolate and reason from disparate statements, stories, and laws dealing with pregnancy. While there is considerable debate about abortion among modern Jewish ethicists, there is broad agreement about the relevant sources. This means that divergences of opinion reflect different interpretations of the same core texts.

Jewish discussions of abortion generally begin with reference to the same key cases from the Bible, Mishnah, and Talmud. Based on these classical sources, all agree that abortion should not be regarded as murder, and that concern for the pregnant person's life is tantamount. Interpreters diverge, however, on what further conclusions can be drawn from these cases. The selections gathered here not only illustrate this divergence but also address it in meta-reflections about how ideology and subjective experience condition ethical reasoning and interpretation.

For Dena S. Davis, the abortion discussion exemplifies the role of subjective interpretation in case-based ethical reasoning. Writing in the early 1990s, when there were relatively few women trained in Talmud and Jewish law, she argues that the halakhic discussion of abortion is impoverished because of the absence of women's voices and perspectives. This piece provides a helpful overview to Jewish abortion ethics by introducing the three classical sources on pregnancy that are foundational in modern discussions. Writing just a few years later, Rebecca T. Alpert offers a sharper, more targeted critique. Alpert focuses on one leading twentieth-century Orthodox thinker, Rabbi Immanuel Jakobovits,[42] demonstrating

---

42. [Rabbi Immanuel Jakobovits (1921–1991) was the chief rabbi of Britain from 1967 to 1991. See the Introduction for discussion of his pioneering work in Jewish medical ethics. See Fred Rosner's piece in part 4, section 20, for further discussion of his views on reproduction.]

how he changes his discourse about abortion in response to political and social shifts in American society. Even as Alpert excoriates Jakobovits for his repressive attitudes about women, her review of his writings offers an incisive analysis of how principles, ideology, and sociology inform halakhic reasoning.

Alan Jotkowitz acknowledges that ideology may sometimes overtake halakhic rulings but denies that this is the case in recent Orthodox rulings on abortion. Though his piece is a direct response to an initial essay by Ronit Irshai (not reprinted here), his argument can be read as a retort to Alpert as well. In Irshai's initial article, she identifies a trend of intensifying stringency in halakhic rulings on abortion; like Alpert, she suggests that this reflects denigrating views of women. Jotkowitz contends that the range of halakhic rulings on abortion can all be read as valid, rigorous interpretations of precedents rather than as evidence of regressive views of women. This section concludes with Irshai's brief retort to Jotkowitz, arguing that the precedents could in fact support more liberal interpretations that accord more agency and respect to women considering abortion.

The contentiousness of the abortion issue makes it hard to untangle ethical considerations from their political implications. For some thinkers, the relative silence of Jewish tradition on abortion is instructive, indicating that abortion is not a chief area of Jewish moral concern and exposing the degree to which a distinctly Christian ethical sensibility has overtaken the very terms of the abortion debate. Others disagree, regarding abortion as a serious issue that Jewish law and ethics may address effectively through traditional modes of textual interpretation and legal consideration.[43] Because Jewish ethical discussions of abortion largely center on textual interpretation and reasoning, they often entail a level of subtlety and deliberation that is lacking in polarized political debates.

43. For a critique of the dominance of this mode of reasoning, however, see Michal Raucher's essay in part 1, section 1.

DENA S. DAVIS

Abortion in Jewish Thought: A Study in Casuistry

Dena S. Davis (b. 1947) is a professor of bioethics and religion at Lehigh University. Trained in both religious studies and law, she focuses on the ethics of genetics research, reproductive technologies, and end of life decision-making. Her most recent book is Genetic Dilemmas: Reproductive Technology, Parental Choices, and Children's Futures *(Oxford, 2010).*

From "Abortion in Jewish Thought: A Study in Casuistry," *Journal of the American Academy of Religion* 60, no. 2 (Summer 1992): 313–24.

Three paradigm cases, or "narrative-precedents," exert gravitational pull on the discussion of abortion in traditional Judaism: Exodus 21:22–23; Mishnah *Ohalot* 7:6, and Babylonian Talmud *Arakhin* 7a–b.

The passage in Exodus is the most authoritative because it is biblical rather than rabbinic. It reads:

> If men strive, and wound a pregnant woman so that her fruit be expelled, but no harm befall [her], then shall he be fined.... But if harm befall [her], then shalt thou give life for life.

In this case, accidentally causing a woman to miscarry is a civil injury, and the perpetrator must pay a fine. But accidentally killing the woman is a criminal case, and the wrongdoer is subject to death. The fetus is not considered a *nefesh adam* (human person) in Jewish law at any stage in pregnancy. Unlike the woman, the fetus has neither the moral nor juridical status of a person. Consequently, when the woman's life is endangered by pregnancy or childbirth, she has the right to protect herself by destroying the fetus. In halakha this is not only her right but her obligation because the duty to protect one's life and health outweighs all others (the principle of *pikuach nefesh*).

The Exodus passage does not imply that fetal life is held lightly as if it were simply property. David Bleich[44] speaks for the tradition when he says, "Judaism regards all forms of human life as sacred.... Fetal life is regarded as precious and may not be destroyed wantonly."[45] Judaism holds that human life is intrinsically

---

44. [Rabbi J. David Bleich (b. 1936) is a leading Orthodox Jewish authority on Jewish law and contemporary bioethics.]

45. J. David Bleich, "Abortion in Halakhic Literature," in *Jewish Bioethics*, eds. Fred Rosner and J. David Bleich (New York: Hebrew Publishing Company, 1979), 135.

sacred because humans are created in God's image. Sherwin[46] identifies three claims of Jewish theology regarding human life: that each person is unique, that each human life is therefore irreplaceable, and that because of that unique and irreplaceable character, each human life "embodies intrinsic sanctity."[47] Furthermore, when a fetus is destroyed, *its* possible offspring are destroyed as well.

Thus, the Exodus passage on the one hand, and the intense concern for the preservation of human life on the other, set the ontological boundaries within which halakhists can make decisions. Within these boundaries cases exert their gravitational pull, governing the ebb and flow of argument, as halakhists make their points by orienting specific questions to paradigmatic cases. The passage in Mishnah *Oholot* reads as follows:

> If a woman is having difficulty giving birth, one cuts up the fetus within her and takes it out limb by limb because her life takes precedence over its life. Once its greater part has emerged, you do not touch it, because you may not set aside one life for another.

This passage presents the paradigm case to which the principles inferred from the Exodus narrative are applied. The mother's life is threatened (however innocently) by the fetus. Since we know from Exodus that the fetus is not a *nefesh* and can never be preferred over the mother, it follows that the fetus must be destroyed to protect her. The second half of the passage is puzzling, because it is impossible to imagine a situation to which it would apply. If the head has emerged (or its larger part, in the case of a breech presentation) the mother's life may still be in danger, but not in any way that would be diminished by destroying the fetus. The second half of the passage describes a null set, even in ancient times. The practical result is, "An abortion must be performed any time it is necessary, and may not be performed in those instances in which it would be pointless in any case." So the thrust of this passage, as it relates to abortion, is to remind us of the absolute precedence of the woman's life.

There are certain principles for which this case stands. It would be impossible to tug the case in a radically different direction, for example to argue that fetal life has a claim equal to the mother's. But within its directional thrust, there are

---

46. [For a selection from Conservative rabbi Byron Sherwin (1946–2015), see part 4, section 22.]

47. Byron Sherwin, *In Partnership with God: Contemporary Jewish Law and Ethics* (Syracuse, NY: Syracuse University Press, 1990), 175.

many interpretive moves to be made. What is meant by "difficulty in childbirth," i.e., what kinds of threats are serious enough to come under the rubric of this case? A wide range of interpretation is possible. Even Immanuel Jakobovits,[48] one of the most conservative commentators, states that the threat to the mother need not be either immediate or absolutely certain. Further, a grave psychological threat is considered by many decisors to be as weighty as a physical hazard. In an intriguing twist, we learn that for some halakhists not only danger to the mother can be grounds for abortion, but also danger to an existing child who is dependent for life on the mother's milk.

A third paradigm case is the strange hypothetical question of the woman who has been condemned to death and is pregnant. This precedent-narrative has been described as "ghastly," "grisly," and "bizarre" by modern commentators, but ironically its thrust is a compassionate one. In Jewish law, once a prisoner is condemned to death the execution may not be delayed, because it is not permissible to extend the anxiety and mental suffering of the one facing death.[49] A question arises if a woman condemned to death is discovered to be pregnant, should one delay her execution until the birth of the baby? The answer is "No," unless labor has already begun. Furthermore, if there is a possibility that the fetus might be born after the death, "where it would cause bleeding and thus expose the executed mother to be disgraced," then one should "strike the woman against the womb so that the child may die first, to avoid her being disgraced" (B. T. *Arakhin* 7a–b). As Green[50] comments, "The sages are clearly demonstrating their concern for the mother rather than for the child. Saving the child's life does not merit inflicting even a few hours more suffering on her. Likewise, the prospect of her disgrace also bulks larger in the sages' view than any claims of parental life."[51] . . .

As we shall see, the roles of subjectivity and of analogy are well recognized by some modern scholars of halakha. The issue that has been ignored, however, is the interaction between subjectivity, analogy, and the identity of the interpreters themselves. If one part of the community has been left out of the interpretive process, there is a good reason to question the credibility of the results.

48. [See the Alpert article below for further discussion of Rabbi Immanuel Jakobovits (1921–1991).]

49. [For discussion of Jewish views on the death penalty, see the piece by Beth Berkowitz in part 2, section 12.]

50. [Ronald M. Green (b. 1942) is a scholar of religious ethics.]

51. Ronald M. Green, "Contemporary Jewish Bioethics: A Critical Assessment," in *Theory and Bioethics*, ed. E. E. Shelp (Amsterdam: D. Reidel Publishing, 1985), 261.

To argue casuistically is to argue analogically. We take the case before us, sort out its component parts, and attempt to find its geographical place in the "moral taxonomy." Is this case more "like" this precedent-narrative, or more "like" that one? In issues of bioethics, we are dealing with emotions and with uncertainty. Thus, analogic argument is necessarily subjective....

Louis E. Newman,[52] in an extremely perceptive essay,[53] argues that most contemporary halakhists make the error of assuming that the texts virtually interpret themselves, with the decisors acting almost like passive conduits, and the "right" answers a foregone conclusion. In fact, as he shows, the role of interpretation cannot be ignored....

Newman focuses on the difficulty of applying ancient texts to the modern dilemmas posed by medical technology. But there is a deeper, prior problem: *who* is allowed into the interpretive process and whose subjective experience is to count? Newman, Green, and other liberal critics fail to notice that women have been excluded almost completely from the halakhic process. Just as, in American law, feminist jurisprudence and critical race theory present the view that excluding women and people of color from casuistic scholarship has resulted in an ideological interpretation of law that reflects the bias of white males who flourish under the status quo, so I argue that in a culture as powerfully gender-oriented as Judaism, it is reasonable to assume that the body of law would be different had women been part of the interpretive process....

In other words, halakhic reasoning is analogical, interpretive, and ineluctably subjective, but only half the people expected to adhere to it are allowed into the process. This presents problems for its credibility both within and without its own community. True, decisors are enjoined to take women's suffering into account, even to put it first, but it is male "understanding" of female experiences, percolated through the male experience of Jewish culture in which they occupy a very different position. To say that all interpretation is ideological is not to say that women's is any less so, but only to make the point that a casuistic enterprise that invited all its constituents into the process has a better chance of arriving at fair and sensitive conclusions.

---

52. [For more on Jewish ethicist Louis Newman, see part 1, section 1.]
53. [A selection from this essay is reprinted in part 1, section 1.]

REBECCA T. ALPERT

Sometimes the Law Is Cruel:
The Construction of a Jewish Antiabortion Position in the Writings of Immanuel Jakobovits

Rebecca Alpert (b. 1950) is a professor emerita of religion at Temple University. A scholar of American Judaism, she was among the first women to be ordained as rabbi when she completed her rabbinical studies at the Reconstructionist Rabbinical College in 1976. Her research interests include Judaism, sexuality, gender, race, religion, and sports.

From "Sometimes the Law Is Cruel: The Construction of a Jewish Antiabortion Position in the Writings of Immanuel Jakobovits," *Journal of Feminist Studies in Religion* 11, no. 2 (Fall 1995): 27–37.

For the past thirty years, discussions about abortion have been in the forefront of cultural debates in the United States and Europe. Although other issues of reproductive choice (safe and accessible contraception, freedom from forced sterilization, and alternative insemination) may in fact be more central to women's lives, abortion has been the issue in the public eye. The religious Right has been responsible for much of the prominence of this debate. The Catholic Church and Protestant fundamentalist groups have kept public attention focused on abortion, which they have constructed as a moral issue. The participation of churches in the antiabortion movement has been bold and conspicuous, with little regard for issues of separation of church and state. The movement's stated goal is to reverse the legalization of abortion, and its short-term strategy has been to put restrictions on the availability of abortion through legislative initiatives, civil disobedience, and violence. In comparison, the liberal Christian pro-choice position has received scant attention.

Because this issue is so commonly framed in religious terms, it is not surprising that representatives of the Jewish religious community have been asked with great frequency to present the Jewish view on abortion. Because Jews are generally perceived as liberals, it has been assumed popularly that Judaism is a pro-choice tradition. The reality is vastly more complex. Because of the complexities, it is not accurate to describe any one perspective as "the" Jewish position on abortion. It is more accurate to speak of a range of Jewish positions. . . .

Despite this complexity, Jews on both sides of the abortion debate have attempted to present a Jewish position that supports their point of view. It is my goal here to examine the development of one such position in the writings of Rabbi Immanuel Jakobovits (b. 1921). Educated at Jews College and the Etz Chaim Yeshiva in London, Jakobovits became the chief rabbi of Ireland in 1949 and, in 1958, rabbi of the prestigious Fifth Avenue Synagogue in New York City. From 1966 to 1991, he was the chief rabbi of the British Commonwealth. He was the first contemporary Jewish scholar to write about abortion, and he published two significant articles. The first came out in 1959 as part of his classic work *Jewish Medical Ethics*.[54] The second work appeared in 1967 as part of an anthology, *Abortion and the Law*, which included a broad range of articles by leading ethicists, lawyers, and theologians.[55] The 1967 article has been reprinted many times in both Jewish and secular texts. It is considered one of the standard Orthodox position papers on abortion in Jewish law.

By analyzing the differences between the two articles, I seek to evaluate how a traditional Jewish position on abortion was affected by, and sought to affect, public debate. Jakobovits's 1959 article is a serious presentation of the complexities of the Jewish position, but his 1967 article presents the argument that Jewish tradition is unequivocally opposed to abortion under any circumstances except where the life of the woman is threatened.

The difference in Jakobovits's treatment of the subject is directly attributable to changes that were under way in US abortion laws. Prior to the early 1960s, discussion of abortion was in fact theoretical. But restrictions on abortion came under attack by the women's movement and by a growing number of physicians, and states began to change their abortion laws. Whereas in 1959 Jakobovits could write about the complexities of a Jewish view of abortion, by 1967 he felt compelled to present an unequivocal Jewish position that could influence the debate. Although such a position would not be as stringent as the Catholic position, which opposed abortion under all circumstances, it would also not be as liberal as the Protestant position, which supported a woman's right to choose abortion. Jakobovits saw the liberalization of abortion as a threat to traditional Jewish values, which deny women the right to make decisions of this magnitude. He thus carved out a Jewish position asserting that women do not have that right. The position that Jakobovits and other halakhic scholars have taken

54. Immanuel Jakobovits, "Controlling the Generation of Life," in *Jewish Medical Ethics* (New York: Bloch Publishing Co., 1959), 170–92.
55. Immanuel Jakobovits, "Jewish Voices on Abortion," in *Abortion and the Law*, ed. David T. Smith (Cleveland: Western Reserve University Press, 1967).

has had a significant impact on the Orthodox Jewish community and has put pressure on traditional women not to have abortions....

Three primary concerns of Orthodox Judaism motivated Jakobovits to present a different picture in 1967, one that would remonstrate against the acceptance of liberalized abortion. First, any effort to abort a fetus with mental or physical disabilities, no matter how severe, is repugnant to contemporary Orthodox Jewish sensibility. In fact, for many Jews anything that resembles eugenics is an anathema because of the experience of Nazi experimentation. This link was paramount in Jakobovits's mind in 1967 because of the importance of thalidomide babies in the early abortion debate. Although Jakobovits acknowledges that this is only a minor factor in the public discussion, it is still central to his thinking.

Second, and more significant, contemporary Orthodox sensibility recoils from any possibility of sexuality outside of marriage. Although Jewish attitudes toward heterosexuality have been complex and ambivalent throughout the centuries, to the contemporary Orthodox community sex outside of marriage is an anathema and must be deterred at all costs. To the extent that abortion is seen to enable sexually active women to go unpunished, it cannot be tolerated.

Third, implicit in the liberalization of abortion laws was the idea that women would be making decisions about abortion with their doctors. Jakobovits decried medical professionals making these decisions, but he never mentioned women's roles at all. It is clear that women making such decisions is not even a possibility in Orthodox Judaism.

But it would also be very difficult, given the complexity of halakha, for Jakobovits to present an image of Jewish law opposed to abortion. All that could be said unequivocally was that when the woman's life was threatened, her life took precedence over the life of the fetus, and that abortion could not be construed as murder. Jakobovits could still maintain that Jewish women almost never had abortions, but now he also needed to assert that Judaism opposed abortion except when the woman's life was in mortal danger. Jakobovits had to make clear that in traditional Judaism women would not be permitted to make decisions about such weighty matters.

To create such a position, Jakobovits used two strategies. First, he presented a simple, rather than complex, description of the halakhic sources. Second, he abandoned the case method and employed a rhetorical appeal to "Jewish values" to present his position.

In the introductory section of the second article, Jakobovits articulated his concern that things were changing in the area of abortion. He pointed to a "staggering rise in the rate of abortions" and claimed that the motives for this increase and for the movement for legalization were the use of abortion as "a means to prevent the birth of possibly defective children, to curb the sordid indignities and hazards imposed on women resorting to clandestine operators, and simply to contain the population explosion."

He then argues against medical professionals having any right to determine the legality of abortion, claiming that doctors are merely technicians, whereas abortion is a moral issue. He therefore asserts that the decision is better left to "moral experts, or to legislatures guided by such experts."[56] Presumably those moral experts are religious leaders, but the question of church-state relations is never raised. Jakobovits does not consider the possibility that individual women might have some role in deciding these issues for themselves....

Jakobovits never refers to the woman carrying a fetus as a woman or even as a pregnant woman. She is always described as mother. Because she is mother, her fetus is also implicitly always child. The debate is framed in such a way as to give her no autonomous existence nor even to recognize her existence vis-à-vis the fetus she carries.

When the stakes of changing abortion law became apparent to Jakobovits, however misinformed he was as to the facts or potential consequences, his polite discussions of complexity yielded to a simple solution—abortion should not be legalized. Jakobovits's writings illustrate that contemporary events affect the position of thinkers who claim to be interested only in timeless values and that traditional texts are subject to a variety of interpretations, depending on the context.

---

56. Immanuel Jakobovits, "Jewish Voices on Abortion," in *Jewish Bioethics*, ed. Fred Rosner and J. David Bleich (New York: Sanhedrin Press, 1979), 119.

ALAN JOTKOWITZ

Abortion and Maternal Need:
A Response to Ronit Irshai

Dr. Alan Jotkowitz (b. 1964) is the director of the Medical School for International Health at Ben-Gurion University of the Negev and senior physician at Soroka University Medical Center, Ben-Gurion's teaching hospital. He grew up and pursued medical training in the United States before moving to Israel. An avid student and teacher of classical Jewish texts, he publishes extensively in the fields of internal medicine, medical ethics, and Jewish medical ethics.

From "Abortion and Maternal Need: A Response to Ronit Irshai," *Nashim: A Journal of Jewish Women's Studies and Gender Issues* 21 (Spring 2011): 97–109.

[The article presented here is a response to an article by Ronit Irshai, "Gender Perspectives in Halakhic Decision-Making: Abortion as a Test Case," in *New Streams in Philosophy of Halakhah*, eds. Aviezer Ravitsky and Avinoam Rosenak (Jerusalem: Magnes–Van Leer Institute, 2008).]

Dr. Ronit Irshai, in a thoughtful analysis of the halakhic attitude toward abortion, advances the thesis that the halakha has been influenced by a specific regressive attitude toward women. In particular, for ideological reasons, contemporary halakhic authorities have consistently put the fetus's interest ahead of the woman's. Irshai posits that modern decisors have by and large rejected a formulistic approach to halakhic decision-making regarding abortion, because of a specific attitude toward the role of woman....

With regard to abortion, there is clearly room for two viable approaches, and the fact that a *posek*[57] takes a more restrictive view might be due to factors other than gender bias. The *posek* might, for example, feel that this is an example of *safek de'oraita lehumra* (the preference for stringency in cases of doubt concerning laws derived directly from the Torah) or have other, equally valid halakhic reasons for a restrictive approach. By briefly reviewing the classical sources and modern responsa, I will show that there is halakhic precedent for a more restrictive approach to abortion. Therefore, in my opinion, bias is difficult to prove in this case....

Through a close reading of the relevant Talmudic sources, Irshai attempts to

---

57. [A *posek* is rabbi with the authority to decide questions of Jewish law and practice.]

demonstrate that, according to classic Jewish sources, the fetus is not considered a "person."

> A [pregnant] woman who is going out to be executed—we do not wait until she gives birth [to execute her]. A woman who is sitting on the birthing stool—we wait until she gives birth.... This might seem obvious, for [the fetus] is part of [the pregnant woman's] body. But it must be specified, for you might have thought, since it is written: "[When individuals fight ... and a miscarriage results, ...] the one responsible shall be fined according as the woman's husband may exact" [Exod. 21:22], that this indicates that [the fetus] is the husband's property, and therefore we may not cause him to lose [it]. That is why [this rule] is specified. But perhaps it is indeed so [that we should wait, so as to prevent loss to the husband]? Rabbi Abahu said in the name of Rabbi Yohanan, the verse states: "and also both of them shall die" [Deut. 22:22]—[the redundancy] comes to include the fetus.... [Regarding] a woman who is sitting on the birthing stool, what is the reason [that we wait]? Since the fetus has moved, it is considered a different body. (B. T. *Arakhin* 7a)

The implication of this passage is that before the woman goes into labor, the fetus is not considered a separate entity. Irshai makes this cogent assumption. The following passage is also highly relevant to the discussion:

> If a woman is having difficulty giving birth, one may dismember the infant in the womb and remove it limb by limb, because her life comes before the fetus's life. If most of the fetus has emerged, one does not touch it, because one does not put aside one life for another. (Mishnah *Ohalot* 7:6)

Irshai[58] presents two possible understandings of the mishnah:

1. The only reason the mishnah's first clause allows one to abort the fetus is that the mother's life is in danger. Otherwise, abortion is prohibited.

2. There is no reason to assume that the first clause is limited to a situation in which the woman's life is in danger. The reason why an abortion is allowed is that before most of the fetus has emerged, it is not considered a "person."

58. Ronit Irshai, "Gender Perspectives in Halakhic Decision-Making: Abortion as a Test Case," in *New Streams in Philosophy of Halakhah*, eds. Aviezer Ravitsky and Avinoam Rosenak (Jerusalem: Magnes–Van Leer Institute, 2008), 430.

Rashi,[59] commenting on B. T. *Sanhedrin* 72b, in fact takes this second position:

Until the fetus has been born, he is not a *nefesh* (person), and you can kill him to save the mother, but once his head has emerged one may not touch him, because it is as if he has been born, and one does not put aside one person for another.

Irshai prefers the second position, which is consistent with her thesis that the fetus is not a person. However, she neglects to identify the first position with the most important medieval decisor, Maimonides,[60] who states:

If a pregnant women is having difficulty giving birth, one may dismember the fetus in the womb with a medication or by hand, because he is like a *rodef* [a pursuer] trying to kill her, but if the head has emerged, one does not touch him, because one does not put aside one life for another, and this is the way of the world. (Mishneh Torah, *Hilkhot Rotzeaḥ* 1:9)

Maimonides apparently felt that the reason why the abortion is allowed is that the fetus is considered a *rodef*—which would only apply in a situation of positive danger to the mother's life. The authoritative *Shulchan Aruch*[61] (*Choshen Mishpat* 425:2) follows Maimonides's ruling, quoting it almost verbatim. . . .

It is hard to imagine writing a contemporary essay on the halakhic approach toward abortion without an extensive discussion of the revolutionary work of the twentieth-century Israeli authority R. Eliezer Waldenberg.[62] His courageous opinions relating to abortion helped solve many seemingly intractable personal dilemmas and brought him disdain in parts of the rabbinic world. R. Waldenberg felt strongly that the fetus is not considered a "person." Following in Emden's[63] footsteps, he held that an abortion could be performed solely for reason of maternal need, in particular, in the case of a pregnancy resulting from illicit relations (Resp. *Tzitz Eliezer*, IX, 51:3).

The advent of new technologies in the twentieth century raised new halakhic issues relating to abortion. Physicians now have the ability to diagnose severe

---

59. [Rashi, an acronym for Rabbi Shmuel Yitzchaki (1040–1105), was a French rabbi and the foremost commentator on the Bible and Talmud.]

60. [Maimonides, or Rabbi Moshe ben Maimon (1138–1204), was a prominent philosopher and jurist based in Egypt who codified Jewish law.]

61. [*The Shulchan Aruch* is a code of Jewish law written by Rabbi Joseph Karo (1488–1575).]

62. [Rabbi Eliezer Waldenberg (1915–2006) was a halakhic authority who lived in Jerusalem and ruled on many questions about medicine.]

63. [Rabbi Jacob Emden (1696–1776) was a halakhic authority in Germany.]

genetic conditions such as Tay-Sachs disease in utero, facing modern rabbinical authorities with the dilemma of whether to permit elective abortions in such cases. R. Feinstein[64] was strongly opposed, but R. Waldenberg felt differently. In a case of Tay-Sachs, he responded:

> Is there a greater case of pain and suffering than what will be caused to the mother in giving birth to this child, which everyone says will suffer and surely die within a few years? . . . And add to this the pain and suffering that the child will experience. And therefore, if there is a situation where the halakha permits abortion for reasons of pain and suffering and great need, then this should be a classic case for allowing it. And it makes no difference whether the suffering is physical or emotional, because in many instances emotional suffering is greater than physical suffering. (Resp. *Tzitz Eliezer*, XIII, 102:1)

The primary focus here is the needs of the mother, be they physical or emotional. On these grounds, he allows a late-term abortion, in the seventh month of pregnancy, for a fetus with Tay-Sachs.

Waldenberg was subsequently asked about the permissibility of abortion for a fetus with Down syndrome—a much more difficult question, because of the uncertain prognosis of such children and the varied ability of families to cope with them. He was hesitant about giving a general dispensation in this regard, but instead instructed the couple to talk to their own rabbi, who would be better able to assess their ability to cope with the child. However, he noted that there is room to allow abortion in selected cases, because the birth of a child with Down syndrome has the potential to "to destroy the psychological well-being of the wife and husband and also to put them at risk for a serious or not-serious illness and also to destroy their way of life" (Resp. *Tzitz Eliezer*, XIV, 101:2). . . .

Irshai points out that, according to Jewish law, only men and not women are included in the biblical obligation to procreate. She continues:

> In practice, however, women are "captives" of cultural assumptions that take a dim view of their remaining single; they are subjected to their husbands for the purpose of procreation; and, consequently, they are hampered in the use of contraception; moreover, their presence as subjects is scarcely considered in the case of abortion . . .[65]

---

64. [Rabbi Moshe Feinstein (1895–1986) was a prominent Orthodox rabbi and halakhic authority in the United States.]

65. Irshai, "Gender Perspectives," 446–447.

By contrast, I have endeavored to show that, for many distinguished halakhic authorities, the woman's needs are central to the halakhic discussion. Indeed, according to R. Waldenberg, the fact that she is not obligated to procreate does "free" her to take control of her body and, in certain instances, to have an abortion if she so wishes.

As noted above, Irshai begins her essay by claiming that ideology has played a central role in the restrictive attitude of many authorities toward abortion. However, many modern authorities in fact take a very liberal approach toward abortion, allowing even late-term abortions in cases of maternal need. As for those who do take a more restrictive view, there are certainly Talmudic and medieval sources to support this approach. . . .

I do think there is a need in the halakhic discourse for feminine voices, which, as D. S. Davis has pointed out, are sorely missing. However, for many serious halakhic authorities, the needs of the woman are of the utmost concern in halakhic decision-making relating to the difficult question of abortion. I believe their attitudes are consistent with modern feminist thinking regarding the setting of priorities in this highly charged debate.

RONIT IRSHAI

Response to Alan Jotkowitz

Ronit Irshai (b. 1965) is a professor of gender studies at Bar Ilan University. Her scholarship brings a feminist perspective to discussions of reproduction, fertility, and sexuality in Jewish law. Her most recent book, together with Tanya Zion-Waldoks, is Holy Rebellion: Religious Feminism and the Transformation of Judaism and Women's Rights in Israel *(Waltham: Brandeis University Press, 2024).*

From "Response to Alan Jotkowitz," Nashim: A Journal of Jewish Women's Studies and Gender Issues 21 (Spring 2011): 110–13.

I wish to relate to several important points noted by Dr. Jotkowitz and clarify them more fully.

In my opinion, the most plausible reading of the rabbinic sources indicates that a fetus does not have the status of a person under Jewish law. This is the view that emerges from the second option I outlined for understanding Mishnah *Ohalot* 7:6 (regarding a fetus whose birth threatens the mother's life), which

I believe is preferable, in that it accords both with the pericope in B. T. *Arakhin* 7a (about the execution of a pregnant woman) and with a long series of interpretations by both earlier and later halakhic authorities. Even Maimonides's analogy of the fetus to a "pursuer," in the case of a threat to the mother's life, does not, I believe, necessitate attributing personhood to it, and this understanding is supported by the majority of those authorities. A very small number of later authorities ... adopt the more stringent interpretation of Maimonides's position, according to which an abortion may be performed *only* in the case of a threat to the mother's life. However, the dominant position, throughout the ages has been the lenient one, according to which the fetus is not a person, and there is consequently no sweeping biblical ban against abortion.

There has been somewhat of a reversal of this trend in the twentieth century, with an escalating tendency to adopt the stringent approach and to view the prohibition of abortion as being directly ordained by the Torah. Of course, this has implications for the situations in which abortions are permitted, but my argument goes beyond that. In the last generation, halakhic decisors have become increasingly aware of issues relating to fetal abnormalities. Their permission to abort in such cases, and in cases of danger to the woman's health, is based on the determination that the fetus is not a person. One might think that this determination would justify abortion on other grounds as well, but, at least in published decisions (as opposed to oral responses given in individual cases), this has not been the case. For example, R. Moshe Tzuriel[66] writes:

> It is clear that it is not permitted to abort a healthy fetus when there is no danger to the mother's life. Any other justification for abortion—financial considerations, a wish not to hinder the woman's "career" or to preserve an attractive appearance, crowded living conditions, etc.—is unacceptable. In this article we are concerned only with the abortion of a fetus known in advance to have a serious mental or physical defect.[67]

R. Tzuriel goes on to present a very lenient position, stating that the fetus does not have the status of a person and quoting a series of halakhic decisors who permit abortion even when there is no danger to the mother.

I maintain that if the fetus is not a person, it is implausible, at least analyti-

---

66. [Rabbi Moshe Tzuriel is an Orthodox rabbi who teaches in Israel.]

67. Moshe Tzuriel, "Aborting a Fetus Diagnosed with a Serious Defect," *Tehumin* 25 (2005): 64–78.

cally, to differentiate in principle between abortion on the grounds of physical or mental defects, and abortion on the basis of needs not connected to the fetus itself. What is the categorical difference between the two cases? One possible response is that there is some guiding principle by which abortions that go against the value of "the sanctity of human life" may be distinguished from those that do not. But is that value really more challenged by the abortion of a fetus whose birth might harm the mother's dignity or life plan than by that of a defective fetus? And what about the value of preserving a woman's esteem and ability to manage her life in a way that conforms to her intellectual, professional and emotional needs? . . .

To conclude, my arguments relating to halakhic attitudes on abortion may be summarized as follows:

1. The most plausible reading of the rabbinic sources and the generations of halakhic literature deriving from them is that a fetus does not have the status of a person. . . .

2. The increasing tendency of a majority of the greatest twentieth-century halakhic decisors to view the fetus as a person does not follow necessarily from the previous strata of halakhic literature, and it has clear gender implications.

3. Even those decisors who believe that abortion is prohibited on rabbinic rather than biblical grounds discuss it mainly either "from the perspective of the fetus" and the possibility of serious defects or illnesses, or in reference to threats to the woman's health. My argument against this position is two-pronged: (a) If the fetus is not a person and can be aborted if it is defective, then why should this not be allowed in the case of a woman claiming that she cannot raise the child? Why should this determination of the fetus's status work in only one direction? (b) Acknowledging only the woman's bodily needs—that is, her physical and mental health—detracts from her dignity, in that she is not recognized as a subject, a whole person with needs, interests, aspirations, and desires going beyond her reproductive function.

Aging/Ends of Life

There are at least two inescapable features of the human condition: humans age and humans die. These facts often induce complex emotions and psychological responses from denial to curiosity, rationalizations, theodicies, and theologies. These, in turn, have inspired a litany of behaviors, including liturgies, rituals, habits, and biomedical interventions that hasten or forestall the inevitable. And just as our human desires, fears, and uncertainties shape our actions, so too our experiences can shape our understanding of aging and dying. Either way, there is a deep connection between reasoning about aging and dying, and doing something about them.

Of course, Judaism embraces no particular way to think about aging and dying. Nor does the tradition, broadly construed, advocate a singular way to behave regarding them. That said, certain attitudes and rituals have become hallmarks of Jewish orientations toward the life span and its cessation. The tradition includes stories and commandments regarding the importance of honoring the aged, caring intently for the dying, respecting corpses, and providing succor and structure for mourners. Such foundations, though, are not without controversy. What does "honor" mean? What does "caring for the dying" entail? Who qualifies as "the dying"? When, exactly, does a person become a corpse, and what may or may not be done to them? The selections in this section reflect recent shifts on these issues in secular and Jewish thought and law. (For another consideration of these questions, see Louis Newman's essay in part 1, section 1.)

The earliest of these selections is by Byron Sherwin, whose 1974 article offers a survey of "Jewish Views on Euthanasia." In general, euthanasia encompasses a wide range of biomedical interventions that bring about a patient's demise sooner than otherwise. This can include a range of activities, from withholding of measures (e.g., not providing life-sustaining mechanisms or treatments like CPR) to withdrawal (e.g., removing a patient from already applied life-sustaining mechanisms); from supplying (e.g., providing a patient means to end their life) to applying (e.g., directly applying those means to a patient). Sherwin structures his essay so that it concludes with a clear summary of Jewish positions—some of which were and continue to be controversial. While those positions are important to consider, it is how he reached those positions that intrigues us here. Sherwin's overall method is philosophical, specifically epistemological. He asserts that moral judgments (like whether one may hasten another's death) are intelligible only within frames of reference that are assumed to be true. Whether a frame, like "Jewish," is authentic thus becomes a contested matter and needs to be clarified. Sherwin thus first defines and defends his frame so that he can ultimately make claims about euthanasia.

Ruth Langer's 1998 chapter, "Honor Your Father and Mother: Care Giving as a Halakhic Responsibility," examines filial responsibilities of adult children to parents, an otherwise rare set of duties in premodern medicine societies when people did not live very long. Because humans today tend to live longer than previous generations, Langer integrates gerontology into her halakhic analysis to provide a more nuanced understanding of these obligations. This methodological approach illustrates both the relevance Jewish sources have to the current human condition and, conversely, the relevance contemporary science has for thinking about Jewish life, values, and duties.

Jonathan K. Crane's 2013 monograph, *Narratives and Jewish Bioethics*, delves deeply into a classical narrative often employed by ethicists considering the ethics of euthanasia: the Talmudic story of R. Chananya ben Teradyon being burned alive by the Romans (B. T. *Avodah Zarah* 18a). He offers a narrative approach in which authors, texts, audiences, and their interrelationships are closely examined. Crane shows the myriad ways contemporary bioethical authors contort that central story to both support their position vis-à-vis euthanasia and persuade their imagined audiences that theirs is the right way to read that story. That original story, however, is more complicated than many bioethicists would have us believe: it articulates ambiguity and ambivalence more than clarity and certainty. How one reads (about aging and dying) is thus itself an ethical enterprise.

In his 2016 essay, "Can a *Goses* Survive for More Than Three Days? The History and Definition of the *Goses*," Jeffrey L. Rubenstein investigates the source of influential Orthodox ethicist J. David Bleich's claim that the term *goses* refers to an individual who will die within three days. Using what could be termed an archeological approach, Rubenstein sifts through layers of classic rabbinic literature to raise up for close examination different conceptualizations of the term. What he finds is that a strict three-day time horizon is a medieval innovation, a minority opinion, and highly contested. By the essay's end, Rubenstein reflects on the importance and dangers of narrowly defining biomedical terms, especially those that pertain to end of life issues.

BYRON SHERWIN

Jewish Views on Euthanasia

Byron Sherwin (1946–2015) served for several decades as a scholar of Jewish theology, mysticism, and ethics at the Spertus Institute in Chicago. In addition to being a Conservative rabbi, he earned a PhD in the history of culture at Columbia University. His diverse scholarship includes works on the golem, interreligious issues, and Polish Jewry.

From "Jewish Views on Euthanasia," *The Humanist* 34, no. 4 (1974): 19–21.

Many contemporary philosophers assume that moral judgments cannot be rationally or objectively justifiable, that there is no final truth in ethics any more than in physics. A similar claim was made by the medieval Jewish philosopher, Moses Maimonides, in the twelfth century. He rejected the theoretical possibility and therefore the actual attempts of ancient and medieval philosophers to create a rational morality, to find in reason the grounds of obligation and the content of duty. Maimonides taught that morality cannot be derived from reason, that moral statements are neither true nor false.

Once one accepts the assumption that moral statements in themselves are bereft of truth value, one may choose the nihilistic alternative of moral chaos or one may see a frame of reference within which to posit moral statements. In the latter alternative, the frame of reference serves as the basis for evaluating the truth value of the given statement. "Truth" becomes relative to the chosen framework. One commits oneself to the basic assumptions upon which the framework rests. These assumptions are *believed* but not *known* to be true, nor *can* they be known to be true. One makes one's moral decisions *as if* the assumptions upon which his frame of reference rests are true....

The authenticity of a given position or the "meaningfulness" of a given term within Jewish ethics is determinable by whether or not there is precedent for that position within the classical texts of Judaica, by whether the terms used to express that position are operative and meaningful within the framework of normative Judaism. From this it would follow that a view of euthanasia held by an individual Jew or even by many Jews need not necessarily be one that is relevant to or representative of Jewish ethics as presently construed. Such a view may be "moral" and "meaningful" within a framework other than that of Jewish ethics, but unless it can claim authenticity on grounds of its consistency with precedent, the views of a single Jew or of many Jews on euthanasia remain irrelevant to the position of Jewish ethics on euthanasia.

It should be further noted that a characteristic of Jewish ethics or of the ethics of Judaism is to translate, whenever possible, abstract moral generalizations into particular legal obligations. Jewish ethics most clearly articulates itself in Jewish law. Therefore, to determine Judaism's position on euthanasia, one ought to consult Jewish legal literature.

Finally, one must remember that questions and terms often used in articulating a position on euthanasia in other frameworks may be irrelevant in Jewish ethics. Similarly, assumptions made and terms used within the framework of Jewish ethics may be irrelevant and meaningless in other frameworks. One such term, for example, crucial to discussions of euthanasia in Anglo-American legal and philosophical literature, has little or no operative meaning in Jewish ethics. The term "right" is not operative or meaningful in the framework of Jewish ethical or Jewish legal discourse. The question of whether or not an individual has the right to die is meaningless. In classical Hebrew, there is no term for "rights" as it is used in Anglo-American moral-legal terminology. The notion of rights in British and American jurisprudence is based upon historical and political circumstances that are peculiar to them but that remained irrelevant to developments in Jewish moral-legal literature.

Anglo-American jurisprudence, it may be claimed, revolves around questions of rights: What are my rights? What happens when there is a conflict of rights? Does A have the right to do X? Under what circumstances, if any, may B infringe upon my rights? What are C's penalties for infringing upon B's rights? And so on. Jewish law, on the other hand, revolves around the principle of religio-moral-legal obligation rather than the principle of rights. The basic question in Jewish law is not "What are my rights?" but "What are my obligations toward person A or in situation X?" ...

The problem of euthanasia, as all problems in Jewish law, may be properly articulated by asking, "What is person A obliged to do in situation X?" With specific regard to euthanasia, the following questions may be asked: What is an individual dying of a terminal disease obliged to do? What is he permitted to do? What is a physician treating a terminal patient obliged to do? What is he permitted to do? If the life of a terminal patient is ended by the patient himself or by someone else, is the killer a murderer? Are one's obligations different toward a terminal patient being kept alive artificially than they are toward one not being kept alive artificially? Is there any permissible alternative to euthanasia or death for the terminal patient? ...

According to Jewish law, "a dying man is regarded as a living person in all respects." Active euthanasia—causing or accelerating his death in any way—is considered murder. Maimonides, in his classical legal code [M.T. *Avel* 4.5], wrote: "One who is in a dying condition is regarded as a living person in all respects.... He who touches him (thereby causing him to expire) is guilty of shedding blood. To what may he be compared? To a flickering flame, which is extinguished as soon as one touches it." According to another medieval source, even if the patient himself asks to be put out of his agony, one is forbidden to comply with his wishes. "If one suffers great agony and he says to another, 'You see I shall not live; kill me for I am unable to withstand this affliction,' one is enjoined not to touch the patient" (*Sefer Hasidim*, eds. J. Wistinetzki and J. Freiman [Frankfurt am Main: Wahrmann, 1924]). The physician is especially enjoined from practicing euthanasia, even at the patient's request. Though he is exempt from criminal charges for unpremeditated murder, the physician who intentionally terminates the death of his patient may be criminally liable.

According to a later source, "Even if one has been dying for a long time, which causes agony to the patient and his family, it is still forbidden to accelerate his death" (Solomon Gunzfried, *Code of Jewish Law* [New York: Hebrew Publishing Co., 1927]). Just as active involuntary euthanasia is generally forbidden in Jewish law, so is active voluntary euthanasia forbidden. A medieval text, for example, states, "Even when great suffering is visited upon an individual and he knows he will not survive very long, he is prohibited from killing himself" (*Book of the Pious*). The following Talmudic source is used by this and other later sources as a precedent in this regard: "The Romans took hold of Rabbi Hanania b. Teradion, wrapped him in a Torah scroll, placed bundles of branches around him, and set them on fire. They then brought tufts of wool, which they had soaked in water, and placed them over his heart, so that he should not expire quickly. 'Open your mouth so that the fire may enter you and end your agony,' urged his students. The rabbi replied, 'No! Let only Him who gave me my life take it away. But no man should injure himself!'" [B.T. *Avodah Zarah* 18a]

According to Jewish law, life is to be preserved, even at great cost. Each moment of human life is considered intrinsically sacred. Preserving life supersedes living the "good life." The sacredness of life and the uniqueness of the individual require every possible action to be taken to preserve life. Expressing this notion, for example, one text insists upon the rescue of an individual buried under a fallen building (*Shulchan Aruch, Orah Hayyim*). "Even if they find him so crushed he can live only for a short time, they continue to dig." According to a commentary on this passage, if the building fell on the Sabbath, one is *required* to violate the Sabbath even if it means granting him only "momentary life." Though active euthanasia is forbidden, passive euthanasia, in certain circumstances, is permitted by Jewish law. One is permitted, but not obliged, to remove any artificial means keeping a terminal patient alive because such activity is not considered a positive action (*Yoreh Deah*).

In the conclusion of the Talmudic account of the martyrdom of Hanania b. Teradion, the Roman executioner asks the rabbi whether he may remove the tufts of wool from over his heart that artificially prolong his life. The rabbi agrees to this and expires. Later sources interpret his actions as being nonsupportive of voluntary active euthanasia (that is, opening his mouth to let the fire enter) but supportive of voluntary and involuntary passive euthanasia (that is, removing the tufts of wool) (*Avodah Zara*). In other words, though prolonging natural life is always obligatory, artificially prolonging the life of a terminal patient is optional. One medieval source even goes so far as to prohibit any action that may prevent the patient's quick death and artificially lengthen his agony (*Book of the Pious*).

While a physician is enjoined not to actively cause a terminal patient's death, at least according to one Talmudic view, he is not obliged to tend the patient's illness (though he may reduce pain), thus providing the possibility for a quicker, easier death.[68]

One may argue the possibility of active euthanasia in Jewish law by combining related precedent with a form of argument characteristic of Jewish legal discourse. The relevant precedent is the only Talmudic text in which the term "euthanasia"—"an easy, good, or quick death"—occurs (Hebrew: *mitah yafa*). The form of argument is the inference *a fortiori* (Hebrew: *qal va-homer*, literally "the light and the weighty"). An example of this form of inference would be: "Here is a teetotaler who does not touch cider; he will certainly refuse whiskey." The acceptability of applying this form of argument in Jewish legal discourse is stated in the Talmud (*Niddah* 19b).

On the basis of this discussion, it should be evident that the overwhelming consensus of the majority of Jewish religio-moral-legal literature on euthanasia

---

68. The problem, as expressed in classical literature, revolves around the question of whether the practice of medicine is by divine command (*mitzvah*) or by permission (*reshuth*).

is that active voluntary or involuntary euthanasia is prohibited and passive voluntary or involuntary euthanasia is permitted but by no means obligatory....

A final issue that bears discussion is whether active euthanasia, in any form, may be justifiable within the framework of Jewish law. If justifiable, such a view might be construed as a "minority opinion," since it challenges the weight of tradition and precedent. But Jewish law, like American constitutional law, makes provision for minority dissent within its broader framework. If legitimate and "valid" within the framework of a legal system, today's minority view may serve as tomorrow's majority view.

The term *mitah yafa* is used in the course of Talmudic discussion concerning the execution of criminals convicted of capital offenses. In one text, the verse "You should love your neighbor as yourself" (Lev. 19:18) is interpreted to mean that the criminal is to be given a *mita yafa*; the pain usually inflicted by the variety of death sentence is to be reduced both in time and degree of affliction (*Sanhedrin* 45a, 52a). At this point, one may argue either (1) from one comparable case to another or (2) from the "weighty" to the "lighter" case.

> 1. The terminal patient is compared by the Talmud to a criminal condemned to the death penalty, in that his case is hopeless (*Arakhin* 6b). From this equation one might argue that the terminal patient ought to be given at least the same consideration as a criminal about to be executed for having committed a capital offense.
>
> 2. One may also argue that if a criminal, guilty of having committed a capital offense, is shown such consideration, how much more so should one innocent of any capital offense, one who is terminally ill.

Not only may one make a case for active euthanasia in Jewish law, one may also argue that in certain circumstances the killer is not to be considered a murderer. In order to consider an act as murder, according to Jewish law, two conditions must be satisfied: premeditation and malice (see Exod. 21:14). Rabbinic literature specifically exonerates a physician who kills his patient, even if he acted with willfulness, when malice is not also present. Though the medieval codes link premeditation with malice, there is no logical or psychological reason to do so. The rabbinic precedent may stand on its own. Thus under certain circumstances, according to this "minority" view, the physician may be legally (but not necessarily morally) blameless for practicing active euthanasia.

RUTH LANGER

Honor Your Father and Mother: Caregiving as an Halakhic Responsibility

Ruth Langer (b. 1960) is a professor of Jewish studies at Boston College. She earned both her rabbinic ordination and PhD in Jewish liturgy at Hebrew Union College. An expert on Jewish liturgy and Jewish-Christian relations, she focuses her scholarship on changes in liturgical ideas and practices throughout the ages.

From "Honor Your Father and Mother: Caregiving as an Halakhic Responsibility," in *Aging and the Aged in Jewish Law: Essays and Responsa* (Pittsburgh: Freehof Institute for Progressive Halakhah, 1998), 21–41. Reprinted in *That You May Live Long: Caring for Our Aging Parents, Caring for Ourselves*, eds. Richard F. Address and Hara E. Person (New York: UAHC Press, 2003), 113–26, 184–87.

A striking feature of the rabbinic discussions of this mitzvah is the absence of a pronouncement specific to young children's relationships with their parents and, conversely, the relatively detailed attention to situations that pertain more readily to adult children and their elders. We never outgrow the obligation to honor our parents; indeed, the obligation grows more significant as we and our parents age.[69]

The halakhic tradition recognizes that one of the most intense and difficult phases of the child-parent relationship is often toward the end of the parent's life. Age generates physical and mental debilities that create dependency, often accompanied by personality changes that threaten to undermine the familial relationship. But the rabbinic discussions took place at a time when reaching old

---

69. This is not likely to be a result of any lack of awareness of growth in the relationship as a child moves from the total dependency of infancy to the independence of adulthood; the discussion of the Babylon Talmud follows directly on a discussion of parental obligations to their young children (B. T. *Kiddushin* 31b–32a).

This emphasis of the halakhic corpus on the relationship between adult children and their parents is revealed only when one traces the actual discussions of this issue in the major collections of the responsa literature. The largest group of discussions by far in the more recent responsa deal with the question of how to continue honoring one's parents after they have passed away. They indicate that adults are asking the halakhic questions; that honoring their parents has been a significant expression of their religiosity, built up over a lifetime relationship; and that to discontinue the mitzvah because of death seems unnatural to them, deepening their sense of loss. This issue is particularly important for children who have lost parents in the Holocaust.

age at all was rare, and extended chronic illness was relatively uncommon. In our day, when medical advances and longer life spans have dramatically increased the likelihood that any individual parent will spend an extended period in frail physical and mental health, the question of the halakhically required nuances of "honoring one's parents" needs to be reopened with much deeper attention paid to the repercussions of several aspects of the changed reality of our times. By juxtaposing the halakhic tradition and the results of contemporary gerontological research, we can reach new and deeper understandings of the halakhic tradition. These understandings can then help us formulate a late-twentieth-century statement about filial obligations to parents that is sensitive both to the beauties of the Jewish legal-ethical tradition and to the realities of modern life....

The Ten Commandments and Leviticus also use two different verbs, "honor" and "revere." These two verbs also appear in connection with commanded human relationships with God. This not only lends extreme gravity to the commanded relationship with parents, placing it among those commandments that have "no measure" (M. *Peah* 1:1), but also allows the rabbis to develop the details of this relationship by giving greater indication of their practical meaning. Proverbs 3:9 reads, "Honor God with your wealth." Honoring, then, is expressed materially; to honor parents refers to the provision of goods and, even more importantly, of services. The tannaitic tradition establishes that dutiful children express honor by ensuring food and drink, clothing and shelter, and by accompanying parents as they enter and leave. In other words, children have an obligation to tend to their parents' needs. A question we shall need to confront later is whether this demands direct caregiving or just indicates the provision of care.

Here the rabbinic traditions specifically indicate that the parent should pay for the substance of this care; and if the parent is destitute, any contribution from the child falls in the category of *tzedakah*, where in any case provision for one's own family takes priority. The implication of removing the financial element from the commandment to honor parents is primarily that children are not required to impoverish themselves to maintain their parents' accustomed standard of living....

Although these details are important and give substance and shape to the commandments, a few overarching points deserve special emphasis. Maimonides begins his discussion of our issue saying, "Honoring parents is an *important* positive commandment."[70] It is not merely ethically, socially, or naturally

---

70. Maimonides, *Hilkhot Mamrim* 6:1.

important; rather, the Torah's implied equation of relationships with parents and relationships with God elevates the mitzvah of honoring parents. Like every social relationship, but even more so, its implications are not solely in the human realm, but reflect primarily on one's fealty and obedience to God's command. Fulfillment of this commandment comes primarily, therefore, within the rabbinic system, out of an absolute obligation originating in God. The specifics of children's relationships with their parents, whether there is a bond of love or of social obligation based on services received from parents, is essentially irrelevant. Love and prior relationships are indeed a reason for honoring one's parents, but their absence by no means exempts children from the obligation to fulfill the commandment; fulfilling the commandment solely on the basis of love or personal human obligation does not raise it to its highest spiritual level. . . .

It follows, then, that the sentimental element of a parent-child relationship does not enter into the halakhic determinations of the child's responsibilities. Indeed, Jewish law explicitly acknowledges the difficulties and stresses of the parent-child relationship, both under "normal" circumstances and as exacerbated in situations of ill health.[71] It is exactly these challenges to the filial relationship that drive the halakhic system to elevate the commandment to honor parents to such an absolute, insisting that children's honor and respect for their parents must be as unconditional as their relationship with God. The gratitude expressed in filial piety is not a matter of exchange or of love on the earthly level. The emotional health of the parent-child relationship is secondary at best. Responsibility and obligation take precedence and ensure that the needs of the elderly are appropriately met.

Having established the absolute and elevated nature of the filial obligation to honor and respect parents, we need now consider some details of the relationship and, particularly, to ask if it has limits, too. Significant contemporary research on caregiving families looks to understand, measure, and alleviate the stress created when a family must bring into its midst or take responsibility for a now physically or mentally debilitated parent. Although having a dependent, elderly parent has become a normative experience, it is one that exceeds the capacities of many families to cope. This can be attributed to many factors, most

---

71. Exemplified most dramatically in the statement of Rabbi Yohanan, who was orphaned from birth, "Happy is the person who has no parents," to which Rashi comments, "For it is impossible to honor them to the degree necessary, and one is consequently punished because of them" (B. T. *Kiddushin* 31b).

significantly demographic shifts: there are more elderly because people are living longer, but there are fewer caregivers because of declining birth rates. This has increased the odds that children will need to become caregivers and that the caregivers themselves will be older. In addition, death now more often follows chronic, long-term illness, increasing the time span for which caregiving is required. Consequently, "adult children provide more care and more difficult care to more parents over much longer periods of time than they did in the good old days."[72] ...

The rabbinic discussions on this issue were obviously written before the modern demographic shift that so changed the incidence of caregiving. In light of this, it is surprising how little contemporary discussion there is of questions of filial responsibility for extended caregiving, especially in cases like Alzheimer's disease, where the personality changes are so marked, or even in less severe situations where the normal, nonpathological intensification of personality traits in old age can reactivate the childhood love-hate relationship with the parent, making operation under the rabbinic guidelines for honor and reverence difficult. Most modern authorities simply assume that the halakha developed for short-term caregiving applies directly and obviously to contemporary demographics. The parameters set out by the traditional rabbinic discussions are clear. Even if the parent is mentally disabled to an extent that causes the child distress, the child must assiduously preserve a stance of reverence and honor to the parent. ...

Maimonides's interpretation, with which not all sages agreed, but which became mainstream halakha, particularly with Joseph Caro's[73] explicit acceptance of it in his *Beit Yosef* and *Shulchan Aruch*,[74] is that filial obligations to honor and revere parents are an absolute that must be upheld under the most difficult of circumstances. Yet, because Rav Assi is not criticized for leaving his mother,[75] this must be seen as a precedent. He did try to honor her wishes, but she pushed him too far. When that point is reached, it is perfectly appropriate, according to Jewish law, for the child to leave the parent so that the relationship will not deteriorate and the child will not be forced into actions lacking honor and reverence. Maimonides adds a significant point. The child is not free simply to abandon

72. Elaine M. Brody, "Parent Care as a Normative Family Stress," *The Gerontologist* 25 (1985): 21.
73. [See part 4, section 19, footnote 9.]
74. Maimonides, *Yoreh Deah* 240:10.
75. [This is in reference to a story found at B. T. *Kiddushin* 31b.]

the parent. Rather, the child must specifically delegate the care of the parent to others. In arranging this care, the child's serious responsibility is to ensure that these others will treat the debilitated parent appropriately.

Turning to a nursing home placement, in-home nursing services, or some part-time arrangement that relieves the child of full-time caregiving is thus fully appropriate under Jewish law when the child's attempts to provide care will result only in a deterioration of the relationship, causing the child to manifest a lack of honor or reverence to the parent. The point at which this occurs will obviously vary from case to case, and each decision must be reached individually.

JONATHAN K. CRANE
Narratives and Jewish Bioethics

Jonathan K. Crane (b. 1973) received ordination from Hebrew Union College and a PhD from the University of Toronto. He serves as a scholar of bioethics and Jewish thought at Emory University's Center for Ethics. He works broadly in Jewish ethics, bioethics, comparative religious ethics, food ethics, animal ethics, environmental ethics, and narrative ethics. A past president of the Society of Jewish Ethics, he founded and co-edits the Journal of Jewish Ethics.

From *Narratives and Jewish Bioethics* (New York: Palgrave Macmillan, 2013), 19–21, 149–50.

Chapter 2: Narratives, Norms, and Deadly Complications

Details matter. Discerning which details are significant—and why—is our constant challenge as readers of life and of texts.

For this reason it is important for readers of stories to justify their reading strategies. Readers of stories need to make transparent how and why they do or do not attend to certain details of a narrative and not others, or why they disparage narratives altogether. This is part and parcel of the process of clarifying one's hermeneutic or reading strategy.

Acknowledging that one indeed employs a hermeneutic—and we all do, whether we are conscious of it or not—when consuming and deploying stories in persuasive arguments such as bioethics, necessarily distinguishes three nodes or perspectives involved in ethical discourse. There is the author who reads a text, the narrative of the text the author is reading, and the audience to whom the author addresses her argument and reading of that specific text. These three

—author, text, audience—may never meet in person but they nonetheless interact in ethical and bioethical discourse. Narrative theorist James Phelan thus calls for greater care to be given to the "recursive relationships among authorial agency, textual phenomena, and reader response, to the way in which our attention to each of these elements both influences and can be influenced by the other two."[76] For how one reads a text is as much a factor to the bioethical argument as how one thinks of oneself and the nature of the audience one ultimately desires to influence, not to mention what that text is in itself. In regard to Jewish bioethics, we therefore need to question who bioethicists are and whence their authority; we should wonder what the text they cite actually says; and we should inquire how readers might respond to what authors say that text says. What happens, for example, if a bioethicist claims a text says something it does not? Where does that leave the reader? What does it say about the bioethicist? What does it do to the text? Who should protect a text's integrity? What kind of responsibility does an author have to an audience that does not have access to the original text? How should an audience respect and respond to an otherwise revered bioethicist who says the text says something it does not?

There are further questions complicating the interrelationships between author, audience, and text—especially when we take narrative texts seriously. In addition to justifying how they read a particular story, authors also need to defend why they look to that particular story at all. The story's relevance to the moral conundrum at hand may or may not be readily apparent. What about other stories—how does an author use them? Are they mentioned, alluded to, studied in depth, glossed over, or completely ignored? Why? Such questions pertain to the issue of canon, for when bioethicists turn to narratives A and B and not C they perforce construct the organic boundaries of which stories are to be considered relevant for certain bioethical conversations and which should not be so involved. But consumers of a bioethical discourse need to be wary of such canons; perhaps narrative B has little to say about a particular topic despite what bioethicists insist otherwise, and story C really should be considered but hitherto has been ignored. This realization provokes meta-narrative questions that need addressing: if multiple stories are relevant to a particular issue, how are the decisions made that one of them or a select few are more salient than the others? By what criteria do authors privilege certain stories over others? And from

---

76. James Phelan, *Narrative as Rhetoric: Technique, Audiences, Ethics, Ideology* (Columbus: Ohio State University Press, 1996), 19.

where do those criteria come? And when the selected stories point to dramatically different conclusions—who decides which story should trump and thus provide normative guidance, and on what grounds is that decision made? . . .

Some authors embrace ambiguity and bring it forward into their normative bioethical arguments. Most, however, strip stories of their potential polysemy, cutting and reframing them so that only one interpretation or meaning emerges. They eliminate the "ways of looking" and say a story proffers but one way of conceiving a problem or its solution. This impulse to restructure stories so that they countenance singular conclusions paradoxically points to the fluidity narratives bring to normative discourse and the vague boundaries between what they might endorse and what they might proscribe. In brief, just as narratives themselves are composed of selected and interpreted events, readings of those narratives are also nothing but selections and interpretations; readings *are* narratives.

Such questions and caveats both complicate and make interesting the story of how narratives fit in modern Jewish bioethical discourse. Their role can be understood in light of a larger set of questions pertaining to the relationship between and role of narrative in Jewish law. This broader basket of concerns has long concerned Jews; indeed, it is as old as the rabbis. It is not our intention to rehearse the totality of this lengthy debate or to weigh in on it; rather, in the next section we restrain ourselves to highlight only some of the more salient features therein. We then turn our sights to modern Jewish bioethics and its troubled relationship with narratives. As will be shown, stories have long been incorporated in bioethical deliberation though they have not been treated very well. Indeed, most bioethicists appear to have the predilection to point to stories to support their positions on a specific moral issue. Few spend time or effort to plumb the stories for their descriptive richness or prescriptive diversity. Though this reading strategy is lamentable, it becomes potentially lethal when we consider modern Jewish bioethical deliberations regarding care at the end of life, specifically regarding euthanasia. For better and for worse, bioethicists writing on euthanasia read—or misread, as it will be shown—stories, especially a specific one, and in so doing they endanger not only patients already vulnerable to power asymmetries and ill health, but also families of those patients, their physicians, fellow clergy who may or may not be willing or able to disagree with the bioethicists, and others. Understanding how bioethicists read this story and make their normative recommendations is thus a lethally relevant task the urgency of which is all the more pressing with the growing number of people involved with their own or others' dying processes. . . .

When considering the story of Chananya ben Teradyon's fiery end,[77] there are [several] possible ways to connect it with the moral morass that is euthanasia. It can be ignored altogether since we presume it—and any other ancient text, for that matter—cannot have any relevance. Its moral weight being nil, we are left free to render our decisions without it informing us one way or another. ... [Another] approach—autonomy—leaves it to the individual modern Jew to decide the moral weight of this story. Whatever attraction this approach may garner, it does little to build cohesiveness through a community, for I could argue that the story is extremely morally relevant while you could hold otherwise. I would hold that because Chananya endorses intervention in the end euthanasia is therefore palatable, and you would argue against this because you think the story only illustrates the anxiety rabbis held toward intervention, and you'd rather rely upon another story or other laws that appear more relevant to you. Depth theology[78] corrects for the atomism of autonomy since it requires communities—lay and professionals together—to discern and decide a story's relevance to a modern conundrum. Yet balancing authority within this communal deliberation remains a procedural stumbling block, often distracting from the urgency of the situation. We may all agree that Chananya's story is relevant, but we disagree as to how it should be interpreted and by whom—and so we turn our attention to these procedural issues instead of those substantive ones regarding a dying loved one at hand....

Since archetypal stories often obscure subsequent ones, we should be wary, Childress[79] advises, of invoking just any story when we write bioethical tracts. This is because any narrative perforce frames how problems will be perceived, constrains ethical reflection thereon, and indicates ways to resolve those problems. As Cover[80] notes, the selection of a story and its invocation in a normative argument is itself a norm-creating exercise. Instead of invoking a story seemingly arbitrarily, bioethicists must reflect upon and make explicit why they turn to a particular narrative at all and not another. Only then would their interpretation of it gain its normative force in a non-question-begging manner.

77. [This refers to the execution of Rabbi Chananya ben Teradyon. The most popular version of the story is found in B. T. *Avodah Zarah* 18a.]

78. [Depth theology was coined by Rabbi Abraham Joshua Heschel in his essay by this title for *Cross Currents* 10, no. 4 (1960): 317–25.]

79. [James Childress is a professor emeritus of religious studies, ethics, and public policy at the University of Virginia.]

80. [For a selection by Robert Cover, see part 1, section 3.]

JEFFREY L. RUBENSTEIN

Can a *Goses* Survive for More Than Three Days? The History and Definition of the *Goses*

Jeffrey L. Rubenstein (b. 1964) is the Skirball Professor of Talmud at New York University. Holding both rabbinic ordination from the Jewish Theological Seminary and a PhD from Columbia University, he focuses on rabbinic literature, liturgy, and law, ranging from the Dead Sea Scrolls to the Talmud and beyond, with a special focus on stories and narratives.

From "Can a *Goses* Survive for More than Three Days? The History and Definition of the *Goses*," *Journal of Jewish Ethics* 2, no. 2 (2016): 1–37.

The definition of the *goses* is of considerable ethical significance because traditional Jewish sources that permit the withholding or withdrawal of medical treatment (sometimes called passive euthanasia) are, with a few exceptions, limited to the *goses*.[81] Medical treatment generally may not be withheld from individuals not in the condition of *gesisah*. However, advances in modern medical care increasingly make it possible to keep patients alive for extended periods of time and have led to a drastic narrowing of the category of the *goses* if defined in terms of three days. Jewish ethics accordingly would not allow for the withholding of medical care from many patients today who have no hope of recovery, who suffer terrible pain, or who have little or no mental function and quality of life—but who can be kept alive for three days. The awareness of alternative definitions of the *goses* would allow for the withholding or withdrawal of treatment in more cases when medical intervention is futile and serves only to prolong suffering. . . .

The term *goses* appears rarely in classical rabbinic literature, and no attempt is made to define the term precisely. From the contexts it is clear that the term refers to someone who will die soon or imminently—or at least is expected to die soon or imminently. Exactly how soon or how imminent is not addressed. . . .

The notion that a *goses* will die within three days is first attested in the Middle

81. Alan J. Weisbard, "On the Bioethics of Jewish Law: The Case of Karen Quinlan," *Israel Law Review* 14 (1979): 335; Steven H. Resnicoff, "Jewish Law Perspectives on Suicide and Physician Assisted Dying," *Journal of Law and Religion* 13 (1998–1999): 320; J. David Bleich, "Survey of Recent Halakhic Periodical Literature: Treatment of the Terminally Ill," *Tradition: A Journal of Orthodox Jewish Thought* 30, no. 3 (1996): 63: "The distinction between an active and a passive act, as drawn by those authorities, applies to a *goses* and to a *goses* only."

Ages and derives from a tradition attributed to Maharam of Rothenburg (Meir b. Baruch, 1215–1293). The tradition appears in *Sefer ha-Mordechai* of Mordechai b. Hillel (d. 1298), a student of Maharam:

> Once a certain woman was a four-day walk distant from her husband, and some Jews came and told her: "We left your husband *goses*." It was asked of our teacher Meir [b. Barukh] and he instructed her to mourn, since it is stated [in the Talmud *Gittin* 28a] ... "the majority of *gosesin* die." ... If so, in this case, most *gosesim* do not live two or three days.[82]

This tradition appears almost verbatim in the commentary of Asher b. Yehiel (Rosh, 1250–1328), who also studied with Maharam.[83] ... This tradition offers the first quantification of the maximum "life expectancy" of a *goses*, formulated as the presumption that a *goses* dies within three or four days for purposes of mourning. There would appear to be no source or justification for this time frame other than the common practice that developed out of medical experience in the early Middle Ages.

The version of the Maharam's ruling that gives the time as three days became the common tradition among medieval and early modern jurists, presumably because of the influence of the *Tur*.[84] It is codified by Joseph Caro in *Shulchan Aruch*,[85] Y. D. 339:2. ...

The first authority who seems to have defined explicitly the *goses* as one who cannot survive for three days was Joshua Falk (1555–1614)[86] in the *Perishah*, his commentary on the *Tur*: "This implies that it is the nature of *gesisah* to be three days."[87] ...

At all events, we no longer have a ruling specifically about the onset of mourning, potentially limited to this specific issue, but rather an autonomous definition of a *goses*. Note also Falk's formulation in terms of an abstract noun, *gesisah*, which does not appear in his sources. The implication of Falk's formulation, taken in and of itself, is that "no *gosesim* live" more than three days, an inference in tension with the traditions from which it ultimately derives. ...

82. Mordekhai b. Hillel, *Sefer ha-Mordekhai, Moed Qatan, Hilkhot Aveilut*, #864.
83. Asher b. Yehiel, commentary to bMQ, ch. 3, #97.
84. [The *Tur*, short for *Arba'ah Turim* (Four Rows), is a code of halakha composed by Yaakov ben Asher in thirteenth-century Spain.]
85. [See part 4, section 19, footnote 9.]
86. [Joshua Falk was a sixteenth-century Polish scholar and commentator of halakha.]
87. *Perishah* to *Tur*, Y. D. 339.5.

With the exception of Faivish,[88] all jurists, on the basis of the Maharam's ruling, simply grafted a three-day definition onto the Talmud's principle that "the majority of *gosesim* die," transforming it into the idea that "the majority of *gosesim* die within three days." But they still recognized that some *gosesim* live longer and even recover, as the Talmud implies. Only Faivish transformed the Maharam's ruling into an absolute principle that no *gosesim* survive more than three days, which is clearly inconsistent with the Talmud's overall view....

The appeal of the definition of the *goses* as one who will die within three days, no matter what, should be straightforward. It ostensibly provides an objective definition that can be quantified absolutely. It fits with trends in modern medicine, and in modern research in general, which emphasize numbers, statistics, data, and quantification. It avoids potential problems with alternative definitions that define the *goses* in terms of "the dying process" or the nature of his physical condition. These alternatives are imprecise, subjective, and liable to a "slippery slope." The "dying process" is a vague concept, and a judgment as to when a patient has begun that process is inherently subjective. Many patients beyond hope of recovery can nevertheless survive for a long time given our advanced medical technology, so to classify some of these patients as *gosesim* seems to smack of a slippery slope whereby a traditional category has been expanded radically with no clear limit. These are serious and legitimate concerns, and we are all aware of abuses whereby patients with low quality of life too quickly have been allowed to die, or to choose death, without efforts to mitigate the pain or explore other alternatives. With today's soaring costs of health care, there are also pressures to limit expenses for end of life care.

Bleich's concerns about such problems appear in occasional remarks against alternatives to his views. For example, in an article in *Sh'ma* magazine published in 1992, Bleich presents his three-day definition and then writes:

> It may be inferred from the writings of some contemporary writers that they do not deem the likelihood of survival for a three-day period to be incompatible with a condition of *gesisah*. Nevertheless it seems clear that even a severely debilitated, terminally ill patient who may linger for weeks or months cannot be deemed a *goses*. Yet one searches the writings of these authorities in vain for specification of a longevity that removes the patient from status of a *goses*.[89]

---

88. [Shmuel b. Uri Shraga Faivish was an eighteenth-century scholar and author of the *Beit Shmuel*, a commentary on Caro's *Shulchan Aruch*.]

89. J. David Bleich, "May One Refuse Medical Treatment?," *Sh'ma* (December 11, 1992), 19.

Here Bleich recognizes that some authorities rule that a *goses* can live longer than three days, but immediately rejects this view. The third sentence is the crux: if a *goses* is defined otherwise, there can be no "specification of longevity" beyond which a patient is not a *goses*. This, to Bleich, is unacceptable and ipso facto cause for rejecting such views, as they are too vague and subjective....

The point is that if one attempts to define *gesisah* in terms of physical symptoms, one might include patients who are not moribund or experiencing throes of death, and one might even include those whose condition can be reversed with modern medical technologies. In the Middle Ages, these patients presumably would have died imminently and could fairly be called *gosesim*. To apply that type of definition today, Bleich wants us to understand, is problematic.

These problems with alternative definitions are significant and require serious attention. Yet medicine is as much an art as a science, and medical judgments cannot always be reduced to numbers and quantities. A certain degree of vagueness, subjectivity, and danger of the slippery slope may be an inherent aspect of medicine in general, and end of life decisions in particular. Moreover, a rigid three-day definition has certain problems of its own. First, as noted in the introduction to this paper, it may unjustifiably restrict the category of *goses* and eliminate many cases where withholding or withdrawing medical treatment would appear to be the preferred course—cases where there is no hope of recovery, low quality of life, and a great deal of pain—simply because the patient can be kept alive for four days or a week or even more (I recognize there is a degree of circularity in this argument). Second, it is extremely difficult to judge when a patient will die "no matter what" within three days, such that a doctor or rabbi may judge that, apart from a few recognizable conditions, just about no patient can be considered a *goses*. This, in my opinion, becomes a kind of inverse slippery slope such that the category is almost eliminated from practical ethics. For fear that advances in medical technology deliver us to the Scylla of too expansive a category of the *goses*, Bleich may have consigned us to the Charybdis of one too narrow. Ironically, his strategy obviates the potential abuse of the category by almost defining it out of existence.

Acknowledgments

The work of this book began at the suggestion of Michael Marmur and David Ellenson, z"l, editors of a previous volume in this series, and we acknowledge with gratitude their thoughtful encouragement. This wide-ranging project was also made possible through the invaluable assistance of the following individuals, institutions, and organizations:

Sylvia Fuks Fried, Eugene Sheppard, David Briand, and the team at Brandeis University Press guided the project from its early stages to completion. We could not have done this work without their continuing enthusiasm and support for this project.

Portions of this in-progress project were presented at the Society of Jewish Ethics and the Tauber Institute Colloquium at Brandeis University, and we are grateful for the challenging questions and helpful suggestions we received from our colleagues.

Anna Coufal, a rabbinic intern at the Center for Jewish Ethics at the Reconstructionist Rabbinical College, was the consummate editorial assistant, organizing our materials, editing our writing, and raising probing questions about our choices throughout. Anna also served as a model reader, helping us to address the issues and information that students and teachers would be seeking from the volume. This work was supported by the Levin-Lieber Family Program in Jewish Ethics and the David A. Teutsch Fund for Ethical Leadership at the Reconstructionist Rabbinical College.

Support from Brandeis University and the Center for Ethics at Emory University allowed us to meet in person for an intensive work session at Emory. Work-study students at Emory's Center for Ethics—Annie Ye and Charlotte Weinstein—provided research assistance. Molly Paul, a rabbinic student at the Reconstructionist Rabbinical College, also provided research assistance.

We are especially indebted to David Ellenson, z"l, whose generosity of spirit, wisdom, encouragement, commitment to excellent scholarship, and personalized mentorship—and an appreciation of a good joke—were invaluable to us as we bent to this task. It is to David, beloved teacher, scholar, and friend, that we dedicate this volume.

Jonathan K. Crane
Emily Filler
Mira Beth Wasserman
August 2024

ACKNOWLEDGMENTS OF PREVIOUSLY PUBLISHED MATERIAL

Abrams, Judith Z. *Judaism and Disability: Portrayals in Ancient Texts from the Tanach through the Bavli*, 84–88, 152–53. Washington, DC: Gallaudet University Press, 1998. Reprinted by permission of Gallaudet University Press.

Adler, Rachel. *Engendering Judaism: An Inclusive Theology and Ethics*, 169–72, 174–76, 180–81, 190–96, 198–99. Boston: Beacon Press, 1998. Reprinted by permission of the University of Nebraska Press. Published by the Jewish Publication Society.

Alpert, Rebecca T. "Sometimes the Law Is Cruel: The Construction of a Jewish Antiabortion Position in the Writings of Immanuel Jakobovits." *Journal of Feminist Studies in Religion* 11, no. 2 (Fall 1995): 27–37. Reprinted by permission of the *Journal of Feminist Studies in Religion*.

Asch, Adrienne. "Recognizing Death while Affirming Life: Can End of Life Reform Uphold a Disabled Person's Interest in Continued Life?" In *Improving End of Life Care: Why Has It Been So Difficult?*, Hastings Center Report Special Report 35, no. 6 (2005): 31–36. Reprinted by permission of the Hastings Center.

Belser, Julia Watts. "Improv and the Angel: Disability Dance, Embodied Ethics, and Jewish Biblical Narrative." *Journal of Religious Ethics* 47, no. 3 (2019): 443–69. Reprinted by permission of the author.

Benjamin, Mara. *The Obligated Self: Maternal Subjectivity and Jewish Thought*, 23–32. Bloomington: Indiana University Press, 2018. Reprinted by permission of the author.

Berkowitz, Beth. *Execution and Invention: Death Penalty Discourse in Early Rabbinic and Christian Cultures*, 153–54, 159–65, 179. New York: Oxford University Press, 2006. Reprinted by permission of Oxford University Press, conveyed through PLSclear.

Berman, Nadav S. "Jewish Law, Techno-Ethics, and Autonomous Weapon Systems: Ethical-Halakhic Perspectives." In *Jewish Law Association Studies*, vol. 29, *The Impact of Technology, Science, and Knowledge*, edited by Elisha S. Ancselovits, Elliot N. Dorff, and Amos Israel-Vleeschhouwer, 91–124. Forest Hills, NY: Jewish Law Association, 2020. Reprinted by permission of *Jewish Law Association Studies*.

Borowitz, Eugene. *Renewing the Covenant: A Theology for the Postmodern Jew*, 214–17. New York: Jewish Publication Society, 1991. Reprinted by permission of the University of Nebraska Press. Published by the Jewish Publication Society.

Boyarin, Daniel. "Dialectics of Desire: 'The Evil Instinct Is Very Good.'" In *Carnal Israel: Reading Sex in Talmudic Culture*, 61–76. Berkeley: University of California Press, 1995. Reprinted by permission of the author.

Brody, Samuel. "Jewish Economic Ethics in the Neoliberal Era, 1980–2016." *Journal of Jewish Ethics* 7, nos. 1–2 (2021): 39–62. Reprinted by permission of Penn State University Press.

Broyde, Michael. "Just Wars, Just Battles, and Just Conduct in Jewish Law: Jewish Law Is Not a Suicide Pact!" In *War and Peace in the Jewish Tradition*, edited by Lawrence Schiffman and Joel B. Wolowelsky, 1–43. New York: Michael Scharf Publication Trust of the Yeshiva University Press, 2004. Reprinted by permission of the author.

Claussen, Geoffrey. "Musar in a White Supremacist Society: Arrogance, Self-Examination, and Systemic Change." In *No Time for Neutrality: American Rabbinic Voices from an Era of Upheaval*, edited by Michael Rose Knopf with Miriam Aniel, 352–68. Self-published, 2021. Reprinted by permission of the author.

Cohen, Aryeh. *Justice in the City: An Argument from the Sources of Rabbinic Judaism*, 8–14, 69–83. Boston: Academic Studies Press, 2012. Reprinted by permission of Academic Studies Press.

Cooper, Julie. "A Diasporic Critique of Diasporism: The Question of Jewish Political Agency." *Political Theory* 43, no. 1 (2015): 80–110. Reprinted by permission of *Political Theory*, conveyed through Copyright Clearance Center.

Cover, Robert. "Nomos and Narrative." *Harvard Law Review* 97 (1983): 4–68. Reprinted by permission of *Harvard Law Review*, conveyed through Copyright Clearance Center.

Crane, Jonathan K. *Narratives and Jewish Bioethics*, 19–21, 149–50. New York: Palgrave Macmillan, 2013. Reprinted by permission of Springer Nature.

Davis, Dena S. "Abortion in Jewish Thought: A Study in Casuistry." *Journal of the American Academy of Religion* 60, no. 2 (Summer 1992): 313–24. Reprinted by permission of the author.

Dorff, Elliot. *Love Your Neighbor and Yourself: A Jewish Approach to Modern Personal Ethics*, 15–19. Philadelphia: Jewish Publication Society, 2003. Reprinted by permission of the University of Nebraska Press. Published by the Jewish Publication Society.

Epstein-Levi, Rebecca J. "Person-Shaped Holes: Childfree Jews, Jewish Ethics, and Communal Continuity." *Journal of Religious Ethics* 49, no. 2 (2021): 226–44. Reprinted by permission of John Wiley & Sons, conveyed through PLSclear.

Freedman, Benjamin. *Duty and Healing: Foundations of a Jewish Bioethic*, 13, 31–33, 43–45, 48–49, 52–54. New York: Routledge, 1999. Reprinted by permission of Taylor & Francis, conveyed through PLSclear.

Gans, Chaim. *A Just Zionism: On the Morality of the Jewish State*, 111–12, 116, 121–22, 125–27, 129, 131–33, 137–38. New York: Oxford University Press, 2008. Reprinted by permission of Oxford University Press, conveyed through PLSclear.

Gavison, Ruth. "Reflections on the Meaning and Justification of 'Jewish' in the Expression 'A Jewish and Democratic State.'" In *The Israeli Nation-State: Political, Constitutional, and Cultural Challenges*, edited by Fania Oz-Salzberger and Yedidia Stern, 135–63. Boston: Academic Studies Press, 2014. Reprinted by permission of Academic Studies Press.

Gibbs, Robert. "Mending the Code." In *Jews and Genes: The Genetic Future in Contemporary Jewish Thought*, edited by Elliot N. Dorff and Laurie Zoloth, 342–74. Philadelphia: Jewish Publication Society, 2015. Reprinted by permission of the University of Nebraska Press. Published by the Jewish Publication Society.

Glauz-Todrank, Annalise E. "Jewish Critical Race Theory and Jewish 'Religionization' in Shaare Tefila Congregation v. Cobb." In *Judaism, Race, and Ethics: Conversations and Questions*, edited by Jonathan K. Crane, 191–216. University Park: Penn State University Press, 2020. Reprinted by permission of Penn State University Press.

Goldstone, Matthew. *The Dangerous Duty of Rebuke: Leviticus 19:17 in Early Jewish and Christian Interpretation*, 1–25. Leiden: Brill, 2018. Reprinted by permission of Brill, conveyed through Copyright Clearance Center.

Gordon, Lewis R. "Afro-Jewish Ethics?" In *Jewish Religious and Philosophical Ethics*, edited by Curtis Hutt, Halla Kim, and Berel Dov Lerner, 213–28. New York: Routledge, 2018. Reprinted by permission of Taylor & Francis, conveyed through PLSclear.

Gross, Aaron. *The Question of the Animal and Religion: Theoretical Stakes, Practical Implications*, 148–51, 184–89. New York: Columbia University Press, 2015. Reprinted by permission of the author.

Imhoff, Sarah. "Racial Standing: How American Jews Imagine Community, and Why That Matters." In *Judaism, Race, and Ethics: Conversations and Questions*, edited by Jonathan K. Crane, 217–36. University Park: Penn State University Press, 2020. Reprinted by permission of Penn State University Press.

Irshai, Ronit. "Response to Alan Jotkowitz." *Nashim: A Journal of Jewish Women's Studies and Gender Issues*, no. 21 (Spring 2011): 110–13. Reprinted by permission of Indiana University Press.

Jacobs, Jill. *There Shall Be No Needy: Pursuing Social Justice through Jewish Law and Tradition*, 10–12, 14, 16–22. Nashville: Jewish Lights, 2009. Reprinted by permission of the author and Turner Publishing.

Jotkowitz, Alan. "Abortion and Maternal Need: A Response to Ronit Irshai." *Nashim: A Journal of Jewish Women's Studies and Gender Issues*, no. 21 (Spring 2011): 97–109. Reprinted by permission of Indiana University Press.

Kay, Judith. "Jews as Oppressed and Oppressor: Doing Ethics at the Intersections of Classism, Racism, and Antisemitism." In *Judaism, Race, and Ethics: Conversations and Questions*, edited by Jonathan K. Crane, 66–104. University Park: Penn State University Press, 2020. Reprinted by permission of Penn State University Press.

Krone, Adrienne. "Ecological Ethics in the Jewish Community Farming Movement." In *Feasting and Fasting: The History and Ethics of Jewish Food*, edited by Aaron S. Gross, Jody Myers, and Jordan D. Rosenblum, 273–86. New York: New York University Press, 2019. Reprinted by permission of NYU Press, conveyed through Copyright Clearance Center.

Labovitz, Gail. *Marriage and Metaphor: Constructions of Gender in Rabbinic Literature*, 250–54. New York: Lexington Books, 2009. Reprinted by permission of the author.

Langer, Ruth. "Honor Your Father and Mother: Caregiving as an Halakhic Responsibility." In *Aging and the Aged in Jewish Law: Essays and Responsa*, 21–41. Pittsburgh: Freehof Institute for Progressive Halakhah, 1998. Reprinted in *That You May Live Long: Caring for Our Aging Parents, Caring for Ourselves*, edited by Richard F. Address and Hara E. Person, 113–26, 184–87. New York: UAHC Press, 2003. Reprinted by permission of Rabbi Walter Jacob and the Solomon B. Freehof Institute of Progressive Halakhah.

Levey, Geoffrey Brahm. "Judaism and the Obligation to Die for the State." *AJS Review* 12, no. 2 (Autumn 1987): 175–203. Reprinted by permission of the author.

Levinas, Emmanuel. *The Levinas Reader*, edited by Seán Hand, 211–26. Cambridge: Basil Blackwell, 1989. Reprinted by permission of John Wiley & Sons, conveyed through PLSclear.

Levine, Aaron. *Economic Morality and Jewish Law*, 8, 15, 191–214. New York: Oxford University Press, 2012. Reprinted by permission of Oxford University Press, conveyed through PLSclear.

Levitt, Laura. "Love the One You're with." In *The Passionate Torah: Sex and Judaism*, edited by Danya Ruttenberg, 245–58. New York: New York University Press, 2009. Reprinted by permission of the author.

Lev, Sarra. "Talmud That Works Your Heart: New Approaches to Reading." In *Learning to Read Talmud: What It Looks Like and How It Happens*, edited by Jane L. Kanarek and Marjorie Lehman, 175–202. Boston: Academic Studies Press, 2019. Reprinted by permission of Academic Studies Press.

Lichtenstein, Aharon. "Does Jewish Tradition Recognize an Ethic Independent of Halakha?" In *Modern Jewish Ethics: Theory and Practice*, edited by Marvin Fox, 62–88. Columbus: Ohio State University Press, 1975. Reprinted by permission of Dr. Tovah Lichtenstein.

Magid, Shaul. "Ethics Differentiated from the Law." In *The Blackwell Companion to Religious Ethics*, edited by William Schweiker, 180–83. Malden, MA: Blackwell, 2005. Reprinted by permission of Blackwell.

Marx, Tzvi C. *Disability in Jewish Law*, 1–2, 17–19. London: Routledge, 2002. Reprinted by permission of Taylor & Francis, conveyed through PLSclear.

Mayse, Ariel Evan. "Where Heaven and Earth Kiss: Jewish Law, Moral Reflection, and Environmental Ethics." *Journal of Jewish Ethics* 5, no. 1 (2019): 68–110. Reprinted by permission of Penn State University Press.

Mbuvi, Amanda. "*Avadim Hayinu*: An Intersectional Jewish Perspective on the Global Ethic of Solidarity." In *Multi-Religious Perspectives on a Global Ethic: In Search of a Common Morality*, edited by Myriam Renaud and William Schweiker, 85–99. New York: Routledge, 2021. Reprinted by permission of Taylor & Francis, conveyed through PLSclear.

Mittleman, Alan. "Theorizing Jewish Ethics." *Studia Humana* 3, no. 2 (2014): 32–42. Reprinted by permission of Gorgias Press.

Neis, Rafael Rachel. "'All That Is in the Settlement': Humans, Likeness, and Species in the Rabbinic Bestiary." *Journal of Jewish Ethics* 5, no. 1 (2019): 1–39. Reprinted by permission of Penn State University Press.

Newman, Louis. "Woodchoppers and Respirators: The Problem of Interpretation in Contemporary Jewish Ethics." *Modern Judaism* 10, no. 1 (1990): 17–42. Reprinted by permission of *Modern Judaism*, Oxford University Press.

Novak, David. *Jewish Social Ethics*, 22–24, 33–38. New York: Oxford University Press, 1992. Reprinted by permission of Oxford University Press, conveyed through PLSclear.

Plaskow, Judith. *Standing Again at Sinai: Judaism from a Feminist Perspective*, 25–31. New York: HarperCollins, 1990. Reprinted by permission of HarperCollins.

Raucher, Michal. *Conceiving Agency*, 1–5, 9–11, 16–20. Bloomington: Indiana University Press, 2020. Reprinted by permission of Indiana University Press.

Rosner, Fred. "In Vitro Fertilization and Surrogate Motherhood: The Jewish View." *Journal of Religion and Health* 22, no. 2 (Summer 1983): 139–60. Reprinted by permission of Blackwell, conveyed through Copyright Clearance Center.

Ross, Tamar. *Expanding the Palace of Torah: Orthodoxy and Feminism*, 210–12. Waltham, MA: Brandeis University Press, 2004. Reprinted by permission of the author.

Rubinstein, Jeffrey L. "Can a *Goses* Survive for More Than Three Days? The History and Definition of the *Goses*." *Journal of Jewish Ethics* 2, no. 2 (2016): 1–37. Reprinted by permission of Penn State University Press.

Schofer, Jonathan Wyn. "Self, Subject, and Chosen Subjection: Rabbinic Ethics and Comparative Possibilities." *Journal of Religious Ethics* 33, no. 2 (2005): 255–91. Reprinted by permission of John Wiley & Sons, conveyed through PLSclear.

Schonfeld, Toby. "Messages from the Margins: Lessons from Feminist Bioethics." *Journal of the Society of Christian Ethics* 28, no. 1 (Spring/Summer 2008): 209–24. Reprinted by permission of the *Journal of the Society of Christian Ethics*.

Sclove, Lena. "Beyond the Binary of Silence and Speech: What Jewish Liturgy and Spirals Reveal about the Limits and Potentials of Spiritual Caregiving for Survivors of Sexual Violence." In *Applying Jewish Ethics: Beyond the Rabbinic Tradition*, edited by Jennifer A. Thompson and Allison B. Wolf, 67–84. Lanham, MD: Lexington Books, 2023. Reprinted by the permission of Rowman and Littlefield.

Seeman, Don. "Ethnography, Exegesis, and Jewish Ethical Reflection: The New Reproductive Technologies in Israel." In *Kin, Gene, Community: Reproductive Technologies among Jewish Israelis*, edited by Daphna Birenbaum-Carmeli and Yoram S. Carmeli, 340–62. New York: Berghahn Books, 2010. Reprinted by permission of the author.

Sherwin, Byron. "Jewish Views on Euthanasia." *Humanist* 34, no. 4 (1974): 19–21.

Spitz, Elie. "'Through Her I Too Shall Bear a Child': Birth Surrogates in Jewish Law." *Journal of Religious Ethics* 24, no. 1 (Spring 1996): 65–97. Reprinted by permission of the author.

Strassfeld, Max. *Trans Talmud: Androgynes and Eunuchs in Rabbinic Literature*, 183–88. Oakland: University of California Press, 2023. Reprinted by permission of the University of California Press.

Tanhum, Yoreh. *Waste Not: A Jewish Environmental Ethic*, 45–48. Albany: State University of New York Press, 2019. Reprinted by permission of SUNY Press.

Teutsch, David A. "Reinvigorating the Practice of Contemporary Jewish Ethics: A Justification for Values-Based Decision-Making." *Reconstructionist* 69, no. 2 (Spring 2005): 4–15. Reprinted by permission of the author.

Thompson, Jennifer A. "Reaching Out to the Fringe: Insiders, Outsiders, and the Morality of Social Science." *Journal of Jewish Identities* 8, no. 1 (2015): 179–200. Reprinted by permission of Johns Hopkins University Press.

Tirosh-Samuelson, Hava. *Religion and Environment: The Case of Judaism*, 90–92, 260–61. Telford, PA: Pandora Press, 2020. Reprinted by permission of Pandora Press.

Washofsky, Mark. "Internet, Privacy, and Progressive Halakha." In *The Internet Revolution and Jewish Law*, edited by Walter Jacob, 81–142. Pittsburgh: Rodef Shalom Press, 2014. Reprinted by permission of the author.

Weiner, Jason. "Are There Limits to How Far One Must Go for Others? Toward a Theoretical Model for Health Care Providers." *Journal of Jewish Ethics* 6, no. 1 (2020): 94–108. Reprinted by permission of Penn State University Press.

Weintraub, Melissa. "Does Torah Permit Torture?" *Review of Faith & International Affairs* (Summer 2007): 3–8. Reprinted by permission of the author.

Wolpe, Paul Root. "If I Am Only My Genes, What Am I? Genetic Essentialism and a Jewish Response." *Kennedy Institute of Ethics Journal* 7, no. 3 (1997): 213–30. Reprinted by permission of Johns Hopkins University Press.

Wurzburger, Walter. *Ethics of Responsibility: Pluralistic Approaches to Covenantal Ethics*, 9–30. Skokie, IL: Varda Books, 2001. Reprinted by permission of the University of Nebraska Press. Published by the Jewish Publication Society.

Wyschogrod, Michael. "Judaism and the Sanctification of Nature." *Melton Journal* 24 (Spring 1991): 5–7. Reprinted by permission of the *Melton Journal*/Jewish Theological Seminary.

Zagar, Sarah. "Water Wears Away Stone: Caring for Those We Can Only Imagine." *Nashim: A Journal of Jewish Women's Studies and Gender Issues*, no. 37 (2020): 116–31. Reprinted by permission of Indiana University Press.

Zohar, Noam J. "Is Enjoying Life a Good Thing? Quality-of-Life Questions for Jewish Normative Discourse." In *Quality of Life in Jewish Bioethics*, edited by Noam J. Zohar, 19–31. Lanham, MD: Lexington Books, 2006. Reprinted by permission of the author.

Zoloth, Laurie. *Second Texts and Second Opinions: Essays toward a Jewish Bioethics*. Oxford: Oxford University Press, 2022, 232–53. Reprinted by permission of Oxford University Press, conveyed through PLSclear.

Index

abortion, 345–61; antiabortion position and Jakobovits, 351–54; fetus, status as a person, 356–57, 359–61; and maternal need, 355–59; in traditional Judaism, 347–50
Abortion and the Law (Smith), 352
Abraham, 26, 28, 39, 42, 54, 62–63, 65, 335
Abrams, Judith Z., 265–68, 277–78
academic economics, 150
accompaniment, 132–34
accuracy, 253–55
acquisition, 41–45, 101–4, 143–44, 237
activists, 202–4, 244, 273–75, 278
Adler, Rachel, xviii, 23–24, 41–45
adne hasadeh ("humans of the field"), 224, 224n29
adult children, 369–73, 369n69
adultery, 230, 330, 337
advocacy, 142–43
affiliation, 106–7
Afro-Jewish ethics, 283–87
Afromodernity, 286
Agamben, Giorgio, 220–21, 220n18
agency, 14–18, 102, 121, 166–71, 193–95, 285
aggadic (non-legal) texts, 10, 204
Aggy, 190
aging/ends of life, 362–80; caregiving as halakhic responsibility, 369–73; disability rights, 272–75; and euthanasia, 9–14, 364–68; *goses*, history and definition of, 377–80; narratives and Jewish bioethics, 373–76
agriculture, 205–7
agunot ("chained" wives), 103–4
Agus, Arlene, 336, 336n32
ahavat ha-briyot (love of humanity/creatures), 49

AI military ethics, 194
air warfare, 182
Akiva, Rabbi, 75–76, 177–78, 313, 313n12
Alcoff, Linda Martin, 122–23, 122n35
Alpert, Rebecca T., 351–54
American Jewry, 105–7, 168–69
American legal system. *See* Anglo-American jurisprudence
American privacy law, 114n18, 117
Americans Disabled for Attendant Programs Today (ADAPT), 274
Amsel, Nachum, xviii, 87, 87n40
analogy, 349
androgynes, 239–44, 239n60
Anglo-American jurisprudence, 14, 293–98, 365
animals, 215–26; animal experimentation, 201, 329–30; dietary practices, 217–22; and likeness, 222–26
Anthropocene, 210–11
antiabortion movement, 351–54
anti-Jewish oppression, 287–92, 291n94
antinomianism, 6
antiracism, 84–85
antisemitism, 167–68, 170, 287–92
anusim ("crypto-Jewish"), 258, 258n70
apparent body, 257–58, 261
applied ethics, xxiv
Arabs, 161–64
Arba'ah Turim, 378, 378n84
Arendt, Hannah, 169, 291n94
Aristotelian virtue philosophy, xvi–xvii, xxiii
Aristotle, 223
armed conflict categories, 180
arrogance, 82–86
artificial insemination, 330, 337

Asch, Adrienne, 272–75
Asher b. Yehiel (Rosh), 378
Ashkenazi Jews, 258–59, 288, 292
Assi, Rav, 372
atonement, 265–67
"authentic" and "inauthentic" Judaism, 106–7
authentic humanity, 137
authorized war, 180–81
Autonomous Weapon Systems (AWS), 192–95
autonomy: and bioethics, 303; divine will, 64–65; end of life treatment, 273; family in health care decision-making, 316; of humanity, 32–33; individual rights and, 118; model of duty, 309–10; narratives and Jewish bioethics, 376; and reproduction, 14–18; and self-determination, 171
avadim hayinu ("we were slaves"), 135–38

Baal Shem Tov, 32, 32n26
Babylonian exile, 230
Babylonian Talmud, 19, 129–30, 218, 231, 260–61, 347
Baddiel, David, 291n96
Bahya ibn Pakuda, 83–84
bal tashchit (do not waste), 196, 199, 202, 207
bamidah she'adam modeid ba, mod'din lo (measure for measure), 265
baraita (teaching not incorporated into the Mishnah), 132–33, 132n50
Baron, Salo, 108–9, 108n16
Bar-Zev, Asher, 10
Basic Laws of 1992, 162
battlefield ethics, 179–83
Beauchamp, Tom L., 303–4
bees, 206–7
Beit Bukiya, 240, 240n61
Beit Yosef (Caro), 372
Bela Farm, 206–7
Belser, Julia Watts, 276–80
beneficence, 69, 304, 319
Benhabib, Seyla, 343, 343n37
Benjamin, Mara, 68–70

Berkowitz, Beth, 187–91
Berlin, R. Naftali Tzvi Yehudah, 64
Berman, Nadav S., 192–95
Bhabha, Homi, 189, 189n100
biblical culture, 269–70
biblical ritual, 132
biblical wars, 175, 178, 180
Bilhah, 335–36, 339
binary, 289–90
biomedical ethics, 9, 47
Birthright Israel, 258
birth surrogates, 333–37
Blackness, 284
Black people, 283–87, 296
Black women, 238n55
Bleich, J. David, xviii, 103, 103n8, 347, 347n44, 379–80
Bloch, Abraham, xviii
Bloustein, Edward, 117, 117n20
B'nai Yisrael, 135, 138
Bonilla-Silva, Eduardo, 295, 295n98
The Book of Beliefs and Opinions (*Kitab al-'Amanat wal-I'ti adat*) (Saadia Gaon), xvi
The Book of Direction to the Duties of the Heart (Bahya ben Joseph ibn Pakuda), 83–84
A Book of Jewish Ethical Concepts: Biblical and Post-Biblical (Bloch), xviii
Borowitz, Eugene, xviii, 28, 65–67
boundaries of responsibility, 132–34
Bourdieu, Pierre, 219, 219n15
Bouvia, Elizabeth, 274–75
Boyarin, Daniel, 166–71, 166n75, 166n76, 230–33
Brandeis, Louis D., 117, 117n21
Breslauer, S. Daniel, xviii
Brettschneider, Maria, 238–39, 238n57
b'rit ahuvim (lover's covenant), 44–45
Brody, Samuel, 150–54
Broner, Esther M., 27, 27n18
brothers' keepers, 342–43
Broyde, Michael, 179–83
Brumberg-Kraus, Jonathan, 218–19, 218n11
B. T. *Arakhin*, 347

B. T. *Bava Batra*, 153–54
B. T. *Bava Metzia*, 7, 219
B. T. *Berakhot*, 323
B. T. *Hullin*, 218
B. T. *Ketubot*, 109–10
B. T. *Shevu'ot*, 260–61
b'tzelem Elohim (divine image), 184, 213, 225–26
Buber, Martin, xvii, 30, 30n22, 209, 236n51, 239
Burden-Stelly, Charisse, 84–85
Burke, Tarana, 123, 123n38
business ethics, 150–54
butchery, 218
Butler, Judith, 166–71, 166n76

Cahill, Lisa Sowle, 316–17, 316n17
Calarco, Matthew, 221, 221n21
Camp, Claudia V., 104, 104n11
Canaanites, 85–86
capitalism, 151–53, 289
care, narratives of, 210–11
caregiving as halakhic responsibility, 369–73
caregiving relationships and infertility, 342–44
Caro, Rabbi Joseph, 311, 311n9, 372, 378
Catholic Church, 341
Chananya ben Teradyon, Rabbi, 366–67, 376, 376n77
character/virtue, 72–86; good judgments, xvi–xviii, xxiv; Jewish normative ethics, 209; moral philosophy, xxiv; *musar* in white supremacist society, 82–86; and norms, 49; rabbinic ethics, 74–77; Talmud study, 78–81
charitable giving, 148–49
charity, 318–19
cheresh (person with a hearing and/or speaking disability), 267
childbirth, 347–49
childfree Jews, 108–11
child-parent relationship, 369–73

children, 108–10
Childress, James F., 303–4, 376, 376n79
chosenness, 65–67, 286
Christianity/Christian Americans, 122, 243–44, 297, 341
church-state relations, 351–54
circles of certainty (Freire), 79
cities, 129–34
Citizenship Law, 158–59
civilians, 181–83
classism, 287–90
Claussen, Geoffrey, 82–86
climate change, 196, 202, 210
clinical ethics, 306–9, 321–25
Coastal Roots, 205
Cohen, Aryeh, 129–34
Cohen, Hermann, xvii
Cohen gene, 260
Collins, Patricia Hill, 288
colonialism, 285
commandments: halakha, basis of, 172; to honor parents, 370; Jewish moral norms, 27; Jewish social ethics, 51–53; and obligation, 175; to reprove, 118–19; ritual and ethical distinction, 61, 95; against violations of human dignity, 184. *See also* mitzvah; obligation(s); responsibilities
commandment to the king, 83–84
commensal concerns, 218
Committee on Medical Ethics of the Federation of Jewish Philanthropies of New York, 331–32
communal continuity, 108–11
communication, 96
communities, 95–211; and economics, 139–54; and the environment, 196–211; and families, 99–111, 315–16; and society, 58–60; and solidarity, 126–38; and speech, 112–25; state power and violence, 172–95; and Zionism, 155–71
compassion, 269–70
Compassion in Dying, 273–74
conceptions, 295

confession, 122
conflict, 308–9
congregation-based communities, 89–91
conscience, 28, 64–65
conscientious objection, 194
consensus, 324
consent, 237
consequentialism, xxiv, 72, 145
Conservative Jews, 29–30
consideration for the "fearful," 175–78
constructions of being human, 213–301; and animals, 215–26; and disabilities, 262–80; gender and sexuality, 227–44; and genes, 245–61; and race, 281–92
Contemporary Jewish Ethics (Kellner), xvii
converts, 285
Cooper, Julie, 166–71
Cooper, Risa Alyson, 206
corporeality and divinity, 250
Covenant/covenant, 54–71; covenantal ethics, approaches to, 60–65; Jewish social ethics, 51–53; and Levinas, 56–60; maternal love, 68–71; as relationship, 65–67
Cover, Robert, 37–41, 309–10, 376
cowardice, 177–78
Cox, David, 248
Crane, Jonathan K., 373–76
createdness in the image of God, 192–93
creation, doctrine of, 201
creation stories, 196, 215, 227
crip, 276–80
critical race theory (CRT), 281, 293–98, 350
critique, strategies of, 189–91
Cruzan, Nancy, 272
Cunningham, Claire, 276–80, 276n77
Curtis, Jess, 276–80

da'at (knowledge), 267–68
Dan, Joseph, 47
Davis, Dena S., 18, 347–50, 359
day laborer (*po'el*), 147
death penalty, 187–91

decapitation, 187–89
decision-making, 273, 315–16
Declaration of Independence of May 1948, 162
Declaration of the Rights of Man, 338
deontological ethics, xxiv, 72, 145
de-orayta (obligation rooted in Scripture), 311, 311n10
depth theology, 376, 376n78
desacralization of nature, 200–201
desire, dialectics of, 230–33
destruction of the Temple, 26, 99
Deuteronomy, 39, 42, 56–58, 70, 82–83, 92, 132–33, 139, 142–43, 148, 176–77, 188, 207, 260–61. *See also* Exodus; Genesis; Leviticus; Tanach (Hebrew Bible)
diachronic justice, 159
dialectical tradition, 231–33
diasporism, 166–71, 166n76. *See also* Jewish diaspora
dietary practices, 217–22
difference(s), 221, 223–26
din (law), 7–8
disabilities, 262–80; and abortion, 353; in ancient texts, 265–68; disability activist and lobbying groups, 273–74; disability arts, 276–80; disability difference, 278–79; end of life treatment, 272–75; in Jewish law, 268–71
discrimination, 275, 289–90n91, 295–97
diversity of Jews, 285
divine, one acts in the world as, 32–34
divine destiny, 40
divine imperatives, 60–65
divine love, 32–34, 68–70
divorce, 44, 102–4
DNA, 256, 257–59
doing Jewish ethics, 3–18; ethic independent of halakha, 5–9; interpretation, problem of, 9–14; reproductive agency, 14–18
Dorff, Elliot, xviii, 18, 27–30, 314
Douglas, Mary, 248, 248n66
Down syndrome, 358

dualist tradition, 231–33, 231n46
Du Bois, W. E. B., 283–84, 283n84
duties that human beings owe to God (*bein adam la-makom*), 95
Dworkin, Ronald, 13, 13n9, 50
dying. *See* aging/ends of life

Ecclesiastes, 245
economics, 139–54; business ethics, 150–54; economic justice, 141–44; economic morality, 145–49; living wage ordinances (LWOs), 145–49
Eden Village Camp, 205
Eichmann, Adolf, 291n94
Eidels, Rabbi Shlomo (Maharsha), 133, 133n52
Elazar ben Shamua, Rabbi, 240
election, 286
Ellenson, David, 17
Elshtain, Jean Bethke, 247–48, 247n64
embodiment, 250
Emden, Jacob, 357, 357n63
empowerment, 24, 123–24
end of life treatment and disability, 272–75. *See also* aging/ends of life
environment, 196–211; environmental activism, 204; environmental ethics, 91–94, 202–4, 208–9; Jewish community farming movement, 205–7; Judaism and the sanctification of nature, 199–202; religion and, 208–11
Epstein-Levi, Rebecca J., 108–11
Eretz Yisrael, 161–64
erotic, 236–39
ethical acquisition of wealth, 144, 152–53
ethical monotheism, xvii
ethical norms, 19–34; covenantal basis of, 61–63; ethics differentiated from the law, 31–34; and feminism, 22–27; modern personal ethics, 27–31
ethical values, 87–94; environmental ethics, 91–94; values-based decision-making (VBDM), 89–91

ethnicity, 66–67, 136
ethnocultural groups, 159–60
ethnography, 17–18, 18n10, 337–41
eugenics, 248–51, 353
eunuchs, 239–40n60, 239–44
euthanasia, 9–14, 364–68, 375–76, 377; active euthanasia, 366–68; passive euthanasia, 10, 367, 377
evolution, 252
execution of a pregnant woman, 349
execution of criminals, 368
Exodus, 135–38, 141, 172, 347–48. *See also* Deuteronomy; Genesis; Leviticus; Tanach (Hebrew Bible)
Ezrat Nashim, 336n32

Faivish, Shmuel b. Uri Shraga, 379, 379n88
Falk, Joshua, 378, 378n86
families, 99–111; acquisition in rabbinic marriage, 101–4; communal continuity, 108–11; family, role of in healthcare, 315–16; insider/outsider distinctions, 105–7
The Fathers According to Rabbi Nathan, 74–77
Faur, José, 51–52
Feely-Harnik, Gillian, 217–18, 217n7
Feinstein, Rabbi Moshe, 358, 358n64
feminism and Orthodoxy, 233–36
feminist bioethics, 314–17
feminist Judaism, 22–27
feminist jurisprudence, 350
feminist position on sexuality, 235–39
fertilized eggs, 330–31
fetus, status as a person, 356–57, 359–61
First Nation peoples, 285
Focus on the Family, 243–44, 243n63
food and sex in Talmudic literature, 231–32
food practices, 217–22
Foucault, Michel, 122, 122n33
foundational anthropology, 341
Fox, Marvin, xvii
France, 338
Freedman, Benjamin, 306–10, 316

freedom and human dignity, 286
freedom of choice, 53
freedom of expression, 116–17
Freehof, Solomon, 10
free-market economy, 144, 153–54
Freire, Paulo, 79, 79n36
Fromm, Erich, 62, 62n32
fruit trees, 92–94, 92n51, 207

Gans, Chaim, 157–61
Gavison, Ruth, 161–65
gay and lesbian relationships, 237
Gemara, xv, 7, 35, 57, 59, 78
gender and sexuality, 227–44; androgynes and eunuchs, 239–40n60, 239–44; and confession, 122; constructions of in rabbinic literature, 101–4; desire, dialectics of, 230–33; embodiment in Judaism, 250; feminism and Orthodoxy, 233–36; gender hierarchies, 100
General Assembly of the United Nations, 161–63
genes, 245–61; gene therapy, 252–56; genetic essentialism, 247–51; mending the genetic code, 252–56; racialist logic of Jewishness, 257–61
Genesis, 26, 33, 99, 141, 172, 184, 195, 215, 222, 243, 276–80, 326, 339, 340–41. *See also* Deuteronomy; Exodus; Leviticus; Tanach (Hebrew Bible)
Genesis Rabbah, 26, 26n17
gene talk, 258
gene therapy, 252–56, 330
genetically modified food crops (GMOs), 245
genetic body, 257–59
genetic self, 248–51
genetic technologies, 245
genotypes, 247–48
genre of Jewish writing in English about economics, 150–54
gentiles, 287–92, 291n94
geographical boundaries, 131–32
Gershon ben Judah, Rabbenu, 336, 336n34

gesisah, 377–80. See also *goses* (imminently dying or moribund)
gestational surrogacy, 334
Gibbs, Robert, 252–56
Glauz-Todrank, Annalise E., 293–98
Global Ethic, 135–36, 135n55
gnosis, 267, 267n73
God: commandments, 51–53; creation stories, 196, 227; divine communication, 234–35; divine love, 32–34, 68–70; honoring parents, 370–71; Jewish concept of election, 286; Name of God, 255; obligation to die for the state, 175–77; partnership with, 204; relationship with, 31, 62, 65–66, 105, 371; religion and environment, 208–9; sanctity of nature, 201
God's will, 27–31, 51, 61
Goldstone, Matthew, 118–21
good and evil, 230–33, 247
good judgments, xvi–xviii, xxiv
goodness, 131
Good Samaritan principle, 185
Gordon, Lewis R., 283–87
Goren, Shlomo, 330, 330n24
goses (imminently dying or moribund), 10–11, 377–80
graded ultimate obligation, 178
Gray-Rosendale, Laura, 122–23
Greek philosophers, xxiii
Green, Ronald M., 349–50, 349n50
Gross, Aaron S., 217–22
Guantanamo, 183

Hagar, 335–36
Hampson, Daphne, 235, 235n48
HaNasi, Rabbi Yehudah, 10, 188–91, 240–41, 255
Haninah bar Chama, Rabbi, 225–26, 225n36
haredi women, 15–18
Harlan, John Marshall, 114n18
Hart, Mitchell B., 281, 281n82
Hartman, David, 203, 203n114
Harvey, Jennifer, 290–92

Hasidism, 31–34, 31n25
hatred, 33, 120, 247–48, 288–89, 291
Hauptman, Judith, 101, 101n1
healing and sexual violence, 121–25
healing arts (*ars medica*), 299
health care providers, 318–21
hekdesh (consecrated), 43
Held, Virginia, 344, 344n39
Henry, Paget, 284, 284n86
hermeneutics, 130, 249, 338–40, 373–74
hesed shel emet (true kindness), 287
eshbon ha-nefesh (accounting of the soul; personal reckoning), 49, 73, 83–84
heterosexuality, 353
hidden transcripts, 187–89
hierarchy, 92–93, 213, 234
hilkhot tzniyut (laws of modesty), 116
Hillel, 249–50, 334
Hippocrates, 299, 303
Hobbes, Thomas, 178, 342–43, 342n35
Holocaust, 108–9, 292
horizontal classification, 223, 226
Horowitz, Bethamie, 106
Hosea, 41
hospitality (*hachnasat orchim*), 126
human behaviors, xvi, 38–40, 68–70, 247, 250, 341. *See also* piety
human beings and nature, 201–2
human dignity (*kvod habriyot*), 115–17, 184–85, 190, 270, 274–75, 286
humane subject, 219–20
humane urbanism, 130–31
human exceptionalism, 225
human innovation, 53
human life, 347–48
human right to rule over and manipulate nature, 201
humility, 82–86, 115–16

identifications: Jewish critical race theory, 297–98; with the outsider, 137; racialist logics of Jewishness, 260–61
ideology, 359

idolatry, 230–31, 248
image of God, 184, 192–93, 215, 223–26
Imhoff, Sarah, 257–61
immigration, 157–61, 164
imperative to choose life. *See* preservation of life
impotence, 32–33
incarnational ethics, 32–34
inclusion, 237–38, 269–71
indirect duties, Kant, 209, 209n124
infertility, 326, 329, 335
informed consent, 273, 303
Ingold, Tim, 217, 217n5
insider/outsider distinctions, 105–7
intermarriage, 100, 106
internet, 112, 114–17
interpersonal responsibility, 118–21
interpretation(s), 375; in contemporary Jewish ethics, 9–14; ideological, 350
interpretive community, 324
intersectionality, 135–36, 135n57, 287–92
intersex bodies, 244
interspecies reproduction, 225
intimacy, 132–34, 227
in vitro fertilization (IVF), 329–32, 338
Irshai, Ronit, 18, 355–61
isolation, 287–90
Israel: covenantal perspective, 66–67; and disability, 266; immigration to, 157–61; Israeli-Palestinian conflict, 166–71; Law of Return, 158–61, 158n74; and love, 68–71; obligation to die for the state, 175–77; partition resolution, 161–65; reproductive technologies, 337–41; and Zionism, 155, 157–61
Israel ben Eliezer, Rabbi, 32n26
Israeli Supreme Court, 184–85
Israelites, 59, 66, 68–71, 100, 172, 175–77, 260–61, 277, 296

Jacob, 265–67, 276–80, 335–36, 339
Jacobs, Rabbi Jill, 141–44, 147–48, 147n64, 151–54

Jakobovits, Immanuel, 299–300, 332–333, 332n26, 345n42, 349, 351–54
Jerusalem, 14–18
Jewish Americans: critical race theory (CRT), 293–98; and religionization, 293–98
Jewish bioethics, 299–325; and abortion, 345–61; aging/ends of life, 362–80; ethnographic methods, 17–18; medical ethics, 303–25; narratives and, 373–76; and reproduction, 326–44; reproductive agency, 16
Jewish bodies, 258–61
Jewish community farming movement, 205–7
Jewish continuity, 105–11
Jewish culture, 89–91, 108, 350
Jewish diaspora, 66–67, 157–61, 166–71, 250
Jewish emancipation, 67, 168, 292
The Jewish Encyclopedia of Moral and Ethical Issues (Amsel), xviii, 87
Jewish endogamy, 100
Jewish ethics: abortion and maternal need, 355–59; abortion in traditional Judaism, 347–50; acquisition in rabbinic marriage, 101–4; Afro-Jewish ethics, 283–87; androgynes and eunuchs, 239–44; antiabortion position and Jakobovits, 351–54; authenticity, 106–7; battlefield ethics, 179–83; biomedical ethics, 9, 47; birth surrogates in Jewish Law, 333–37; business ethics, 150–54; caregiving as halakhic responsibility, 369–73; caregiving relationships and infertility, 342–44; clinical ethics, 306–9, 321–25; communal continuity, 108–11; continuities and influences in modern Jewish ethics, xv–xviii; covenantal ethics, approaches to, 60–65; Covenant as relationship, 65–67; critical race theory and religionization, 293–98; death penalty, 187–91; defining, xxii–xxvi; desire, dialectics of, 230–33; and diasporism, 166–71; dietary practices, 217–22; differentiated from the law, 31–34; disabilities in ancient texts, 265–68; disabilities in Jewish law, 268–71; disability arts, 276–80; duty to provide health care, 318–21; economic justice, 141–44; economic morality, 145–49; end of life treatment and disability, 272–75; environmental ethics, 91–94, 202–4, 208–11; ethnographic methods, 17–18; and euthanasia, 9–14, 364–68; and feminism, 22–27; feminism and Orthodoxy, 233–36; feminist bioethics, 314–17; fetus, status as a person, 359–61; genetic essentialism, 247–51; *Global Ethic* of solidarity, 135–38; good judgments, xvi–xvii, xxiv; *goses*, history and definition of, 377–80; independent of halakha, 5–9; insider/outsider distinctions, 105–7; interpersonal responsibility, 118–21; interpretation, problem of, 9–14; at the intersection of classism, racism, and antisemitism, 287–92; in vitro fertilization (IVF), 329–32; Israeli-Palestinian conflict, 166–71; Jewish community farming movement, 205–7; and Levinas, 56–60; likeness as a key to humanness, 217–22; living wage ordinances (LWOs), 145–49; and marriage, 41–45; maternal love, 68–71; mending the genetic code, 252–56; methods of reasoning, 3–18; military ethics, 179–83; modern period, xvii–xviii; modern personal ethics, 27–31; moral philosophy, xxiv; *musar* in white supremacist society, 82–86; narratives and Jewish bioethics, 373–76; narratives and *nomos*, 37–41; and nature, 208–11; and norms, 19–34, 46–49, 61–63; obligation of the city toward others, 129–34; obligation to die for the state, 175–77; particular identity, 166–69; partition resolution, 161–65; *Pirkei Avot*, xv–xvi, 152; privacy on the internet,

114–17; quality of life, 310–13; rabbinic ethics, 74–77; racialist logic of Jewishness, 257–61; reproductive agency, 14–18; reproductive technologies in Israel, 337–41; sanctification of nature, 199–202; self-determination, 157–61; sexual violence, 121–25; social ethics, 50–53; Talmud study, 78–81; techno-ethics, 192–95; theorizing, 46–49; and torture, 183–86; and values, 87–94; values-based decision-making (VBDM), 89–91; valuing the past, 235

Jewish feminism, 22–27

Jewish identity, 135–36, 166–71, 191, 250, 258–59, 292

Jewish institutions, 106

Jewish labor law, 146–48

Jewish law (halakha), xxv–xxvi, 3–4, 35–53; and abortion, 347–50, 355–61; antiabortion position and Jakobovits, 352–54; birth surrogates in, 333–37; caregiving as halakhic responsibility, 369–73, 369n69; covenantal ethics, 61–62; disability in, 268–71; and divorce, 102–4; environmental ethics, 202–4; ethical acquisition of wealth, 144, 152–53; ethic independent of, 5–9; and ethics, 35–53; ethics differentiated from, 31–34; ethnographic methods, 17–18; eunuchs and androgynes, 241–43; and euthanasia, 10, 365–68; God's will, 27–31; halakhic commitment, 8; halakhic formalism, 17; in vitro fertilization (IVF), 329–32; Jewish community farming movement, 206–7; Jewish normative ethics, 209; Jewish social ethics, 50–53; living wage ordinances (LWOs), 145–49; and marriage, 41–45; narrative in, 375; narratives and *nomos*, 37–41; and norms, 19–20, 46–49; obligation to provide health care, 319; principles of Jewish economic law, 144; privacy, 115–16; process of forming a partnership, 44–45; quality of life, 311–13; reproductive technologies, 341; self-defense, 180, 182, 185–86; techno-ethics, 192; and torture, 184–86; and war, 179–83. *See also* commandments

Jewish media, 105–7

Jewish Medical Ethics (Jakobovits), 299–300, 352

Jewish memory, 22–27

Jewish moral norms, 27–31, 63

Jewish myth of origin, 250–51

Jewishness, 67, 107, 136, 165, 167–70, 257–61, 257n69

Jewish normative ethics, 46–49, 208–9

Jewish sages, xxiii

Jewish self-rule, 171

Jewish tort law (*Nezikin*), 203

Jewish tradition, xv; attitudes to the disabled, 268–70; conservationist practices, 208; Conservative approach, 30; Jewish feminism, 21–27; and Jewishness, 260; and selfhood, 249; and values, 90–91; view of identity, 135–36; and war, 179–82

Jews and Blacks in the Early Modern World (Schorsch), 281

Jews and Race (Hart), 281

Jews of color, 257n69, 258–60, 297

Job, 75–76

Jonas, Hans, 209–10, 209n122

Josephus, 187

Jose the Galilean, Rabbi, 177

Joshel, Sandra, 102–3

Joshua, 56–57

Jotkowitz, Alan, 355–61

The Journal of Jewish Ethics (JJE), xviii

Judaism: and abortion, 347–50; and duty, 310; and economics, 144, 150–54; and embodiment, 250; and family, 315–16; health care providers, 318–20; and human life, 329, 361; nature was created by G-d for man, 329–30; normative Judaism, 208

judgment, 30, 204

jurisprudence, Dworkin, 13, 50

jurists, 378–79

just city, 129–34
justice, 25, 49, 84, 129, 131, 141, 304

Kagan, Rabbi Yisrael Meir, 112
Kahana, K., 6
Kant, Immanuel, xvii, xxv, 47, 209, 209n124
kashrut, 26, 49, 216, 219
katan (minor), 267
Kaufman, Debra, 106
Kay, Judith, 287–92
Kellner, Menachem, xvii
ketubah (marriage contract), 44, 44n29, 101, 101n2, 104
kiddushin (sanctification of marriage), 43–45
ki ha'adam etz hasadeh (Deuteronomy 20:19), 92
kilayim (prohibited mixing), 224, 224n31
killing of the priests of Nob, 193–94
killing of Uriah the Hittite by King David, 193–95
kingship, 177
King Solomon, 333
kinship relations, 339–41
kinyan. *See* acquisition
kinyan hakadosh baruch hu (property of God rather than of human beings), 185
Kluger, Rabbi Shelomo, 312
kosher practice, 217–22
Krone, Adrienne, 205–7
Kugel, James, 119, 119n23
kvod habriyot docheh lo taaseh (human dignity the power to displace other religious commandments), 184

labor markets, 146–47, 154
Labovitz, Gail, 101–4
Langer, Ruth, 369–73
lashon hara (evil speech), 112
late-term abortions, 358–59
Law of Return, 158–61, 158n74
laws of damages, 204
Leah, 334–36, 339
legal positivism, 50–51

Leibowitz, Yeshayahu, 3, 5, 5n1
Lemba, 258–59, 258n71
levayah (escorting the dead toward burial), 133–34, 133n54
Leve, Sarra, 78–81
Levey, Geoffrey, 175–79
Levinas, Emmanuel, xvii, 30, 56–60, 129–31, 203, 209–10, 225
Levine, Aaron, 145–49
Lévi-Strauss, Claude, 215
Leviticus, 119–20, 190, 341, 370. *See also* Deuteronomy; Exodus; Genesis; Tanach (Hebrew Bible)
Levitt, Laura, 102, 102n4, 236–39
liberal Jew, 48, 106, 115–16
liberal political theory, 342–43
liberationists, 287–88
Lichtenstein, Aharon, xvii, 5–9
Lieberman clause, 104, 104n10
lifnim mishurat hadin (beyond the letter of the law), xvi, 3, 7–8, 28, 46
likeness, 222–26
Lilith Magazine, xvii
lived realities, 16–18
Livermore, Mary, 190
living wage ordinances (LWOs), 145–49, 145n61
Lorde, Audre, 237–38, 237n54, 238n55
lo talin (withholding wages), 148
love, 32–34, 68–71, 371
lower ecology, 199–200

Maggid of Mezeritch, 32
Magid, Shaul, 31–34, 31n25
Maharam of Rothenburg (Meir b. Baruch), 378–79
Maimonides (Moshe ben Maimon), 357n60; and abortion, 357, 360; Aristotelian virtue philosophy, xvi–xvii; caregiving as halakhic responsibility, 370–73; charitable giving, 148–49; and euthanasia, 366; *The Guide of the Perplexed* (*Dalālāt al-Hā'irīn*, or in Hebrew, *Moreh Nebukim*),

xvi–xvii; military ethics, 181–82; and morality, 364; municipal responsibility, 133; partnership with the divine, 204; *Sefer Ha-Mitzvot* (Book of the Commandments), 313n11

Manichaeism, 284, 284n85
Marcionites, 70
marginalization, 294–95, 297
marriage, 41–45, 101–4, 236–39
Marx, Karl, 289, 289n90
Marx, Tzvi C., 268–71
maternal love, 68–71
maternal need, 355–59
matriarchs, 335–37, 339
M. *Avot*, 74–75, 152
Mayse, Ariel Evan, 202–4
Mbuvi, Amanda, 135–38
McGinity, Keren, 106
McRuer, Robert, 276, 276n78
medias res, 137, 137n59
medical ethics, 303–25; clinical ethics, 306–9, 321–25; duty to provide health care, 318–21; feminist bioethics, 314–17; medical technologies, 350, 357–58; quality of life, 310–13. *See also* disabilities; Jewish bioethics
medical professionals, 353–54
Mehta, Samira, 106
Meir, Rabbi, 132–33, 133n51, 255
Mendel, R. Menahem, 32–34
Mendelssohn, Moses, 46
Mesharsheya, R., 56, 59–60
#MeToo movement, 112, 123
Micah, 64, 115
midah k'neged midah (measure for measure), 265–67
middle agency, 290
Middle Ages, 377–80
midrash halakha, 91–94
Midrash Tanhuma, 260–61
midwives in Exodus, 137–38
Milgrom, Jacob, 120–21, 120n30
Million Dollar Baby (film), 272, 274

mimicry, 189–91
minimum wage legislation, 146
Mishnah, xxiii; biblical ritual, 132–33; death penalty, 189–91; Deuteronomic exemptions, 177–78; and disabilities, 267–68; effective methods of acquisition, 42; interpretation of the Torah, 253; Judaism as a tradition of law, 35; and procreation, 334; territorial doubles, 224
mitah yafa, 368
Mittleman, Alan, 46–49
mitzvah: in Afro-Jewish ethics, 286–87; attitudinal accompaniment of the performance of, 47; of honoring parents, 369–73; participation in, 270; performative aspect of love, 68–71; promoting quality of life, 310–13; of *pru urvu* (be fruitful and multiply), 108, 110. *See also* commandments; obligation(s); responsibilities
M. *Kiddushin*, 299
M. *Niddah*, 225
model of duty, 307–10
Modern Jewish Ethics: Theory and Practice (Fox), xvii
modern personal ethics, 27–31
modern state, 172
modesty (*tzniyut*), 115–16
M. *Ohalot*, 347–48, 356, 359–60
monarchy, 176–77
monogamy, 239, 336–37
moral agency, 194
moral authority, 62–64, 107, 269
moral imagination, 193, 340
morality, 5–8, 16–18, 61–64, 105–7, 145–49, 354, 364
moral philosophy, xxiv–xxv
moral sensibilities, 234
Mordechai b. Hillel, 378
Moses, 22–24, 29, 54, 56–57, 141–42
Mount Ebal, 57–59
Mount Gerizim, 57–59
M. *Peah*, 370

M. *Rosh Hashanah*, 33
M. *Sanhedrin*, 193, 357
M. *Sotah*, 132, 132n48, 267
Murnaghan, Sheila, 102–3
Murphy, Trevor, 225–26, 225n37
musar (moral discipline), xvii, 82–86
mutability, 242–43
M. *Yoma*, 95

Naess, Arne, 93, 93n53
Nahmanides (Moshes ben Nahman), xvi, 7, 7n4, 148
narratives and Jewish bioethics, 373–76
narratives and *nomos*, 37–41
nationality-based priorities in immigration, 158–60
nation-state, 162, 167–72
Natural History (Pliny), 225–26
naturalization, 159–61
natural law theory, 50–53, 61, 338
nature, 200–202, 208–11
Nazi experimentation, 303, 353
Neis, Rafael Rachel, 222–26
neoliberalism, 150–54
Newman, Louis E., 9–14, 350
The New Republic, 247–48
nomos (normative universe), 37–41
non-Jews, 159–61, 218–19, 258–60, 289, 297
nonmaleficence, 304
normative authority, 61–65
normative discourse, 375
normative Judaism, 46–49, 208, 364
normative religious ethics, 16–18
normative universe, 37–41
Norton, Bryan, 93
Not Dead Yet, 273–74
"Notes Toward Finding the Right Question" (Ozick), xvii
Novak, David, xviii, 50–53
nuclear family model, 109

obedience to the law, 61–64
obligation(s): caregiving as halakhic responsibility, 369–73; of the city toward others, 129–34; to defend human life, 184–86; to die for the state, 175–79; and euthanasia, 364–66; Jewish continuity, 110–11; to procreate, 330, 332, 358–59; to protect one's life and health, 299, 347; to provide health care, 318–21; to seek peace, 181. *See also* commandments; mitzvah; responsibilities
obligatory war, 180–83
omni-sufficiency of the halakha, 46–48
ona'ah (laws around fair pricing for goods and services), 146–47n63, 146–49
one-fifth rule, 319–21
ontology, 210
oppression, 238n55, 287–92, 291n94, 295
oral law, 58
Oral Torah, 29, 29n21
"Order of Redemption" (*Seder Yeshu'ot*), 204
ordination of women as rabbis, 25
Orthodox Judaism, xxv, 28–30, 333, 353
Other, 81, 129–31
outreach, 106–7
ovum surrogacy, 333–34
ownerless places, 132–34
Ozick, Cynthia, xvii

Palestine, 155–56, 161–65
Parashat Shoftim, 83
parents, 369–73
participation, 267–70
particular identity, ethics of, 166–69
particularism, 126
partition resolution, 161–65
partnership law (*hilkhot shutafut*), 44–45
Passover seder, 25, 135
paternalism, 316
patriarchs, 335–37
patriarchy, 233–34, 237
Peel Commission, 164
peoplehood, 170–71, 260
perfection, 254, 268
Perishah, 378

personal morality, 306–8
personal privacy, 114–17
personhood, 360
Pesach (Passover), 135–38
Peskowitz, Miriam, 102–3
Pharaoh, 137–38
Phelan, James, 374
Philo, 187
philosophy, 342–44
physician-assisted suicide, 275
piece-worker (*kabbelan*), 147
piety, xxiii, 31–32, 60, 85, 270, 371
pikuach nefesh (lifesaving), 311–13, 347–48
Pirkei Avot, xv–xvi, 152
Plaskow, Judith, xvii, 22–27, 236–39, 236n51
Pliny, 223, 225–26
polis, 129n43. *See also* just city
political economy, 152
political Zionism, 166–71
polytheism, 200
Porter, J. R., 119–20, 119n26
posek (rabbi with the authority to decide questions of Jewish law and practice), 355, 355n57
positive commandment, 133, 313, 320, 370
postcolonial theory, 187
post-structuralism, 216n2
potentiated double consciousness, 284
poverty, 142–44
precedents, 9–12, 17, 306, 347
pregnancy, 14–18, 111, 232, 347–50, 356–58
preservation of life, 6, 61, 299, 311–14, 348, 366–67
Pri Ha-'Aretz (lit. "fruits of the land"), 32
privacy, 114–17
private and public setting, tension between, 120
process theology, 236
procreation, 108, 227, 232–33, 326, 330, 334–37, 358–59
pronatalism, 108–10
protectionism (*hezkat yishuv*), 126
Proverbs, 112, 370

pru urvu (be fruitful and multiply), 108. *See also* reproduction
purchase model of marriage, 103
pursuer model, 180, 182, 360

quality of life, 310–13
queer/crip reading of Jacob wrestling with the angel, 276–80
Quinlan, Karen Ann, 273, 273n76

Rab (Abba bar Aivu or Abba Arikhah), 254, 254n68
rabbinic Judaism, 129–34, 218, 232–33
rabbinic literature, xxiii; androgynes and eunuchs, 239–44; biblical prohibition against withholding a worker's wages, 148; constructions of gender in, 101–4; and *da'at*, 268; fetus, status as a person, 356–57, 359–61; God's will, 29; Jewish ethics relying on, 18; laws of damages, 204; obligation of the city toward others, 129–34; obligation to provide health care, 319–20
rabbinic responsa, xxiii–xxiv
rabbis: acquisition in rabbinic marriage, 41–45, 101–4; biblical ritual, 132; caregiving as halakhic responsibility, 369–73; and classification, 222–26; and economics, 153–54; laws of execution, 187–91; obligation to die for the state, 177–78; ordination of women as, 25; participate in the sages' system, 267–68; rabbinic ethics, 74–77; reproductive agency, 15–16; and sexuality, 232; species groupings, 223, 223n28; and surrogacy, 333–34; and torture, 184–85; and women, 24–26
race, 281–92; Afro-Jewish ethics, 283–87; at the intersection of classism, racism, and antisemitism, 287–92; Jewish critical race theory, 293–98; racialist logic of Jewishness, 257–61; and religionization, 293–98
Rachel, 334–36, 339

racial impostor syndrome, 136
racialization, 294–95
racism, 220, 259, 281, 287–92
Ramban, 47
Ramsey, Norman, 295
Rashi (Rabbi Shlomo Yitzchaki), 24, 24n16, 133, 224n29, 357, 357n59
Raucher, Michal, 14–18
reading strategies, 373–76
reality, 284–85
realization of the self as other, 286–87
rebuke, 118–21
Reconstructionist congregations, 90
Reform individualism, 28–31
refutability, 194
religion, 63, 208–11, 296, 296n103
religionization, 293–98
Religion of Reason: Out of the Sources of Judaism (Cohen), xvii
religious approaches to bioethics, 314–17
religious authority, 17, 77, 107, 116, 338
religious ethics, 16–18
religious questions, 105–6
"representative" Judaism, 136
reproduction, 326–44; birth surrogates in Jewish Law, 333–37; caregiving relationships and infertility, 342–44; human as a creature in God's image, 225; in vitro fertilization (IVF), 329–32; Jewish continuity, 108–10; reproductive agency, 14–18; reproductive failures, 240; reproductive technologies in Israel, 337–41; and sexuality, 232
resistance, 191
responsibilities: caregiving as halakhic responsibility, 369–73; community and society, 59–60; interpersonal responsibility, 118–21; Judaic approach to nature, 208–11; placed on the city, 132–34; realization of the self as other, 286–87; relationship with God, 66; techno-ethics, 193–95; that bind human beings to one another (*bein adam la-havero*), 95. *See also* commandments; mitzvah; obligation(s)
responsible investing, 202
restraint, 115–17, 154
revelation, theology of, 233–35
revelation at Sinai, 22–24, 235, 260–61, 271
reversal, strategies of, 189–91
"The Right Question Is Theological" (Plaskow), xvii
rights, 306–10
Rivlin, David, 275
Rolston, Holmes III, 92–93
Roman executions, 187–91
Rosenblum, Jordan, 218, 218n9
Rosenzweig, Franz, xvii
Rosh Hashanah, 206
Rosner, Fred, xviii, 329–32
Ross, Tamar, 233–36
Rubenstein, Jeffrey L., 377–80

Saadia Gaon, xvi, 64n34
Sabbath, desecration of the, 311–12, 329, 331, 367
Sacks, Jonathan, xviii
safek de'oraita le umra (preference for stringency in cases of doubt), 355
Safran Foer, Jonathan, 217
Samson, 266–67
Samuel, 176, 193–95
sanctity of human life, 185, 329, 361
Sarah, 335–36, 339
scala naturae, 213
Schiavo, Terri, 272
Schofer, Jonathan Wyn, 74–77
Schonfeld, Toby, 314–17
Schorsch, Jonathan, 281, 281n81
Schwartz, Baruch, 119n25
Schwarzschild, Steven, 197, 197n106
science, 248–49
Sclove, Lena, 121–25
Scott, James, 187–90
The Sea Inside (film), 272
second-wave feminists, xvii–xviii

secular bioethics, 319–20
secular Jews, 286, 296
secular law, 204
Seeman, Don, 337–41
Sefer Chofetz Chaim, "Book of One Who Desires Life" (Kagan), 112
Sefer ha-Mordechai, 378
self: Covenant as relationship, 65–66; realization of the self as other, 286–87; self-defense, 165, 180, 182, 185–86; self-determination, 157–65, 170–71, 191, 273–75; self-examination, 82–86; selfhood, 65–66, 249–51; self-respect, 117, 158, 202, 270, 274; self-restraint, 115–17
servant-surrogacy, 339–40
Sessions, George, 93
sex: outside of marriage, 353; and procreation, 336–37; sexual violence, 121–25. *See also* gender and sexuality
sex changes, 240–44
sexism, 220
Shaare Tefila Congregation v. Cobb, 293–98
Shammai, 334
shared project, 130
Sherwin, Byron, 348, 348n46, 364–68
Sheva Berakhot (Marriage Blessings), 41–43
shifkhah (handmaid), 335–37
Sh'ma magazine, 379
sh'mitah (the sabbatical year), 143
Shoresh Jewish Environmental programs, 205–7
shoteh (person with mental illness or disability), 267
Shulchan Aruch (Caro), 311, 311n9, 357, 357n61, 372, 378
siddur (prayer book), 124
siege, 181–82
Sifre, 93–94, 93n56, 224
sifrut hamusar (literature of moral exhortation), 47
silencing, 122–23
Simeon, Rabbi, 56, 59
sin and disability, 265–67

situatedness, 342–44
slaughter of animals, 218
slavery, 136–37, 289
social ethics, 307–9
social justice, 141–44, 207
social justice literature, 150–54
social location, 287–88
social media, 95–96, 112–13, 114
social science, 105–7
social support policies, 109
society, 248–51
Society of Christian Ethics (SCE), xviii
Society of Jewish Ethics (SJE), xviii
solidarity, 126–38; *Global Ethic* of, 135–38; obligation of the city toward others, 129–34
Soloveitchik, Joseph B., 47, 47n30, 203
sovereignty, 46–48, 66, 170, 172
speech, 112–25; interpersonal responsibility, 118–21; privacy on the internet, 114–17; sexual violence, 121–25
Spinoza, Baruch, 93
Spitz, Elie, 333–37
state power and violence, 172–95; battlefield ethics, 179–83; death penalty, 187–91; obligation to die for the state, 175–79; techno-ethics, 192–95; and torture, 183–86
Steinberg, Avraham, xviii
strangers, 25, 133–34, 270
Strassfeld, Max, 239–44
structural changes, 288
structural dynamics, 287–92
subjectivity, 349
subordinate groups, 189
succession, 40
suffering of animals, 206–7
summons, 79–81
surrogacy, 333–37, 339–40
survivors of sexual violence, 121–25
suspension of the ethical, 62–63
symmetry, 265–67
systemic change, 82–86, 142–43

Talmud, xxiii; and abortion, 355–56; environmental ethics, 203–4; and euthanasia, 366–68; food and sex in Talmudic literature, 231–32; Jewish moral norms, 28; Jewish myth of origin, 250–51; natural law theory, 61; responsibility placed upon the city, 132–33; Shabbat desecration, 312; three-day definition for *gosesim*, 379; and women, 24; working the heart, 78–81

Talmudic tort law, 203–4

Tamari, Meir, 151–53

Tanach (Hebrew Bible), 19, 23–24, 38–40, 69, 118–19, 175–77, 204, 215, 265–67, 340. *See also* Deuteronomy; Exodus; Genesis; Leviticus

Tanhuma bar Aba, R., 271, 271n74

Tannaim, 152

Targum Yonathan, 334, 334n29

Tay-Sachs, 358

techno-ethics, 192–95

Ten Commandments, 370

Tendler, Rabbi Moshe D., 331, 331n25

territorial doubles, 224–26, 224n30

Tetragrammaton (YHWH), 255

Teutsch, David A., 89–91

teyku ("the matter stands"), 324

theocentric orientation, 61–62, 64, 196, 209

theories and methods of Jewish ethics: character/virtue, 72–86; Covenant/covenant, 54–71; ethical values, 87–94; ethics and law, 35–53; forging ethical norms from Jewish textual sources, 19–34

Thompson, Jennifer A., 105–7

ticking bomb scenario, 186

Tirosh-Samuelson, Hava, 208–11

T. *Kilayim*, 224–26

Torah: and abortion, 360; and arrogance, 82–83; biblical prohibition against withholding a worker's wages, 148; covenantal ethics, 60–61; creation stories, 196; death penalty in, 188; dignity of the poor, 142–43; and the disabled, 271; God's will, 29; honoring parents, 371; impact on emotions and desires, 75–76; Jewish endogamy, 100; Jewish memory, 22–27; and Levinas, 56–60; obligation to provide health care, 319; performative aspect of love, 70–71; and procreation, 334–37; property ownership, 143–44; quality of life, 311–13; and religionization, 296; Torah study, 109–10

Torah scroll, 252–56

torture, 183–86

Totemism (Lévi-Strauss), 215

traditionalism, 236

traditional marriage, 340–41

trans theology, 244

trauma, 121–25

tumtum (person of indeterminate gender), 242, 242n62

Tuskegee Syphilis Study, 303

tza'ar ba'alei chayim (compassion for animals), 196, 206

tzedakah (gifts to the poor), 115, 143, 207, 370

Tzuriel, R. Moshe, 360, 360n66

ubuntu, 287

universalism, xxv, 66, 126

universalistic rationality, xvii

UN Special Committee on Palestine (UNSCOP), 164

upper ecology, 200

values-based decision-making (VBDM), 89–91, 89n46

valuing the past, 235. *See also* Jewish memory

Vayikra Rabbah, 238

verbs, 136–37, 370

vertical relationships, 223

virtue ethics, xxiv, 72

wages of workers, 148–49, 153–54

Waldenberg, R. Eliezer, 357–59, 357n62

Walzer, Michael, 177, 177n81
war, 179–83. *See also* biblical wars
Warren, Samuel D., 117, 117n21
Washington v. Glucksberg, 275
Washofsky, Mark, 114–17
"The Way You Look (at me) Tonight," 276–80
"weak" anthropocentrism, 93
wealth, 143–44, 145, 152–53.
 See also economics
wedding ceremonies, 41–45
Weiner, Jason, 318–21
Weintraub, Melissa, 183–86
welfare economics, 145–46
Western Christianity, xxv
Western moral philosophy, xxv
Western philosophical tradition, xxiii
Westphalia treaties, 172
white Jews, 290–91
whiteness, 284–85, 290, 294–97
white privilege, 290
white supremacy, 82–86, 288, 290, 292
Whose Life Is It Anyway?, 272
wilderness, 143
Wilkinson, J. Harvie III, 295
Wolfson, Elliot, 219, 219n13
Wolpe, Paul Root, 247–51
womanism, 288n88
women: abortion and maternal need, 355–59; antiabortion position and Jakobovits, 352–54; biblical obligation to procreate, 332, 358–59; halakhic approaches to the status of, 48; halakhic process, excluded from, 350; insider/outsider distinctions, 106; Jewish feminism, 22–27; and marriage, 41–45, 101–4, 236–39; ordination of women as rabbis, 25; and Orthodoxy, 234–36; reproductive agency, 14–18; women's movement, 339, 352
world religions, 210–11
Written Torah, 29, 58, 83–85
Wurzberger, Walter, 60–65
Wyschogrod, Michael, 199–202

Yaakov ben Asher, 378n84
Yakerson, Masha, 258
yetzer hara (potential for evil), 233
yibum (levirate marriage), 335, 335n31
yirat shamayim (fear of Heaven), 49
Yohanan, Rabbi, 7, 356, 371n71
Yoreh, Tanhum, 91–94
Yosef, Ovadiah, 330, 330n23

Zagar, Sarah, 342–44
Zionism, 155–71; Covenant-ideal, 66; Israeli-Palestinian conflict, 166–71; Jewish diaspora, 157–61, 166–71; Law of Return, 158–61, 158n74; partition resolution, 161–65; political, 166–71; self-determination, 157–65, 170–71
Zohar, Noam J., 310–13
Zoloth, Laurie, 30, 321–25